Special Index

The Dixie Frontier

THE

Dixie Frontier

A SOCIAL HISTORY

*of the Southern Frontier from the First Transmontane
Beginnings to the Civil War*

by

EVERETT DICK

*Research Professor of American History
Union College, Lincoln, Nebraska*

Special Index

CAPRICORN BOOKS : NEW YORK

Dedicated

to the descendants of

John Dick

traveler on the Wilderness Road

and pioneer

of Old Kentucky

Foreword

FOR three hundred years—from the time of the first English settlement at Jamestown until the last land was homesteaded early in the twentieth century—the frontier was the most important single factor in the formation of the "American way of life"; indeed, it holds the key to the interpretation of American history.

For the first half of this period Europeans busied themselves with peopling the area west of the Appalachian Mountains. With the close of the French and Indian War, in spite of the King's royal proclamation to the contrary, this pent-up population began to trickle across the mountains and down into the valleys on the headwaters of the Tennessee River. By 1775 this stream of population had welled up again and, finding an outlet through the Cumberland Gap, flowed gently down the western slopes onto the plains of Kentucky. Other streams of immigrants from Georgia and the Carolinas on the south and from northern Virginia by way of the Ohio River on the north flowed toward the Mississippi.

During the Revolutionary War and the period of Indian fighting for thirteen years afterward Kentucky continued to be settled while the area north of the Ohio River, occupied by the Indians, was little settled. As from time to time Indian treaties made land available across the Ohio, there was a migration of Southern people into Ohio, Indiana, and Illinois until roughly the southern two fifths of these states became virtually a part of Dixie in culture and civilization. For example, in Abraham Lincoln's home county around Springfield, Illinois, this stream of settlers from the South, of which Lincoln himself was a part, met the Yankees. Timothy Flint, writing in 1827, said: "Kentucky, Tennessee, Missouri, the upper part of Alabama, and all Arkansas, have distinct manners in which the nationality of Kentucky is the ground color." As a matter of fact, he might well have broadened his statement to have included southern Ohio, southern Indiana, and southern Illinois, and northern Mississippi and northern Louisiana. Since western Georgia and northern Florida were not opened until central Missouri was being settled, they, too, are rightfully included in this area which I have chosen to call "the Dixie Frontier."

The great majority of the people who settled just west of the mountains were from the foothills and mountain valleys just to the east of the Alleghenies, where the people were just emerging from the raw conditions of that recent frontier. Likewise the majority of those who settled the three trans-Mississippi states were from the area just to the east, where a degree of civilization and culture was only beginning to appear.

Ordinarily the upland and mountain regions were settled first. The bottoms were avoided because they were thought to be too low and swampy to be healthful. Then too, the jungle was so dense that as one old settler expressed it, "you couldn't a stuck a butcher knife to the handle in the canebrake that covered the whole face o' the yearth." In contrast to the lowland jungle, the uplands were more inviting. There was little underbrush and a settler could drive a wheeled vehicle by the nearest route from place to place through the open forest. The streams were clear and cool and the climate comparatively healthful.

An attempt has been made to follow the frontier as it slowly crossed the mountains and moved ceaselessly westward until the whole area had begun to emerge from frontier conditions. At the time the Civil War cut short the era of settlement, the frontier period may be said to have ended. In many places frontier conditions obtained for years, but the westward tramp of population passed to the plains following the Civil War.

Preface

NEARLY sixty years ago, in *The Winning of the West*, Theodore Roosevelt brought to the attention of Americans the important and dramatic part played by the first settlers west of the Appalachian Mountains. No small part of the narrative dealt with the borderers of Kentucky and Tennessee. The present volume is an attempt to present the everyday life of those first settlers and of the pioneers of the entire region, which was distinctly Southern in its characteristics and culture.

This cultural area does not coincide with the political area that is commonly known as Dixie. In many ways the culture of southern Indiana, for example, is more like that of Alabama than it is like that of Michigan although Indiana is classed geographically and historically with Michigan as part of the Old Northwest.

The Dixie Frontier was one of the most romantic and heroic of the entire continent. No attempt has been made to follow the course of political history. The aim is to give a picture of daily life, with the struggle of the settlers for survival, their attempt to grab the rich resources, their honesty and dishonesty, their points of excellency and their obvious defects. Out of the heroic struggle against savage

Indians and an inhospitable nature there came forth the Southern American.

A studied attempt has been made to avoid cluttering up this study of the American frontier with the frontier ways of the French and Spanish in the area since these are exceptional rather than typical.

The sources are largely biographies, diaries, letters, records of interviews, monographs, county histories, official documents, travel accounts, newspapers, and the publications of historical societies and state historical departments.

The drudgery of research has been lightened by the many courtesies and helpful interest of the officials and librarians of the universities and state historical departments or historical societies of the states concerned, the Library of Congress, the National Archives, the Wisconsin State Historical Society, the libraries of the University of Nebraska, the Nebraska State Historical Society, the Filson Club, and other public and private libraries.

I wish especially to thank Dr. Benton Wilcox, librarian of the Wisconsin State Historical Society, and his excellent staff for their efficient help and many courtesies. I am indebted in a very real way, also, to Dr. Thomas D. Clark, head of the department of history of the University of Kentucky, for his courtesies, the use of his private collections, and many suggestions arising from an intimate acquaintance with the social history of the frontier of the South.

Above all, I wish to acknowledge my indebtedness to the Rockefeller Foundation for a grant-in-aid that made possible the research and writing of this volume.

My wife, Opal Wheeler Dick, has been my constant companion and assistant on my research in the field as well as doing a vast amount of copying and editorial work on the volume. More credit is due her than is possible to give in this last but not least paragraph.

EVERETT DICK

Union College
Lincoln, Nebraska

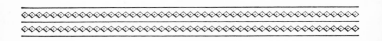

Contents

PAGE

Chapter I. THE PROMISED LAND 3
Forests—Grasslands—Game—The long hunters—Land claims—Surveying land—Conflicting claims—Tennessee land system—The Indian countrymen of Alabama and Mississippi

Chapter II. A NATION ON THE MARCH 13
Reason for migration—Watauga—Travel on Wilderness Trail—Hardship of travel—Migration down the Ohio River —Flatboat travel—Indian attacks—Southern migration across the Ohio River into the Old Northwest

Chapter III. THE SQUATTER 23
The hunter-trapper settler—Squatters' dislike of civilization —Many moves—Loved hunting—First homes—Cabin furnishings—Half-savage ways—Hunting buffalo—Bear—Deer —Wild hogs

Chapter IV. STATION LIFE IN TENNESSEE AND KENTUCKY 38
A typical station—Indian attacks from Ohio—Ways of Indian fighters—Indian mode of warfare—Siege of Boonesborough—Loss of life—Nashboro—Kate Sherrill and John Sevier

PAGE

Chapter V.   THE PLANTER MOVES WEST   53
Why the planter migrated—Natchez settlement—Squatter
and speculator—Planter moved overland—Planter moved
down the Ohio River—Travel difficulties over the mountains to Alabama—The slave leaving the East—Slave cara-
vans

Chapter VI.   LAND GREED   63
Land policies—Intruders on Indian lands—Squatters—Land
boom of 1818—Speculators collaborate to cheat the government—Land-office business—Pre-emption—Indians defrauded of land—Land-office arrears

Chapter VII.   BEGINNINGS OF PLANTATION LIFE   78
Planter settlers—Log houses—Early crops—Whites and
Negroes work together—Slave management—Slave women
—Log houses weatherboarded—Patriarchial system—Cul-
ture of the planters

Chapter VIII.   THE SLAVE AS A PIONEER   87
Leaving the old home—Slave caste—Relation of slaves to
masters—Working conditions—Morals—Regulations—Social and religious privileges

Chapter IX.   FRONTIER AGRICULTURE   98
Clearing and first planting—Plowing—Corn cultivation—
Corn harvest—Wheat-growing—Harvesting—Threshing—
Making rails—The milk cow—Range industry

Chapter X.   GOING TO MARKET   107
Pack trains—Driving stock—Opening New Orleans market
—Flatboat business—Navigating flatboat—Visits between
boats—Traveled by day and night—Amusements—Sights at
New Orleans—Boatmen return on foot

Chapter XI.   ECONOMIC LIFE   115
Barter—Specie from New Orleans—Cut money—Trading
—Early stores—Procuring goods—The keelboat—Tin peddlers—Clock peddlers—Yankees hated—Boat peddlers—Paper money—Wildcat banks

CONTENTS

PAGE

Chapter XII. GOOD TIMES   125
Log-rolling—Carrying logs—Pranks—Frolic—A raising—
Husking—Singing before the husking—Picking cotton seeds
—Other bees—Dances—Party games—Courting—Bundling
—Early marriage—Backwoods wedding—Plantation wed-
ding—Long visits—The barbecue

Chapter XIII. SPORTS   139
Sports barbarous—Animal-baiting—Gander pull—Shooting
match—Road-camp fight—Throwing the tomahawk—Cockfighting—Animal hunts—Horse-swapping—Horse-racing

Chapter XIV. THE FRONTIER TOWN   148
Early towns preceded settlement—Later towns followed
settlement—Town promotion—Competition between towns
—Little Rock primitive—Early Lexington—Town utilities
—Fire protection—Market—Lawless towns

Chapter XV. PROFESSIONAL AMUSEMENT   158
Animal show—The circus—Waxed figures—Magicians—
Early players—Difficulties of the showman—Flatboat plays
—Medicine shows—Gambling—Gambling holes—Card
games—Gambling on steamboats—Cheating

Chapter XVI. SCHOOLS   170
Educational decline on the frontier—Country school—
Yankee teachers—Subscription school—Raising the school-
house—Boarding round—Log schoolhouse—Harsh disci-
pline—Punishment—Loud school—Teaching manners—
Long hours—Amusements—Turning the master out—Select
schools—Academies—Transylvania College—Girls' schools
—Tutors—Children go away to college

Chapter XVII. RELIGION ON THE FRONTIER   181
Frontier irreligious—Baptists and Methodists—Religious
meetings—Church announcements—Slaves and masters
worship together—Negro service—Business meeting—
Church discipline—The church and liquor—An ignorant
ministry—Unscholarly preaching—Hardships of the circuit
rider

PAGE

Chapter XVIII. THE GREAT REVIVAL   195
The origin of camp-meetings—Religious phenomena—The
jerks—Holy laugh—Camp-meeting ground—Camp-meeting
program—Confusion in worship—Rowdies disturb meetings
—Estimate of Great Revival—Revival meetings

Chapter XIX. TRAVEL AND ACCOMMODATIONS   204
Early trails—Express and mail—Primitive wagon roads—
Stagecoach travel—Rough travel—Mud wagon—Stage-
driver—Arrival of the stage—Taverns—Buildings—Toilet
facilities—No privacy—Eating and drinking

Chapter XX. SICKNESS AND DEATH   215
Pioneers unhealthy—Home doctoring—Home doctor book
—Scalded feet—Many doctors—Low professional require-
ments—Quacks—Bleeding—Malaria—Care of the dead—
Funerals

Chapter XXI. FRONTIER JUSTICE   225
Fights—Cruel punishments—Cases settled by common sense
—Poor jails—Courts primitive—Judges not professional—
Law fees paid in livestock—Trials a source of entertainment
—Law training—Trials a farce—Vigilante justice

Chapter XXII. POLITICS AND ELECTIONS   236
Self-government—Watauga—Territorial government—Ig-
norant legislators—County court—Tax-gatherer itinerated
—Electioneering—The still hunt—People politically minded
—Voting

Chapter XXIII. FRONTIER MANUFACTURES   244
Making salt—Gunpowder—Maple sugar—Molasses-making
—Grinding corn—Floating mills—The mill a social center
—Textile-manufacturing—Tanning—Distilling whisky

Chapter XXIV. WHITES AND INDIANS   256
Indians friendly—Whites kill Indians—Scalping—Whites
take scalps—Indians capture whites—Running the gantlet
—Women not violated—Friendly relations between the
races—Indians scare whites

CONTENTS

PAGE

Chapter XXV. Frontier Military Life   262
Militia organization—Small units—Hunting shirts—Rangers
—Spies in the woods—Signs of Indians—Robertson's jour-
neys—Discipline of militia—Muster a military mockery—
Soldiers' ragged drill—Barefoot soldiers—Muster a social
occasion—Representative Indian campaigns

Chapter XXVI. The Frontier Woman   274
On the trail west—Starvation voyage from Kentucky to
Natchez—Ohio boats attacked—Woman encourages men to
fight—Women load guns—Lonely life in the forest—
Woman hero of an Indian attack—Help husbands in the
field—Make clothes—Childbearing

Chapter XXVII. Border Food   287
Wild fruit—Buffalo—Other game—Garden truck—Dried
food—Different ways of cooking corn—Raw foods—Nuts
—Honey—Sour milk—Too much whisky

Chapter XXVIII. Pioneer Dress   293
The hunting shirt—Breeches rare—Moccasins—Barefoot—
Homespun—Women's wear—Few store goods—Better
dress among planters

Chapter XXIX. Frontier Ways   299
Few crude dishes—Laundering out of doors—Fireplace fur-
nishes light—Beds—Gums for containers—No locks—Chimney on fire—Family worship—Hospitality—Travel by sled
—Blanket over the saddle

Chapter XXX. Frontier Speech   310
Cracker talk—Speaking in superlatives—Metaphors from
the forest—Figures from Indian fighting—Figures from
steamboating—Cracker dictionary—A keen sense of humor
—Anecdotes—Overuse of "elegant"—Plunder—Tarnation
—Rivermen bragging

Chapter XXXI. Frontier Characteristics   321
Whites as cruel as Indians—Rough society—Theater riot—
Open-hearted to unfortunate—Inquisitive—Dislike of for-
mality—Sham despised—No display of affections

PAGE

Chapter XXXII. FRONTIER CHARACTERISTICS (Concluded)   330

Shiftlessness—Desire for self-government—No servility—Limited class distinctions—Military titles desired—Each new settlement a little republic—Exploitation—Individualism—Old customs looked upon lightly—Uncomplaining—Personal honor valued—Provincialism—Belief in republican form of government

BIBLIOGRAPHY   341

INDEX   Follows page 374

The Dixie Frontier

I

The Promised Land

THE first Americans who crossed the Appalachian Mountains were thrilled with the beauty and the richness of the vast area beyond. Typical of this attitude is an entry in the journal of Thomas Hanson: "All the land that we passed over to-day is like a paradise it is so good and beautiful."

Southward of an irregular line drawn east and west from northern Missouri through central Kentucky an immense forest covered the entire area to the Gulf. Certain treeless areas north of this line in Kentucky were called the barrens and in Missouri and Illinois were known as the prairies. These areas were great meadows whose grass rose to a height of from two to four feet. In the lowlands of the forest grew dense canebrakes and small brushwood, matted together with a veritable network of vines and briers forming an almost impenetrable jungle. The canebrakes were unbelievably tall and dense. The mother of Mrs. A. O. P. Nicholson of Maury County, Tennessee, remembered that the cane was as high as the house. The bridle path from Claiborne to Suggsville, Alabama, in 1808 was so narrow and the cane so dense that the saddlebags of travelers had worn the cane on each side of the trail. The cane was so high that a man on horseback could barely reach the tops with an umbrella. Early residents of Kentucky reported that cane grew ten to twelve feet high and as thick as hemp.

The celebrated traveler Christian Schultz on his voyage down the Mississippi River in 1808 noted that the growth of cane began to increase every day after he moved south of the Ohio River and increased in height until it was thirty feet high and the stalks were about four or five inches in circumference. The growth then began to diminish until the thirty-first parallel was reached, when it disappeared altogether. The dense cane formed the lair of wild animals such as bears, wolves, and panthers. A man did not venture into the jungle lest he lose his way or forfeit his life to the wild beasts.

The first hunters in Kentucky pronounced the region a veritable hunter's delight. In 1869 Daniel Boone was quoted by Filson, Kentucky's first historian, as saying:

> We found everywhere abundance of wild beasts of all sorts through this vast forest. The buffaloes (or bison) were more frequent than I have ever seen cattle in the settlements browsing on the leaves of the cane or cropping the herbage on the extensive plains, fearless because ignorant of the violence of man.[1]

Flocks of turkeys numbering scores fed fearlessly in the open between irregular lines of elk and buffalo, and bears rolled "nigger head" stones over and ate the grubs and field mice that were thus uncovered. When the famous long hunter Abraham Bledsoe first visited the site of Nashville, he said he found a one-hundred acre area so crowded with buffalo and other wild animals that he was afraid to dismount for fear of being trampled underfoot.[2] Other witnesses declare the whole Southern area to have been one vast game paradise.

There is a grave question whether the country could have

[1] Brent Altsheler: "The Long Hunters and James Knox," *Filson Club Quarterly*, V, 173–4.
[2] Ibid., pp. 171–4.

been settled as readily as it was had it not been for the cane and the game. The latter supported human life until crops and domestic animals were raised and the cane supported domestic animals. Without these it would have been almost impossible to bring out over the mountains and through the wilderness enough provisions to keep the settlers and their stock from starving in winter.[3]

The grand opportunities for hunting, trapping, and trading came to the ears of the venturesome in the East, and soon hunting and trapping expeditions made their way into Kentucky and Tennessee, and traders pushed into the lower South. These early hunters were known as "long hunters," perhaps because they were gone from their homes for such long intervals. They were absent many months, some hunting continually for more than two years. Some authorities give the year 1770 as the date of the first expedition of long hunters. That autumn forty men from southwest Virginia set out under the leadership of James Knox, equipped with horses, traps, blankets, and dogs. They erected a skin-house and by the early part of 1771 had it filled with as many packs of pelts as they could carry home to Virginia. During the following five years more than eighty persons went from the Atlantic coastal states to hunt and trap in Kentucky and Tennessee. The long hunters usually organized into bands of ten, twenty, and forty for protection and convenience of transportation.[4] Once each five weeks they were to round up, deposit their pelts, and exchange experiences.

Smaller groups and even individuals wended their lonely way into the wilderness fastness in pursuit of skins. Their feats were in many ways even more remarkable than those of the bigger groups of long hunters. Daniel Boone is the most famous of these. He loved to roam without restraint through the wild forests. He started at daybreak when the dew was on the leaves and stole noiselessly upon the wary deer. He

---

[3] John D. Shane interview with James Wade in Draper MSS. 12CC38.
[4] Altsheler, op. cit., V, 169–70.

spent months alone in the forest in this carefree happy manner. A party wandering through the forest one day heard a
singular sound and a man named Mansco crept carefully
toward it while the others remained behind. What was his
amazement to find Daniel Boone lying on the flat of his back
on a deerskin, singing at the top of his voice.[5]

Sometimes Daniel's brother, Squire, or perhaps one or two
others went with him. In 1770, when they did so, it looked
as if the Indians had found their camp. They made another
one and took every precaution to conceal it. They made a
fire only at night to conceal the smoke, and even then
sheltered it so the flames could not be seen. They obliterated
the path running into their retreat. They broke their trail
by walking some distance in a stream, making great jumps
by swinging on the hanging wild grapevines, and, where possible, by walking on smooth stones and fallen trees. Close
to the camp all footprints were covered by leaves. If Indians
were in the vicinity, Boone, like one of the wild animals he
trapped, slunk off to the impenetrable safety of the dense
canebrake. Sometimes, like the mother bird that draws an
enemy away from her young, he built a campfire openly
and then, like a wily fox, slipped off a mile or two and slept
in the jungle of cane without a campfire.[6]

The bulk of the hides procured were deerskins. The process of preparing these for market was no light task. Both the
hair and the outer skin, in which the hair was rooted, known
as the grain, were scraped off with a knife. When dry, the
hide was rubbed across a "staking board" until the skin was
pliable. This process, known to hunters as graining, stripped
it of unnecessary weight and more readily prepared it for
packing. Such skins were known as half-dressed, and a pack
horse could carry about a hundred, averaging two and a half
pounds each. In 1770 they sold for about forty cents a pound.

These half-dressed skins were not cached in the ground

---

[5] Draper Notes, XXXII, 480.
[6] John Bakeless: *Daniel Boone* (New York, 1939), pp. 57–8.

as was customary in the Rocky Mountains a half century later, but were placed on poles elevated above the ground. After several layers had been placed on each other, a pole was fastened on top to keep the pile compact. Then, by means of tugs or lines thrown over the top, other poles were suspended to weight the skins down. The pile was protected from the weather by elk skins or peeled bark. When enough had been gathered for a pack, they were folded, baled up, and stored on platforms out of reach of the wolves and bears. Here they were protected from the weather until the trappers carried them to the settlements. About fifty skins formed a pack, and a horse carried one on each side.[7]

On at least one occasion Daniel Boone was gone from home nearly two years. He loved the wilds and was as much at home there as the average city dweller is in his home. This does not mean, however, that he never got lost, although he was a bit reluctant to admit it. After his recital of the adventures incident to one of his long hunts, an auditor, knowing he had no compass, asked him if he ever got lost. The reply was characteristic of the optimism of the American frontiersman: "No, I can't say as ever I was lost, but I was *bewildered* once for three days."

Americans have always been land-hungry. Perhaps this is because the emigrants from the old countries of Europe associated their landless condition in the old home with their poverty, and now in their new home they had a consuming desire to become landholders. As time went on, land-hunger increased until it became a mania. The leaders and outstanding men of the community frequently were engaged in securing as much land as possible, either for possession or to sell it at a handsome advance in price. Speculation was the great American enterprise from the middle of the eighteenth to the middle of the nineteenth century.

It is interesting to note that on John Sevier's second incursion into the Hiwassee country in eastern Tennessee,

[7] Charles A. Hanna: *The Wilderness Trail* (New York, 1911), II, 222–3.

the Indians had no more than fled before the voracious
pioneers began to blaze out numerous tomahawk claims, or
improvements as they were optimistically called. They hoped
in this way to establish ownership by conquest rather than
by purchase.

George Washington and Patrick Henry were leading
figures in land speculation in their day. The latter was ab-
sorbed in this activity the last third of the eighteenth century. When as Governor of Virginia he commissioned
George Rogers Clark to wrest the Old Northwest from the
British, it is almost certain he had an eye to Western lands
as well as to the execution of a patriotic stroke. These speculators dreamed of towns, cities, and highly improved countryside rising where their surveyors ran their lines. These
would in turn further enhance their holdings.

For a century it had been customary for the pioneer in
the area east of the mountains to mark off claims and hold
them by raising a crop of corn or by cutting his initials on
several trees near his clearing. This secured to the settler a
homestead of four hundred acres for which a clear title was
secured on payment of a small sum, and entitled him to a
pre-emption of one thousand acres adjoining for forty dollars
per hundred acres. Many times the claimants did not take up
their residence for months, perhaps did not even build a
cabin, and made no payment. Yet these "tomahawk rights"
and "corn rights" were recognized by other settlers. These
practices continued in Kentucky and Tennessee, which belonged to Virginia and North Carolina respectively at that
time. Although legally allowed only one claim, and that by
actual settlement, many went here and there marking off
the best land and traded or sold it to later comers.

Soldiers of the French and Indian, Revolutionary, and Indian wars were granted warrants that entitled them to unoccupied land. Big speculators bought up the land warrants
for a fraction of their actual value by offering cash. Armed
with a good supply of these warrants, the big speculator

sent a surveyor to search out the best lands and claim them. This program was accentuated by the fact that paper money was at a discount and yet was accepted at face value by the land office. The woods were literally filled with these surveying parties marking off claims. They went here and there taking the pick of the land: two thousand acres for this man, six thousand for that one, and eight hundred for still another. Sometimes a surveying party ran across another, ceased work, and went a little farther away to survey.

Several things operated to bring about great confusion in Kentucky land titles. In the first place there was no system of surveys, and this resulted in the greatest confusion of odd-shaped tracts. Then, too, the description of boundaries was based on natural objects such as stones, creeks, and trees, which were likely to become obliterated. For example, Daniel Boone in his field notes of July 9, 1776 states:

> Survaide for Mager [Major?] Bullock a Cartin trickt of Land Lying on the Waters of Moddy [Muddy?] Crick. Joyning Jesse Benton on the West End Beginning at a Black oke and Running West 204 pole to a White oke thence south 302 poles to a hickerry thence Este 204 poles to two white oke saplings thence 302 pole to the beginning.[8]

When trees died or were cut down, when rocks were moved or streams changed their courses, the ground work was laid for disputes. Worse than that, however, was the fact that there was no way to avoil overlapping surveys or indeed overlapping claims. When a claim was registered at the land office it was with the understanding that it was valid subject to the condition that it had not been entered by anyone else. If later claims were laid to the same tract or portions of it, they were invalid. But how was one to determine whether a piece of land had been entered, since there were no state-wide survey records available? This led to

[8] Boone MSS., Vol. XXV, Draper MSS., Wisconsin State Historical Society Library.

duplication of claims. Sometimes prior claimants did not fulfill the exact legal requirements and lost their rights for this
reason. Sometimes good farms were laid out, improved, and
finally after bitter lawsuits were lost by reason of later
surveys after as many as twenty years of occupancy. It is
well known that Daniel Boone and many of the other pioneers who bore the brunt of the hardships of the early occupation of Kentucky lost all of their numerous landholdings.

North Carolina laws allowed each head of a family to
claim 640 acres for himself and 100 acres for his wife
and each child. He received a title to the land when he paid
forty shillings per hundred acres. Land in addition to that
amount cost one hundred shillings instead of forty. The in-
efficient surveying system was conceded by the legal provision that a claim paid for by a warrant could be shifted to
a new claim if it was discovered that the first entry was made
on land already claimed by another.[9]

The North Carolina law, applicable to Tennessee in 1782,
had the advantage over that of Kentucky, however, in that
an official surveyor marked off the land. The system was:
(1) A claimant would go into the woods and mark out
roughly the boundaries of the desired tract. (2) This rude
survey when submitted to the entry-taker at the land office
was called an "entry." He made a record of the entry and
issued a warrant for the survey. (3) The official surveyor
connected with the land office then made a survey and submitted a plat to the secretary of state, who issued a grant.
(4) The title was complete when the grant was recorded in
the office of the register of the county where the land lay.[10]

In Georgia the land was the property of the state, which
opened up various tracts for entry at stated intervals and
allowed all who presented themselves to draw lots. The small

[9] Theodore Roosevelt: *The Winning of the West* (New York, 1894),
III, 11.
[10] Thomas Perkins Abernethy: *Frontier to Plantation in Tennessee*
(Chapel Hill, N.C., 1932), pp. 50–1.

fraction who were successful, upon payment of a moderate fee, secured a title.

In the cultural area of the Old Southwest—all of the states except Kentucky, Tennessee, and Georgia—the land was the property of the United States and was surveyed by the efficient rectangular survey. By means of plats kept in the land offices there was no danger of double entry or defective titles. A discussion of the disposition of the public domain in the other states is found in a later chapter.

In western Georgia, Alabama, and parts of Mississippi were to be found contemporaneous with the coming of the first settlers to Kentucky and Tennessee a sprinkling of men known as "Indian countrymen." These were men who for various reasons had left civilization to live among the Indians long before the true American pioneer came. Some were fugitives from justice. Others left home to get away from family trouble or to forget some great sorrow. Still others loved life in the far-off wilds among primitive people with its romance and trade profits. Some were honorable men who married Indian women and, establishing homes, reared respectable half-breeds. Others were disreputable men who lived like animals and accordingly exerted a bad influence on the Indians. They usually settled at strategic points on trade routes and engaged in ranching and trading. They were received as members of the Indian tribes and in time their offspring played an influential part in Indian history.

Chief McGillivray of the Creeks was a son of one of these Indian countrymen. His sister Sophia, a beautiful half-breed maiden, lived with him at Hickory Ground in 1776. During an Indian council a young South Carolinian of Huguenot ancestry, Benjamin Durant, appeared in the Indian country on a romantic errand. He was a champion in feats of physical prowess in his country and had come to seek out a certain man who lived at Hickory Ground who was said to be his superior. Sophia was there in all her youth and beauty, dressed in fine apparel. After a tremendous struggle Durant was declared victor. His splendid form, fine physique, and handsome face, as brown as her own, captured the heart of the Indian maiden, and soon they were married. Sophia was long the interpreter for her brother, who had lived so long among the whites that he spoke the Indian language indifferently. She was thus a most influential figure in the tribe, probably next to the chief himself. Durant cultivated several bends of the Alabama River and became a wealthy man.[11]

Many of these prosperous Indian countrymen together with their half-breed offspring cushioned the friction between reds and whites. On the other hand, some of them were unprincipled, with no loyalty to either race. They lived as outlaws, and each race blamed the other for their crimes.

[11] Colonel A. J. Pickett: "Notes on Alabama," MSS., Vol. II, Alabama Department of Archives and History.

II

A Nation on the March

A VARIETY of causes operated to lure the settler over the mountains through the forbidding wilderness to the promised land. First was the desire to own land, a greater opportunity for one's children, riches by speculation. Daniel Boone well expressed the popular attitude: "Now is the time to secure all this country; we've got it, let's keep it!" In 1779 Colonel Floyd wrote to Colonel Preston that his claim for 1,400 acres of land had been approved and he was immediately offered six fine young Virginia-born Negroes for it. He further wrote: "You never saw such keenness as is here about land."

Some, like James Robertson, turned westward to escape the abuses and oppression of corrupt government which had brought on the Battle of the Alamance between the Regulators and the colonial authorities in North Carolina. Some went into the wilds as an escape from disappointment, to begin over again when failure had struck, or to escape the toils of the law. Even Daniel Boone, whose love of the wilds and the life of a hunter were enough to draw him thither, got out of the country just ahead of a creditor who had the legal papers made out to attach his property. The document has been preserved. The words "no goods" have been written on the back. A warrant sworn out for his arrest for debt bears the words: "Gone to Kentucky." [1] For years it was common in Virginia for an inquiry as to where a certain man had gone, to receive the answer: "He's gone to hell or Kentucky."

At first two little streams of migration trickled down out of the mountains into the West. By 1800 these had reached flood tide and were pouring a veritable torrent onto the lowlands of Kentucky and Tennessee. The earliest effective crossing of the mountains took place in spite of the Royal British Proclamation of 1763 forbidding settlement west of the mountains. The crossing was through gaps leading from western Virginia and North Carolina to the headwaters of the Tennessee River. The first settlers filtered into this area of eastern Tennessee, known as the Watauga region, during the decade of the 1760's. After a short pause, in the seventies, this settlement's pent-up force broke over to the north at Cumberland Gap and, making a channel through the wilderness, flowed out upon the lowlands of Kentucky. In the eighties settlement flowed from this base in eastern Tennessee west into central Tennessee on the Cumberland River. In the meantime, in the seventies, a new stream of settlement had begun its flow down the Ohio River. This was to become by all odds the greatest stream of settlement flowing into the area treated in this volume.

Once having determined to migrate, the pioneers bent all efforts in preparation. When the McAfee families made ready to go, in the spring of 1776, they busied themselves day and night making an extra supply of linen, flannel blankets, bedclothes, and clothing of all kinds. They needed enough to last for a number of years during the hard pioneering period until the raw product could be raised to make these things in the new home. Just as they started, Mrs. George McAfee was confined. The others left her, but at the first opportunity when a long halt permitted, her hus-

[1] Bakeless: *Daniel Boone*, p. 90.

band hastened back. He met her on the way, for the courageous woman had set out on horseback only three days after her confinement, taking her baby along.

The road into Kentucky, known as the Wilderness Road, was laid out by Daniel Boone in 1775 and is a monument to the skill and practical engineering ability of an uneducated pioneer. It required skill to lay out a road through more than two hundred miles of wilderness in such a way that for over a century it remained almost unchanged. It was a mere trail through the trees and around the mountains, suitable only for horse or foot traveler. It was only roughly cleared with axes, and not until about 1800 was it improved for wagon travel.

It was customary for large parties to gather in eastern Tennessee and travel together through the unsettled areas of Kentucky or middle Tennessee. For years the territorial government provided an annual escort for settlers traveling from eastern Tennessee to the Cumberland area in central Tennessee. The time of departure was advertised for weeks in advance. In the eighties little boards with the distance painted in black were nailed to the trees every three miles on the trail to middle Tennessee.

When a sufficient number had gathered to form a protected party, they organized for the journey through the wilderness to Kentucky. In the company in which one unknown chronicler traveled in 1784, there were about five hundred. One hundred and thirty-four were active, well-armed men. The rest were old men, women, children, besides Negroes. A day was spent in organizing, choosing officers, and making regulations for the journey. That evening it was found that a number of them were breaking out with the measles. They finally decided in spite of this difficulty to proceed slowly and camp at night by the roadside with a mounted guard of thirty men who would keep a great number of fires around the encampment and cry out every five minutes: "All is well!" in an endeavor to scare the Indians.

Many of the company sick with the measles rode from morning till night in the rain. In one place the trail ran along a creek, which the travelers crossed no less than fifty times in one day by very bad fords. The road varied all the way from rugged ascents and almost impassable descents to low miry stretches up to the horses' knees at every step. The unknown traveler said that he had hard work to make a mile in an hour. Out of twenty-two days, he said, there were "only 4 in which it did not rain and thunder excessively." [2]

The procedure on the trail was somewhat as follows: The big boys drove the stock at the van of the party. This was very difficult. John Floyd ruefully wrote after his first trip to Kentucky that "whoever drives cattle here ought to have patience in great abundance." Jonathan Robertson, the ten-year-old son of James Robertson, had great difficulty with a heady old ram, which, in spite of everything the boy could do, would sally off into the brush, forcing James to dismount and follow through the vast wilderness on foot. Finally when he got the obstreperous animal back on the trail, he was sometimes miles behind the caravan.

Everything they would need in the new country had to be carried by pack horse. David and Nathaniel Hart of Kentucky, in 1777, had their cabin burned by Indians. Five hundred apple-tree scions that had been carried through the wilderness by pack horse were ruined.

The younger children were placed in cages or baskets made of hickory withes and fastened on the sides of gentle old horses or else they were seated between large rolls of bedding fastened before and behind them. The women sometimes walked and sometimes rode, carrying the babies. Some of the men, with rifle in hand, guarded the pack horses, while a large proportion of "the guns" as each man able to bear one was called, were used as scouts and walked spread out on the front, flanks, and rear to intercept any Indians who might be waiting to attack such a vulnerable group.

Many were the trials endured by those who traveled through the wilderness. Many were poor and did not realize the difficulties they would have to meet. Often illy clothed, half-starved men, women, and children trudged along barefoot. For days the travelers marched through the rain and mud and camped in the dripping dismal woods at night.

A short fragmentary diary kept by William Calk on the way to Kentucky in 1775 gives a vivid picture of the problems of the march. In the party was Abraham Hanks, maternal grandfather of Abraham Lincoln.

fryday ye 24th [March]. . . . Come to a turabel mountain that tried us all almost to death to get over it & we lodge this night on the Lawrel fork of holston under a grait mountain & Roast a fine fat turkey for our suppers & Eat it without aney Bread. . . .

thursd 30th [March] we set out again & went down to Elk gardin and there Suplied our Selves With Seed Corn & irish tators then we went on alittel way I turned my hors to drive before me and he got Scard Ran away threw Down the Saddel Bags and broke three of our powder goards and ABram's flask Burst open a walet of corn and lost a good Deal and made aturrabel flustration amongst the Reast of the Horses Drake's mair ran against a sapling and noct it down we cacht them all again and went on and lodged at John Duncan's.

Wed. ye 5th [April]. Breaks away fair & we go down the valey & camp on indian Creek we had this creek to cross many times & very Bad Banks. ABrams [Hanks'] saddel turned & the load all fell in we go out this Eavening & Kill two Deer. . . .

Fryday, ye 7th this morning avery hard snowey morning we still continue at camp Being in number about 40 men & some neagroes, this eaven Comes aletter from Capt.

Boon at Caintuck of the inding doing mischief and Some turns back

Satrd 8th. We all pact up & started corst Cumberland gap. . . . We Met a great maney people turned Back for fear of the indians but our Company goes on Still with good courage. . . .

tuesday 11th. . . . abrams mair ran into the River with Her load & Swam over he followed her & got her & made her Swim Back agin. . . .

Wednesday 12th. . . . We meet another Companey going Back   they tell Such News ABram & Drake is afraid to go aney further. . . .

thursday 13th   ABram & Drake turn Back

In spite of hardships and dangers the Wilderness Trail poured a stream of immigrants into Kentucky. A traveler on his way to the rendezvous where companies assembled

kept an account of the number of souls I overtook in one day going to that country [Kentucky]; and though I was the whole day in riding about thirty miles, but very little faster than a waggon could drive, I overtook two hundred and twenty one. They seem absolutely infatuated by something like the old crusading spirit to the holy land.[3]

Judge Harry Innes wrote on December 7, 1787:

The Emigrations have been great this Fall—to the 1st of this Inst. 10,000 souls have been counted to cross Clinch—about 2,000 came down the River—say 3,000 of the 12,000 were Citizens of this District returning home which is a large calculation, & the increase is 9,000 including those gone to Cumberland, who are but few.[4]

With all of this traffic, however, the far larger stream moved down the Ohio River, particularly during the period after 1800. Prior to the close of the Revolutionary War al-

[3] Ibid., p. 93.
[4] Judge Harry Innes to John Brown, Danville, Kentucky, December 7, 1787, MS., Kentucky Historical Society.

most all of this migration went to Kentucky, but after 1788 an increasingly larger proportion settled in the area north of the Ohio River until by 1800 the major part was going there. This route was much easier than the tedious all-land route, and yet it presented its problems. The beginnings of the journey required an overland jaunt of from a few miles to a few hundred miles. In the earlier years this was managed with pack horses, but later by wagons. Upon reaching the vicinity of Pittsburgh the immigrants either built or bought a flatboat. Such a craft was built on a slope near the water, of whipsawed and hewed timber. It was constructed bottom-side up and turned over before it was launched. Oakum or old rope was driven into the cracks with a hammer.

The ark or family flatboat was the most popular. It was made less than fifteen feet wide (but varied in width) in order to negotiate the falls at Louisville, which had a fifteen-foot channel between the rocks. Fifty feet was a popular length. The boat appeared rectangular in shape from above, but the bottom was shorter than the top and the ends consequently sloped enough to aid the craft to glide on the water. Around the outside of the deck were upright posts about six feet high, and to these posts heavy planks were pinned as a protection against the fire of the Indians. Portholes for firing pierced these planks. A roof often covered a part or all of the boat. After 1796, when danger of Indian attack had ceased, the bulwarks were no longer built. Timothy Flint observed, in 1825, that it was no uncommon spectacle to see one of these craft floating along with a large family, old and young, servants, and livestock of all kinds, reminding the spectator of Noah's ark. The deck looked like a farmyard scene, with its stack of hay, hogpen, cowyard, and implements. At one end was a fireplace for cooking, and quarters for women. Very often two or three families co-operated in buying an ark at a cost of about seventy-five dollars. Often they could be sold for almost as much some distance down the river.

Jacob Young's parents floated downstream on such a flatboat in 1797. Fifty-two persons and fifteen horses were on board. There was no danger of Indian attacks, but owing to those in years previous, the party was apprehensive. It was late in the season and the weather was very stormy. They often had a wild time. Horses pranced and attempted to jump out, women screamed at the top of their voices, and cowardly men stood on the bow excitedly crying in confusion: "To the right!" "To the left!" Young, who was the steersman, became so angry that he "swore terribly" as the women cried aloud and prayed for mercy.

In good weather when the water was sufficient the journey was pleasant. When D. Meade moved his household and property on two boats, he had a punt that played constantly between his boats and the shore. Someone, he said, was ashore ten times a day, sometimes on one side and sometimes on the other. In the early days, however, Indian attacks were frequent and deadly. A boat dared not tie up on the northern shore and some even were attacked and boarded while moving. A favorite trick of the Indians was to get a white man who was their captive or had turned renegade to appear on the shore and, pleading distress, beg piteously to be taken aboard. Those who paused to be good Samaritans were destroyed.

In 1784 on the Ohio shore the Indians attacked three boats. Two were taken and the third lost every man on board except a certain Reverend Mr. Tucker, a Methodist missionary who was on his way to his circuit in Kentucky. He was wounded in several places, but when the Indians pushed off from shore in a canoe and attempted to board the flatboat, the women loaded their dead husbands' rifles and handed them to the minister, whose aim was so deadly that every shot dropped an assailant. The Indians grew disheartened and gave up the attack. After the battle Tucker fell from sheer exhaustion and the women took the oars and made a landing at Limestone, Kentucky. A few days later the heroic circuit rider died of his wounds, mourned by his benefactors.

Low and high water brought problems also. Sandbars, snags, whirlpools, and angry waves caused heavy labor. Sometimes the unwary or inexperienced tied up at night to an undependable, insecure hitching-place only to find themselves drifting helplessly in the darkness. From this experience comes the expression characterizing a man as undependable: "He isn't a bad man, but he'll never do to tie to."

I. B. Miller wrote in his journal in the autumn of 1789:

Then sailed for Kaintucky. Arove at Limestone the 18th., after 10 days of the fertigueinest time I ever saw.

During the period following the War of 1812 many Kentuckians and other Southerners who had during their military service seen the rich land in the area north of the Ohio River moved into southern Ohio, Indiana, and Illinois, giving these areas an upper Southern culture. During this era the little rivulet of migration into Missouri began to increase until it became a flood, with the principal source Virginia and the Carolinas or descendants of those originally from there who had paused in Kentucky or Tennessee en route.

In 1819 a Missouri observer noted that

Immense numbers of wagons, carriages, carts, etc., with families, have for some time past been daily arriving. During October it is stated no less than 271 wagons and four wheeled carriages and carts, passed near St. Charles. . . . It is calculated that the number of persons accompanying these wagons, etc., could not be less than 3,000.[5]

George W. Dameron remembered one party of about sixty who came to Missouri from North Carolina about 1830. About half the number were slaves.

These migrations were chiefly by covered wagon although some floated down the great rivers that drain Kentucky and

[5] E. M. Violette: "Early Settlements in Missouri," *Missouri Historical Review*, I, 51.

Tennessee and, arriving at their confluence with the Ohio, made the remaining journey by wagon. By the thirties and forties emigrants often went to Missouri, Arkansas, and other frontier states on steamboats.[6]

[6] For a more detailed description of immigrant life on the steamboat, see Everett Dick: *Vanguards of the Frontier* (New York, 1941), chapter vii, and *The Sod-House Frontier* (New York, 1937), chapter i.

III

The Squatter

KEEN observers again and again mention that the westward movement of population in the United States flowed in waves. First came the missionary, hunter-trapper, trader, and Indian countryman, or squaw-man as he was known in the territory north of the Ohio River. These lived with the Indians and so far as American civilization was concerned were practically part of the Indian life. They were not a part of the great homemaking program that had its roots in agricultural pursuits. They did not think of themselves as settlers. They often spoke of returning east to "the settlements" for supplies or to market the products of their business. And yet these "vanguards of the frontier" formed an entering wedge for the first settlers.

The next wave was made up of the first crude homemakers, the squatters. They were agriculturists in a small way, and yet they loved the wild free life of the hunter and detested the plow. This class has aptly been termed "the cutting edge of the frontier." An Englishman thought that these settlers of Big Prairie, Indiana, in 1817 were about half-Indian in their mode of life. They were not very cordial toward the "land-hunter." They wanted the whole range of the forests for themselves and their cattle. He found ignorance, indolence, and disorder, with a total disregard for cleanliness in their houses and persons. He found them kind, honest, and hospitable, however. The Indian agent Schoolcraft mentioned that when he was leaving a hunter's house, the latter not only refused to take any money for the accommodation but took him to the smokehouse, handed him a knife, and remarked: "Go in and cut." Still another saw in the squatters "a race of men possessing remarkable traits of character and manners which are a compound of civilization and barbarism." They continually tramped on the heels of the Indians and not infrequently had to be removed from Indians lands by the government because they had possessed the land before the Indian title had been extinguished.

On Big Bottom, near Chariton, Missouri, in 1819, was a cornfield of nearly a thousand acres under a common fence. More than twenty families each cultivated a plot in this large area. They lived in cabins around the field. Children in almost countless numbers showed their tangled and matted locks, dirty faces, and squalid dress as the stranger passed through the area.

The name "Hoosier" was often applied to these backwoodsmen even as far south as northern Louisiana and southern Arkansas. Everywhere the general characteristics of this tribe were the same, east to Georgia and from Mississippi and Alabama north to Illinois and Indiana.

When population came, the squatter's troubles began. No longer could he pasture the government land; but he had to keep his cattle and horses on his own premises. The game that gave him subsistence was driven away. The increase in population brought with it government, with its taxation, regulations, and a whole calendar of restricting laws. However great the benefits of government, they could not begin to compensate the squatter for the loss of his freedom. He would sell out his rights to someone who wished to buy his claim from the government and once more betake himself to the wilderness where there were bears, deer, and other game and fur-bearing animals in abundance.

The Ramsay family from 1808 to 1820, in twelve years, moved and lived on nine different places, finally ending up in southeast Mississippi. As neighbors began to settle from two to five miles from him, the hunter-farmer became uneasy. A European tried to dissuade a settler who was considering moving to Mississippi, in 1832, from moving to a region unknown to him. The settler's reply was characteristic: "I have no elbow-room. I cannot move about without seeing the nose of my neighbor sticking out between the trees." Daniel Boone expressed the philosophy of the squatter when he said: "I think it is time to remove when I can no longer fall a tree for fuel, so that its top will lie within a few yards of my cabin."

The typical hunter-farmer was expert with the rifle, capable of the periodical exertion that hunting required, but strongly inclined to take his ease by the fireplace when there was meat in the cabin. Patient and easygoing, he would submit to a great deal of inconvenience before he would rouse himself. His agricultural pursuits seldom got beyond a little clearing or deadening for a corn patch, but when out in the woods with his rifle, he was strictly in his element. The hunter's wife was much more inclined to inquire of the stranger whether he had noticed any signs of game than any of the things ordinarily of interest in the feminine world.

The squatter based his actions on the preferential treatment accorded for generations to "cabin rights." Not all squatters were perennial drifters, however. Some were poor, not from lack of ambition, but through misfortune or lack of opportunity. These prospered and often remained in their new homes to become members of the middle class, or advanced into the large planter group. Some, however, without initiative to move on west to rise in the economic scale, became the lower stratum and progenitors of the poor whites and tenant classes of the South today.

The settler liked to arrive in the new country in the spring. He would then select the richest, best-lying, well-watered land he could find for his claim. He would then make a small clearing for a house and truck patch and deaden a small area for a cornfield.

In the meantime the family had to be housed temporarily. Along the rivers in certain places the rocks projected out over the banks. Hunters and early settlers sometimes lived in the shelter of these for months. They were known as rock houses. It was in a shelter of this kind that Dr. Thomas Walker and his associates of the first American "land looking party," which came into Kentucky in 1750, lived for a time.

Another type of shelter was the half-faced camp. It could be made in several ways. The typical one, however, was made by setting two forked posts in the ground and placing a transverse pole across the crotches. Then boughs of trees, butts upward, were leaned from the ground against the horizontal pole. Evergreens were preferable if available. If they were not, bark or the skins of animals served.[1] A fire in front of this rude shelter threw its heat upon the occupants.

Another shelter was made of poles and shakes. Even the earliest hunter-settlers had an ax or two and some iron wedges. Others owned or could borrow a crosscut saw. A large oak was felled and the settler's wife or a neighbor helped saw and split it and by means of the wedges rived off boards. Boards of this kind, commonly called shakes in the North, were three or four feet long and six or eight inches wide. Four forked poles were then cut and set in the ground. Two of these, which were to support the front of the roof, were perhaps two feet longer than those which were to support the rear. Two transverse poles were then placed on the four forks, and boards laid across these formed a roof for protection against the rain. In Alabama a family

[1] John W. Monette: *History of the Discovery and Settlement of the Valley of the Mississippi* (New York, 1846), II, 12.

often spent weeks in such a shelter, and after the cabin had been built they sometimes used this for a kitchen. If the weather required it, they placed poles or boards crosswise and pegged them to the uprights.

The kind of permanent house depended upon the available help. If the squatter had only the help of his wife, he cut near the building site mere poles of a size they could handle. If there were even a few settlers, however, he cut logs and notched them, and the house was put up at a house-raising. A log pen was laid up, and if a crosscut saw was available, the windows and doors were cut afterward. If not, he had short logs cut, which were laid up and propped in place as the pen was built. The door and window facings were "scalped" as the cabin went up, and these were pegged to the logs on each side of the doorway. A door was hung on wooden hinges. In Alabama, Mississippi, Louisiana, Arkansas, and Tennessee the wooden unglazed windows hung on wooden hinges like the door and were known as shutters. There were cracks between the logs where the chinking had fallen out, and as one Alabama sufferer said, the large cracks in the shutters and door let in additional cold to the shivering, suffering, defenseless household. In fact, he said, there seemed to be just warmth enough inside of those thoroughly ventilated cabins to attract all the cold blasts in the country for miles around. Inside every cabin, he declared, there was nothing but a huge mass of concentrated winter weather and suffering humanity.[2]

A little farther north the window openings were sometimes closed with deerskin scraped thin or with heavy greased paper. Even in Missouri, however, more often than not there was nothing even suggesting transparency to close the opening. In the northern area the fireplace often occupied the whole end of the house and would take a log twelve feet long. When burned in two in the middle, the ends could

[2] F. D. Srygley: *Seventy Years in Dixie* (Nashville, Tenn., 1893), p.136; Kathleen Graham: *Notes on a History of Lincoln Parish, Louisiana* (place and date of publication not given), pp. 27-8.

be pushed together. The cabins often had two doors, one on each side of the house, and an ox or a horse was used to "snake" a log right into the house by leading the animal through the cabin and unfastening the chain when the log was in the center of the cabin. The log was then rolled up to the fireplace.

In the lower South heating was not such a problem. In fact, some lived for months without window shutter or door. The chimney was made of sticks and clay, known as "cats and clay." The sticks were well embedded to keep the fire from burning them. The fireplace itself was made of clay, well pounded. Many pole houses were roofed with bark and the skins of wild animals. In the better houses the roof was made of riven boards three to four feet long. Each layer of boards was held in place by "butting poles." These weighted down one layer of boards and kept the next higher one from slipping down.

After a time, as his family increased, the squatter who stayed in the area and became prosperous built a second cabin and connected the two by a covered passage eight or ten feet wide. This, commonly known as the dogtrot, was a cool place for the family to eat in summer. From this type of dwelling originated the expression: "the three P" order of architecture—two pens and a passage. Such a house was also sometimes known as a saddlebag house, owing to its shape. In a house of this type one pen was used for the general living-room and the other as the kitchen and dining-room. Sleeping-apartments in the attic were reached by means of a ladder. Later a veranda was placed on the front and there were the rudiments of the standard Southern dwelling.

As the visitor approached the hunter's cabin he was greeted by a pack of dogs, which set up such a chorus that one would have thought a pack of wolves or panthers was approaching; and not until they were peremptorily and repeatedly recalled would they desist. These dogs were kept especially for protection against the Indians and for hunting

bears. As game grew scarcer, they were used to chase deer
and especially to trail wounded animals. These hounds were
valuable, and the hunter was very fond of them. He would
share his food with them, and they followed him everywhere, even to church, weddings, and funerals. It was no
small task to provide food for a pack of from six to a dozen
dogs, and many times the hunter was forced from his ease
by the fire out into the hunt solely in order to provide meat
for his dogs.

The visitor approaching the hunter's house noticed a large
number of deer antlers and deer feet lying here and there.
On the house and on scaffolds around it were an innumer-
able quantity of deer, bear, and other skins. Although the
cabin was nearly filled with shy dirty children, the hospitable settler and his wife made the visitor at home. On step-
ping inside he saw a number of deer and buffalo horns on
the walls used for racks and hangers. On a pair of these over
the fireplace rested "Old Beelzebub" and any other guns the
hunter might own. On other hangers were shot-pouches,
leather coats, dried meat, and other articles comprising the
wardrobe, arsenal, and larder of the family.

On the floor were the skins of animals. To one side of the
fireplace was the cupboard, consisting of a row of shelves
with a few simple dishes made from wood, although there
might be a few pieces of pewter brought from the old home
and kept for special occasions. In the corner was a "one-
legged" bed made by using two walls of the cabin to support the side and head of the bed. A single post supported
the corner of the bed that was not fastened to the cabin
walls. Poles were laid across the bed rails, and on these was
placed a tick filled with leaves, dried grass, cattail down,
moss, or turkey feathers. Under the bed were stored various
supplies in gourds. In a large gourd, perhaps two feet in
diameter, the salt was stored. Smaller ones held shot, powder,
and various other supplies.

Hanging near the fireplace where the cooking was done

was a small cooking-salt gourd with its circular hole high up on one side for the insertion of a finger. Also near the fire on the floor was the meal gourd or meal gum. A gum was a container made of a hollowed-out section of a log, set upright and fitted with a bottom and a lid. Gums were preferable to gourds near the fireplace, for they were more substantial and could be used for stools. Gums were used to house bees also when a swarm was brought into captivity. When an overnight visitor went to the well to wash the next morning, someone poured water over his hands from a gourd. On the wall forming a part of the cupboard section were to be seen two deerskin containers made by taking the hide off as nearly entire as possible and sewing up the holes. One of these contained bear's oil and the other honey. From the roof hung circles of dried pumpkin, strings of dried apples, shucky beans, and other food stores for winter.

Frank Nixon, of Limestone County, Alabama, had his cabin decorated in an interesting way. He had killed a large bear, utilized its skin and meat, and cleaned the entrails, which he had stuffed and dried in graceful festoons around the inner walls of his cabin. In order to relieve the somber yellow hue of these ornaments he interspersed them with red pepper pods.

One man remembered that when he called, a squatter honored his guests by bringing out a big bearskin and placing it before the fire for their bed. The bear had been especially hard to kill and had slain his favorite dog. Then the old hunter threw down a pack of coonskins for his guests to use as pillows, the long tails hanging all in the same direction like so many striped snakes.

The intellectual status of the perennial squatter was pitiful. Almost always beyond the school and church, his children grew up without learning and moral training and without any desire for them. Schoolcraft noted that in his short tour of a few weeks in Arkansas and Missouri, in 1818, two instances had occurred where in childish disputes boys had stabbed each other with knives. In neither case was reproof administered. Rather it was looked upon as a promising trait of character.[3] And yet the squatters had vigorous intellects, bold and original ideas, and a vast fund of information drawn from nature. They had an eloquence peculiar to their environment, drawing illustrations from nature rather than from the classics, as was the custom of the times. A Methodist minister who visited in southern Illinois and Missouri in 1818 found that the younger members of the family, although grown, had no use for books or "any such trash."

A. J. Smith, a great bear-hunter of northeastern Arkansas, who usually went barefoot, bareheaded, and armed with a huge hunting knife, sold the Governor of the commonwealth some cattle and hogs. One day he called at the Governor's home to collect. His hair and beard were long and shaggy, and the Governor's wife was thoroughly frightened at his appearance but let him into the house. The hunter very carefully folded back the carpet and leaped over it to a seat by the fireplace, remarking: "Lady, I don't want to dirty up your quilt." The first lady was certain he was a horsethief and had his horse locked up. Her panic was not abated until her husband returned home and cordially greeted the pioneer.

Superstition generally held sway. Witchcraft was still believed in. One man told Schoolcraft that his rifle was so bewitched that he could kill nothing with it and he suspected that a neighbor, out of malice, had cast a spell on it. A belief in the sovereign virtue of certain metals prevailed. One woman had a brass ring that she had worn for several years which was a specific cure for cramps. Some thought that soap-making had to be done at a certain period of the moon's phases, stirred only with a sassafras stick, only one way, and by only one person.[4]

Most of the squatter's energy was used in hunting, but he

[3] Henry R. Schoolcraft: *Journal of a Tour into the Interior of Missouri and Arkansaw* (London, 1821), p. 49.

[4] Mrs. Bonita Musgrave: "A Study of the Home and Local Crafts of

spent some time digging ginseng, or "sang" as they called it. Daniel Boone dug it and was also a buyer among his neighbors. They also dug yellowroot. Incidental to his hunting, in spare time the squatter cleared a little patch for corn and truck.

The Easterner was astonished at the makeshift arrangements of the pioneer on the cutting edge of the frontier. He made his horse collar of braided shucks, the harness tugs and ropes of hickory bark or the raw skins of animals. An observer noticed a horseback rider coming through the forest with a bridle made of hickory bark, the stirrups and saddle-tree cut from the forest tree, and the saddle seat made of the skins of wild animals. Wagons or carts were made entirely of wood. The wheels were made of cross-sections sawed from a gum tree. The probate records of Ouachita Parish, Louisiana, reveal a condition that existed in many sections. Many of the settlers who died left goods to the value of less than one hundred dollars.[5]

An incident in Illinois in 1818 shows the inventive character of the early settler. James Lemon was breaking a piece of stubble ground and at noon left his homemade harness on the beam of his plow while he went to dinner. His son, a wild, mischievous youth who had been engaged in keeping the stubble from accumulating on the plow, stayed behind and hid one of the corn-shuck collars, thinking that he might rest while his father made a new collar. On returning and finding the collar mysteriously gone, the plowman mused a short time, and then, very much to the disappointment of his lazy son, deliberately took off his leather breeches, stuffed them with stubble, straddled them over the horse's neck for a collar, and plowed the rest of the day in his shirt tail.

Hunting was the life of the borderer, however. The buf-

the Pioneers of Washington County, Arkansas," MS. (Master's thesis, University of Arkansas, 1929), p. 60.

[5] Probate Records, Ouachita Parish, Monroe, Louisiana; Glenn Gardner Martel: "Early Days in Columbia County, Arkansas," MS. (Master's thesis, University of Arkansas, 1933), p. 37.

falo ranged in considerable numbers on the prairie lands of the area along the Tennessee, Kentucky, Ohio, and Missouri rivers, but soon they were either killed off or pushed on westward before the white occupation. Buffalo-hunting, therefore, was not a major activity for a very long period or over a very large area.

The earliest hunters waited at the licks and killed a few as the animals came for salt. A little later dogs were used. A company mounted on horses and with additional pack horses and their dogs would ride to the buffalo ranges. One hunter would creep up softly and fire into the midst of the herd. Then the whole company would rush in upon them with their dogs. This would throw the herd into confusion and each hunter would pick out a buffalo and kill him. Then the dogs would attack, and while the buffalo were engaged in fighting the dogs, the masters would have time to reload and kill others. After the chase was concluded, they would split the animals, take out the entrails, throw the meat across pack saddles, and carry it home. Only a small fraction of the meat was saved from this wanton slaughter. So quickly were the buffalo killed or chased away from the settlements that at the meeting of the first legislative assembly of Transylvania, Daniel Boone offered a bill, which became a law, protecting the buffalo. In that society of rugged individualism, of course such a restriction was bound to be ignored, and in a very few years the last buffalo in Kentucky had been killed.

When the group had arrived home after a successful hunting trip, there came the division of the kill. The program by which distribution was made was called "cut and call." One man, the caller, was blindfolded and placed behind a tree. Another stood by to act as referee and see that the caller did not peek. A third wielded an ax and a knife. When he had cut a piece, he cried out: "Who's here?" The blindfolded man who was judge and jury shouted the name of the one who was to receive it. This continued until all had been distributed. Unless liquor entered the picture, all went smoothly.

Bears were to be found generally over the entire Southern area. In the fall these animals would fatten on the fruit, nuts, and honey of the forest, and in the early winter they went into hibernation in a hollow tree or cave. Once in a while during the winter the bear would get out of its home and walk about and then return to its nest. The favorite time to hunt the bear was in the winter just before it went into hibernation or when it emerged for a short time. In the spring and summer the animal was lean and the skin was unprime. David Crockett was probably the most famous bear-hunter of all time. While he moved west with the frontier time after time, he established his fame as a bear-hunter on the Obion River in the northwest corner of Tennessee about 1825. The canebrakes there near the Mississippi were literally teeming with bears. Crockett, a member of the state legislature, exchanged his toga for buckskin hunting shirt and breeches, called his eight large dogs, "as fierce as painters" (panthers), and was off for the canebrakes. Trained bear dogs would not trail any other animal, and once they had taken up the trail they never gave it up until the bear was at bay. Only a good dog would fight a bear, and even he would avoid a direct attack from the animal, but would worry it until his master could come up and dispatch it. Sometimes the dogs ran a bear into a cave, and an intrepid hunter went in, shot the bear, and dragged it out with a rope. Legend has it that Mammoth Cave, in Kentucky, was discovered by a bear-hunter who followed the bear and dogs into the cavern in 1799. When Crockett had killed a bear he would blaze a trail on saplings back to his hunting camp and take four or five pack horses with him to bring back the meat. He then built a platform to keep the meat out of reach of wolves. Four forked stakes were driven into the ground, poles were laid across, and other poles laid across these. Crockett killed one bear that weighed as much as 650 pounds.

During the week between Christmas and New Year's in 1825 he killed seventeen. During that winter he killed one hundred and five bears.

Wild turkeys and deer abounded over the whole Southern frontier. In northern Louisiana turkeys were frequently run down by hunters on horseback and noosed by a rope thrown by the riders with astonishing dexterity while at full speed. Turkeys were wary birds and hard to shoot. Only the wise and persevering hunter was able to kill them. They were trapped with considerable success, however. An enclosure about ten feet square was made by piling up rails on the plan of a log house and placing a layer over the top of the pen. A trench was then dug from the outside into the pen under the bottom rail. Just inside the pen the trench was covered with a board or with sticks. Corn was then scattered in the trench and within the pen. The turkeys would follow the trail of corn into the pen and, finding themselves in a cage, would walk along the sides trying to get out, but were so stupid they never thought of going toward the center of the pen and walking back down the trench. The hunter had only to hit them on the head and kill them. A number were sometimes taken at the same time in this way.

There were several methods of hunting deer. In the still hunt the woodsman attempted to slip up on a herd and kill one. A platform or blind from which to shoot the wary animals was often utilized near a water hole or lick. Dogs were used to chase them by a point where the hunter lay in ambush. Another method was fire hunting, which was most effective on a dark night. A slave or a fellow hunter held high a long-handled skillet of burning "light wood" in an area the deer frequented. The animals were blinded and attracted by this and stood still to look at it. Their eyes shone like coals of fire and the hunter aimed between them.

Another species of animal hunted was wild hogs. These animals, which ran wild in the woods, were often hunted with gun and dogs just like game. When first turned out, the hogs were marked with certain cuts in the ears, and these marks were registered. The following earmark recorded in the court records of Pulaski County, Kentucky, is typical: "On motion of Peter Kemey his ear mark (to wit) a half crop in the right ear and a swallow fork and underkut in the left ear is ordered to be recorded." [6] In some areas the owners kept their swine in a semi-tame state by calling them up and feeding them from time to time. They thus learned their master's call or horn blast and would come at his command. In some places, however, these hogs became as wild as deer. It was said that the woods hogs of northern Louisiana were descended from southern European hogs. Whether that was so is questionable, but certainly by the early nineteenth century they were numerous and as wild as undomesticated animals. Some attribute the origin of the razorback hog to this herd. While this is doubtful, these hogs were very similar. When people wanted pork, they would take a gun and dogs and go into the woods. The dogs bayed the animals and the hunter could slip up and kill one or two before the herd took flight. A dog not well trained would sometimes be killed by them. Sometimes a man was treed and kept up there several hours before the angry porkers gave up their quarry. An Alabama observer remarked that one who had never seen a charge of one or two hundred excited, enraged hogs has no idea of the fury of their attack.

Another activity of the borderer was hunting bees. Honeybees are not indigenous to America, but were brought here by Europeans. Enough of them escaped, however, to stock the woods, and as the frontier moved westward they moved just ahead of the line of white settlement. Harrod brought the first bees into central Kentucky in 1784 or 1785 from the Monongahela country. The wild bees must have escaped from there to the West.

The bee-hunter took some honey and honeycomb in a wooden box into an area where he thought he could find

6 Pulaski County (Ky.) Court *Order Book*, I, 7, September 24, 1799.

bees. He deposited the sweets and burned a little of the bees-wax. The scent was sure to attract bees if they were in the area. He sprinkled some flour on their wings to make them more visible and to identify them and watched them take a "bee line" toward their home, laden with honey. He then followed the white bees with his bait until he came to the hollow tree in which they lived. He marked the tree and cut and robbed it in the fall when it was full of honey. Honey and maple syrup were practically the only sweets on the frontier.

IV

Station Life in Tennessee and Kentucky

ALL of the frontier settlements west of the Blue Ridge Mountains from the beginning of the French and Indian War in 1754 until nearly 1800 were subject to Indian attack. As a result, settlement was made in stockaded communities, which were known as forts in the northern area and east of the mountains, but usually were called stations in the Old Southwest.

A typical station consisted of a rectangular enclosure of from one half to two acres, made up of cabins and stockades, with blockhouses at the corners. A range of cabins formed one or more sides. If the cabins did not form a solid wall, they were connected with a row of logs set on end close together and sharpened at the top. This palisade and the outer walls of the houses were ten or twelve feet high. At two corners, at least, were blockhouses, two stories high. The lower story was made similar to a cabin, but the upper extended out about two feet beyond the outer walls of the cabins and stockades. An opening was made in the floor of this projecting story just outside the wall to enable the occupants to dislodge any attackers who might attempt to seek shelter under it. The projecting structures also enabled the occupants to fire down two sides of the exterior of the enclosure, making it possible to kill anyone who might attempt to climb the walls or set fire to the palisades. All roofs were made to slope inward to guard against the enemy's firing the fort. A large two-leaved folding gate made of thick slabs split from logs was swung between the parallel ends of two cabins. It was protected by a platform and sentry-box above, and was built nearest the spring. There were no windows or doors in the outside wall except a few small sally gates, which were used when the great gate was closed. At appropriate distances and heights the walls of palisades, cabins, and blockhouses were pierced with loopholes. These holes were small on the inside, but enlarged as they passed without, in order to give sweep to the fire. They were kept plugged. During an attack, when the plug was removed, many guns would sometimes fire right at the openings, which were often watched from ambush. Outside the walls, at a distance too far to provide protection for attackers, were scattered a number of cabins. Such was the typical station, and such in a general way were the famous stations of Watauga, Nashboro, Boonesborough, and Harrodsburg. In places less exposed or less inviting to attack a station consisted of a single blockhouse with a cabin or two. A whole station was built without the aid of a single nail or spike of iron.

A number of settlers made their homes in the cabins of the enclosure and, if no immediate danger threatened, went outside to their employment during the day. Others had their homes outside and went into the fort only when there were alarms and "Indian signs." At such a time the gates were closed and securely barred at sunset each day.

Indian attacks on the Kentucky stations, especially from 1775 until 1783, were a part of the larger struggle between the British and their Indian allies on the one hand and the Americans on the other. The Indians of the Old Northwest were egged on by British headquarters at Detroit, and toward the end of the war American settlers under the command of George Rogers Clark invaded and captured the British posts in Illinois and Indiana and chastised the Indians of Ohio. Even after the Revolutionary War peace did not come until General Wayne signed the Treaty of Fort Greenville in 1795, making peace with the Northern Indians, and General John Sevier won the victory over the Southern Indians at the Battle of Nickajack in 1794. At any time for a quarter of a century Indian war was likely to flare out at a moment's notice, and for weeks and even months open warfare existed.

An Indian army could not be kept long in the field and was likely to attempt to make a raid and return to its own territory. Often a large party would proceed rapidly to the center of the white settlements and then separate into small scalping parties. The faithful scouts would get warning to the larger stations of the approach of a large body, but when it broke up into small groups it was almost certain that some isolated ones would be caught unaware. Suddenly these phantom warriors prowling through the dark aisles of the forest came upon the lonely cabin, ambushed the men as they left their homes to hunt or work, and, falling upon their defenseless women and children, killed and scalped those unable to make the arduous journey back to their wigwams, and marched the stronger ones into captivity. Some of them were tortured and burned alive, but most of them were adopted into Indian families to take the place of lost ones.

Men lived with their rifles in their hands, ready to mount and ride to the aid of a distant station or to pursue a war party making for their lair with prisoners and horses. A man often stood guard with a rifle while another milked the cow or plowed the field. It was as unusual to see a man without a rifle at that time as one without his hat today. And it always had to be loaded and ready. The man caught with an empty rifle might easily pay for his negligence with his life. Michael Cassiday one day met a powerful Indian in a fairly open place in the forest. Each leveled his gun at the other, but Cassiday, to his consternation, found that his pocket handkerchief was tied around the lock and so prevented him from cocking it, and he feared to untie it lest the Indian see that his gun was useless and fire. They remained pointing their guns at each other for some time in a desperately grim tableau. Finally, when the Indian did not fire, Cassiday suspected something was wrong with his gun and began to take off the handkerchief. Then the Indian "treed" (hid behind a tree). Cassiday, now ready to fire, got a shot at the Indian, wounded him, and when he made at the redskin with his scalping knife, discovered the Indian had the ramrod stuck in his gun.

When men went through the woods in company, they agreed between them which one should fire if game appeared. This precaution was taken lest they should all be caught with empty guns and become an easy prey to Indians. Then, too, the settlers were always short of ammunition and it would have been a great waste to spend more than one shot on a deer. When shooting at a mark the participants placed the target in front of a tree and then dug the balls out of the wood again. After the famous siege of Boonesborough the pioneers picked up 125 pounds of lead that had been shot at the stockade. Various ruses were used by the Indians to kill unwary whites. Sometimes they would imitate the call of turkey or other wild animals and in that way lead their victims into position and shoot them.

Once Kasper Mansker of Tennessee was "gobbled up" by an Indian. An excellent scout, he was suspicious of the sound of the turkey he heard, and approached so cautiously that he located the very tree behind which the human gobbler stood. The distance was greater than an Indian would be likely to fire, but it was just right for "Old Nancy" and she was ready to "speak to him." Mansker was certain the Indian had seen him and the old scout feigned to pass around him, but the Indian began slyly to slip from one tree to another slightly in advance of the old hunter. In the midst of this life-and-death game Mansker, who had kept his left eye on the Indian, got an opportunity and "Nancy spoke to him." Shortly afterward Mansker had the Indian's old gun on his gun rack in his cabin.

This incident brings to our attention the fact that because of a chronic shortage of ammunition the Indians never loaded their guns as heavily as did the frontiersmen. The report was never so loud and had a peculiar flat crack. As a result, good woodsmen could tell by the sound in an instant whether a shot was fired by the Indians or the whites.

Sometimes Indians would catch a belled horse and, hiding it in a thicket, would wait out of sight, ringing the bell. When the owner came to catch his horse, he was killed. It was the custom among woodsmen never to make a noise in the forest, but to slip noiselessly along, taking every possible precaution to prevent surprise. Robert Jones, of middle Tennessee, had been cautioned not to be so noisy, but forgetting the good advice, he called when near the home of David Wilson, thus giving notice of his presence, and was killed by the Indians. The hunters' caution of pioneer days has become the political maxim of later days: "Never hallo until you are out of the woods."

Life at a station was a co-operative enterprise. The land near the fort was divided up among the members of the station, and there, while some tilled the soil, others stood guard with rifles. At night all went into the stockade under military escort. Leaders in settlement and in military affairs attempted to keep settlement compact around the stations and thus present a united front against the Indians. It was utterly impossible to realize this ideal, however, for even in the midst of Indian attacks the land-greedy settlers were going here and there staking out claims, and frequently some daring and much-needed individual would find a beautiful location and take his family out to live in a lonely cabin miles away from the station. As the mother stations grew in population by the arrival of newcomers, they swarmed and formed other stations with some of the "old settlers" acting as a sort of cadre in the formation of the new unit.

During the winter and at any other time they dared to do so, many families lived at their own "clearing," as their farms were called. Samuel Gibson remembered that when he was a boy his father's family lived about a mile from the stockade; when a messenger brought the dread message that Indians were about, his father would let the members of the family out one at a time until all were on their way to the fortification. Then the father, gun in hand, would bring up the rear. The flock had its instructions. If they heard any noise they were to run aside into the bushes and hide like partridges. When they got to the gate the sentry told them to squat down until all had assembled. Then he got down from the sentry-box and opened to them. It was good to hear the creak of the hinges as the great doors swung shut behind them and they were in the haven of safety.

Not infrequently the ominous message came in the dead of night. There was the sound of horses' hoofs on the still night air, a cautious knock at the door or back window. Quickly the family was awake and in motion. The father grabbed his gun and other equipment. The mother and the older children dressed the younger ones. All of this had to be done in the dark, for they dared not light a candle. And it was done with speed and silence. Care was exercised not to wake the baby. As for the rest, it was enough to say "Indians!" and not a word was heard afterward. The younger ones were wrapped in bedding and carried by the older ones, and quickly, hand in hand, the little procession wended its way through the pitch-black forest to the safety of the palisades. The terror of these occasions created a deep and lasting impression on the children. Sometimes the entire community belonging to a station were at their homes in the evening, and the next morning every family was in the fort. The next day armed parties were sent out to bring in the most valuable household belongings.

When the Indians attacked a station, they usually attempted to surprise the defenders. This was sometimes accomplished, at least to a degree, for the people were unbelievably dilatory and careless about keeping up the stations. Often stumps behind which Indians could hide were left near the stockade; weeds, which were used as a screen by the Indians, were allowed to grow within rifle-shot of the walls. The people at Boonesborough never even began to dig a well within the fort until faced with an Indian attack three years after the fort was built. Hickory-bark lead troughs conveyed the rain water from the roofs into rain barrels, and this insipid liquid was used for drinking. Carelessly, even this scanty storage supply was often not filled.

A favorite trick of the Indians was to send a few of their number within sight of the fort as a decoy. The frontiersmen, never noted for their discipline and restraint, were altogether too likely to rush out and give chase. Then the larger body of Indians would cut them off from the fort and, having surrounded them, would attempt to capture them. If the whites were wise and stayed in, it was no time before there was not an Indian in sight. Then if imprudent fighters went out, thinking the Indians had gone, they might be killed or captured. When a small band captured horses or people and started back to their country, the whites were sure to give chase if men were available. It was often possible for unmounted Indians, by walking in water or by other ingenious means, to cover their trail, but if they were riding or driving horses it was impossible to hide the spoor.

On Sunday afternoon, July 7, 1776, Jemima Boone (daughter of the famous scout), who was suffering from a cane stab in her foot from going barefoot, persuaded two friends, Frances and Elizabeth Calloway, to join her in a canoe ride so she could bathe her feverish foot in the cool water of the Kentucky River. While their attention was called elsewhere, the canoe drifted onto a sandbar near the northern shore. Suddenly five Indians sprang into the water from their hiding-place, and in spite of Elizabeth's vigorous use of the paddle the girls were overpowered and hurried northward. As they hurried along, the girls tried in every possible way to make a trail that could be followed. In this they were not disappointed. The men at the fort heard the screams of the girls and there was great excitement. Samuel Henderson, the sweetheart of Betsey Calloway, was shaving and had one side of his face shaved. There was no time to finish. Daniel Boone rushed into the woods barefoot. Six others accompanied them in their Sunday-best homespun clothes, following the trail on foot like a pack of hounds. Others followed on horseback. On Tuesday morning while the Indians and their captives were eating breakfast, they were surrounded by Boone and his men, and the girls were rescued unharmed. Only one Indian escaped. There was general rejoicing at Boonesborough as there came to a close as romantic an episode as any book of fiction can furnish. Three of Boone's men, John Holder, Samuel Henderson, and Flanders Calloway, were the lovers and later the husbands of the three girls.

The favorite method of attack on a fort was to march to the vicinity of the station during the night and at daybreak, when the people of the fort least expected it, to rush onto the stockade, yelling and brandishing tomahawks with the hope of finding the gate open or the fort unprotected.

Perhaps the most classic of all Indian attempts to take a fort was the siege of Boonesborough. The British encouraged and aided this attack. General Hamilton, the British commander at Detroit, sent twelve Frenchmen with a string of pack horses to carry ammunition and supplies. There were probably about three hundred Indians. On September 7, 1778 this overwhelming force laid siege to Boonesborough with its thirty men, twenty boys, and a few women. They attempted first, by a show of power, to overawe the defenders and secure their surrender. When they failed in this, the army very ostentatiously left. The settlers did not take the bait, however, and waited within closed gates. Within an hour the Indians were as thick as ever, and from behind trees and logs and through tangled woods bullets were directed at every crack and porthole. At night the woods glowed with savage campfires. The attackers, evidently not realizing how weakly defended the station was, dared not assault it. The defenders sent urgent requests to the settlements on the Holston for aid. The pioneers made a wooden cannon by hollowing out a gum log, bound it with wagon iron, loaded it with musket balls, and fired into the besiegers. It did real execution and scared the Indians frightfully, but burst at the second shot. After a few days the people in the fort noticed that the water in the river near the shore was muddy and realized that their assailants were tunneling from the river under the fort with the idea of either blowing it up or throwing a force into the stockade. The defenders began digging a counter tunnel. The heat was excessive and the diggers were nearly exhausted. Finally a rain brought relief from the heat and water to the defenders.

One night the assailants attempted to fire the fort by carrying lighted torches close enough to hurl them against the stockade. This was exceedingly dangerous because the torchbearer, even though he dodged and danced about in the night, made an excellent target for the fort's riflemen. From the bluffs across the river the enemy shot blazing arrows onto the roofs of the houses in the fort. Some of these torches and blazing arrows were made of flax captured from a settler's cabin and wrapped in the inner fiber of shellbark hickory, which was oily and burned readily. Others were filled with powder, and a piece of punk was placed in the combustible missile, which would after a time burn into the powder, cause an explosion, and fire—a sort of incendiary bomb set off with a time fuse. The roofs were within the sweep of a hail of enemy bullets and there was nothing with which to put out a fire except inflammable brooms, although sometimes it was possible to push a burning shake off the roof from the inside with a pole. To go out and attempt to extinguish a fire along the outside wall of the stockade meant almost certain death. John Bakeless tells us that on that night the light of the torches, fire arrows, and flashes of rifle fire lighted up the fort so that the people could see to pick up a pin.[1]

In that hour of need, legend has it, the ingenuity of Squire Boone, brother of Daniel, paid dividends. He had unstocked some old muskets and placed plungers in them, effectually making squirt guns that would shoot a considerable stream of water. These, placed at convenient spots, were manned by the women, who filled them from the rain barrels.[2]

This did not solve the problem of putting out fires along the outside of the wall, and when John Holder, looking down from the blockhouse, saw that a torch had landed against a cabin door and that it was blazing to the top, he ran down, dashed into the cabin, and, at the risk of his life, dashed a bucket of water on it and saved the fort. It seemed, however, as though it was only a matter of time before a breach would be burned. Then, too, the water and food grew scarce and man and beast were suffering. Over a week of loss of sleep, anxiety, work in the heat, and the strain of the situation had worn the people out in body and spirit. They looked in vain for reinforcements from the Holston. Dissention broke out. Through the ever narrowing space between the two parties of sappers, the diggers heard the sound of the enemy getting nearer. The outlook was dark; indeed, the final crisis appeared at hand. Would the Indians blow up the fort with a well-placed blast or would they rush the exhausted, starving defenders? To heighten the gloom, rain poured down in torrents, favoring the Indian mining crew in digging into

---

[1] Bakeless: *Boone*, p. 219.
[2] Willard Rouse Jillson: "Squire Boone," *Filson Club Historical Quarterly*, XVI, 154.

the fort without being heard. The long night finally dragged its weary way through and September 16 dawned a beautiful, quiet, sunshiny day. The wet weather had caved in the mine, and the fickle Indians, never too fond of work, had become discouraged and abandoned the siege. From the great mass of inflammable material they had gathered, it appeared they aimed to emerge from the mine at the edge of the wall and burn it down so they could enter through the breach and take the fort. Cautiously, daring scouts took their lives in hand and reconnoitered to see whether the enemy had really gone. When it became certain that the fort was saved, great was the rejoicing. For nine days this ill-manned post had been closely invested.

At times for months ceaseless vigilance had to be maintained. The diary of Captain John Cowan of Harrodsburg reveals the following happenings from March to June 1777:

March 6. Two men killed at Shawnee Springs.

March 7. Indians attempted to cut off small party from the fort, some cattle killed and horses taken, four men wounded.

March 18. Two men arrived from Boonesborough with accounts of one man killed and one wounded.

March 28. Thirty or forty Indian stragglers attacked the fort. They killed and scalped one man. They took another man prisoner and then killed him.

April 3. There was an alarm about daylight.

April 8. News came that one man was killed at Rye Cove.

April 9. Indians were about.

April 25. Fresh signs of Indians were seen at two o'clock. They were heard imitating owls, gobbling like turkeys, etc. At four a sentry spied one and shot at three soon after.

April 28. Indians within 200 yards of the fort.

April 29. Indians attacked the fort and killed one man.

April 30. A messenger from Boonesborough arrived with the news that forty or fifty Indians attacked the place, killed and scalped one man, and wounded four.

May 1. Scattered parties of Indians were seen.

May 4 and 6. Indians seen several times these two days.

May 16 and 18. Indians seen and heard.

May 27. There was an alarm this morning. An express arrived from Boonesborough and reported that the place was attacked from Friday until Sunday morning.

June 2. Indians were seen around the fort. An express from [General] Logan said the Indians attacked and killed one man and wounded two. He reported that in the recent attack on Boonesborough only three men were wounded, but that the Indians tried hard to burn the fort.

June 5. An express returned from Boonesborough and said he went within one and a half miles of the fort and, seeing many Indians, did not venture in.

June 20. A man from Logan's reported one wounded man died. One was missing. Part of his coat was found in the woods.

June 22. This evening the Indians killed and cut off the head of Barney Stagner above the big spring.

June 25. A party of Indians crossed the river going toward the settlements.

On May 31, 1780 John Floyd wrote from Bear Grass, Kentucky: "Hardly one week pass [sic] without some one being scalped between this and the Falls [Louisville] and I have almost got too cowardly to travell about the woods without company." [3]

On December 8, 1780 he wrote that that week was the first since March that they had been without an alarm. A natural death was so uncommon that an old lady who dwelt in one of the stations, when asked what was the most beautiful sight she had seen in Kentucky, answered that it was a young man who had died a natural death. There he lay unblemished by tomahawk or scalping knife. It was to her

[3] Floyd Correspondence, Draper MSS. 17CC128, Wisconsin State Historical Society Library.

a novel and pleasing sight. By 1782 it seemed that the whites would be run out of Kentucky. Boone wrote the Governor of Virginia that Kentucky must be either reinforced or abandoned.

In 1790 Federal Judge Innes wrote Washington officials that the Indians had killed fifteen hundred in the seven years since he came to Kentucky.

The story was the same in Tennessee. Guild says that for fifteen years within seven miles of Nashville one person was killed in every ten days. Some fourteen to twenty persons who had been scalped and recovered lived in the Tennessee settlements about 1800. Indeed, about 1780 one by one the stockades were abandoned and so many left the country that it seems likely that the Cumberland settlements around present-day Nashville would have been abandoned had it not been for the magnificent leadership of Robertson. By his courageous words, resolute example, and aggressive action he held the settlement together. When the corn failed, the settlers got their food from the forest. Quantities of walnuts and other nuts were gathered. Hunters brought in a large quantity of bears, buffaloes, deer, and other game.

Dogs were used in Tennessee both for scouting and for fighting the Indians. The dogs were placed on the outside of the fort to give warning to the sentinels of the approach of Indians. Horses and cows, also, by their uneasiness often gave signs that the redskins were at hand. Cattle would snort and scamper toward the stations at their approach. The Indians much disliked to be pursued by the settlers' bear dogs. They were not still long enough for the Indians to get a fatal shot at them, and if by chance the redskins wounded one, it only made the rest of the pack more fierce and the dogs were at the Indians' throats so furiously that they had no chance to reload. Then was the time for the white man to do his deadly work.

On April 2, 1780 at Nashboro (Nashville) the Indians employed a favorite trick. A large party of Cherokees approached the fort at night and lay hidden in the forest. In the morning three of them fired at the fort and ran. Twenty of the impetuous defenders mounted horses, rushed after the decoys, and dismounted to fight. The main group of Indians then cut off the whites from the fort. The latter attempted to break through the circle and get back to the fort. In the excitement of the doubtful moment the women in the fort turned out the dogs and, grabbing axes and guns, stood by the gate and loopholes. The dogs, seeing the line of Indians drawn up to keep their masters out of the fort, dashed out in a furious onset, to the discomfiture of the red men. This fortunate diversion enabled the whites to rush through the lines into the fort.

Sometimes a man was pursued so hotly that the defenders dared not open the gate to let him in. James Roy found himself in this fix. He threw himself in a prone position behind a stump near the fort and lay there four hours while Indian bullets kicked up the dust around him, and his mother anxiously watched from the inside. Finally the defenders dug a hole under a cabin wall and he wriggled to safety. Sometimes in rescuing a wounded man outside the fort a rescuer would hold up a feather bed before him as a shield against savage bullets.

At the siege of Watauga in 1776, tradition tells us, Kate Sherrill, a tall, winsome girl with brown hair and a form as graceful and supple as a hickory sapling was surprised and pursued by Indians. As she ran like a deer toward the stockade, John Sevier, then a young widower, from a loophole shot her foremost pursuer, and when she leaped up and caught the top of the stockade, he helped her over and caught her in his arms. A little later she became his bride, his own Bonny Kate, as he fondly called her.

In spite of the seriousness of the times many tricks were played at the stations by men who went out and hid to scare the braggart, the inexperienced, or the coward. This was dangerous. On one such occasion a spy coming toward the station saw a lad with his gun coming toward him. Thinking to scare the youngster, he gave an Indian yell and treed. The spy was dressed in buckskin and the boy thought indeed it was an Indian and also took to a tree. When the spy looked out from his retreat to see the boy run, the youngster, who was on the lookout, fired and the spy fell dead on the spot.

The first few years the settlers were often pinched for food. The winter of 1780–1 was known as the hard winter. The snow was banked high, ice and snow locked the food from the animals of the forest, the streams were frozen solid, and even firewood had to be chopped out of encircling ice. Many of the forest creatures froze or got so poor they were hardly fit for food. Hogs and cattle around the station froze. The settlers managed to keep from freezing, but the corn gave out and there was nothing but the almost useless game to stave off starvation.

V

The Planter Moves West

THE various reasons that caused the landless man to move west operated upon the planter. There were the younger sons who had no ancestral estate. Some had fallen into debt and, salvaging what they could, went west to begin anew. Then there were those benevolent masters whose slave family had multiplied until it had outgrown the Eastern plantation. They wanted to keep their black family together and, rather than sell some of their hands, they decided to move to an area where broad acres could be found to fit their needs. But most potent of all attractions of the West was the lure of land. To the east, particularly in the Piedmont region, the land was wearing out. With Kentucky competition, tobacco prices fell, but ever rising cotton prices lured the planter to the new cotton West. Even before the War of 1812 rumors of wealth and opportunity in the Tennessee River Valley in Mississippi Territory gave it the name "Happy Valley," and the Alabama basin was declared the Arcadia of southern America.

It seems that the majority of planters who carried with them the plantation system came from the Piedmont and brought few slaves. Their broad acres and large numbers of slaves were gained in the deep South. Many of them had no slaves at all. In fact, those without slaves were about equal in number to slaveholders in 1830. A good example of the building of a plantation was the experience of Alexander Porter, a lawyer of Nashville. Competition was formidable and in an endeavor to better his situation he began to consider moving to Louisiana, which had recently been purchased from France. He saw that that area would soon be admitted as a state and that he might grow in importance with the new territory. He had sought the advice of Andrew Jackson concerning the proposal, and Old Hickory had enthusiastically urged him to go to one of the new territories. He made preparations to go immediately. A little later he met Jackson, who with his usual enthusiasm exploded: "What! Alick, not gone yet? This won't do. When you determine, act quickly; somebody may get in before you. And remember Alick, you are going to a new country —and a country, too, where men fight. . . ." [1]

As early as 1792 an American colony settled on the Tensaw River and also above Natchez, Mississippi. They mingled with the Spanish, French, and British there, and lived in the rudest kind of log cabins. For a livelihood they cultivated indigo for export and also made tar. The real flow of American settlement, however, did not begin until the first and second decades of the nineteenth century.

By 1810 Louisiana and lower Mississippi were spoken of in the most glowing terms among Americans. Nathaniel Cox wrote in 1806 that one gentleman who worked twenty-eight hands expected to clear that year from ten thousand to twelve thousand dollars, in addition to molasses, which he calculated would feed and clothe his Negroes. He said cotton that year would clear from two hundred to two hundred and fifty dollars per hand.

The professional squatter and the speculator ordinarily went hand in hand ahead of the planter. The squatters pre-

[1] Wendell H. Stephenson: *Alexander Porter, Whig Planter of Old Louisiana* (Baton Rouge, 1934), p. 10.

pared the way by blazing trails, producing food on which the planter's "family" subsisted until he could get a start, and in other ways opening the path of settlement. He had cleared some land and usually for a consideration was willing to sell and repeat the process a little farther beyond. The speculators had hunted out the best lands and were ready to sell for a profit. Some planters bought land directly from the government at land sales, and, indeed, many slave-holders were squatters in that they resided on government land for some time before they secured the title to their holdings.

The planter who had money and slaves at stake in taking such a radical step often made a trip to investigate what the new country was like and discover whether he could buy good land at a reasonable price. If he did not go he wrote to friends or acquaintances who had moved before.

François Xavier Martin wrote to Colonel John Hamilton of Elizabeth City, North Carolina, on March 22, 1811, that the quickest way to reach the Mississippi River and the rich land beyond in Louisiana was by horseback, with a pack horse to carry provisions, but that if he did not wish to rough it, a chair was the easiest and quickest way, although much slower than by horseback. He says he went west in a chair and covered twenty-five miles a day. The main objection was that a person could not reach a house to stay at each night while traveling over the Natchez Trace, and he advised taking a tent and a four-gallon keg of water behind the chair. This was evidently a sedan chair.

Planters had moved into Kentucky and middle Tennessee in the 1790's and the first decade of the nineteenth century, but it was not until the next decade that west Tennessee and the lower South began to receive large numbers of settlers. It was a common thing for the big planter, once having selected his land, to send an overseer and his slaves ahead to clear the land, plant crops, build cabins, and, in short, re-produce there, in a measure, the plantation in the East. In a

year or two, when conditions became more livable, he and
his household migrated. In that case the overseer and slaves
were the real pioneers. For example, Colonel Samuel Meredith, of Amherst County, Virginia, in 1789 sent his overseer,
Dr. Philip Roots, and a number of slaves to improve his
two-thousand-acre grant. This estate, later known as Winton, was located seven miles north of Lexington.[2]

Some of these early migrations were made by the Wilderness Road. Others were down the Ohio by boat. David
Meade with feelings of great misapprehension left his plantation in Prince George County, Virginia, on June 8, 1796.
A succession of broken wheels and axles relieved the monotony of the journey. Of the seventh day he wrote that he
went over eleven miles of "the worst road I had ever seen
particularly the ascent & descent of Negroe Mountain . . .
here one of our hired waggons overset without injury to any
person or thing although there were several little negroes at
the top of it."

On the twelfth day they embarked on the Monongahela
River at Redstone in two large boats (forty by thirty-four
feet, whereas the usual width was twelve feet) with the
company, goods, and carriages. A white man and two Negroes drove the horses to Wheeling, where the deeper water
of the Ohio would accommodate the boats with their added
cargo. The first day out of Redstone they stuck on a gravel
bar and a snag, but freed their craft without any great delay.
On the evening of the third day they arrived at Pittsburgh,
where they spent nearly a whole day purchasing stores. On
the morning of the sixth day they arrived at Wheeling and
loaded the horses, which had arrived two or three days
earlier. The boats leaked so badly they had to be unloaded,
and a day was spent in calking them. The horses were landed
to pasture on the banks of the stream each evening. On
July 4 they arrived at Limestone and started out with very

² J. Winston Coleman, Jr.: *Slavery Times in Kentucky* (Chapel Hill,
1940), pp. 15–16.

poor horses and tattered carriages. On July 7, after just one month on the road, they joyfully reached Lexington and rented a building as temporary headquarters while the planter arranged his new home.[3]

A North Carolina party with sixty colored people, en route to Alabama by water, was less fortunate. Crossing the Blue Ridge Mountains, they took flatboats at Knoxville and sent the horses down the river by land. Landing at Muscle Shoals, they packed their goods on the horses and started for the Tombigbee settlements. They embarked in long canoes a little above the site of Aberdeen, Alabama, were wrecked, lost their goods, tools, guns, and all their effects except the clothes on their backs. One white child and twenty-one Negroes were drowned. Filled with gloom, they pressed forward through the dense forests. They were saved from starvation only by their faithful dogs, which killed rabbits, opossum, and raccoons. After a hundred and twenty heart-breaking days they reached their destination.[4]

Some went down the tributaries of the Ohio into that stream and the Mississippi to the new land on the border of the lower valley of the Mississippi. Some went from the Atlantic seaboard to Gulf ports by sea. Still others left Georgia and traveled overland to Montgomery, Alabama, Natchez, Mississippi, or beyond.

The consideration with which some Eastern slaveholders treated their slaves would have surprised the Northern abolitionist. Leonard Covington, of Aquasca, Maryland, when giving consideration to moving west, wrote to his brother who had settled in Mississippi asking him about the country. One of the foremost questions was whether the Negroes fared well there. He wanted to know whether they generally

[3] Bayard Still (ed.): "David Meade to his Sister," *William and Mary Quarterly*, XXI, 318–33.

[4] Timothy Horton Ball: *A Glance into the Great South-East or Clarke County, Alabama, and Its Surroundings, from 1540 to 1877* (Grove Hill, Ala., 1882), p. 75.

appeared as happy and contented as they did in Maryland. He further asked his brother whether his slaves would willingly return to Maryland and whether they were satisfied with the change and with their treatment.

It was not unusual for the planter, when he was considering moving west, to present the matter to his black family and ask them whether they were willing to move to the new country. When Colonel Thomas Dabney decided to leave Virginia for the territory of Mississippi he called his slaves together and told them of his intentions. He told them he did not intend to take one unwilling servant, but that his plan was to buy all husbands and wives who were connected with his people at their owners' prices, or if any of his people preferred, they could find a master or mistress who would buy them and they could stay in old Virginia. No money consideration, he declared, would stand in the way of keeping the families together and contented. In this case as in most instances where the master was considerate, every slave decided to go with the master.[5]

Negroes were very much attached to their birthplace and their homes and there was much distress at leaving. One old slave in recalling the day he left Virginia told an interviewer long years after freedom had come to him that it was a sorrowful troop that left Virginia that day. After the break was made, however, they were encouraged to sing and have a good time. The aisles of the woods fairly rang with their songs. They had been told of the wonders in the new land —that all sorts of good things were in store for them in that land of milk and honey. Soon their dejection disappeared, and light-hearted and carefree they traveled along day after day.

During the great migration just before 1820 many moved from Georgia and the Carolinas in the most primitive manner. Pack horses and hogsheads were often used to carry personal effects. The latter were an adaptation of the then

[5] Susan Dabney Smedes: *A Southern Planter* (New York, 1890), p. 48

common method of marketing tobacco. A long rod was inserted lengthwise in a huge waterproof hogshead. This rod projected far enough at each end to allow it to serve as an axle, and a pair of shafts were fastened to it. An ox pulling in the shafts drew the revolving trunk over hundreds of miles through the Indian wilds to the planter's final destination. In this manner William Coate and his family, of the Newburg district, and Drury Allen and his wife and five children, from the Edgefield section of South Carolina, moved to Clarke County, Alabama.

During the flush times of the thirties, when west Tennessee and portions of Mississippi and Alabama were in the process of settlement, the Carolinas and Georgia seemed to be emptying themselves into the reservoirs to the west. Wagon after wagon, each full of women and children, passed through the older Alabama settlements headed toward the unsettled areas. Month after month and year after year with each recurring autumn this ceaseless hegira continued. Power, who traveled westward on an Alabama road in 1834, noted that he found the road covered with migrating parties. Well-informed residents with whom he conversed on the subject estimated that not less than ten thousand families had left the Carolinas and Georgia that season. After a few years in which migration was interrupted by the panic of 1837, the great stream of movers began to pour over into Arkansas and northern Louisiana. Many on their way to Texas stopped in those regions either temporarily or permanently.

There was no typical line of march or method of transportation. These varied with the wealth and notions of the planter. The Williams family traveled more than three hundred miles through a trackless wilderness to reach western Tennessee. The journey began in the old settled portion of Mississippi in January, and the long train of movers slowly pushing through the lonely stretches of pine woods Joseph Williams described as follows:

In front rode my father, on his faithful and sure-footed dapple-gray mare, with heavy holsters swinging across the pommel of his saddle, with their black bear-skin covering. Stern, thoughtful, and reticent, with indomitable will, he had resolved to convoy his precious charge safely through whatever of peril or difficulty that should menace him. Following close behind was a large black carryall, containing mother, grandmother and the young children. . . . We made some days as much as ten miles, oftener, however, not more than six or eight. We were not unfrequently delayed for several days when difficult crossings of streams were to be made.[6]

At night the slaves slept in tents surrounding their master and mistress. Adam Hodgson wrote that in 1820 on the banks of the rivers he usually found a curious collection of sulkies, carts, Jersey wagons, heavy wagons, horses, oxen, mules, little planters, Negroes, and Indians. Often a wealthy planter and his wife would bring up the rear of a long cavalcade.

Power described the typical caravan as consisting of from two to four tilt wagons, long and low-roofed, each laden with goods. The white folk and their house servants were stowed over the freight of these wagons. On the march these vehicles were preceded and surrounded by field slaves, varying in numbers from half a dozen to fifty or sixty. A couple of mounted men brought up the rear. He was surprised to note that frequently when he visited a camp at night he found an air of good humor and contentment in spite of the discomfort and privation.

While the Taylor family was on its trek from Georgia to Alabama, the father and the two eldest sons rode in front. Then followed two wagons with their Negro drivers, the mother on horseback, and two younger children on pack horses. The Negro women and children followed, some on foot and some on horseback.

[6] Joseph S. Williams: *Old Times in West Tennessee* (Memphis, Tenn., 1873), pp. 8–10.

Often the Negroes walked and carried a load proportional to their strength,[7] although a well-to-do planter sometimes hauled all his slaves in wagons while he rode horseback and the white family traveled in a carriage. Some of these big planters brought with them the family physician and the private teacher.

Featherstonhaugh tells us that on a winter day he met an almost unbroken line of emigrants with at least a thousand Negro slaves trudging on foot. They were wet from fording streams and were shivering with the cold. On this day they must have been wet constantly, for the traveler said that on that one day he had forded from forty to fifty streams, which were swollen from rains. On the other side of the picture, Aunt Harriet, a slave of Colonel Thomas S. Dabney, recalled that he furnished every slave with an umbrella: "All had umberillas, ebery one, an' when it rain you see all dem umberillas go up." When they got to Richmond, Colonel Dabney told his slaves that this was their last town and they could buy what they wanted. Aunt Harriet said she bought some cups and saucers, plates, and a coffee pot to have when she got to "Beulah land."

In contrast to this magnanimous treatment, some masters kept a patrol around the camp, and to prevent the escape of any slaves one of the overseers called the roll two or three times every night. Everyone was awakened while the names were called and they answered.

The planter who came a long way by road faced many of the difficulties that the earlier emigrants had experienced. The Reverend John Owen, with his wife, two small children, his mother-in-law, and three or four slaves, left his home in Norfolk County, Virginia, on October 24, 1818. He was soon plunged into a series of difficulties that tired his soul. His cart broke down again and again. It turned over twice, and a third time the horse ran away and broke it all to pieces. Before he reached east Tennessee, he declared, "the Devil

[7] Srygley: *Seventy Years in Dixie*, p. 267.

turned loose." Straying horses, "infernal roads," and the break-down of vehicles plunged him into deepest despair and made him envy "the Bruit creation their freedom from care and anxiety of mind." On November 22, 1818 he wrote:

> Started early bad roads Old mair fell down carriage run back very much alarmd Mother & Ann Coupling Bolt broke detaind much distressed & low spirited almost wish I was dead or that fate had bloted the day in which I was born out of the calendar & left a perfect blank. . . .

He arrived at Tuscaloosa, Alabama, the day after Christmas after nine weeks' traveling, and became a prominent planter at Tuscaloosa.[8]

The plantation system and Negro slavery were quickly transplanted from the East to Alabama. By 1824 the slaves outnumbered the whites in the Montgomery area. Nevertheless, not all who came to Alabama were large slaveholders. The great profits and increased slaveholdings were made after these men came to the lower South.

Sometimes a planter simply sold his old plantation and started out with his family and possessions to seek a new home. Basil Hall met such a man with about fifty slaves. When questioned as to where he was going, the planter told him that he was bound for Florida and although he had no definite idea where to locate, he was sure a man could not possibly go wrong in such a fertile and unoccupied country.

[8] "John Owens Journal," Southern History Association *Publications*, April 1897, pp. 88–97.

VI

Land Greed

As has been noted, the land in Kentucky and Tennessee for the most part passed from public to private ownership under the direction of the state. The same was true of frontier Georgia. This general plan was begun in connection with the parts of Alabama and Mississippi that were owned by Georgia until it was turned over to the United States Government in 1802. According to the agreement made at that time, Alabama and Mississippi were to be treated, in general, the same as the territory north of the Ohio River with the exception of the clause forbidding slavery. This provided that the area should be formed into states eventually. The land became the property of the United States and was surveyed by the excellent rectangular system. In the meantime, while the area was under the control of Georgia, that state had proceeded on the prodigal land policy of selling to big interests for a song large tracts in the present area of Alabama and Mississippi.[1]

The Georgia Legislature in 1789 made large grants of

[1] The policy of giving away great quantities of land was followed within the boundaries of present Georgia. Between June 20, 1789 and March 21, 1796 three and one half times as much land was granted as was then embraced in the area of the state. Samuel Guyton McLendon: *History of the Public Domain of Georgia* (Atlanta, 1924), p. 119.

land in the Mississippi country to the so-called Yazoo Land Company. Later it was discovered there was much fraud in securing the vote in the legislature, and the state would not accept the proffered cash nor consummate the deal.

When the United States secured the land, it attempted to apply the following land and Indian policies: [2] (1) The rights of the Indians were to be safeguarded. (2) No one was to settle on the public domain until it had been surveyed and purchased by the settler. (3) The land was to be surveyed into townships of thirty-six square miles. Each square mile, consisting of 640 acres, was known as a section and divided into quarter sections. (4) Land was to be sold to the highest bidder, with a minimum price of two dollars an acre.[3] (5) If, when a certain tract was offered for sale, no one bid on it at the auction, it was open to private sale at the minimum price thereafter.

Land offices were established by the government in the general vicinity of the land to be sold. The office was very plainly furnished, with perhaps a desk and a bookcase. Sometimes an old family bureau was used for a desk. A register, corresponding to a clerk, and a receiver, corresponding to a treasurer, represented the government and were in charge of the "tract" and sales books. In these books was kept an accurate record of every plot of land in the district. Land-office officials were required to keep a register of the weather also. In many parts of the country these were the first weather-observation points, and our earliest records come from them. Before the sales, interested persons would procure a chart of the land to be offered for sale and would range through the forests looking for the best land and marking their choices on their plats. Before the great sales of the thirties in Mississippi several hundred persons were engaged in this business, known as land-hunting or land-

[2] There were minor changes in the policy from time to time, but in general this is a correct statement.
[3] This was reduced to $1.25 an acre in 1820.

looking. Sometimes these land-hunters hired the surveyors, who knew the whole country, to lead them to the best land.

The time of sales at the different land offices in a given region was staggered and men could buy at one sale and then ride on to one at the next land office. A sale lasted for two or three weeks. When the sale opened, the auctioneer designated which range and township he was going to sell first and then, commencing at section one, proceeded to thirty-six, selling each section or portion of a section to the highest bidder.

In flush times often three or four thousand persons, living in tents and booths, might be seen scattered over the plain around the land office at Cahaba, Alabama. Some, as the season might dictate, basked in the sunshine or lolled in the shade while waiting for the proceedings to progress to a point of interest to them. As the sale progressed, men were continually going and coming. It was a perfect harvest for the merchants, taverns, and liquor dealers. It was customary when buyers had made a good investment to purchase a barrel of whisky, knock out the head, and invite all to drink whisky and water with him without money and without price. Quickly every man procured a tin cup and helped himself.

The first difficulty that appeared was the disregard of the borderers for the rights of the Indians. The fighting frontiersmen felt that there was no good Indian but a dead one and it was a shame that the Indians should be allowed to deprive them even temporarily of the use of so rich a possession. Judging by their actions, their motto might well have been the words of Caleb of old as he stood before the Promised Land: "Let us go up at once, and possess it. . . ." Time after time officials warned the intruders to get off Indian territory. As early as September 1, 1788 Congress issued a proclamation forbidding intrusion on the Cherokee hunting grounds in Tennessee and ordering the settlers to remove at once. The squatters ignored the order, and instead of compelling them to obey its dictates the central government in 1791 made a treaty with the Cherokees by which these Indians gave up the land in question. An old bill presented to Governor Blount of Tennessee by two deputy marshals reads:

"For 8 days service in removing the frontier citizens off the Indian land agreeably to the order of Governor Blount of the 1 December 1795—$3 per day each—48." [4]

In 1804 John Sevier, of Tennessee, warned the settlers to remove from Indian lands, reminding them of their promise to do so when a United States official had visited them previously.

In 1809 R. J. Meigs removed seventeen hundred people from the Cherokee and Chickasaw lands. In July 1827 the United States Government sent troops into Indian lands in Alabama, ousted the settlers, and burned their houses and crops in what was known as the Intruders' War.

As early as 1835, squatters intruded on the Indian land in northwestern Missouri. Soldiers from Fort Leavenworth removed them, but they returned and occupied the area until the Platte Purchase of 1836 extinguished Indian title to the region. The problem was an ever recurring one. The democratic government was never able to bring itself to the point of consistently enforcing its laws when they operated against its insistent, willful children.

A second problem, even after the Indian title was extinguished, was that of keeping the land-hungry pioneers from moving onto the public domain and taking possession of the choicest lands before the sale. This was a habit that had been in vogue for many years. The proprietors of Pennsylvania and the big landholders of Virginia and North Carolina had been plagued with these squatters. Such species of titles as "cabin rights," "corn rights," "sugar-camp rights," and "tomahawk improvements" were bought and sold like genu-

[4] McClung Collection, MS., Knoxville Public Library, Knoxville, Tennessee.

ine property, although they were based on mere occupancy rather than ownership. As a result there had grown up in colonial days a custom of allowing pre-emption rights to squatters.[5] This precedent in colonial procedure bobbed up to harass the national government.

The new government struggled with the problem. Intruders were warned to move off the public lands. The army was sent to drive them off. An act passed in 1807 provided for a hundred-dollar fine and six months' imprisonment for an offender who did not move within ninety days after being warned. This was merely a threat and was of little effect. The squatters had little money for fines and there were no jails to confine them.

In May 1810 the Secretary of War wrote to General Wade Hampton: "The intrusions on the Public Lands in every direction have grown to a serious evil."

In spite of the efforts of the central government the practice became so general and the attitude of all the people in the territory so benevolent toward it that the legislature of Mississippi Territory had by 1816 given district representation to counties in which not a single man resided who was not an intruder. This not only lent a shade of respectability to their action, but actually placed a political premium on trespassing. A few dozen men in an area were enabled to elect a member to the legislative assembly. Thus, in consequence of their illegal removal to the lands of the United States, they acquired possibly one hundred times the political consequence and power that they would have had by lawfully remaining on land actually owned by them.

With popular opinion as it was, when offenders were brought to trial in their own area, juries would not convict them. Judge Harry Toulmin wrote from Mississippi Territory in 1816 to President Madison: "How can a jury be

[5] Amelia Clewley Ford: "Colonial Precedents of Our National Land System as It Existed in 1800" (Doctor's thesis, University of Wisconsin, 1908), *Bulletin* of the University of Wisconsin, No. 352, History Series, II, 128–9.

found in Monroe county to convict a man of intrusion,—where every man is an intruder." [6]

In reply to government warnings, removals, and threatened prosecutions, the settlers said that the government was tardy in throwing the land upon the market and that they could not find available good land except at high prices from speculators.

When the land did come into the market, these squatters were anxious to obtain at a low price, the minimum if possible, the land on which they had made their improvements. They argued that if their land was worth more than the minimum it was because they had made it so with their labor, and that they had earned a special concession because they had been a buffer between the Indians and civilization, and their very presence had made the unoccupied land more inviting and therefore more valuable. They countered the government warning to move by asking for a special pre-emption act that would guarantee the squatter his claim at the minimum price. On March 3, 1803 a special pre-emption act for land south of Tennessee was passed. This rewarded obstinate intruders by providing that all who were living on their claims on October 27, 1795 were allowed to buy as much as 640 acres at the minimum price—two dollars an acre. After 1820 the minimum price of land was a dollar and a quarter an acre. In 1830 a more general pre-emption act was passed that allowed all settlers who were living on any part of the public domain to buy not more than 160 acres on which his improvements were located, at the minimum price—then a dollar and a quarter an acre.

The settlers sought this consideration because of the activities of speculators who came to the land auctions with ready money, bid against the squatter, and ran the price up higher than the squatter could afford to pay. In this way the

---

[6] Judge Harry Toulmin to the President. WD: AGO, Old Records Div. ALS. Carter: *Territorial Papers*, Vol. VI, Territory of Mississippi, pp. 646–7.

speculator profited by the foresight and industry of the settler, while the settler lost his "improvements."

This partial pre-emption act did not protect any except those who had been squatters in 1829. As the great land rush of the thirties progressed, the struggle between speculators and squatters continued.

There is little evidence on the Southern frontier of the widespread existence of well-organized squatter or claim clubs, with their rules and governing officials, such as secured by force pre-emption rights to settlers in the Northern and plains areas. In a few places, however, the squatters banded together in a loose way against the speculator. At Cahaba, Alabama, in 1830, the planters resolved to allow no one except the then present occupants to view the land or take the numbers of the sections. They entered into a written agreement to take measures that would secure to them their improved land at a dollar and a quarter an acre. One man in each township was elected to bid for the land. The rest were pledged to be at the sale at the land office armed and to shoot any man who dared bid against him. A fund was raised to defray any expenses that might occur in violating the law. By force of arms they drove off the land every man who attempted to examine it. A number of men who went on the land to examine it with a view to bidding on it at the sale "put up" at a private house. At midnight a company of thirty armed men surrounded the house, took the numbers away from the prospective buyers, and compelled them to leave at that hour on penalty of death. Here, then, was a full-blown claim club such as flourished north of the Ohio River.

One man in Butler County, Alabama, who rode over a hundred miles to the land office, was outbid by a speculator and lost his place. Another settler in the same neighborhood, seeing how his neighbor was treated, determined not to suffer a like fate and so resolved himself into a one-man claim club. When his land was put up for sale, he mounted a barrel with rifle in hand and calmly announced that he would put a bullet through the first man who bid against him. This one-man claim club succeeded very well.

Speculators knew they had the settler at a disadvantage and in some places an organized band exacted hush money from the settler by promising not to bid on his land if he would give the speculators an amount equal to the minimum government price of a dollar and a quarter an acre. If the farmer did not have the money to pay these two prices, the extortioners would take a mortgage on his land. The state of Alabama by legislative acts tried to prohibit these practices, but it was not entirely successful.

At the earlier land sales south of Tennessee, especially on the Tennessee River about Huntsville, in 1818 and 1819, the craze for land created a fever similar to that of the California gold rush of 1849. Sales at from ten dollars to thirty dollars an acre were common and plots frequently brought as high as seventy. One eighty-acre tract brought $150 an acre and another $251 an acre. Nevertheless, in spite of these high prices for plots here and there, the average price per acre for the year 1818 at the Huntsville land office was only $7.78.

At these sales two or three groups of speculators were bidding against each other, but it was not long before they got together and by agreement quieted competition to the point that very little land sold for more than the minimum price. As early as April 30, 1808 the Secretary of the Treasury stated that it was a common occurrence at the public land sales for companies to form to buy land for purposes of speculation, and that the effect was to eliminate competition among those who had thus associated themselves and much lessened it even among others. Such combinations, he noted, could not be prevented by law, but President Jefferson directed that the superintendents of land sales discountenance them as far as possible and that by no means was it proper for superintendents to be concerned in any such companies or any operations that were designed to lessen competition. These combinations apparently were quite general and continued down through the years.

By the thirties the practice was notorious. It became so bad that the government finally authorized its agents to bid against the combinations when they thought it advisable. One of the worst features of the swindle was the fact that many of the land-office officials were in collaboration with the swindlers and betrayed the interests of the government they were paid to protect. On a few occasions, however, land-office officials, after a quantity of land had been sold, stopped the sale when it became obvious that a combination existed.

By this time the actual settlers had won certain concessions from these speculator organizations, and the speculator-squatter combinations answered the purpose of the claim clubs among settlers north of the Ohio River.

At the land sales at Cochuma, Mississippi, in the fall of 1833, occurred a good example of the general practice. The speculator company signed a contract by which each member agreed to put into the fund not less than a hundred dollars nor more than a thousand. The aggregate sum was to be used to purchase land. Thus all competition on the part of members would be eliminated, and since most of those at the auction were members, competition was practically reduced to nothing. The company consisted of citizens of Tennessee, Alabama, and Mississippi. Four commissioners were appointed to do the bidding. The lands purchased were to be auctioned off by the company to the highest bidder and the profits divided between the members in proportion to the amount of stock they owned. Actual settlers were allowed to have at the minimum price the eighty acres on which they lived if they would promise not to bid. If their improvements covered one hundred and sixty acres or more, they were to have not more than one hundred and sixty acres.

These actual settlers were to hand to the agents of the

company the numbers of this improved land they wished to purchase. At that particular sale the company bought three quarters of the land sold. They seldom had to pay more than a dollar and a quarter an acre. The company then conducted an auction open to all comers and sold their purchases. The net result was that the government auction was in large measure a farce, and the real auction was that of the speculators. At Columbus, Mississippi, in 1834, the government land sale closed Saturday evening, and the same evening from the steps of the courthouse, only fifty or sixty steps from the land office, the speculators conducted the real auction. Dividends of $465 for each thousand dollars invested were declared as a result. Since these speculator companies limited the amount of money that could be invested by one man and since they protected the actual settler, they may be said to have approximated the claim clubs of the area north of the Ohio River.

A swindle practiced on the government at times was that of having irresponsible individuals attend the sale and bid high prices for land and then disappear altogether and allow their colleagues, the speculators, to secure the land at private entry at the minimum price.

In 1841 a general pre-emption act was passed by Congress that allowed the settler to measure off a claim for a home anywhere on the public domain and by fulfilling the proper conditions be sure of possessing it at the time of the land sales. This law allowed the pre-emptor to pre-empt but once and required him to promise to make the land his home and not take it with the idea of selling it to someone else. He was not eligible to take a pre-emption if he already owned 320 acres of land. He furthermore had to improve the land. Upon these conditions he was allowed to buy a quarter section at the minimum price. It was the guarantee, then, that the actual settler could select his land long before it was thrown on the market or even surveyed and be sure of securing it for a dollar and a quarter an acre instead of bidding on it at the auction.

This opened up a vast array of abuse and fraud. In 1836 Land Commissioner E. A. Brown found that in the region of Opelousas, Louisiana, nearly all the free Negroes, Spaniards, and Indians who inhabited the area were employed by speculators to claim the best land. Whole armies of men, slaves, and hirelings, were used by these unscrupulous persons to reap the golden harvest. There were such pretenses at cultivation or improvements as planting a few vegetables, scattering perhaps a few handfuls of grass seed, burning off a little patch of cane, and placing rails around a plot hardly larger than a garden. Henry Howell, of Alabama, in an attempt to fake improvements, planted pumpkins in November when the ordinary winter weather would have killed the first leaf.

A feature of the pre-emption acts of the thirties, which opened the portal to a world of corruption, was the provision that where two persons had made improvements on the same quarter section, one should be entitled to what was called a pre-emption float. This was a floating right that permitted the holder to enter a like quantity of land on any of the surveyed but unsold lands. This gave the holder the privilege of going anywhere, selecting the best land, and attaching his float to it, thus securing it upon payment. Often actual settlers who had not paid for the land on which they were living found themselves dispossessed by one of these floating claims, which required no improvements since they had allegedly been made previously on the disputed claim that gave rise to the float. The commissioner found cases where men who lived fifteen or twenty miles apart went before a justice of the peace and swore they lived on the same quarter section. Upon presentation of this false evidence, one would receive a pre-emption float. Quantities of affidavits were printed and distributed to paid agents, who with the co-operation of ignorant or corrupt justices of the peace secured floats wholesale for speculators. Within six months at Opelousas three hundred and fifty such claims were made. The commissioner believed that not so many as thirty of these in the whole Louisiana district were honest.

Moreover, despite sworn statements that they had not pre-empted before, many pre-empted in one district, sold the land at a big advance, moved on to the next, and repeated the program time and time again.

Prior to 1820 land could be purchased on the installment plan, with four years to pay. Many purchasers paid down only the first annual payment. Often they farmed and had the use of the land for years. Technically their land reverted to the government, but their claims to it were respected. They thus cheated the government out of the use of the land. At times buyers supplicated the government for relief laws. In response the time for payment was extended. Particularly after the big land boom of 1817 and 1818, when land sold at high figures, buyers sought a reduction in the price of land. The land law of 1820 abolished installment buying and allowed those who had not paid for their land to turn back to the government such part of it as they could not pay for and use the amount paid on the relinquished part to apply to the purchase of that retained. Later laws reduced the high prices paid in boom times by thirty-seven and a half per cent. Later, further reductions were made.

When Louisiana, Arkansas, Missouri, and parts of Mississippi and Alabama came into possession of the United States the land that was claimed was held by various sorts of tenure: French, Spanish, or British grants, Indian titles, and squatter rights. The United States attempted to protect all bona fide claims, but greedy, unscrupulous individuals rushed in and took up land or concocted fictitious claims of one sort or another.

An example or two will indicate the problem of these claims. A certain John or James Bowie sold many dubious claims to people in Arkansas. These were all disallowed although influential men had bought them and used every exertion to validate them. Baron de Bastrop, visiting Kentucky, sold a large tract of northern Louisiana land to Abraham Morehouse. The latter made about one hundred sales between 1804 and the time of his death, in 1813. Daniel Boone in Missouri held a vast grant from the Spanish Government. He lost the principal part of this through his failure to fulfill the technical details necessary to complete his title.

In order to untangle this maze of claims, fictitious and bona fide, the United States appointed a commission to look into each claim and allow or annul it. Its work was done well, and later court decisions upheld those of the commission.

Occasionally when the United States made a treaty with a tribe of Indians, wringing from them the promise to give up their lands, they made the concession that each Indian who was of age or the head of a family should have a right to select a plot of land to be reserved for him. The government sent locating officers to locate the Indians on the land as provided by treaty. These locators often connived with other unscrupulous white men to rob the Indians of any real benefit they were supposed to derive from the agreement. According to the arrangement, the Indians could sell the land under the supervision of the government agent. Speculators would get an Indian to impersonate the real owner before the agent and sell to the swindler for a song. The real owner was thus beaten out of his headright. When an uprising of the Indians occurred as a result of this fraud, a federal investigator was sent to the scene. His report incriminated men of respectable standing.

Another species of dishonesty was locating minors and those who were not family heads on land. For example, the two Indian wives of Peter Reid, a white man, each got a claim. The locators apparently located dummy Indians and then got their land conveyed to speculators. These claims not only swindled the Indians and the government, but sometimes gave rise to floating claims that deprived actual settlers of their pre-emption rights.

Unfortunately the land-office officials were often in alliance with those who unscrupulously attempted to possess land at the minimum price, and they were often dishonest in other respects. In 1835 a congressional investigating committee found that the worst abuses were in Alabama, Mississippi, and Louisiana, but that with the exception of one office in Ohio there was no evidence of frauds north of the Ohio River.

Such irregularities as the following on the part of the land office itself occurred: A buyer approached the receiver at Washington, Louisiana, and wanted to buy a tract at the minimum price of $1.25, but could not raise the money. He agreed to pay $1.75 at a future date. The receiver accepted his note for $1.75, marked the tract sold, marked the buyer's receipt $1.75, but entered the price in the books as $1.25. The receiver, of course, kept the difference, and the government received no money until the $1.75 was paid.

Many receivers bought numerous tracts of choice lands at private entry and sold them to buyers at attractive advances. This was done without any monetary investment by the receiver. He simply marked tracts with an S, held them out of the market until he could sell them at an advance, and then pocketed the difference.

As a matter of fact, receivers were chronic embezzlers. Thirty-five receivers had been in arrears for three years or more prior to the 30th of September 1833. The largest amount was $52,062.04, one something over thirty thousand, six between twenty and thirty thousand, and eight around ten thousand.

As early as 1803, settlers of Mississippi sent a memorial to Congress asking for a homestead law on almost the same plan as that passed fifty-nine years later. The proposal was agitated from time to time, but did not become a law until Civil War days. Now and then settlers and legislative bodies urged Congress to pass a graduation act. This likewise was not passed until the middle of the nineteenth century. It provided that after land had been offered for sale a number of years and still remained unsold, the price should be reduced automatically from time to time until the price was low enough to attract buyers.

In 1854, when it became known that under the terms of this law one could purchase forty acres for five dollars, there was a tremendous rush to the land offices. At St. Louis the crowd was so dense in the street in front of the land office that the police had to clear a passage for wagons to pass. The regular officers were entirely unable to handle the tremendous volume of business. Even after assistants had been hired, it was impossible to keep up with the impetuosity of the buying throng. And thus through the whole frontier period ran the driving urge to speculate and to possess the land.

VII

Beginnings of Plantation Life

SOME planters migrated to Kentucky and Tennessee. Some small farmers also developed into large landholders. In time some of these planters moved on into Arkansas and Missouri. The upper South was not, however, the true plantation area. The lower South, with its cotton and cane, is more generally known as "the plantation South."

Professor F. L. Paxson describes settlement in the cotton kingdom as occurring in two phases: first, the small land-owner occupied the land, clearing it with free labor and bringing it into cultivation; second, the cotton planter purchased of the original settlers a number of adjacent holdings, moved his slaves onto the purchases, year by year increased his holdings, and year by year embedded himself more deeply in what came to be known as the plantation system.[1]

On the whole, settlement of the cotton kingdom truly went through these two phases. As a corollary to Professor Paxson's generally accurate description, it may be pointed out, however, that some planters were actually squatters. The receiver of the St. Stephens, Alabama, land office in 1824 wrote to the Commissioner of Public Lands recom-

[1] Frederick L. Paxson: *History of the American Frontier* (Cambridge, Mass., 1924), pp. 205-7.

mending that the lands on the Tombigbee and Alabama rivers be surveyed and placed on sale. He further stated that these lands had been partially settled by "wealthy planters." The receiver of the Tuscaloosa land office wrote that the settlers on land that was to be sold shortly had lived on it ten years without paying taxes or rent and had invested the crop income in slaves. Planters no doubt sometimes attended the land sales and bought up a contiguous area for a plantation. Many plantations were in a process of being cleared for years. Each winter the slaves cleared a portion to be known next year as the new ground. Furthermore, even in the plantation area there were always many small farmers with few or no slaves. The studies of Harriet and Frank Owsley show that the majority of slaveowners, even in the black belt, were farmers rather than planters.[2] As a matter of fact, the area was settled by great planters, small planters, and farmers in one grand intermingling, with small farmers often in the lead.

One of several very early settlements in the cotton South was an island of settlement around Natchez, about twenty-five miles deep and one hundred miles long. On the west was Spanish territory and in all other directions was Indian territory. The settlers came from the seaboard about the time of the Revolutionary War. Most of them were simple hill people, but among them were some of considerable property. By 1803, large plantations had grown up there. Visitors wrote that it was a common thing for a planter to own a hundred slaves. Between 1800 and 1810 population increased 252 per cent in the Natchez district.[3] The great influx of settlers in Mississippi came in the 1830's, however. Around 1800, Americans secured grants in Louisiana from the Spanish Government and began to settle there. Abraham

[2] Frank L. and Harriet C. Owsley: "Economic Basis of Society in the Late Ante-Bellum South," *Journal of Southern History*, VI, 39–40.
[3] Nell Angela Heidelberg: "The Frontier in Mississippi," MS. (Master's thesis, 1940, Louisiana State University and Agricultural and Mechanical College), pp. 8, 9, 22, 34, 35.

Morehouse, of Kentucky, who was a central figure in this movement, settled in Morehouse Parish.

The first great rush into Alabama was in the northern area along the Tennessee in 1816–18. So great was the ingress of settlers that the Indians and the few old settlers were unable to furnish enough corn for food. During this period immediately after the War of 1812, cotton was selling at a good price and, with the cotton gin coming into general use, the stage was set for the plantation era. There was a tendency for the rich to settle on the bottoms and other choice lands while the poorer settlers were pushed back upon the higher ground and became the small farmers.

When the planter had become possessed of his acres, he immediately selected the site for the house, garden, and outbuildings and set his hands to cutting a gash in the dark forest and underbrush to make room for them. The father of Joseph Williams, who settled in the forests of west Tennessee in 1830, had all this done, his house built, and all hands planting the crop within a month.

The first house was ordinarily a double log cabin with perhaps a lean-to behind one or both cabins, and an attic constructed above. The log plantation house persisted for years. Frederick Law Olmsted, who traveled in Mississippi and Louisiana in the fifties, noted that the plantations were large, but except for size there were few signs of wealth. The greatest number, he said, had small, mean houses. Charles Daubeny, a famous European scholar, also noted that the homes of the planters in Louisiana were mean, associated with large assemblages of Negro huts. Philip Henry Gosse in his *Letters from Alabama* mentioned that the homes of even the wealthy planters were built of rough unhewn logs, and many had big cracks between the logs and not a single window. There was a square hole, he said, two feet wide, with a shutter, which, when open, furnished light although there was no need for it since the crevices between the logs afforded ample light. During the day many a slowly moving spot of light upon the floor showed the progress of the sun toward the west. It was in just such a house as this that the only territorial Governor of Alabama lived during the years of his administration. This was indeed the era of a log-cabin aristocracy.[4]

The two-pen log house was destined to affect vitally the architecture of the plantation houses. As the planter increased in affluence he added to the structure other square log pens, identical with the first two, and cut doorways between them. In time he had amplified it into a four- to eight-room house. Later he built a spacious veranda across the front. When sawmills came in, many of these log structures were weatherboarded and became the white mansion houses. A comparatively few planters, most of them between 1845 and 1860, built new houses, although usually on the same general plan as the log houses. They were long and rambling rather than well-knit structures. The effect of the log house is seen in a roomy hallway flanked by spacious rooms, usually square and regular in design. The second story was made on the same plan. The full veranda, with its high ceiling and tall white posts, further lent to the spacious effect.[5]

In erecting the house the big planter was not obliged to rely on the help of his neighbors to lay up the logs; consequently the house-raising bee was eliminated among the larger planters although in vogue among the small farmers in the region. Sometimes, indeed, a planter went with his slaves to help his neighbors, but this was not general. The slave quarters and other outbuildings were built at a convenient distance from the "big house."

Clearing the ground was largely hand work and was carried on by slaves. The clearing was done in the usual way, with the slaves rolling the logs.

The first crop consisted largely of foodstuffs. In Con-

---

[4] Albert Burton Moore: *History of Alabama* (University, Ala., 1934), p. 133.
[5] Thomas Perkins Abernethy: *The Formative Period in Alabama, 1815–1828* (Montgomery, 1922), pp. 26–7, 59–60.

cordia Parish, Louisiana, the early planters cut the cane and, when it was dry, burned it. A sharp stick was then used to make holes, and the grains of corn were dropped into them.

Each year a little more land was cleared and production of the various crops tended to reach a routine procedure. Nearly equal acreages of corn and cotton were raised—about six acres of each for every field hand. The reason for this was that a gang of slaves could plant and tend more cotton than they could possibly pick, and it was economy to use part of their time in producing the chief foodstuffs used on the plantation. Corn was used for making meal for breadstuff and also to feed the hogs from which came the other main food—pork.

In preparing the soil for cotton the ground was listed and a drill run down the furrows. It was cultivated partly by plow and partly by hoe. The bolls began to open the latter part of August, but the plants matured gradually and the fields had to be gone over several times in order to prevent damage to the fiber. This was the busy season. All available help was secured. Even the Indians were hired to help in the earlier times. The larger planters had their own gin house, and after the cotton was ginned and squeezed into 350-pound bales by horsepower, it was taken to the landing.

In Georgia and probably other parts of the cotton kingdom the "task system" was used. The hands were rated according to their ability and given daily tasks proportionately. The fields were divided into quarter-acre tracts and the number of tracts that constituted a reasonable day's work were assigned. By hustling, the slave could finish his work fairly early and have the rest of the day for himself.[6]

In the frontier days everyone worked and nothing was more common than to see white men, often the owners, and slaves working together in the field. Public opinion was such that the social standing of a white man was not affected adversely.

[6] Ibid., pp. 135, 61–7.

While the slave could not be independent, he could, and did, economically live a carefree life, and it was his master who worried about his needs. When George N. Gilmer was married, his parents gave him and his bride the plantation and thirty-five slaves. In Gilmer's words:

> In a year or so we, by learning to manage ourselves, could easily manage our servants—or slaves if you will have it so, but in truth we were the slaves. We had to do the nursing in time of sickness, to supply food and clothing. Upon us was all the care and anxiety. We had a hard and slavish time of it . . . and it was about all we could do to make the income meet the outgo. . . . Negro children now came piling in on us. . . .[7]

Some planters issued to each slave a weekly allowance of a peck of meal and three and a half pounds of pork. The hands were allowed gardens and could sometimes by hunting or fishing increase their food supply. Possum and watermelon were favorite special dishes, but corn and pork were the regular fare month in and month out. Some owners allowed the slaves to cook this food in their cabins; others objected to this on the ground that it took time from their work in the field, and that the food was not so well cooked. In such a case one or two Negroes did the cooking for all. The noon meal especially was cooked and carried to the slaves in the field.

The earlier frontier crops in Louisiana were corn, indigo, tobacco, rice, cane, and wheat. Afterward indigo was abandoned and rice and wheat largely so. Tobacco was finally crowded out in favor of cane and cotton, both of which lent themselves to the plantation system and slave labor. Farther north in Arkansas and Missouri the plantation could hardly be said to exist. There the frontier crops were like those in Kentucky and Tennessee: first corn, followed by wheat.[8]

[7] George N. Gilmer: "Autobiography," MS., Alabama Department of Archives and History.

[8] Hemp followed these crops in Kentucky and Missouri and flourished

Plantations varied from the two-family establishment to the huge estate. In the first instance, the colored family lived in a log house almost identical with the white folks' house, and the white woman cared for the colored children along with her own and cooked the meals for both families while the colored woman and her husband worked side by side with the planter in the fields. On rainy days or when field work was of a kind she could not do, the colored "aunty" helped her mistress. Such a planter was "on the make" and worked his slaves and himself hard. As the financial situation eased, the aunty went to the field less and her cabin became the kitchen of the plantation. The food was cooked there and carried to the white folks.[9]

In time more slaves and more acres were added and the plantation gradually became an estate with an honorable name such as Oakwood or Chestnut Hill. Log additions were made to the white folks' house from time to time. The row of log slave quarters was extended. In time the big house was weatherboarded, a veranda and tall posts built on, and the whole painted white. The old slaves who had helped the master in less prosperous times and their children became the household servants or petty officers in charge of gangs of field hands. Surrounding the "mansion" were barns, a smoke-house where the pork was cured, a gin house where the gin and press were operated, and various other outbuildings. Such an organization was largely independent of the outside world, a self-sustaining community.

Samuel Gibson, after whom Port Gibson, Mississippi, was named, raised everything used on his plantation but sugar and coffee. He had a large orchard with peaches, plums, apples, melons, and nuts. His flocks furnished milk, butter,

particularly after cotton-raising reached considerable proportions farther south and there was a demand for bale rope and bagging to prepare cotton for the market. James Franklin Hopkins: "A History of the Hemp Industry in Kentucky," MS. (Master's thesis, University of Kentucky, 1938), pp. 37–8.

[9] Hamilton Wilcox Pierson: *In the Brush* (New York, 1881), p. 49.

cheese, and meat. In the forest was game in abundance and hunting recreation for his slaves. Mrs. Gibson supervised the making of all clothes.[10] Life amid such surroundings was highly patriarchial, simple, and rustic. It presents the most beautiful and ideal picture of slavery at its best. Professor Daubeny says that when Judge Porter returned from his journeys on the circuit, his black family came out to greet him and that the judge, obviously beloved by his dependents, shook hands with everyone like a feudal lord among his serfs, receiving their expressions of joy at his return and inquiring with interest into the family concerns of each of his hundred and sixty Negroes.[11]

Many gained riches fast in the great cotton boom, and some of these newly rich had a tendency to form an arrogant aristocracy, with all the unlovely characteristics of the newly rich in any age. To the Southern planter nothing was more certain than that heaven smiled on the aristocratic society he had set up, and that it was the most ideal in all the world.

The big planters visited and traveled about the country a great deal, perhaps staying overnight at a neighboring plantation. They usually subscribed to several Eastern or English papers, were well read, and intelligently discussed markets, politics, and plantation economics. Class distinctions began to appear even while there were miles of forest between the plantations and in many respects frontier conditions existed. Another evidence of a change of the status of the planters was a decline in backwoods hospitality. Frederick Law Olmsted found the planters and their overseers, although gracious enough to those of their own class, very unhospitable to strangers. It was with great difficulty that he found a place to stay overnight. Many owners did not live on their plantations, and those who did would not allow a benighted stranger to stay overnight.

At this time luxuries and good living began to appear.

[10] The *Record* (Port Gibson, Miss.), February 18, 1887.
[11] Stephenson: *Alexander Porter*, pp. 120, 121, 126.

When R. L. Allen of the *American Agriculturist* visited Oak Lawn, three hundred miles above New Orleans, in Louisiana, he said he found that the Yankees by their usual shrewdness were doing a brisk business exchanging congelations of the wintry North (ice) for crystallizations (sugar) of the sunny South. A Negro with a bunch of peacock's feathers in his hand, which he continually waved over the food and every part of the table, kept the numerous flies off while the family was eating. Silks and fine fabrics were imported from France. The day of the frontier had disappeared on the large estates even though they were but spots surrounded by the great forests.

VIII

The Slave as a Pioneer

THE first Kentucky settlers brought with them their slaves, and these had a part in the desperate twenty-year struggle between the whites and the Indians. In 1777, when a census of the inhabitants of Harrodsburg, Kentucky, was taken, ten per cent of the population was slave. The outstanding slave hero of those bloody days in Kentucky was Monk, a powerful young Negro belonging to Captain James Estill of Estill's Station. In some way he had learned the mysteries of making gunpowder, and from saltpeter, found in a cave in southern Kentucky, and sulphur he produced the first gunpowder ever made in that state. On several critical occasions he supplied Boonesborough and Estill's Station. One morning the Indians met Monk hauling water to Estill's Station and asked how many were in the fort. He looked wise and counted out forty on his fingers to them. At the time there were only four sick men in it. The Indians, bluffed by the Negro's stratagem, contented themselves with killing the livestock outside the fort and fled, carrying Monk away captive. When Captain Estill heard of the attack he pursued, overtook them, and gave battle. In the heat of the struggle Monk's voice rang out above the crack of the rifles: "Don't give way, Massa Jim, there's only about twenty-five of the redskins, and you can whip 'em!" After a losing battle of three hours, in which Estill was killed, the surviving whites fled from the field. In the midst of battle Monk escaped from his captors and carried one of the whites, whose thigh had been broken by a rifle bullet, almost the whole distance of twenty-five miles to Estill's Station.[1]

While a settler by the name of Woods, who lived near Crab Orchard, Kentucky, was away one day, Indians attacked his cabin. As an Indian forced his way into the door, a lame Negro with bare hands bravely defended Mrs. Woods and her daughter Hannah. The Negro grappled with the Indian, but fell heavily under his savage attacker's onslaught. Although underneath, he held his assailant tight in his arms, calling loudly for "Miss Hannah" to get the broadax. With two strokes the Indian was dispatched. In the meantime the mother closed and barred the door.[2]

At Eufaula, Alabama, during an Indian scare a Negro man and a little girl were inadvertently left in the stampede to Columbus, Georgia. When the Negro heard the war whoop and saw the little girl playing around the yard, he put her in a sack, slung it over his shoulder, and disappeared into the swamp. He worked his way nearly to Columbus, when he was met by the frantic searching party.

In spite of an attempt by many humane owners to make their slaves happy and not to take those west who did not care to go, were many heartaches. Many tears were shed as the party looked for the last time at the old home before leaving it and the numerous pleasant associations there. When they arrived in the heart of the forest to carve out a new home, the isolation far from their kin and acquaintances brought great homesickness. An old man in recounting his youth recalled visiting in the slave cabins and hearing the black people mourn for their "Ole Virginny" homes and their loved ones. Many times he wept in sympathy with

[1] Coleman: *Slavery Times in Kentucky*, pp. 6–8.
[2] Ibid., pp. 10–11.

them. James Bland in his "Carry Me Back to Ole Virginny" well portrays the homesick longing for the old home, which they had no real hope of ever seeing again.

Even in the Old Northwest, in spite of its prohibitory ordinance, in the southern portion, where the Southern influence was felt most deeply, a form of slavery persisted in a limited way. This was made possible by indenture or apprenticeship laws. Under this arrangement a master could appear before the court with his slaves and make an indenture whereby they agreed to serve him a certain length of time. John Morris and Silvey, a "Negroe" woman about twenty-four years old, appeared before the court of Gallatin County, Illinois Territory, on June 22, 1815, and signed an indenture whereby she was to serve him until June 22, 1855. The law provided that should a slave refuse to make an indenture, the master was allowed sixty days in which to remove him from the territory. Children born of indentured servants were to serve the master of the mother, males until they were thirty and females until they were twenty-eight. In some instances, at least, these Negroes, who because of their ignorance were an easy prey to the unscrupulous, were kept in servitude for years after the indenture had run out. In 1818 the indentured servants in the territory amounted to one fortieth of the population.

The slaveowner hesitated to use the term "slave." He chose rather to speak of his chattels as "our black people," "the black members of our family," "my black family," "the servants," or "the hands." "Boy" was a general term for a male under forty; a female of this age was called "woman." Older males were called "daddy" or "uncle," but never "mister" or "man." Older females were called "aunty," "granny," or "old lady."

Slavery had its own caste system. There were three classes of slaves: The first were those hired out by their masters to work for someone else. Perhaps the master was not in need of help with their particular qualifications at the time or was in straitened financial circumstances. Some were hired out as cooks, mechanics, or nurses. Some trusty ones were allowed to hire out themselves. They were required to pay a certain amount to their masters, and if they were able to earn more, they could keep that for themselves. The plantation hands were divided into two groups: the house servants and the field hands. The house servants were the slave aristocracy. Often they had grown up with their white folks. In close contact with their owners, they imitated them, were trusted with responsibility, and enjoyed a great deal of freedom. In turn they were loyal and devoted. They, in their own parlance, "belonged" to the white family. They took great pride in their rank and were equally disdainful of field hands and "poor white trash." When a stranger asked a house servant if he knew a Negro who was to be sold, he replied: "No, he field nigger; I nebber has no 'quaint-ance wid dat class."

In conversing with another a slave liked to brag about how much the master paid for him, how important his job was, how important his master was, and what a large plantation he was a part of. In this way he built himself up into a particular caste.

The field hands were the third and lowest class. "Field hands," "niggers," "force," "hands," and "people" were all terms applied to them, but the title "slave" was never used.

When the planter grew rich and increased in goods, there was a tendency for him to leave the care of his estate to an overseer and lose contact with his help. Then there often was less of a personal touch, more regimentation, and less humanity in handling the help. The man who owned a smaller farm and owned eight or ten slaves tended to work with them, take holidays with them, and treat them much as his own sons. And yet the Negroes on a great plantation, who experienced much more severe treatment, prided themselves on their high station and looked down with contempt on "dese yere pore folks' niggers."

The manner of work and the degree of its severity depended largely on the size of the plantation. The small planter tended to run his establishment in an informal fashion, while the large establishment necessarily had to regiment its hands. The master or overseer organized the work the night before, and the next morning at dawn the bell sounded for rising. The work day began at sunrise. At noon the plantation bell recalled the field workers. They were allowed two hours at noon, and labor ceased at sunset.

Many times, especially on medium-sized plantations, the workers were divided into small groups to work rather independently. On March 14, 1840 a Mississippi planter noted in his diary:

> Three boys plowing in oats in pasture, 2 deadening in new ground; when finished, commenced to clear up briar thickets in cotton field; Jacob laying off hill by gin house; Gilbert and Viney throwing three furrows together; Ned sick; women and children knocking down cotton stalks.[3]

The diary indicates that in the early winter there was the work of cotton-picking, ginning, and pressing. This ran over into January. After that came clearing the new ground, grubbing, deadening, and cleaning up ground cleared the year before. Then came log-rolling, mauling rails, pulling and knocking down cotton stalks, hauling manure and cotton seed, burning log heaps, and plowing. In the spring and summer there were the tasks of hunting cattle, cultivating crops, shearing sheep, building a cattle shed, digging a cistern, spading the garden, sowing turnips and fall potatoes, harvesting, and gathering corn. In the autumn came the big work of the year—cotton-picking. The women and children burned the brush and logs, cleared the brush, beat down cotton stalks, dropped corn, scattered manure and cotton seeds, and drew up the sweet-potato beds.

[3] Franklin L. Riley: "Diary of a Mississippi Planter, January 1, 1840, to April, 1863," *Publications*, Mississippi Historical Society, X, 316.

The old people were given such easy tasks as weaving, caring for the stock and chickens, doing chores, or other light work. Some states required male slaves to work on the public roads a certain number of days each year. On rainy days there was some leisure time. On the Burleigh plantation in Mississippi at these times all the women were brought into the big house and taught to sew. There was not a woman on the place who could not mend neatly her own and her husband's and children's clothing.

In the autumn during cotton-picking time overseers sometimes organized the Negroes into groups according to their speed and offered prizes to the fastest pickers. For the men there were trousers, scarfs, hats, and roundabouts, and for the women dress patterns or other inviting things.

In the upper South and among small planters, where the Negroes lived more like one of the white folks, morality among the slaves was comparatively good. Farther south on some of the big estates no more attention was paid to virtue and marriage relationships among Negroes than among cattle and horses. The males with the best disposition and physique had a plurality of wives, and there were no old maids on the plantation of such a master. This free-love arrangement caused a great deal of jealousy, fighting, and disorder among the slaves. Other masters, even at a financial sacrifice, encouraged chastity and fidelity.

Actually, a slave marriage was not legally binding. Sometimes the master simply read a few passages of Scripture, had the couple jump over a broomstick, and declared them husband and wife. Jumping over the broom seems to have been a favorite method in Kentucky. A Lexington minister married hundreds on the terms: "Until death or distance do you part."

House servants were given a stylish wedding in the dining-room of the big house, with all the accompaniments. Little Negroes held the candles while the preacher read, and a sumptuous meal followed. An old aunty was recounting to the daughter of Old Massa the story of the wedding he had given her:

> I had a weddin'—a big weddin'. . . . Your pa gib me a head weddin,—kilt a mutton—a round o' beef—tukkeys—cakes. . . . I had all the chany off de side board, cups an' saucers, de table, de white tablecloth. I had on your pa's wife's weddin' gloves and slippers an' veil. De slippers was too small, but I put my toes in. . . . Marster brought out a milk pail o' toddy an' more in bottles.[4]

The household servants often exerted a powerful influence on their masters. Often they were more than half white, and constant association with the planter's family brought a high degree of culture and refinement. The relationship of many of them to their masters was intimate and confidential. Often they had been childhood playmates and chums of the master, and there was a tendency for these positions to become hereditary when once established. These servants were never whipped and were honest, truthful, dignified, and courteous.

Each of the young ladies of the large plantation had her maid, who was anxious that her young "missus" should excel all others. Under the manipulation of her loyal and ambitious servant, she came forth, if not a veritable Princess Charming, at least transformed into a lovely, becoming candidate for matrimony. The maids frequently employed every art to see that their young missus made a matrimonial alliance that was favorable to them. This was of the highest importance to servants, as it involved the question whether they were to have a kind or an unkind master. If the suitor pleased them, they poured into his ears the highest praises of young missus and treated him with every courtesy. If, however, they found out he was a man of bad habits and an evil temper, one who would make a hard master, they poured into the ears where it would be most effective all they knew to the gentleman's discredit.

[4] Smedes: *A Southern Planter*, p. 55.

The casual reading of the laws and regulations concerning slavery would lead one to think the slaves were subjected to the most rigid tyrannical rules. Investigation reveals, however, that these rules were not enforced except where the slave population was the heaviest and at times when an insurrection was feared. Laws, for example, forbade Negroes from going off the plantation without a written pass.

Patrols, called patterols by the slaves, were organized by the whites, and these night riders endeavored to enforce the regulations.[5] When old Uncle Rastus, of Clay County, Missouri, prayed, he was prone to say: "Oh, Lord, we thank thee for the New Jerusalem, with its pearly gates and its golden streets, but above all, we thank thee for that high wall around the great big city, so high that a patterroler can't get over it."[6] Such a citizens' organization was bound to deteriorate as the routine grew irksome, and the slaves were allowed a wide range of freedom as long as no dangerous symptoms of an uprising appeared—a danger that was ever present, especially in vast areas where the blacks outnumbered the whites ten to one.

Slaves were forbidden to have liquor, but in some way they got it. An old Negro held the candle for Frederick Law Olmsted while he went to bed at a plantation. He got nicely settled for the night and was ready to drop off to sleep when, after a short interval, the light reappeared and Uncle Abram, bending over him holding the candle, winked and shook his head in a mysterious manner. "Hush, massa," he whispered. "You nain't got something to drink, in dem saddle-bags has you, sar?"

---

[5] I remember, as a small boy on my mother's lap, hearing her sing a song she learned as a child from the Negro aunties when she visited the slave quarters. The song ran:

> Run, nigger, run,
> The patterol'l ketch you;
> Run, nigger, run
> 'Fore the break of day.

[6] W. H. Woodson: *History of Clay County, Missouri* (Topeka, 1920), p. 89.

Probably the most grievous feature of slavery was the fact that one human being was placed almost entirely in the power of another. The master could—and unfeeling masters did— separate families at will. Furthermore, the Negro had no right to testify against a white man in a court. This made it possible for a white man to flog a slave unmercifully or to be too free with the slave's wife, without any recourse to the law. A mean or heartless master or overseer could even whip a Negro to death without fear of just punishment. Far removed from restraint by public sentiment, he made life miserable by his tyrannical acts. That such things did not appear more often than they did was for the same reason that horses and other dumb animals are ordinarily well treated—because of the natural humanity of the owners.

And yet the average slave had a surprising number of liberties. He was allowed holidays at Christmas, Easter, the Fourth of July, and election time. Picnics and barbecues were allowed on the green grass in the shade of the forest trees. These were accompanied by athletic events and a bran dance. The best masters allowed a half holiday each Saturday and gave the Negroes a garden plot where they could work for themselves during that time. They could often raise and sell enough produce to make sizable amounts. Walter Lenoir of Columbia, Missouri, allowed his servants to make maple sugar for themselves. Some made and sold ginger cakes on election day or at the militia muster. In the upper South the Negroes generally turned out to the cornshucking, were received on equal terms with the whites, and with antics and songs amused them. At harvest time whisky or some other treat was given the hands. With the proper arrangements, and a white man present, they could gather at some central plantation and dance to the music of the fiddle and triangle or the banjo until midnight on Saturday night.

Probably the most cherished privilege the frontier Negro enjoyed was hunting. In Tennessee only one slave on each plantation was permitted to hunt with a gun, and that not at night with a light. But with a good possum dog to lead the way to the quarry, the moonlight nights of autumn and winter were made gay by the rollicking crowd of hunters. The "tree bark" of the hound brought the crowd to the game. With luck, by shaking the tree, or by a tug on the grapevine, down came the possum with his ruse of playing dead. Quickly he was sacked and the jolly crowd moved on for more 'simmon-fattened possums to sack. In his spare time the Negro was allowed also to hunt bees, gather the honey, sell it, and keep the proceeds.

The slave was allowed church privileges. Larger plantations had their own colored churches, but the commoner custom was for the slaves to belong to the same church as their masters and to sit in a designated section.

Another enjoyable occasion was the camp-meeting. The *Farmers' Gazette* of Sparta, Georgia, in reporting a camp-meeting in 1807, stated that there were about three thousand persons, white and black together, camped on the ground at night. A New Englander, J. H. Ingraham, who was prepared for the worst with respect to the evils of slavery, wrote of attending a ball. The happiest people in the ballroom were the Negroes, he said. "You who live in a free state have no idea of the privileges this class are permitted in a slave state by the white people." The slaves moved about the room at will and a favorite aunty would even ask: "Please, missis, stand dis way a little bit so I can see." And the "missis" would comply as "readily as if a lady had asked her."

Timothy Flint, a Northerner, said he had heard before he visited the lower Mississippi Valley, in 1826, appalling stories of the cruelty and barbarity of the masters toward their slaves. He said he had seen instances of cruelty, but the slaves in general had the most cheerful countenances and were apparently the happiest people he saw. Knowing that Northern slaves were cowed with the threat of being sold down the river, he was prepared to find cruelty and misery, but he found conditions in the lower country to be more tolerable than in that above. He summed up his observations by stating that where the master was a considerate, kind man, the patriarchal authority on the one hand and affectionate veneration on the other rendered the relation of master and slave not altogether so forbidding as we have been accustomed to consider it.

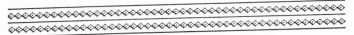

IX

Frontier Agriculture

WHEN the settler had selected the land for his home, the first task was to make a clearing. Having selected a spot for the house, he set about "to fell the trees outward." He cut the trees into logs, split some clapboards or shakes for a roof, and was ready to invite his neighbors to the house-raising. In many cases a barn was not built for years. The cattle and horses either ran in the forest or were kept in a rail pen. Sometimes a makeshift shelter was formed by placing a brush and grass roof over a portion of the pen.

Next came the clearing of a plot for garden truck and another for a patch of corn. The wise backwoodsman selected the nearest area of large straight oaks, which he felled and split for rails. The trees that were a foot or less in diameter were cut down. The larger ones were girdled and died shortly afterward. An area of these was known as a "deadening." The area among these trees was often farmed for a number of years, and in a windy time dropping limbs were a menace to the workman. A Missouri frontier stump speaker closed his remarks with this meaningful exhortation: "Well, men, love God, hate the devil, and keep out of a deadening in time of a thunderstorm." [1] After a windstorm

[1] Interview with G. G. Dick, La Harpe, Kansas, July 15, 1942.

came the tedious back-breaking business, on the part of the boys, women, and girls, of "picking up the chunks," as it was called. The shrubs and brush were dug out with a heavy grubbing hoe. These, together with the limbs cut from the felled trees, were piled up by the women and children.

In the lowlands the cane was cut with an ax or cane-knife and the roots were dug out with a mattock. The cane was allowed to lie and dry out for perhaps two months, and then on a windy day it was set on fire. The flames of the terribly hot fire burned the lower limbs and even the bark off the largest trees, killed them, and left the ground covered with ashes and ready for planting. Generally thereafter the progressive settler tried to clear an area each winter. This, the following year, was known as the new ground. When the logs were in appropriate lengths, the log-rolling took place.

Corn was the ideal first crop. No special preparation of the ground was necessary. Many, like the Lowes of Caldwell Parish, Louisiana, went into the deadening and without plow or any other implement except a sharp, flattened hickory stick jabbed that into the ground, dropped the grains into the holes, and tramped on the ground. Furthermore, little or no cultivation was necessary on new ground. No machinery was necessary for harvesting. And corn made excellent food for man or beast. Moreover, the process of preparing it for food was more simple than with wheat. After the first season it was necessary to plow the ground. This was often done with the crudest kind of homemade plow. A forked hardwood sapling of the proper size was selected. One prong of the fork was cut about fifteen inches long and, when sharpened, served as a share. The other fork was cut longer and formed a beam. Handles were attached near the crotch. This implement, as crude as those used two thousand years before, loosened the soil slightly. It was succeeded by the jumping shovel plow, which had an arched coulter that struck the roots and made the point jump them. An improved plow was known as the "bar-share" plow, which has been described as a profanity-provoking mechanism with a long iron share and a wooden moldboard, which, when it struck a root or stump, brought the handles up with a vigorous jerk, stopping the team. The operator, unable to stop so quickly, was thrown onto the handles, knocking the wind out of him. Or perhaps it struck a smaller root that momentarily slowed down the team, but when it was stretched to its full tension, the root would snap and the two ends would whip the plowman's shins unmercifully.[2]

In an attempt to "check" [3] the corn, the rows were marked lengthwise of the field by plowing furrows four feet apart. It was then rowed crosswise and a boy dropped the corn at the furrow intersections while a man covered it with a hoe. Sometimes cross rows were not plowed, but a peeled stake was set at the side of the field and the dropper walked across the rows dropping the seeds in a line crosswise of the field as straight as possible. Corn was cultivated by crude plowing, and the hoe was used a great deal, especially on stumpy, rooty ground. A small boy was often required to ride one of the horses during the plowing, and when the plow struck a stump, the hames would give the day-dreaming boy a lusty punch in the pit of the stomach.

Harvesting corn consisted in four distinct operations: (1) Just before the blades began to turn yellow, the hands went down the rows stripping off the green leaves from the ears down. These were gathered in bunches and placed in a crotch between two stalks to dry. This was known as pulling fodder. (2) A few days later a sled was drawn through the patch to haul in the fodder. Each bunch was bound with a damp withered blade and hauled to a little shed at the back of the cabin or stacked around a pole. (3) A little later the tops of the stalks were cut off down next to the ears. These were shocked in the field and the nude stalks were left stand-

---

[2] Srygley: *Seventy Years in Dixie*, pp. 162–3.

[3] This is the technical term for the program of planting the hills in rows crosswise as well as lengthwise, giving the field the appearance of a checkerboard.

ing in the field, supporting the ears. (4) In the frosty days of autumn the ears, shuck and all, were snapped and stored in a crib made of rails, there to await the corn-shuckin'. Fodder was largely used in place of hay for work- or riding-horses. The cows were largely fed on "browse." This was simply the small limbs and bark of certain trees that were cut in the winter months. Beech, slippery elm, white elm, and pignut, or white hickory, were thought best.

In some areas wheat was raised to be used for making the much appreciated biscuits, gravy, and pastries. It was said that in many places the ground was so rich that wheat could not be raised until four or five crops of corn had been grown —that prior to this it grew so rank it all went to stalk.

When it was sown, the plowed ground was harrowed with a large piece of brush from the trees. Then a peeled stick was stuck in one end of the field and the sower, with a bag of seed suspended at his left side, walked slowly toward the white stick, broadcasting the wheat. If it was on the prairie, where the field was large, this was sometimes done from horseback. The seed was covered by dragging the brush over it again.

In earliest times the grain was cut with a hand sickle. The reaper grasped a handful of grain in the left hand, cut it off, and laid it in a little pile. Upon cutting a swath through the field and reaching the other end, he hung his sickle or reaping hook over his shoulder and, gathering up the loose grain as he walked away, he bound it into bundles, using the straw for bands. There was a maxim of the harvest field that no boy would ever become a good reaper until he cut his left hand. Later the cradle came into use on ground free from stumps. Around the stumps the sickle still held its own. The advantage of the cradle lay in the fact that the wooden fingers and blade left the loose grain lying in a swath with the heads in one direction in good order for binding. A man could cut on an average two acres a day with the cradle.

Harvest time was made a sort of festive occasion. Several

cradlers came in to help, and when one man's grain was done, the crew moved on to the next place. This was occasioned by the fact that when grain was ripe, there was no waiting. It had to be cut before a sudden storm leveled it to the ground. One man's wheat often ripened early and another's late. It was therefore advantageous to trade work and get the grain cut with dispatch. The assembling of a crowd made for much good-fellowship and work in company, which was indeed welcome to the lonely pioneer. A jug of whisky, to which the hands helped themselves at will, extra eats, and races between cradlers, or competition between cradlers and binders, brought pleasant diversion.

The cradle inaugurated division of labor. The binder followed the cradlers, binding the gavel much as had been done before. The bundles were later set up in shocks until time to haul them to the threshing-floor. Every neighborhood had its champion binder and cradler. Sometimes contests were waged between these titans of the harvest. The grain, after standing in shocks in the field until thoroughly cured, was hauled on a little sled, or later a wagon, to the threshing-floor. In earlier times a rail pen three feet high was built and covered with rails laid close together. A number of bundles were thrown onto this and laid side by side with the heads in one direction.

The grain was then beaten out with a flail, and kernels and chaff dropped through the cracks into the pen below. A flail was made by cutting a hickory sapling about seven feet long and an inch and a half in diameter. About two feet from the butt end, at a point where the handle was to end and the club begin, a hinge was formed by beating the pole with the back of an ax until it was perfectly flexible. The flail was rotated in the hands by a peculiar motion as the grain was beaten.[4] This hard work was often done in the hottest weather, for the grain had to be perfectly dry.

When the threshing was finished, the straw was separated

[4] Peter Hite, MSS., McCormick Library, Chicago, p. 2.

by winnowing. In this process one man would pour wheat and chaff in a small stream from a vessel onto a sheet or skin. Two others fanned vigorously with a sheet. They would take hold of opposite ends of the sheet, stretch it tight, and by a peculiar motion of the arms, working with all their might, manage to make enough breeze to blow out the chaff. The program was made easier if the day was windy. In time, cleaning was simplified by running the material through a fanning mill.

As the cradle succeeded the sickle, so threshing with horses displaced the flail. On a circular spot twenty to twenty-five feet in diameter the loose top soil down to the clay was raked off with a hoe. The clay was then leveled and tamped down until it was hard like a cement floor. The dirt scraped off was banked up around the outside until the threshing-floor looked like a circus ring. Then enough bundles were thrown in to make "a batch." A row of bundles was laid down as close together as possible with the heads pointing toward the center of the ring and the butts against the ridge. When this outer circle was complete, an inner row was made by turning the butts toward the center and lapping the heads just over those of the other row. In the center of the ring there was left a spot eight or ten feet across, in which the threshed grain and chaff were placed. Sometimes a man stood in the center and with a whip kept the horses, two abreast, on the move. More often one or more boys rode and led horses around the tiresome circle. When the tramping feet had worn the straw thin, the crushed straw was removed and the wheat and chaff were thrown into the center of the ring.

The earliest fences were made of brush piled around the outer edge of the clearing. This was very unsatisfactory since the succulent crops were a standing invitation to both domestic and wild animals to break through the frail barrier. This makeshift was soon followed by a rail fence. The tools required were a good ax, a maul, two or more iron wedges, and the same number of hardwood wedges, known as "gluts." The maul was made by selecting a hardwood limb about six inches through and the length of an ax helve; one end of this was whittled down into a handle similar to that of an ax, and enough of the butt was left untouched to form a heavy wooden hammer.

In splitting rails an ax was used to make the first crack in the log near the large end. Into this beginning of an opening an iron wedge was driven. The glut was driven in next to hold the crack open while the iron wedge was transferred elsewhere to open the crack further. The iron wedge took the brunt of opening the cracks, and the gluts did the secondary work. A large boy could finish seventy-five ash or forty-five honey-locust rails in a day. A log chain was hooked around the ends of six or eight rails and a horse dragged them to where they were to be laid up. The commonest fence was that variously known as the worm, snake, or Virginia fence. It was made in a zigzag pattern with the ends of the rails resting one across another at an angle and often held in place by slanting posts at the corners where the rails met.

The milk cow was lured to the cabin each morning by keeping her calf impounded near there. Daniel Drake, who in the first half of the nineteenth century became one of America's most famous physicians, remembered how as a Kentucky youth it was his task to take the calf by the ears and hold it until his mother had got a sufficient head start on the hungry young bovine to guarantee favorable competition for the lad's mother, who milked the right side while the calf worked the left. It was so consistently a woman's job to milk that Dr. Drake said it was considered "girlish" for a boy to milk and that his mother, as well as himself, would have been mortified if any neighboring man or boy had caught him at it. Strange as it may seem, this unwritten law, while proscribing milking, permitted the boys to churn. The universal custom was to feed the cow "slop" at the cabin door. This consisted of broth, dishwater, cabbage leaves, potato parings, and other scraps from the kitchen, such as is given today to the hogs. In the fall for several weeks pumpkin was a principal cow feed. At times cows were also fed some corn. An old man recalled that his happiest days were those of long ago when he sat by the fire "nubbin' " the cow (feeding her small ears of corn) through the cracks between the cabin logs, while his wife outside did the milking.[5]

The other cattle and horses were allowed to run in the forest on the range. Small troughs were cut in the trunk of a fallen tree and occasionally salt was placed there, making what was known as a "lick log." This formed a sort of community center around which the stock ranged instead of scattering too far away.

In northern Louisiana and in Arkansas during the first half of the nineteenth century there were large numbers of wild horses. These were difficult to bring into captivity, but, once broken, became useful. The wild bands were a menace to domesticated animals because the latter sometimes succumbed to the temptation of joining a band and wandered off. Horses were branded and cows and hogs were marked with various cuts and gashes.

Hogs ran wild in the forest, nearly starving in winter and summer, but fattening up in the autumn on mast or nuts in the woods. When it was time to butcher, a group of men and boys took their barrels and salt into the woods, killed the hogs, and packed away the meat for the market.

Progressive frontiersmen attempted to raise enough sheep to furnish wool for making woolen clothing. It was very difficult to protect sheep from their enemies, however. Bears and especially wolves were a constant menace. If the house was built on a hillside the sheep were kept under it. Otherwise they were kept at night in a strong log pen beside the

---

[5] Virginia Clay McClure: "The Settlement of the Kentucky Appalachian Highlands," MS. (Doctor's thesis, University of Kentucky, 1933), p.113.

house.[6] The men were accustomed to dig a wolf pit and rid the country of "varmints" before trying to raise sheep and tame hogs.

In the earliest times pack horses and small sleds were used for transportation. John Hutchins, who lived near Natchez about 1800, raised three crops of cotton before he had any way of taking it to the gin. Finally he improvised a home-made wagon with solid wheels—narrow cross-sections sawed from the trunk of a large tree. The body was a large basket woven from cane. Near Lexington, Kentucky, James Wasson was using the same sort of wheels on a cart in 1780. The probate records of Ouachita Parish, Louisiana, indicate that not a few wagons of that region in 1814 were made without iron.[7] A type of sled used in Missouri before the era of the wagon was known as a lizard. It was made of a V-shaped forked tree and furnished with a bed of brush to haul a load. The horse was hitched to the apex.

[6] William Flinn Rogers: "Life on the Kentucky-Tennessee Frontier near the End of the Eighteenth Century," MS. (Master's thesis, University of Tennessee, 1925), p. 53.
[7] Inventory of Estates, Probate Records, Ouachita Parish, La.

X

Going to Market

THE pioneers had no sooner got settled in their new homes than the problem of transportation and markets became acute. During the first few years of settlement in most areas the products for export consisted principally of hides, pelts, beeswax, bear's oil, and ginseng. In return such indispensable articles as salt, iron, powder, and lead had to be brought to the settlements. In Kentucky and Tennessee the products were at first carried by pack horses over the mountains to the East. In the autumn several families would associate together. A master driver was selected from among them, and one or two young men and sometimes a boy or two were asked to assist. The horses with their two-hundred-pound packs marched in single file along a narrow path through the forbidding forest, over craggy steeps, and through the mountain defiles. Each horse carried a sack of shelled corn for provender. Some feed was deposited at convenient places for use on the return journey.

A large wallet, well filled with jerked bear or deer meat, boiled ham, and cheese, furnished the food for the drivers. The master driver rode ahead leading the string. Each successive pack horse was tied to the one before him. An assistant rode behind to keep an eye on the loads and urge on any lagging animal. At night the horses were hobbled and their bells unstopped; free from their burdens, they grazed about camp while the drivers slept around a roadside campfire. The standard number of horses for the two drivers was ten or twelve.

The next product was livestock. By the time the Indians had been defeated, in the nineties, the drovers began driving their herds of hogs, cattle, and horses into the Eastern and Southern seaboard regions. An immigrant westward said his journey was almost interrupted by immense droves of seven or eight hundred on the way to Baltimore. F. A. Michaux, in 1802, mentioned the droves of stock driven over the Wilderness Road to South Carolina. On the western part of the route the hogs ate acorns and other nuts in the forest, and the cattle and horses grazed on the cane by the way. On the eastern end of the journey the drovers bought corn from the farmers along the way. The drive was made in the autumn. A westbound traveler in 1822 claimed he met droves of four or five thousand hogs moving over the National Road. He said he was informed a hundred thousand had been driven from Kentucky alone. Davy Crockett drove stock from Tennessee to Virginia. One traveler remarked that although the cattle were very wild, timber-raised, and the drives were made from four to five hundred miles through forest lands and across numerous rivers, yet very few were lost. In almost all the new country where there was the least opportunity to market the stock, these drives were made.

County fairs were started early and like the fairs of medieval days were really markets. The first session of the Tennessee general assembly gave the citizens of Blount County permission to hold two fairs each year for the purpose of selling all kinds of goods and merchandise. They were to last two days each and were to be held in March and October. In Missouri horses and mules were exhibited on the green during court week.

But a local market would not do in an almost exclusively

agricultural country where everybody had the same thing to sell. There was naturally little exchange of goods. In the eighties and nineties the whole West clamored for the opening of the Mississippi River to Americans as an artery of commerce. The federal government was not able immediately to secure the concession from Spain, which owned the territory on both sides of the river at its mouth. When the national government seemed deaf to their cries, the Westerners threatened to take things into their own hands, even to the extent of leaving the Union if necessary to secure their end.

To General James Wilkinson, an unscrupulous schemer, goes the credit for opening New Orleans, at least in a limited way, to American trade. In 1787 he established the town of Frankfort with its shipping facilities on the Kentucky River. He then bought up and sent to New Orleans a shipment of tobacco, hams, and butter. He returned with much show of prosperity for a country still in the throes of frontier existence. He rode in a chariot drawn by four horses and attended by slaves, and was greeted as a hero who had gained greater concessions from Spain than had the federal government. He had received nearly five times as much for his tobacco as it was worth in Kentucky. The next spring (1788) he started with twenty-five large armed flatboats and a fighting force of a hundred and fifty men. In collusion with certain New Orleans merchants he had received private privileges. This was the first big expedition. By means of bribery and deceit, by claiming that the party was a group of immigrants coming to settle in Spanish territory, and by taking the oath of allegiance and receiving certificates of citizenship, they were allowed to proceed.

Fortunately for all concerned, the Mississippi River was soon opened to everyone, ushering in the day of the flatboats. These were often known on Western waters as Kentucky boats. Farther north and east they were called arks. Several neighbors would unite in building the boat and in arranging the voyage. Each put on board his own produce at his own risk. One owner went as captain and supercargo, and about six hands accompanied as a crew.

These boats were started on their voyages on all the large rivers whether they flowed into the Gulf of Mexico direct or into the Mississippi or one of its tributaries and thence on her broad bosom to New Orleans. By 1825 the traffic was so immense that at New Madrid as many as a hundred flatboats landed in a single day. Timothy Flint strolled to the wharf on a spring evening and saw them arriving in fleets. They tied up there side by side until the surfaces of the boats literally covered acres. They had come from regions thousands of miles apart. Some boats had come bringing from southwestern New York lumber, from northern Alabama cotton, from Tennessee and Kentucky pork, flour, whisky, hemp, tobacco, and rope, from Illinois and various other places cattle and horses, from Missouri lead and pelts. Some boats were loaded with ear corn, others with barrels of apples or potatoes. There was frozen or boiled cider by the boatload, dried fruits, and every agricultural or manufactured product of the whole area. Roosters were crowing, cattle lowing, horses stamping in their stalls, and swine squealing. There were boats fitted especially for and loaded entirely with turkeys that gobbled furiously.

In the early evening the hands walked from boat to boat making acquaintances, forming mutual-assistance agreements, or traveling comradeships for the rest of the trip to New Orleans, making inquiries, possibly meeting someone they had seen before. After an hour or two spent in that way they jumped on shore and proceeded to celebrate. Sometimes they became riotous and a regular battle between townsmen and boatmen ensued. After midnight the uproar died down and the boatmen proceeded to their boats. Once more the fleet would unite at Natchez and New Orleans, but although they drifted down the same river day after day not far apart, yet they might never see one another again. At daybreak the bugles sounded. Everything was life and activity. In half an hour all were under way and nothing was seen but the monotonous current of the river.

The captain of the boat on which the traveler Baily rode in 1797 agreed with three other boats that they would stick together and put ashore at the same place each night. The signal for stopping was the firing of a gun by the boat in the lead when she found an appropriate place to stop. This gave time for all to maneuver into position to tie up close together. There they spent the evening pleasantly in company.

Often on the Mississippi a number of boats were lashed together and floated along as one. A traveler who was once on board a fleet of eight found it quite a walk from one end to another of this floating town. On one boat they were butchering hogs, another had a cargo of nuts, apples, and cider, and still another was a retail dram shop. These alliances often started in a frolic and ended in a quarrel; then the aggrieved party unlashed his boat and went his way. When several boats floated along separately, it was customary for them to visit one another with skiffs.

As the boat floated along it was often hailed and questions were asked concerning where it was from, who the captain was, where it was bound, and with what it was laden. This often ended in lively repartee, obscenity, blackguarding, and even an exchange of rifle-shots. Often a captain was happy to take a passenger for the sake of company and also to help man the boat in cases of difficulty. When it was learned that many were "on the float"—that is to say, a large number of boats were coming—these craft traveled day and night in order to arrive at the market before it was glutted. On a gloomy dark night with no lights to direct, the crew would strike with an ax and could tell by the reverberation which shore to pull out from. One boat ran 360 miles without landing once. In Louisiana about 1810, flatboats were lighted up at night by beacon fires kept burning in an iron basket suspended on a pole. On a sunny spring day, with the boat floating gently along, all was calm and the life of the boatman was rosy indeed. One acquainted with flatboating described such a scene: One boatman played a violin and the others danced. They flirted with the girls on the bank and joked with men on other boats. Just as the craft disappeared around the bend, the bugle with which each boat was provided sounded. Such a scene with no presentiment of danger held irresistible allurement for the lad on the bank.

Flatboating was not all joy and sunshine, however. Snags, rapids, sandbars, wind and waves, and exposure for long hours during the driving snow or cold rain made the work anything but a picnic. Although there was some personal danger, the greatest bugbears were the delays and hard work in getting a grounded boat afloat or a damaged boat repaired. The captain or owner lived in constant dread of the destruction and loss of property that often meant his whole fortune. John Bedford on his journey down the Cumberland in 1807 passed a flatboat that had been lodged on a sandbar for twenty days.

In time the New Orleans market became glutted and only the first boats received a good price for their goods. Before long, foreign markets were found, and flatboats continued and even increased in number during the thirties after the steamboat came in.

The backwoodsman who made a trip down the river was like a country boy who goes to a big city today. He had no idea that the houses in New Orleans or Mobile were not made of logs and chinked with mud or that all people did not eat from wooden or pewter tableware. To him tea and coffee were slops that did not stick to the ribs. Cups and saucers were a sign of unmanly luxury or effeminate ways. And yet the stripling upon his return home after a trip had great things to tell his wide-eyed friends. An up-river man who for the first time saw a sailing ship at New Orleans inquired if the sailors unfurling the sails had beds up there. Almost all thought the big cities wicked, but many were ready to "go it to the limit." One writer remarked that sober, quiet deacons at home would too often throw religion aside when they embarked on the annual trip down-river.

When the cargo was sold at New Orleans, the boat was usually broken up for lumber. Several small towns in the neighborhood of New Orleans were practically built from lumber received in that way. The members of the crew walked back to their homes. Those from Kentucky, Tennessee, and north of the Ohio River took the Natchez Trace home.

Those who went home through the wilderness carried quantities of specie and, to defend themselves from thieves, banded together in companies and chose officers. Sometimes there were several hundred together. Mules and a hardy tough breed of Indian and Spanish horse, known as the "Opelousas horse," were used to carry the money and "plunder." Some rode horseback, but many could not afford a horse. Extra horses were taken to carry the sick. The first six or seven hundred miles was through an ideal malarial country and the group anxiously hurried along for fear of its grip. Many died on the way. Others who were ill were left to the care of the Indians or a stray hunter. Those who survived such a plight were often so emaciated that it took months for them to reach home. In spite of all these dangers, the prospect of adventure and of returning home with fifty Spanish dollars in gold lured an ever increasing number to man the boats, which over a period increased twenty-five to thirty per cent annually.

In 1811 a naturalist in Tennessee met some of these boatmen returning. They looked to him as dirty as Hottentots, like savages, with an eighteen-day-old beard, dressed in canvas shirt and trousers, black and greasy and sometimes in tatters; their skin was sunburnt wherever exposed and they carried a bundle wrapped in an old blanket. When they came to an unfordable stream, they attempted to cross on a fallen tree. Failing in that, each entered the water with his budget on his head. When they lost bottom they dropped their burden to their shoulders and took to swimming. They sometimes crossed fourteen or fifteen such streams in a day and swamps unequaled in any country. After sleeping on the floor in a house, a dozen boatmen one morning arose complaining of not feeling well. They gave for the reason the fact that they had slept indoors. By 1827, Timothy Flint records, most of the boatmen returned by steamboat.

Some of the rivers, particularly in Louisiana, had obstructions of fallen trees, which hindered navigation. This mass of tangled logs wedged together until the whole river channel was blocked for miles. These were known as rafts. In time ligneous material covered the wood, and often willow trees, many of them ten inches in diameter, grew up from these "floating bridges," as they were called. Some of these actually formed good bridges that were passable at all seasons. The most famous of these was the raft on the Red River that was 160 miles long. It was cleared out by Henry M. Shreve as part of the internal improvement program of the United States Government.[1]

The settlers who lived a distance from the rivers had to haul their products to the rivers. Every autumn long lines of freight wagons hauled cotton from the interior to the Alabama, Tombigbee, Yazoo, Pearl, Coosa, and Chattahoochee or their tributaries. Sometimes these trains hauled their loads as far as a hundred miles. Cotton wagons usually hauled ten bales and were drawn by six or eight yoke of oxen or mule teams. The teamsters made their camp by the road each night in an enclosure formed by their wagons. The group surrounding their cheery fire made a pretty picture. Most of the drivers were slaves, but many small farmers hauled their own crop. Some of the drivers were professional white teamsters. Their mule teams were decorated with bright glistening bells high up over the hames, which made the air merry with their jingle.

[1] The raft was not a single obstruction but a series of rafts with open places between. The timber portion occupied from a third to a half of the whole space.

XI

Economic Life

THE almost entire absence of specie greatly hindered business and financial transactions on the raw frontier. The most common substitute for small coins was coonskins. Almost everything from marriage licenses to the salary of public officers was reckoned in coonskins. It was as common then to estimate a man's wealth in coonskins as in dollars today. One man who lived in that era said that he almost wondered whether the country could have developed without those little animals which were so universally regarded as an unmitigated evil and yet whose skin was converted into a blessing. Where beaver were abundant their skins were used as the unit of money, and a certain number of deer, fox, or raccoon skins were reckoned as worth a beaver skin. Sometimes a skin-buyer bought a man's furs and gave him a warehouse receipt. This was passed from hand to hand as money.[1]

Bear's oil, beeswax, and ginseng were also used to pay for services or goods. A Missouri receipt read: "Good for six pounds of catfish, at St. Louis, the 25th of September, 1799." One pioneer remembered seeing a horse sold at auction in Paris, Kentucky, for so many cows and calves.

[1] Mary Verhoeff: *The Kentucky River Navigation* (Louisville, 1917), p. 65, footnote.

Certificates of service of militiamen on active service were redeemable in produce and were circulated as money. When tobacco culture came in, tobacco and tobacco receipts became a popular medium of exchange. In Nashville cowbells and axes were used to buy commodities. A "faithful rifle and a clear toned bell" were traded for a tract of land. Land itself was often used as money. The expression was often heard in trade: "three twenties," "six forties," referring to acreages of land. In Mississippi cotton ginners' receipts were given to a man who left his cotton to be ginned (four months were allowed the ginner, by law, to do the work). These ginners' receipts were passed from person to person as currency.

After the Mississippi was opened to trade, Spanish specie was brought into the settlements. General Samuel Hopkins wrote in September 1801 that it was reported that seventy horses and mules loaded with money had arrived in Kentucky and Tennessee that year.[2]

When a traveler gave the mistress of an inn a dollar, she gave it to a Negro and told him to "chop it." "Chop it! Ma'am I want it changed." She made no reply, but had the servant cut out her change. He did this very dexterously and returned the dollar with a large chunk of it cut away. When the traveler learned this was the practice of the country, he got the handy Negro to transform two more dollars into pieces. He found this very convenient for use in his travels. Each eighth was worth twelve and a half cents and was called a "bit." This system gave rise to the terms "two bits" or "four bits" in use to this day, meaning twenty-five or fifty cents. The objections to "cut money" were that the sharp edges of the wedge-shaped "bits" wore pockets out and it was necessary to carry them in buckskin wallets. Then, too, the unscrupulous cut the coin into nine eighths or five quarters. The state of Kentucky recognized the practice by

[2] General Samuel Hopkins to his son Sam. G. Hopkins, September 1, 1801, MS., Kentucky Historical Society, Frankfort, Ky.

authorizing the state auditor to exchange cut silver received for revenue with the Bank of Kentucky at a discount of three per cent for small round coins. The discount was occasioned by the frequent dishonest practice in cutting the coins. In 1806 a merchant of Lexington carried a hundred pounds of "cut silver" to Philadelphia.

Many stores were located at boat landings, crossroads, or other strategic points. These vended a few goods in the front "saddlebag" of the residence while the family lived in the back "saddlebag." There was a saying in Alabama that when a person approached a settler's house, a rooster was sure to fly up on a perch in the front yard, flap his wings, and crow: "Master's got a store." In Mississippi the storekeeper never had a fire in the store, but left the front door open whether the weather was wet or dry, warm or cold. Newcomers and the poorer classes did their trading at these crossroads stores. The larger and more wealthy planters did most of their trading at a large center through commission merchants. This was done particularly in the thirties and forties. The planter sent his cotton together with a bill of goods to the commission merchant, who sent the goods back by the next steamboat.

In the country store almost the entire business was done without money. The terms "buy" and "sell" were nearly unknown. Nothing but the word "trade" was heard. Even storekeepers in good-sized towns advertised that the highest price was allowed for skins, beeswax, linsey, and 700 linen. If a man brought more products than he could trade out, he was invited to sit down and drink up the change, or the storekeeper tried his salesmanship on the customer. A great deal of dickering was done in closing a deal; the storekeeper finally cut his price, which was originally set with that in mind, to meet the customer's final offer. When the trade was over, the storekeeper gave an order on the store for the value of any products not traded out. Employers often paid their workmen in orders on the storekeeper, tailor, and shoe-

maker. This was called "paying in trade" and often worked
to the disadvantage of the workman, for he often had to pay
higher prices for his purchases that way; yet he was forced
to trade with only certain stores.

When a customer came in to trade, it was not unusual for
the storekeeper to take him to the back part of the store and
give him a drink of whisky to start the trade off more
briskly. Women were given a handful of raisins or almonds.
Places where liquor was vended were variously called doggeries, groceries, and confectioneries. As a matter of fact,
sweetmeats were sold at confectioneries, but emphasis was
placed on wet goods.

The earliest stores seem to have been tramp vending
establishments. That is, the merchant came out from Baltimore or Philadelphia with a stock of goods, rented the front
of someone's cabin on Main Street, and sold out all or as
much of his goods as possible and returned to the East for
another stock, taking with him the furs or produce he had
taken in. In 1807 the famous naturalist Audubon brought
such a stock of goods to Louisville and sold it out. The size
and variety of the stock were not very imposing. Robert C.
Paine in 1818 opened the first store in Conechu County,
Alabama. His store was built of pine poles unstripped of their
bark, and had a dirt floor. His stock in trade consisted of a
little coarse sugar, a little coffee, and a scanty assortment of
dry goods suited to the necessities of the times.

Even in Alabama goods were brought in by packhorse or
wagon from Savannah and Charleston. Early shipments of
flour were sometimes brought in by the most devious routes.
On April 27, 1822 a flatboat of flour arrived at Montgomery,
Alabama. The wheat was raised in Virginia and milled on
the Holston River in Tennessee near the Virginia line. The
flour was then floated to the Hiwassee and poled up that
river and the Okoa fifty miles before being carried overland
to a tributary of the Alabama where the flatboat was built
that carried it down to Montgomery.

Shortly after 1800, merchants began to run barges and keelboats on round trips to New Orleans and Mobile. It took about fifty to seventy days to make the trip upstream from Mobile to Montgomery These boats went down loaded with cotton and pork and returned bringing sugar, coffee, and other merchandise.

The keelboat was a long, slender craft, sharp fore and aft. It had a narrow gangway or walk just within the gunwale completely around the boat. On this the boatmen walked as they poled the boat upstream. Fixing his pole on the bottom of the stream and placing the knob at the top against his shoulder, the boatman, stooping low, walked slowly to the stern of the boat, where he lifted the pole and walked down the walk on the other side to repeat the operation. In deep water oars were used, and in shallow places where the bottom dragged, the craft was pulled ahead by warping—that is, by fastening a rope from the vessel to a tree on the bank and dragging it slowly forward by means of pulleys. When there was a smooth path along the bank they cordelled. In this procedure a long rope extended from the mast in the center of the boat to the bank, where the crew, walking in single file, pulled the boat along. When this kind of craft was covered with a low house or cabin between the gangways it was called a barge.

When the barge *Lovely* made a trip up the Mississippi in 1807, it had a crew of eighteen—a patroon or captain, a cabin boy, and sixteen oarsmen. The work of the crew was hard and grueling as the boat crept along at snail's pace day after day. The journalist on the *Lovely* wrote on July 14: "Another poor day's work of only a few miles. . . . Poor business this, the Patroon cursing the boat and the hands cursing the boat thus ends this 24 hours." [3]

From Nashville to New Orleans merchant owners sent such barges as the *Industry*, the *Willing Maid*, and the *Fast-going Mary*. In spite of its name neither the last boat nor its

[3] *Journal* of the *Lovely*, July 14, 1807.

sisters were very speedy. It took six months for the round trip. The times of departure and arrival of these boats were gala days in the frontier town.

With the coming of barge transportation, quantities of goods, from city luxuries to everyday necessities, were brought in. There was everything imaginable in the stores then, from needles and pins to panes of glass, great earthen jars, and iron kettles. Along the line of eatables were dried fish, molasses, rice, coffee, sugar, salt, tea, spices, liquors, raisins, and many other foodstuffs. There was a good assortment of yard goods, copperas, brimstone, Bibles, bridle bits, tinware of all kinds, playing cards, powder, lead and flints. The stock included hardware, dry goods, groceries, boots and shoes, drugs, and confections, under one roof.

One store in Columbia, Missouri, in 1836, sold from four to five thousand dollars' worth of goods per month. Besides this there were ten others selling from two thousand to twenty-five hundred dollars' worth a month. In addition, there were fourteen others in the county, all doing a good business. The big merchants become wholesalers to wayside storekeepers, who took out a little stock of goods by pack horse or cart.

Peddlers sprang from the frontier environment as naturally as weeds in a newly made garden. As a rule, in the earlier years these were Yankees, who carried their wares in packs or trunks on their backs and were called pack peddlers. Later they used pack horses. The Irish or Scotch-Irish also did a great deal of peddling in the South. By about 1836 the German Jew made his way into the scene. By that time the peddler carried so many items that he had to take to a wagon. The Yankee pack peddler was originally a tin peddler. He carried his wares on his back in two large tin trunks, each weighing fifty pounds. Gradually he widened his scope and also sold buttons, needles, scissors, combs, children's books, shoelaces, jewelry, Jew's-harps, knives, ribbons, piece goods, woodenware, and other "Yankee notions." Connecticut was the tin-manufacturing center of the United States and became the headquarters of the peddling industry. Peddlers took some cash but more often received goods in trade. Skins, feathers, ashes, old brass, linen rags, beeswax, ginseng, and other frontier products were received and disposed of at the first market.

The clockmaking business arose in Connecticut also. Seth Thomas became the first well-known clockmaker. The earlier clocks had hardwood gears. By 1837 Thomas was making the works of brass. Peddlers traveled all over the United States selling the improved timepiece and repairing old clocks. On the frontier the man who had a clock was considered prosperous, and when one family got one, others in like economic circumstances followed suit. Indeed, putting glass panes in the windows and a clock in the house were sure signs of prosperity. The peddler left the clocks on trial where he could and returned later to receive payment or take up the clock. He seldom took the clock out of the house once it was left. As a rule he received a down payment and took a note for the rest. Collis P. Huntington, of Connecticut, laid the foundation for his later wealth by traveling over the West and South as a peddler and collecting notes on clocks. When he went to California in 1849, he peddled en route. Later he became famous as a railroad-builder.

The Yankee peddler had a bad name everywhere. He was charged with deception, cheating, lying, and swindling. He was the butt of national jokes, and a well-known visitor reported that the whole race of peddlers was proverbially dishonest. They were said to sell wooden nutmegs, trinkets for gold, stagnant barometers, and broken watches supposed to be good timekeepers. No doubt a good deal of this antagonism was occasioned not by the peddler's out-and-out dishonesty but by his persuading the backwoodsman to buy at a price the purchaser later realized was too much. Wooden clocks sold for thirty dollars. Ten thousand of these were sold in the beginning of 1831. In an attempt to stop this,

South Carolina passed a law forbidding any Yankee peddler from selling a Connecticut clock in that state. The shrewd New Englanders sidestepped it nicely, however, by leasing them for ninety-nine years.

The pewter tinker was a welcome wayfarer. He took broken pewterware and mended it or molded it into a different utensil. He made his way from house to house, carrying his molds on horseback or on foot. He also did soldering work and straightened and repaired tin and brass as well as pewter.

In the 1780's John Fitch, inventor of a steamboat, made a map of the Northwest Territory and sold eight hundred copies of it as he traveled through the frontier area. Canvassers traveled through the country selling highly lithographed, leather-bound, gilt-edged family doctor books, histories, and other works. In the forties and fifties, when frontier conditions existed in many parts of the country, the American Bible Society (founded in 1841) developed the colportage system with the aim of placing the Bible in every home. By boat, wagon, and horseback the colporteurs traveled. Their report for 1859 showed that three million families had been visited and eight million Bibles or New Testaments had been distributed by that date.

Peddlers sometimes traveled by canoe, stopping here and there to sell their wares. Some peddlers did business in a larger way, graduating into full-fledged storekeepers with a flatboat arranged as a dry-goods or general-merchandise store with counters, shelves, and drawers like a store on land. Such a boat, when nearing a plantation, would blow a bugle or conch shell to give notice of its approach, and the wives and daughters would go to market, taking their produce to trade for the finery the floating store afforded. One writer mentioned that these stores flew a white flag. A planter's daughter told a traveler that four or five of these floating shops would sometimes pass her father's house in a day. Tin shops, circus boats, and blacksmith shops also served the settlers. The last shod horses and made axes, scythes, and other tools.

When a customer asked a business man the price of a certain article, the merchant, instead of making a direct answer, asked what kind of money was offered. When this was ascertained, the price was stated. The so-called wild cat banks flourished everywhere, printing and distributing notes with no specie or other assets to back them up. As a result, although certain notes were accepted at face value for a time, they soon began to depreciate. As confidence decreased, paper money depreciated all the more. Some Alabama business houses in 1821 advertised that they would not accept Tennessee bank notes. Some banks in the same state advertised they would accept only their own paper money or specie or paper money backed by specie. Such a situation brought chaos in the business world. It took an expert in currency matters to act as a receiver or cashier at that time. When Sol Smith, manager of a theatrical company, itinerated in Alabama, he found so many different kinds of paper money in circulation, together with a great deal of counterfeit currency, that he had to secure the services of a money-wise gentleman of that area to advise him which money he should accept at the box office and at what discount it should be received.

Senator Thomas Hart Benton of Missouri described the irresponsible institutions that turned out such quantities of paper money as "banks of moonshine, built upon each other's paper, and the whole ready to fly sky high the moment one of the concerns becomes sufficiently inflated to burst." In an effort to remedy the situation Alabama established a state bank, but unfortunately its paper soon depreciated. The situation was similar in the other states. Because of bank troubles, after 1837 Mississippi was practically without banks and was dependent on other states for her circulating medium other than gold and silver. After the panic of 1837 various citizens, and particularly business houses, issued small bills to be used in change. These, commonly called "shin plasters," served for a time, but at best were only as good as the issuing agent. Finally, owing to forgeries and other irregularities, they were in many places forbidden by law.

Since banks were often far away and not safe, various devices were used to safeguard money. Sometimes it was buried in iron kettles, or hidden under the hearth or puncheons. One of the most interesting methods of "banking" gold and silver was to bore holes in large blocks of wood, fill the holes with coins, and drive tightly fitting pegs into them. Then the pegs were sawed off close. This left no way to remove the money except by splitting the log, which could not be done without creating an alarm. These blocks were kept near the owners' beds.

XII

Good Times

THE outstanding feature of frontier social occasions was the fact that with the exception of a wedding almost all of the very earliest were connected with work. The whole community gathered to do a piece of work for one person and he in turn expected to help all of his guests when they had a piece of work to do. In the North these were called "bees," but that term was almost never used in Dixie.

One of the first of these in a frontier area was log-rolling, which prevailed until the last vestiges of frontier life had disappeared—long after the necessity that first produced it had passed away. Despite the fact that it was the hardest work on the frontier, it was an occasion of mirth and festivity and kept alive feelings of sympathy and neighborliness. The man who preferred to do his own work without asking his neighbors to help and in turn aiding them was considered a mean, selfish, unsocial being.

The log-rolling season in a community began in February and lasted perhaps six weeks. As soon as the logs were rolled on the clearing of one man, the whole crowd went on to the next and so on from day to day. In preparing for the occasion the owner of the field cut notches on the top of the large logs about every ten feet and started a fire on each notch. When the fire was well started, a dry limb was laid across the log. Morning and evening dry limbs were laid in the widening gap until the log was burnt into lengths. After about a week the fires had done their work. This was called "niggering off." It saved chopping or sawing the logs into carrying lengths, but often left them so black that the hands and faces of the workmen were sooty black before night. One day before the log-rolling the owner walked over the clearing with his ax and cut any spots where the fire had failed to burn through.

The logs were carried with handspikes. These were stout dogwood sticks about five feet long, three inches through at the center, and made smaller and smoother at each end with a drawing-knife. The men would pry up the log length and place the ends of the handspikes under it. Then the men arranged themselves on opposite sides of the log, a man at each end of every handspike. At a given signal they lifted it and carried it to the log heap. The men next to the log heap rested their ends of the handspikes on it and went around to the other side and with their united strength all raised the outer ends and slid the log to its place on the pile. The pile was completed by placing on it the heavy portion of the treetop.

Astonishing loads were carried. Sometimes a log was so large a man could not see across it, and to a bystander on either side it looked as if the immense log was crawling along with a single row of men walking on one side. Sometimes the men straightened up with a log that was heavier than they could carry and they stood several seconds under the fearful strain unable to take a single step. The man who could "pull down" any men in the community in a "log tote" was singled out as a man of prestige. Men were sometimes strained and ruptured in this dangerous work.

There was always more or less exhibition of one's prowess, bantering, and jokes at these gatherings. One joke was slyly to give one's partner the short end of the stick, or perhaps the fun-maker would poke one end of the stick in some manure and secretly shove it under the log to his partner. From such good-natured pranks arose such expressions as "tote fair," meaning to do one's honest part, "I got the dirty end of the stick," or "he shortened the stick on me," meaning he used foul play to gain his ends.

In the cotton country the master often came to a log-rolling bringing two or more hands. As one man said, good whisky was cheap and abundant and there was an "awful supply" on hand generally. Nearly everybody enlivened the occasion by drinking brimming gourds of the backwoods elixir of life. The host provided the dinner and supper. A favorite dish was known as bergu or burgoo. It was pot pie made from a mixture of vegetables of all kinds and wild meats such as squirrel, turkey, venison, and the like, highly seasoned and cooked in a big iron kettle out of doors.[1]

After the "toting" was finished, came the frolic. By the light of huge log fires there took place the counterpart of our modern track and field meet. The young man who could throw his man in a wrestling match, "pull him down" at the end of a hand stick, or outsprint him in a race was honored as the first lad of the settlement. This was manifested by a cheer from the old men, a pat on the shoulder from the women, and the shy approving smiles of the fair maidens. In the dance that followed he had his choice and rode triumphantly home on horseback with her.

Laying up a log house was another task that often required more than the manpower of one household. The logs were cut the proper length, and when the neighbors gathered they organized, appointed a leader and certain other key men, and began to notch and fit the logs and lay them up. At the proper time the windows were cut, the fireplace constructed, the roof covered, and the floor laid. Sometimes, particularly if the family had just arrived and was poor, the

[1] John Allison: *Dropped Stitches in Tennessee History* (Nashville, 1897), p. 19; Thomas D. Clark: *The Kentucky* (New York, 1942), pp. 381–2.

neighbors each brought in something to eat and thus aided the family that was beginning again under great difficulties.

Following the "raising" came the "house-warming" or dedication of the new home. On this occasion the new settler or the bride and groom entertained the whole community. There was a roaring fire in the fireplace. A supper of venison or bear meat with appropriate accompaniment, including plenty of liquor, was enjoyed. The guests brought such presents as would aid in setting up housekeeping. For the host there were the necessities for the chase: a powder horn scraped thin and polished, a leather shot-pouch, tinder-box, and woolen socks. The woman received some of the more common household equipment, such as a spider, trenchers, gourd vessels, buckskin moccasins, and bright-colored knitted mittens. In some places where the community built a house for the bride and groom and set them up in housekeeping, the house-warming took place before the couple was moved into its new home. At any rate, following the feast came an all-night dance. Usually a couple of Negroes played fiddles or a fiddle and a banjo.

When the corn was "snapped" it was piled in a rick by the log pen that served as a granary. When a night had been fixed upon, word was sent around announcing the corn-shucking. Three or four scaffolds were built around the corn pile and covered with dirt. On these, fires of pine knots lighted up the darkness until it seemed almost as light as day.

As the huskers arrived, each was handed the green bottle to take a drink of whisky. When enough people had arrived, two young men "chose up." They divided the rick as evenly as possible by placing a rail across the pile, and decided the choice of ends of the pile by tossing up a chip, one side of which had been spit upon. A second toss decided who should have first choice of the huskers.

There was intense rivalry as the contestants began at the middle of the pile and worked toward the end. Dr. Daniel Drake said it was there that he learned as a boy that competition is the mother of cheating, falsehood, and broils. Corn was thrown over into the crib unhusked, the rail was moved toward one's own end of the pile, or the corn was surreptitiously kicked under the rail toward the other end. If charged with any of these irregularities by the other side, the suspect immediately denied it. Soon the plaintiff was calling the defender a liar. Then, or at the end of the race, ensued a fight.

When the pile was cut in two, the two parties turned their backs upon each other, and while they kept time with their hands, a chorus of voices rose that on a still night could be heard a mile. The oft-replenished green bottle circulated freely as the goal was in sight. Faster and faster flew the dexterous hands. When the winning contestants had thrown their last ear, they lifted their captain onto the shoulders of some of the stoutest men and he, with the bottle in one hand and his hat in the other, was carried triumphantly around the other party amidst victorious shouts. After that came the supper, which always included burgoo.[2]

Sometimes banjos and fiddles accompanied the shucking. When a lad found a red ear, he put it in his pocket, and when the contest was over, at the supper, in the presence of the whole assembly, he presented it to the maiden of his choice and for this act of gallantry was permitted to kiss her publicly.

An old resident of Pontotoc County, Mississippi, recalled that before the shucking began, it was customary in that area for two men to form a saddle with their hands and carry the host around the corn pile while all the others formed a column and followed singing:

> Oh, I'm gwin' to the shuckin',
> I'm gwin' to the shuckin' of the corn.

In that section no liquor was drunk until a jug of whisky was found at the bottom of the pile, which, when uncovered,

[2] Daniel Drake, M.D.: *Pioneer Life in Kentucky* (Cincinnati, 1870), pp. 54–6.

was given to the owner of the corn, who passed it around. Then the supper was eaten.

Where slaves were not too numerous, they were freely allowed to attend the shucking and participate the same as white men. After the supper there was frolicking similar to that at a log-rolling.

In the cotton country in the early 1800's, before the gin had come into general use, picking seeds out of the cotton with fingers was an every-night, after-supper job. The cotton was divided into "tasks" and each member of the family was given his share. After a hard day's work, as the family sat around the open fireplace working until late at night, heads began to nod, and members of the family had to be prodded to get their stint completed. To relieve the monotony of such tedious work the custom of combining work with pleasure in the form of a cotton-picking arose. The young people met at one house or another to pick cotton seeds by night. The cotton was spread on the floor in front of the fireplace to dry thoroughly so that the seeds could be picked out rapidly. It was then parceled out in equal parts and a spirited contest ensued to see who would get his portion picked first. The winner not only was acclaimed champion but was allowed to kiss any girl he might choose.

Other bees were flax-pulling, cotton-picking, sap-collecting, sugaring off, wood-chopping, apple-paring, and "apple butter biling." Sometimes there were races between mowers, cradlers, or hacklers (men dressing flax to be spun into linen). There were also plowing contests. All of these were followed by feasts prepared by the women and girls. Sometimes a road-building bee was called to clear the fallen trees from a road after a storm or to cut a new road, although these matters were in time taken over by the local government. At Muscle Shoals, Alabama, in 1825, such a bee was held to remove the logs and other obstructions from Spring Creek in order to admit boats up to the town. The promoters —possibly the town company—asked all to furnish as many hands with axes as possible and promised "plenty of well barbecued meat and good whiskey." [3]

The feminine accompaniment of practically all bees was the quilting. The hostess had her quilt blocks pieced and set together ready for the coming of the neighborhood women. The quilt was fastened to four frames of wood and hung from the pole rafters by means of four ropes. The women then sat around the quilt on all four sides and the ropes were adjusted until the quilt hung breast-high. As the flying needles finished one arm-length along one side, that portion of the quilt was rolled up and a new arm-length begun. Just as some men were more skillful than others at a house-raising and were chosen to notch the corners, so some women were clever at finishing the quilt corners. It was a hard day's work for ten women to quilt one quilt. If the quilt was not completed, it was drawn up overhead by the ropes.

The most popular social pastime was the dance. Often it took place in connection with bees, but sometimes it was held on a holiday, in the evening or in the daytime. The usual type of dance was the square dance commonly known as a hoe-down or breakdown. Fortesque Cuming observed that teachers of dancing met with more encouragement than teachers in literary or scientific fields. One type of dance was known as a bran dance. Modern usage in an attempt to recall bygone days has mouthed this into "barn dance." It was often held in a newly completed cabin if the floor was smooth enough. Otherwise it was held in the woods. A plot of ground was smoothed off and a quantity of bran or sawdust was spread over it to make it more elastic. People came early and stayed long at these frolics or "hops," as they were called. When John Sevier returned from the Indian campaign of 1788, having been gone all season, his friends gathered to see the old warrior. An old fiddler from Virginia happened along, and a dance of one week ensued. The guests turned their

[3] Nina Leftwich: *Two Hundred Years at Muscle Shoals* (Tuscumbia, Ala., 1935), p. 68.

horses loose in the cornfield and Sevier led out in such dances as "the White Cockade" and "Flowers of Edinboro." [4]

A half century later in Arkansas people walked twenty-five miles to dances and stayed a week. They danced all day and all night. After the first twenty-four hours some slept while others danced and the festivities were kept going. Thomas Nuttall, the scientist, noted that in 1819 during a dance in Arkansas Territory the whisky bottle was handed around and without the inconvenience of using glasses was passed from mouth to mouth, exempting neither age nor sex.

Sometimes instead of a dance there was a fiddlers' contest. The names of the tunes such as "Sugar in the Gourd," "Possum up a Stump," and "Leather Britches" reflect the spirit of the backwoods.

Some, on account of religious or other convictions, preferred party games to dancing. In these the awkward green boys chose the timid blushing girls for partners and marched with them in a circle singing such songs as "Hog Drivers," or "Old Sister Phoebe." There was little tune, time, or pitch, and as a musical entertainment these exercises were a failure, but they were popular because they gave every boy a chance to kiss the girl of his choice, and the girls did not mind either.

Besides these singing party games there were other kissing games such as "picking grapes" or "hanging onto the doorknob." In the former a couple was chosen and a strong homemade hickory chair was placed between them. They then clasped hands above the chair and began to climb up into the seat of the chair a rung at a time. Each time they balanced themselves on a new rung the boy reached over and kissed the girl. At last, arriving at the top, the boy hugged and kissed the girl. Going down rung by rung, they kissed as before. Hanging onto the doorknob was another of the many games whose real excuse was to enable couples to kiss. A boy grasped a doorknob with his right hand, extended his left over his right shoulder, and asked the girl of his choice

[4] Draper MSS., 7XXA, Wisconsin State Historical Society Library.

to hold it with her right hand. She in turn crossed her left arm over her right shoulder and asked a boy to hold on. This was carried on until everybody in the room was "hanging onto the doorknob." The first girl kissed the boy holding the knob and then turned and kissed the one behind, who passed it on. The kiss then made its way to the tail of the queue and returned to the boy at the head, who stooped and kissed the doorknob.[5]

A European visiting in the West felt that there was little sentiment and much business in frontier wooing. A backwoodsman with whom he talked said he would ask the lady the first time he went to see her if she would have him. If she would not, there was no use to go back. Another foreigner stated that if a man called on a girl twice he was expected to declare himself, and if he was not accepted he was expected to cease his visits in order that her prospects for marriage might not be ruined.

To the Eastern educated man frontier courtship in the plantation area was difficult. An eligible young doctor, educated in a Philadelphia medical school, confided to his diary:

I have gone the rounds visiting amongst the ladies—and came out much as I commenced. A free and easy system of sociability is good on some accounts, but, a degree of ceremony is better suited to my tastes. Here I cannot call on a young lady without having to encounter the whole family. . . . I do not know how upon earth I could court a lady here, unless by proxy. . . . The old folks are so plentiful.[6]

When a young man went to call on a backwoods girl, her father and mother sat by the fire. The father often spun yarns while the mother sat and smoked her pipe. After a while the old folks went to bed, leaving the couple sitting by the fire. In time the fire died down and the boy and girl would lie across the bed and pull the covers up over them. There they lay whispering sweet nothings. Or perhaps while

[5] Thomas D. Clark: *The Kentucky* (New York, 1942), pp. 130–1.
[6] H. V. Wooten: "Private Journal of Life and Doings," MSS., II, 30–1.

the girl's family were up, in order to secure a little privacy in the one-room log cabin, the young couple would lie on or in the bed—fully dressed—and talk, and sometimes go to sleep in such bliss. This custom, quite common on the frontier from 1750 to 1800, was known as bundling. Although never endorsed by the highest classes, it was deemed harmless by the middle and lower classes.

In some places on the raw frontier it was customary for the young man who wanted a girl to "publicly give her a fair fall, and noose her," as these young backwoodsmen were in the habit of catching a wild young colt.

A very interesting account of one of these socio-athletic events comes to us from a Kentucky station. Sarah Mc-Cracken, six feet and one inch tall, but comely, had been wooed unsuccessfully by many a man in the community. It was understood the man who would win her had publicly to throw her and put a lasso around her. At a frolic a young man named Reynolds determined to capture her. With a rope of twisted buffalo hair he edged up to Sarah. She, with arch coquetry, egged him on with: "Come on. Faint heart never won fair lady!" The contest was spirited. Although not so stout as he, she was agile and "flirted" him, to use a frontier expression, when he seemed on the verge of victory. For a time the contest seemed drawn and finally, when Reynolds seemed sinking beneath the prowess of this fair Amazon, she tripped and fell full length on the white clover carpet of the woodland. While the forest rang with acclamations, the lover took advantage of the situation and noosed the now meek maiden without further ado. Some of the fair ones privately insinuated to the bride that the slip of the foot was intentional, but they received only a knowing look and the assurance she never had repented the fall.

Women married young on the border. The first marriage in Kentucky was that of Elizabeth Calloway to Samuel Henderson. She had been rescued from the Indians by her lover and others three weeks before. She lacked one week of

being sixteen years old. The next year Jemima Boone and
Fanny Calloway, the other girls taken captive by the Indians, each married at the age of fourteen. As was often the
case, these girls married mature men, although men married
younger than now. Bishop Asbury, who traveled into Kentucky in 1783, said: "It is marvellous to see how the desire
for matrimony reigneth in this country." One contemporary
gave the average marriage age as fifteen for girls and seventeen for men.

But if the maiden married quickly after maturity, she
could not begin to compete with the widow. The first marriage at Harrodsburg was that of the widow of Hugh Wilson. He had been killed and scalped one month before. Sometimes these raw frontier marriages took place without too
much regard for the letter of the law. At the first marriage in
Blount County, Alabama, the minister, upon being implored
to perform the ceremony, refused on the ground that he had
not the authority. On continued urging, he agreed on condition the couple would enter a heavy bond that they would
marry again legally when the opportunity offered. A little
later, when the organization of the county was completed,
the minister, clothed with proper authority, on his way home
from the county seat, stopped at the home of this couple in
the night, got them out of bed, and married them again.

Sometimes a couple had to go a long way to find an officer
clothed with the necessary authority to marry them. On the
occasion of the first marriage in Henry County, Missouri,
the couple came four days' journey on ponies. They inquired of the Indians whether there was a man with the
proper authority and were referred to Henry Avery as a
"heap big white man, plenty law."

At a backwoods wedding the groom and his party assembled at the home of his father and, dressed in the best
frontier style, rode horseback along the bridle path toward the bride's house. They planned to arrive there at
noon, for that was the usual hour for the ceremony. Some-

times the narrow trace was closed off by friends or enemies tying grapevines across it, firing off guns, and in other ways forming an "ambush" for the party.

Another ceremony that took place before reaching the bride's home was the "race for the bottle." A bottle of whisky embellished with ribbons was the prize. Two young men on horseback made the run. An Indian yell announced the start of the race. Over fallen logs, through dense forest and brush, the mile race took its course. The rougher the course, the greater the opportunity for a display of horsemanship. The first to reach the prize returned in triumph with it to the company and, on approaching, announced his victory with a shrill whoop. He paused at the head of the column and gave the bottle first to the groom and then to each succeeding couple. After each had taken a dram, he put the bottle in the bosom of his hunting shirt and took his place in the party.

After the ceremony came the wedding feast of an abundance of wild game and vegetables eaten from a crude table made with broadaxes. Then followed the dance, which lasted until morning, but the bride and groom were not allowed to dance all night. About nine o'clock a group of young ladies "stole off" the bride, took her up a ladder, and put her to bed in the loft. Then a deputation of young men in the same manner "stole off" the bridegroom and put him in bed by the side of his bride. They withdrew and the dance continued, but now and then "Black Betty," the name given to the whisky bottle, was sent up the ladder. Food was also taken up, and the couple were compelled by their jolly friends to eat more or less of whatever was offered.

The next day came the "infare," when the whole wedding party journeyed to the home of the groom and enjoyed a feast and a frolic there. One observer reported an actual case of a couple beginning life in the forest. The young man, he said, had rented a piece of land and loaded their few possessions on a sled pulled by an old blind mare. A bed, oven, bucket, skillet, part of a side of meat, a gourd of lard, and part of a gourd of sugar completed the list of goods. The couple climbed on top of the "plunder" and set out over the mountainous road to their home in the woods. While going down a steep place, just as the groom leaned over to give his bride a reassuring kiss, the sled struck a stump and turned upside down, smashing gourds, breaking the skillet, and scattering goods everywhere. The old horse no doubt would have run off and completed the ruin if he could have seen which way to run.

In the plantation area weddings were more elaborate. The groom and his attendants wore white trousers and coats of homespun jeans with the shirt collars turned over the coat collars and extending back to their shoulders. The guests began to arrive early in the afternoon, many from long distances. Most of them rode horseback. Young ladies carried their clothes in a carpetbag hung on the saddle horn and were accompanied by their colored servants, who took their young misses to a dressing-room and soon had them in charming attire. The wedding took place in the early evening and supper followed. The wedding attendants waited on the bride's table. A large number were seated at the table, but it had to be reset a number of times. Not until after midnight did the colored servants have their turn at the table. Following the feasting came dancing or kissing games. Many of the guests stayed overnight or even for several days.

In fact, there is much evidence of long visits. Dr. Wooten in his journal spoke of spending Christmas and the "balance of the year riding about amongst our friends." Such visits were called "going abroad."

The barbecue was popular, particularly in the lower South. A large trench was dug and filled with wood. The fuel was set afire and at sunset, when the trench was filled with live coals, a slaughtered ox was placed on a spit lengthwise of the bed of coals. All night long, Negroes basted the cooking beef incessantly and stirred the embers frequently.

Lurid fires lighted up the dark night, and as the darkies joyfully plied their tasks, the sweet melody of weird African songs echoed among the forest trees and floated out on the night air. By noon the next day the ox had been thoroughly cooked, and such juicy, tasty meat could not be found in the best tavern in the land. These feasts often took place on holidays such as the Fourth of July, but they were also a feature of political campaigns. As an aftermath of such a forest banquet there flowed quantities of bad whisky and worse oratory. Fourth of July celebrations were often the occasion of speech-making and an endless number of toasts. Revolutionary War heroes were the center of honor at these times.

Backwoods debating societies, spelling schools, storytelling, and singing helped to while away the time. Hunting stories predominated, but for a novelty these children of the forest enjoyed stories about Jack and the beanstalk and his adventures. Songs about Robin Hood were common, and tragical songs were especially popular. These were denominated "love songs about murder." Whist was played among those rising into the backwoods aristocracy.

XIII

Sports

ON the raw frontier sports tended toward the bloody, crude, barbarous, and cruel, such as bear-baiting, dog-fighting, gander-pulling, cockfighting, wolf and dog fights, and rough-and-tumble fights. These earlier sports were succeeded in time by more refined sports, such as shooting for the beef, the turkey shoot, horse-racing, the ring tournament, playing games, and athletic contests.

Beasts for animal fights were secured in traps made by building a pen of logs and baiting it or digging a hole in the ground and so artfully baiting and covering it that the animals would fall into it. The latter was known as a pitfall. In bear-baiting, the bear was shut in a pen and five or six dogs at a time were turned in for half-hour rounds. A prize was given to the owner of the dogs that made the best fight. At a bear-baiting near St. Charles, Missouri, in 1833, forty big hounds were set on the bear. Finally, tired of the gore, the owners ended its life. Seven dogs were mutilated so badly that they had to be shot, and most of the others were wounded in a lesser degree. The narrator asserted, however, that all the spectators agreed that it had been the greatest sport they had experienced in years. Sometimes the spectators were served liberal portions of barbecued bear following the fight.

In early Tennessee history the father of William Martin accepted the challenge of a braggart who maintained that his dog could lick anything, man or beast. He went into the ring bare-handed and was choking the dog to death when the owner begged for its life.

When a wolf was caught in a pit, its hind legs were drawn up by means of hooks and the tendons cut so it could not escape when released from captivity. It sat on its wounded hind quarters and snapped at its enemies right and left. Hunters claimed this gruesome sport was necessary for training dogs.

In Tennessee a game in keeping with early barbarous days was known as snick-a-snack. Each participant provided himself with a case-knife and sat around a large table. At a given signal they began cutting and slashing at each other over the head, face, and knuckles.

At a militia muster, the mill, the county seat on court days, or the crossroads store the champions of various communities strutted, bragged, and issued challenges, which were surely and quickly accepted. Sometimes these were merely rough-and-tumble wrestling matches entered into without anger. John Wilson of Clay County, Missouri, said that in a fist fight there was a rule that there should be no hitting below the belt until "the word went round, 'bite, kick and gouge'; then everything was fair." At times the principals were professional fighters and the fight, stimulated by liquor, became barbarous. These were known as gouging matches. Isaac Weld testified that on the frontier men fought like bears, punching, kicking, biting, and gouging. The acme of accomplishment was to throw one's antagonist down and, catching the fingers under the jaw or in the hair, use this fulcrum to gouge the eyeball out onto the cheek with the thumb. If this could not be done, the fighter tried to bite off a nose or an ear. In order to stop this barbarous practice, legislatures passed laws providing penalties for mayhem.

Bullies, especially in the river towns, were wont to strut about like a cock, issuing challenges and picking quarrels. At Little Rock, Arkansas, one of these gentry, spoiling for a fight and armed to the teeth with pistols and bowie knife, stepped into a tavern. After reciting his good points, he challenged: "I reckon I can chaw up the best man in this room." No one venturing to dispute his remarks, he continued: "I've killed eleven Indians, three white man and seven painters [panthers]; and it's my candid opinion you are all a set of cowards." Then picking out a little doctor in the crowd, he walked up and jostled him. This was too much for the doctor, who had been on the "pynt of bustin' his byler" ever since the bully began "to carry on." This incident resulted in a challenge to a crude frontier duel. The two men, naked except for trousers, the upper part of their bodies greased with lard, and armed with a brace of loaded pistols and a bowie knife, were to take their places in an absolutely dark room to fight it out. The butchery was to begin at a signal from one of the seconds outside. For fifteen minutes there was a deathly silence. The survivor of this battle later testified he could not see a thing and there was not a bit of sound after each had cocked his pistol. Finally he caught a glimpse of the cat eyes of his enemy and fired, but received a shot in the shoulder. A second shot was answered with one in his thigh and, weak from loss of blood, he sank prostrate to the floor. Silently and slowly the other came toward his intended victim with knife in hand, ready to dispatch him. Realizing his extreme danger, with a supreme effort he raised himself, and there were those eyes just before him. Striking with all his might, he thrust his knife through his incautious assailant's heart and felled him. When the seconds came in, they found the doctor weltering in his blood, but still holding his knife up to the hilt in the dead bully's body.

Featherstonhaugh observed in 1837 that the gander pull was a sort of tournament on horseback. It was popular from Georgia to Illinois and Missouri. A path was laid out on the exterior of a circle a hundred and fifty feet in diameter. Two sapling posts were set about twelve feet apart on each side of the path and a slack rope hung from pole to pole, with its middle directly over the path. A live gander, with all the feathers picked off its head and neck, was then produced. A gourd of goose grease was brought out and the bird's neck greased until it was as slippery as an eel. The bird was then tied by the feet to the slack rope in such a manner that it vibrated in an arc of four or five feet. The head hung down just low enough so that a rider, standing in the stirrups, could barely reach the long-suffering gander's neck. Those who wanted to enter the contest paid twenty-five cents each to the manager, who gave a prize to the one who pulled the gander's head off while riding around the circle at a gallop. As the horses got near the gander, two men stood by the path with whips and lashed any horse that gave evidence of slowing down for the grab. Finally, when all was ready, the circle of horsemen rode around a time or two before the signal was given to pull. When the manager called: "Blaze away!" the fun began. Only an expert rider on a well-trained horse could even grab the gander's neck. Hardly anyone could hold onto the slippery neck while going at such speed. It withstood many severe wrenches before the gander's wailing ceased. Even after the neck was broken, it was some time before the head was pulled off. In the meantime large crowds of both sexes and colors enjoyed hours of the amusement, cheering, betting, and watching in tense excitement. Not many women attended, however. Some dexterous fellows with well-trained horses could grasp the neck with such skill and strength that they could pull off the neck with the windpipe screaming after separation from the body. This was considered the highest possible attainment at a gander-pulling.

The rifle was the very center of frontier life. It was used there before it came into general use elsewhere. Many of these weapons, remarkable as it may seem, were actually made in the larger blacksmith shops. The rifle was actually a man's best friend, and a boy early learned to use it. A well-grown boy of twelve or thirteen was furnished with a small rifle and shot-pouch, became a fort soldier, and had his port-hole assigned to him. The lad who went squirrel-hunting and shot his game in any other spot than the head was ridiculed. It was quite customary for experienced hunters to bark a squirrel; that is, to shoot the tree just below the animal and stun it so that it dropped to the ground with its skin unin-jured. Audubon saw Daniel Boone do this repeatedly when Boone was an old man. When their supply of powder would allow it, riflemen, by way of recreation, would very often cut a piece of bark from a tree, make a bull's-eye on it with a little powder wet with saliva, and shoot at this mark, picking all the bullets out of the wood for use again.

So skillful did some of these marksmen become that they did unbelievable stunts. One of these was to snuff a candle without putting it out. Audubon saw one man at a distance of fifty yards snuff a candle three times out of seven, while all the other shots either put the candle out or cut it im-mediately under the blaze.

Other stunts were driving a nail, and cutting a bullet into halves on a knife blade. In the former a common-sized nail was driven two thirds of the way into the target at forty paces. Placing a bullet very near the nail was considered the work of an indifferent marksman. Bending the nail was some-what better, but nothing less than hitting it square on the head and driving it into the target was considered satis-factory. One out of three shots usually hit the nail, and if there were six marksmen, two nails were frequently needed before each man could fire. After the winner was ascertained, the group usually retired to an adjoining house and spent an hour or two in friendly intercourse before dispersing. Blane said that in 1822 a hunter offered him a dollar every time he missed a dollar at one hundred yards if Blane would give him one every time he hit it.

"Shooting for the beef," commonly known as a shooting match, was a well-known diversion. For several years after the Revolutionary War, on account of the scarcity of lead, the beef was divided into "six quarters"—the sixth consisting of the lead fired at the match. This was the last prize. The "fifth quarter" consisted of hide and tallow. The other prizes were the four quarters of the beef. Each man prepared his own target. This was usually a board about a foot wide burned black. On this a piece of white paper was placed. The distance was almost invariably sixty yards. The size of the square for this distance was two and a half inches. In the center of this a rhombus or diamond-shaped figure one inch wide was cut. This was known as the bull's-eye or diamond. Usually there was a group of spectators who cheered and showed their interest in a lively manner. Two judges were selected from this group to see that the contest was fair. During the match the contestants kept up a running conversation, commending a good shot, ribbing a poor one, and often bragging about their own guns. One "allowed" that "Old Hair-splitter" would hit the bull's-eye while another bet on his "Old Blood Letter" and still a third was sure his "Old Panther-cooler would strike plumb center." Close shots were measured with a thread and in that way decided by the judges. The beef was usually not on the ground, but was butchered later. The price per shot was determined by the number of tickets sold; twenty-five cents was often the price. Some men were such expert shots that they were given a quarter to withdraw or promise not to enter the match. The contestants almost always shot from a rest. After the last shot the judges took the boards, measured, and announced the decision. The turkey shoot was a match similar to shooting for the beef except that originally a live turkey was shot at; later a target was used.

In those days after the Revolutionary War when men assembled, odd contests bred of the savage Indian-fighting frontier took place. At a gathering to open a road near Newcastle, Kentucky, in 1797, the men camped overnight on the grounds. In the dark, while burning brush and logs, they divided the crowd into two companies, chose captains, made rules, and fought a sham battle with firebrands. They made a rule that no man could throw a stick without fire on it in order that they might learn how to dodge. They fought in perfect good nature for two or three hours until the fires burned down, brands were scarce, and the fighters began to violate the rule. Some were badly wounded, blood began to flow freely, and a real fight seemed about to begin. At that moment the loud voice of the road boss was heard ordering every man to retire to sleep. They dropped their weapons, rekindled the fires, and lay down to rest.

Indians often attained great skill at throwing tomahawks at a victim. By giving the tomahawk a certain whirl and throwing it at a given distance they could strike an object with the blade. White boys practiced for hours until, like the Indians, they got so they could stick the tomahawk into a tree with astonishing frequency. Throwing "shoulder stones" was a sport similar to the shot put. "Flinging the rail" was perhaps a crude counterpart of our javelin throw, except that the rail was much heavier and could not be thrown so far. They played leapfrog (high-over-the-head style) and a game known as kicking the hat, in addition to the common sports of foot-racing and jumping.

One of the most popular games was "long bullets." In this game the players competed to see who could jerk a cannon ball the greatest distance. While the young men danced all night, the older men put in the time cockfighting. The sport was conducted in a ring known as a pit, and spectators stood around the outside. The rooster's spurs were sawed off to within half an inch of the leg, and steel gaffs, or long slender instruments needle-sharp, which enabled a cock to knife his antagonist, were fastened to the legs. An advertisement in the Montgomery *Republican* of May 19, 1836 informed the public that "a main for $500.00 will be fought at Montgomery Court-House, on Saturday next. Nine feathered champions will be shown by each party."

The squirrel frolic and wolf hunt were co-operative hunts in which the whole countryside took part. In the former, sides were chosen and at the end of several days' hunt a count was made to see which individual and which side had the most tails and scalps. The *Kentucky Gazette* of May 17, 1796 reported that the hunters of such a frolic rendezvoused at Irvine's Lick, and the total number of squirrels killed in one day was 7,941. In the wolf hunt the inhabitants of a region would surround a given area with a thin line of men and slowly converge on the center. The men drew closer together as the cordon grew smaller and tighter. As wolves tried to break through the line they were shot.

Horse-swapping should not be overlooked as a major sport. For a long time, one old settler reminisced, it was almost a mania in Tennessee. It was indulged in as an exciting game and was a universal amusement.

John Sevier's diary gives a glimpse into the diversions of his day. He played ball and billiards—surprising as it may seem on the frontier in 1794—and bet on horse-races and cockfights. Another game of his day was "rattle and snap." A game called fives was probably the game of ball commonly mentioned. Fives consisted in batting a ball against a wall, something like handball. Sevier and his son John beat Messrs. Aitken and Anderson four games of "ball" on August 22, 1795.

Pushpin was played on the caved crown of a hat. Each player commanded an army of pins, which he maneuvered in such a way as to conquer the other's men by dropping one across them.

Horse-races came in very early in a country where everybody rode horseback. As early as 1783 a racecourse existed at Harrodsburg. Hugh McGary, a civil officer of some standing, was found guilty of betting a mare worth twelve pounds on a race run on this course in May of that year. Often, owing to the lack of a cleared area, these races took place on the main city street and all business was suspended for such an event. But soon a stop was put to this, and special tracks were laid out and jockey clubs organized. In the plantation South the big planters soon laid out private tracks, imported blooded horses, and had their Negroes train them. A famous race took place in 1788 between Andrew Jackson, riding his own mare, and Colonel Robert Love. To the intense anger of Jackson, Love's horse won. Women did not attend these sports events in the earlier years, and they were the scenes of much drinking and rowdyism. Even in the forest whatever finery a man could afford he was inclined to use on the trappings of his saddle horse—his saddle, martingale, and bridle. The weaker sex was not one whit behind in riding a caparisoned steed well.

In the latter part of the frontier period—in fact, as the frontier was passing—the tournament came into being. Elaborate preparations were made. Gallant knights in splendid plumed costumes rode to the tourney. The queen of love and beauty was crowned with much pomp and ceremony by the successful knight. There were two events in these tourneys: the quintain tested the rider's skill in striking with the lance or sword a post or dummy figure as he galloped by; running at the ring consisted in capturing on the point of the lance a suspended ring while riding at a full gallop. Each knight had a chosen lady, who watched her knight at the tournament. He wore her colors and, if successful, chose her to be the queen of the tournament. A coronation ceremony and ball followed.

XIV

The Frontier Town

IN early Kentucky and Tennessee the town preceded the settlement of the rural areas. This was due to danger from Indians. Such early towns as Harrodsburg, Boonesborough, Knoxville, and Nashboro were roughly similar to the medieval European town. The area in and around one of these stations was plotted and each settler could hold one or more "in lots" or building plots on the townsite and one or more "out lots" or farming areas. During the stirring days of savage warfare houses were built on these "in lots" and improvements were made on the "out lots." During the day the inhabitants went to their little clearings or worked a field in common near the station under an armed guard. At night they returned to the station and, as in medieval times the drawbridge was lifted behind the returning farmer, so the great gates reached out their protecting arms behind the tired pioneer after a day of clearing ground.

As more people arrived from the East and the stations became crowded, these centers swarmed. A little group led by intrepid frontiersmen established a new station. Such was the station established by Squire Boone, brother of Daniel, some distance from Boonesborough.

After Indian hostilities ceased, in the last decade of the

eighteenth century, squatters and other settlers scattered over the country and settled in the woods wherever they pleased. There was a tendency during this period for towns to follow settlement or accompany it. Such strategic points were chosen as salt deposits, crossroads, mill sites, river fords or ferries, the confluence of rivers, and falls of navigable streams. Here where travel was broken, or where the settlers gathered to have their grain ground or to boil salt, trading centers naturally sprang up to serve the public and often developed into towns.

When there were enough people in an area to form a new county, a county seat was located by the legislature. This was at a convenient place, often the home of a settler or at a spot in the wilderness, and was almost certain to grow into a town.

Even during the earlier years town founders and promoters were not unknown, but by the time of the "Great Migration" after the War of 1812 these promoters flourished. In that period again there was a tendency for towns to precede settlement. The town-booming mania reached great proportions in the thirties and fifties. Indeed, town-making became a regular business of speculators. In southern Indiana hundreds of towns were started. So fervid was speculation in 1818 that the Richmond *Enquirer* warned:

> There is an astonishing rage at the present day for the establishment of new towns. Does a man possess a tract of land convenient to river transportation; if he is a man of enterprise, he starts the plan of a town; lays off his land into lots and expects to make his fortune by selling out. What pains to puff his situation; to dress off with every advantage of health, navigation and fertility which the most plastic imagination can supply.[1]

Very often the town was boomed by several men who associated themselves together, forming a town company. On a given day the lots were sold at auction. The company

[1] Leftwich: *Muscle Shoals*, pp. 37–8.

reserved certain lots, for which they drew. All purchasers of lots had to agree to improve them by building acceptable structures on them.

To cite an example, Columbus, located on the Chatta-hoochee River on the boundary between Georgia and Alabama, is typical. The town was incorporated by the Georgia legislature. Sixty days were allowed to survey the townsite and prepare for the auction. The visitor who arrived just before the sale found that an area five miles square had been surveyed. He was conducted down the main street, a long aisle four feet wide that had been cut through the oak forest. On reaching the center of the "city" the guide went into raptures about the future greatness of Columbus: "Here you are in the center of the city." He assured his auditor that this street was to be sixty yards wide and a league in length. Cross streets had been staked off perpendicular to the main street through the forest. Stumps, brush, and even trees stood in the streets. True to the pioneer tradition, squatters came in and occupied the townsite area. They had built their houses in clusters. Some were made partly of bark and partly of planks. Since none owned a lot and might not be able to buy the lot on which his house sat, many houses were built on trucks, a sort of low carriage with small log wheels, for the avowed purpose of moving them. There was a general under-standing that forty days would be allowed to move the houses. At least sixty frames of houses were lying in piles on the ground. These had been made by carpenters to sell to those who bought lots. Anvils were ringing and the wood was filled with stagecoaches, wagons, carts, gigs, and other vehicles. Grocery stores and bakeries were numerous, and over several doors was the sign "Attorney at Law." At that time there were nine hundred inhabitants and it was expected that from three thousand to four thousand would be there to buy lots and inhabit the new city.

When Arfwedson visited there in 1832, he found a population exceeding two thousand, and the streets, which four years before were merely staked out, were so filled with loaded wagons that it was almost impossible to pass. It was hardly believable it was the same place described by Captain Hall in 1828.

Not all towns were so fortunate. Many towns that were advertised as located favorably, with a good landing, a never failing water supply, and a healthful situation on an anticipated highway, never got beyond the stage of "paper towns." Indeed, sometimes after all the lots were sold in the town, there was never a house on the site. The price at which lots sold was amazing. Even with stumps in the street, no gutters, and the thoroughfares ungraded, prices soared to the skies. At Courtland, Alabama, a hundred lots brought $93,000 in 1818. Cahaba was laid out as the capital of Alabama in 1818, and after ninety days half a lot sold for $5,025.

Frequently there was bitter competition between two towns. Sometimes it was for the county seat. Sometimes, if they were adjacent, they fought for the post office or for a newspaper. All of these things helped "make" a town. For example, the towns of Tullahoma and Pittsburg, Mississippi, were located on adjoining sites with only a street between them. As the towns grew, rivalry between them increased. Pittsburg secured the post office and a newspaper, but the Tullahoma people paid the newspaper proprietor to move into their town and attempted to gain the post office. It is said they hauled it into their town at night in an endeavor to locate it there. At any rate, it was moved for a short time, but soon returned to Pittsburg. There was tense feeling between the towns, with no-trespassing signs posted on the line to keep the citizens of one from the other. Finally the two towns were united, with the name Granada. Alabama, Philadelphia, and East Alabama, adjacent towns, were united under the name of Montgomery.

Names were given to towns as the notion struck the proprietor or citizens. In 1820 when the first steamboat steamed up the Ouachita River to Fort Miro, so great was the rejoicing at a frolic that night that someone suggested the name of the town be changed to that of the boat, *Monroe*, in honor of the occasion, and it was done. In that manner Monroe, Louisiana, received its name.

In appearance the frontier town was not imposing. After eight years of its existence, all of which time it had been the capital, Little Rock was described by an early printer: "The trees are not half cut down in the town yet. Instead of streets, we walk in one cow path to another from house to house." [2]

A visitor to Lexington in 1797 found that there were fifty houses, partly frame and partly hewn log. The leading citizens dwelt in log cabins and wore hunting shirts and leggings. A traveler remarked about the "row or two of smoky cabins, dirty women, men in britch clouts, greasy hunting shirts, leggings, and moccasins."

As late as 1834 in St. Louis dead horses, cows, and hogs sometimes lay on the streets for days, polluting the air. On Market Street, just beyond Chateau's pond, was a slaughter house, and the offal caused a fearful stench. There were no sidewalks, and domestic animals roamed the streets at will. A man wrote from there that he never went out at night without a lantern for fear of falling over sleepy hogs and cows. In the cotton region large piles of rotting cotton seed made a foul smell, which was termed a "detestable and pestiferous nuisance" by the editor of the Montgomery *Republican*. As late as 1843 the streets of the Alabama capital were so full of deep holes that an ox team pulling a wagon on the main street drowned in one.

The cities often owned or hired a few Negroes, who, under the charge of the constable, worked on the streets and city utilities. At night watchmen policed the town. When a green country boy went to Lexington the first time and

---

[2] Hiram Whittington to his brother, April 21, 1827, *Arkansas Gazette,* April 17, 1932.

heard the shrill unearthly cry of the watchman calling the
time of night and the weather, he was nonplussed. In the
small town the watch or patrol, as it was sometimes called,
was drafted from among the citizens. Every person was
subject to this duty for a period of from one to three months,
but in Tuscaloosa, Alabama, upon payment of one dollar
he was exempt for one year.

The minutes of the town council of Grenada, Mississippi,
indicate that five men were to serve for one month, each man
to serve every other night. It was their duty to ring a curfew
bell at nine o'clock in the evening and whip all slaves who
were out after that time without permits. It was the duty
of the constable to take note of all conduct and prosecute
wrongdoers. Any informer received half the fine assessed.

There were no street lights, and those abroad at night
were compelled to carry a crude lantern in order to travel
in safety. It is small wonder, then, that denizens of pitch-
black towns turned to an "illumination" as a chief means of
celebrating. In Columbia, Missouri, in 1836, on the occasion
of the conclusion of a railroad survey into the town two
candles were put in every window, and at about equal distances on the principal street ten tar barrels were fired at
once. Their lurid flames lapping up and the billowing black
smoke created a lively and exciting scene. Its very brilliance,
so we are told, opened every eye to the great advantages of
a railroad.

The water supply was one of the great problems of the
town. In the stations water was caught in rain barrels from
the house roofs. In other places the inhabitants carried water
from a stream or spring. Later, wells were dug here and there
about town and provided with a curb and buckets and still
later with pumps. Frankfort had the first waterworks in
Kentucky. In 1804 a water line was laid down from a spring
and reservoir above town. The pipes were wooden tubes
made of cedar logs. A one-and-a-half-inch hole was bored

through the center and they were fastened together with wooden pins.[3]

It was almost an invariable rule that little attention was paid to fire protection until a fire had burned a portion of the town or of a neighboring town. As a result of such a calamity and the urging of the local newspaper, the city fathers made provision for a fire-fighting organization. The first fire companies were volunteer groups who upon the first sound of the alarm were to rush to the scene of the fire with buckets and form a bucket line from a well or the river to the burning building. Later hooks and ladders were furnished to each company, and still later came the fire engine, with long handles on each side, which were pumped by hand by a number of men. The water came from city or private wells, and since often these were not near the engine, the bucket line had to pass the water to the engine from the well.

When the fire bell rang, every citizen was required to grab his leather fire bucket and hasten to the fire. The women, five or six feet apart, formed one line, and the men a line opposite them. The buckets full of water were passed by the men to the engine, and the women passed the empty buckets back to the well. If a person was sick and could not attend a fire, it was his duty to hand all the fire buckets belonging to the house to passers-by on their way to the fire. Poor as they were, such arrangements were much better than none. At Huntsville, Alabama, the fire organization had been permitted to decline, and at a fire not a single hook or ladder could be produced. Only ten or twelve fire buckets, a part of them without bottoms, were available. After much confusion a kind of line was formed and citizens passed water in tubs, tin pans, and basins. More than a hundred people stood about and several sources of water were near, but very little got to the engine.[4]

[3] Willard Rouse Jillson: *Early Frankfort and Franklin County Kentucky 1750–1850* (Louisville, 1936), p. 129.
[4] The *Southern Advocate*, Huntsville, Ala., January 13, 1826.

For years many of the earlier towns had no mail service except a private express or pony rider running to the nearest post office. Nashville had no United States mail service for eighteen years. Knoxville did not have any until 1794, and then only every two weeks.

Each town had a market where producers could display goods for sale to the townspeople. The Nashville market was on the public square and was open three days a week from daylight until noon. Country people were not permitted to retail produce at any other place. At Lexington a visitor saw exhibited for sale some cabbage, turnip tops, chewing tobacco, catmint, a few bags of meal, some skinned squirrels cut in halves, some sassafras roots, and a few cakes of black maple sugar wrapped in greasy saddlebags. The observer thought that at another season, however, the variety would have been greater.

Society on the frontier was rough and uncouth. The editor of the Macon, Mississippi, *Herald* on July 24, 1841 called the early times the era of the bowie knife and rejoiced that there was a calm serenity in contrast to the former riotous times. A correspondent of the Montgomery *Republican* wrote:

> From the many *bloody* and serious recounters that have of late taken place in this town, I am induced to believe that our citizens certainly possess the most *war-like* dispositions of any people in the civilized world. Scarcely a day passes, but these champions of the *fist* and *skull* display their *dexterity* in the art of bruising each other, no matter how trivial the provocation.[5]

The editor's note added a hearty amen to this correspondent's article.

Twelve years later, when Harriet Martineau visited there, she said that tales of jail-breaking and rescue were numberless and that a lady of the city told her she had lived there four years and during that time she believed no day had

[5] Montgomery *Republican*, January 25, 1823.

passed without someone's life having been attempted either by dueling or assassination.

A New Englander found Little Rock in 1827 much the same. He wrote:

> Virtuous females were insulted with impunity. . . . Every man carried a gun, either for murdering his enemies or for his own defense, and murder was an every day occurrence. It was a daily sight to see men in full health shot down in the street like dogs. . . . In fact, you cannot imagine a more degraded state of society than we had here in Little Rock a few years back. I was ashamed to let you know the true state of affairs here at that time. . . .[6]

The disputes between towns for the location of the county seat or a state capital were often hot. Such a dispute over the state capital developed between Little Rock and Cadron. Certain St. Louis speculators laid off the town of Little Rock and got the lone settler made postmaster. Although Little Rock was right in the woods, with only two shacks, when the vote was taken in the legislature, the senate was for Little Rock, and the lower house for Cadron. Then the legislature recessed, and during this time the speaker of the house and certain other well-known politicians bought for nominal sums land on the Little Rock townsite. When the legislature reconvened, the members of the house saw the light, did an about-face, and voted to locate the capital at Little Rock.[7]

The typical town supported itself financially by a poll tax of one dollar, a property tax of twenty-five cents per hundred dollars' value of real estate, a four-wheeled pleasure-vehicle tax of fifty cents for each hundred-dollar evaluation, tavern and store licenses of five dollars per year each, a tax of five dollars on each traveling show or theatrical per-

[6] He came to Little Rock in 1827. Hiram Whittington to his brother, May 13, 1830, *Arkansas Gazette*, April 17, 1932.

[7] Dallas T. Herndon: *Why Little Rock was Born* (Little Rock, 1933), pp. 23-4, 50-1; Dallas T. Herndon: "History of the Arkansas Gazette," *Arkansas Gazette*, Little Rock, November 20, 1919, pp. 8, 9.

formance, and in some places a sales tax of a quarter of one per cent on all drugs, groceries, and liquors sold.

Luxuries began to come in rather early. Ice was offered for sale in Tuscaloosa, Alabama, for six and a half cents a pound in July 1835. Ice cream and soda water were advertised to sell as long as the ice should last.

XV

Professional Amusement

THE earliest professional shows on a given frontier seem to have consisted of one man and one or more animals. A man often walked from place to place with a trained monkey, acting dog, or wrestling bear. As time passed, a man brought an elephant through the backwoods country, to the intense astonishment of the people. A dromedary, while less spectacular, received due homage from the populace in early Kentucky.

The next type of animal show following the strolling menagerie was the exhibition of certain animals in cages. In 1805, as John Brethett was on his way east, he saw on the wharf at Maysville a large lion that had been landed from a boat from Pittsburgh. He had never seen such a thing before and was impressed that the lion was rightly called the king of beasts. He wrote:

> Even I myself can boast of having my hand on the fiercest beast in the world. . . . The keeper struck him in order to make [him] roar, then "he with eyes darting fury and a countenance distorted" looked tremendous—yet he would not gratify us with a yell, but growled, and the sound of which was indicative of the mighty noise he could make.[1]

[1] Journal of John Brethett, April 7, 1805, MS., Tennessee Historical Society.

These menageries blossomed out into the full-fledged circus. John Robinson was the first to take a circus over the Alleghenies. He had a half-dozen horses, two wagons, and a group of acrobats, including a clown, and a trick mule. Robinson himself furnished the music. He sat in the middle of the ring scraping on a fiddle and perhaps sang some songs. The circus was often advertised as a hippodrome or amphitheater, but was called a show. A man traveling a few days ahead of the circus distributed bills and tacked them on barns or trees.

The circus traveled in heavy wagons across country from place to place by ordinary roads. The country people lined the way and watched the elephant cross the river. When the procession reached the town, a grand entry was made, with gorgeous chariots, a horseback procession, gaudy trappings, and martial music.

After the circus arrived, the clown went riding about town, and when the crowd gathered, like a pied piper he led them to the tent at the edge of town. At first there was no canvas top to the tent. The performance was behind side walls enclosing an area seventy feet across. There were no seats except a few for ladies. A few boards served for a platform for the tumblers and dancers. The show started with a grand entry. The trapeze artists came on next, followed by the clown, who showered compliments and flings at local characters, tavern-keepers, and merchants. In time benches for spectators were added, and a performance at night was ventured by the aid of hundreds of candles. The arena was filled with simple people who gazed in open-mouthed wonder at the astonishing feats.

An early circus in Arkansas, in 1838, was that of W. Waterman and Company. Its troupe consisted of a two-horse rider, a one-horse rider, a tumbler, a plate dancer, a balancer, and a clown. A writer in the Batesville *News* thought that the one-dollar admission was a trifling sum to pay for such fun. Slaves and children were admitted for half price.

Strolling performers entertained with tumbling, balancing, wire dancing, and singing, much as the minstrels and acrobats did in medieval times.

At Natchez, Mississippi, ventriloquists entertained in 1806, and in 1807 appeared a fireworks display, a wax-figure exhibit, and "a three part program of 'extraordinary' bird imitations; 'Herculean Balancing or Ground Equilibriums'; and 'surprising' slack wire stunts." [2]

The wax-figure show was taken in wagons through the country. These figures were advertised as remarkably accurate likenesses of the characters portrayed. One such consisted of fourteen Scottish chiefs in costume, headed by Sir William Wallace, who was seven feet and two inches tall. This was shown at Tuscaloosa, Alabama, in 1835. In connection with it a model of a 132-gun man-of-war was shown. A sleight-of-hand performer who said he first "construed" the crowd and then did astonishing feats came to grief when he performed the shot-and-catch trick. He proposed to have someone fire a pistol and he would catch the bullet on the end of his knife. The man fired the pistol and lo! it snapped and failed to go off, but in spite of the fact that the bullet was not fired, there it was on the end of the knife.

The first professional theatrical attraction at St. Louis was Eugene Leitensdorfer, a magician. Among other things he advertised that he would raise a chicken, kill it, and bring it back to life. He showed an egg to the audience, placed it in a little box, and closed it. Immediately the yeeping of a chicken was heard. When he opened the box, a tiny chicken appeared. He put the chick in another box, closed it, and on opening it pulled out a broiler. This performance was repeated, the fowl becoming larger each time. Finally before the assembly he cut off the bird's head and put it—head and body—into a box. When this was opened the fowl was brought forth cooked a golden brown, swimming in gravy. A delightful aroma seemed to pervade the house. A local

[2] Nell Angela Heidelberg: "The Frontier in Mississippi," MS., pp. 36-7.

lawyer was invited to carve the bird. When he touched the chicken with the knife, lo! the chicken flew from the dish, splashing gravy over the young attorney. St. Louis was much pleased with this entertainment, and at the close of three months the magician left the city with pockets well filled with Spanish dollars.

The early dramatic performances were given by home-talent companies or Thespian societies. At Gallatin, Mississippi, such a performance was held in an old weatherboarded structure. Three young fellows were kept busy raking down the weatherboarding and yelling: "Glorious!" at the top of their voices at appropriate intervals when applause was called for. The money was used to pay for the scenery, and any remainder was dedicated to charity.

One of the earliest professional dramatic troupes to show on the frontier was that of Samuel Drake, Sr., who played in Kentucky during the winter of 1815–16. A representative was sent ahead two or three days before to arrange a place for the show. The troupe followed in a road wagon drawn by two horses, and a light spring wagon drawn by one horse. One or two of the women rode in the wagons part of the time, but most of the company was expected to walk almost all the way to lighten the loads. They would ride out of town for looks and then walk. The wilderness through which these troupes traveled was so dense that sometimes, on becoming separated from the group, an actor was lost in the woods. One such benighted actor in Florida was actually eaten by wolves.

When the strolling players came to a town, they were enthusiastically received. If there was no available building, the tavern-keeper would help the advance representative patch up a place in which to show. Sometimes a courthouse was used; sometimes the tavern served. A raised platform and extra seats were provided and the scenery came along with the company. There were six scenes: woods, street, parlor, kitchen, palace, and garden. The scenery could be put up or taken down and packed in two or three hours. In time, with increased prosperity, each player had a horse, and the scenery was carried in a wagon.

Drake's company played at Frankfort from December 1815 to March 1, 1816, while the state legislature was in session. Following this they showed for lesser periods at Louisville and Lexington. Between their seasons in these towns, various members would band together in smaller units and put on light shows here and there. N. M. Ludlow organized a troupe that played in Nashville in 1817. He rented an old salt storage house and had a stage and benches built. The benches rose in elevated banks and were reached by an inclined plane. He stated that the finest ladies in the city would sit on a narrow board not over ten inches wide, with no back rest, through a five-act play, and go home delighted.[3]

It was customary at this time to have benefit evenings for the various players toward the end of the season. The actor chose the play and those with whom he was especially popular turned out to make a full house in his honor and for his profit.

The difficulties of the pioneer theatrical manager were many. Sol Smith, a well-known showman, on his way to his string of theaters in the South, stopped at Greeneville, Tennessee, where he played to a crowded house of about two hundred. The doorkeeper's receipts showed that just seven had come through the door; the rest had come through the windows. On his way to Montgomery he carried his scenery in a covered wagon and his players in a coach. They traveled three or four days over corduroy roads in the Creek Nation and one evening found themselves in the midst of two thousand travelers—whites with their slaves—camped in the woods before the Kalebah Hatchee, where a bridge was out. Sol and his troupe surprised all by going from campfire to campfire rehearsing the choruses of the plays they were preparing. By strategy they were able to secure a place to stay

[3] N. M. Ludlow: *Dramatic Life As I Found It* (St. Louis, 1880), p. 113.

overnight in a crowded tavern. The next morning Smith was awakened by a hog's trying to pull his pillow through the cracks in the side of the building into the pigpen below.

On the stage the backwoodsman in buckskin hunting shirt, leggings, and moccasins, with a rifle on his shoulder, received loud acclamation. When Ludlow appeared in this role in New Orleans the audience raised a prolonged Indian whoop. He sang a song of Jackson entitled "The Hunters of Kentucky." As a final gesture he pulled up his rifle and took aim in true Kentucky style. It brought the house down and he had to sing it three times. After that for the next few years he had to sing it almost every night at every place he played. In some towns the play became so real to the backwoodsmen, unused as they were to drama, that they proposed to take matters in hand and right the situation. In Huntsville, Alabama, during a performance of a play portraying a family on the verge of starvation, a gentleman suddenly rose. "I can't stand this!" he shouted in a voice loud enough to be heard all over the house. "Gentlemen, I propose we make up something for this woman." A ripple of laughter greeted his proposal, while voices admonished him to sit down. A friend whispered in his ear that the whole thing was a sham. All this only aroused righteous indignation in the benevolent planter. "Gentlemen, you may 'hush' and 'order' as much as you please. For my part, I don't see anything to laugh at; you see the woman hasn't any thing to eat; and that poor little child of hers seems almost famished. . . . Gentlemen, you may laugh, but here goes my V," and with that he threw a pocketbook onto the stage.

It was not long before these rustic spectators became critics of the drama. When asked what he thought of a certain actor, a spectator replied: "Well, I don't go much to theatricals, that's a fact; but I do think *he piled the agony up a little too high* in that last scene." [4]

[4] Captain C. B. Marryat: *A Diary in America* (London, 1839), II, 234, 235.

A man by the name of Chapman ran a floating theater on the Ohio and Mississippi rivers. His practice was to erect a building on a raft at some point high on the Ohio River and equip it with scenery, costumes, and decoration ready for the season. He started in the fall and at each village or plantation tied up, hoisted a flag, blew a trumpet, and put on his play. Such a theater did not have to pay a special tax to the city since the river was not a part of the town. Sometimes a large steamer, while taking on wood, would ask for a show, and this usually netted a handsome income. When they reached New Orleans, the boat was broken up for wood and the troupe returned on a steamer.

Medicine shows gave free performances on vacant lots and drew large crowds. Each act closed at a most exciting point, giving the dapper, professional-looking medicine man an opportunity to sell various panaceas without fear of the crowd's dispersing. His smooth talk and distinguished looks were such as to convince the most dubious of the goodness of the product.

Gambling was another amusement often carried on professionally. As a rule there were laws against gambling, but in spite of these gambling was widely practiced. This was true particularly in boom times when money was plentiful and large crowds assembled for land sales or other purposes. In some towns gambling houses were set up and the more venturesome wagered money on cards, faro, roulette, and other gambling devices. In Newton County, Mississippi, in the thirties court would be held in the courthouse during the day and at night it would be used for a faro bank. So fascinating and all-consuming did the rage become that even children caught the general infection. Baldwin says he knew of one lad, Jim Ellett, who gave a bystander ten dollars to hold him up to bet at the faro table.[5] At Moulton, Alabama, a man played a simple gambling game with three thimbles placed on his knee and a small paper ball. He

[5] Baldwin: *Flush Times in Alabama*, p. 84.

handled the ball with dexterity and bet that no one could tell under which thimble it was. He made so much money that it was said he purchased a large portion of Tuscumbia, Alabama.

Along the river fronts and on the steamboats gambling reached its most despicable level. While some establishments were run honestly, others were what came to be known as "dead falls" or "wolf traps." A typical one was conducted in a dirty room carpeted with sawdust, furnished with rough wooden boxes, tables, and a few dozen cane-seated chairs.[6] When the sharpers met a "green un," they would take his money by cheating him in little ways. If he was too wise to permit this, they took the chance of winning or losing "on the square." If the stranger won a considerable sum, one of the gang left the room with the money. If he continued to win, the dealer asked someone to take his place while he stepped out a moment to attend to urgent business. As he left he took all the money the sucker had paid in. If the latter passed in his checks and asked for his money, he was politely asked to wait until the dealer returned. One of the ring would raise a cry of robbery, and in the uproar and confusion some supposed friend would whisper that he knew where to find the dealer, that he would go and make him pay up. The victim was then dragged all over the vicinity until he had lost all trace of where the gambling place was.

Sometimes a nervy obstinate customer appeared and caused a great deal of difficulty. In one instance a "roper" led an old Kentuckian into the den where a special game was in progress, having been got up for his personal benefit. He put five dollars into the game, and in spite of petty cheating and thievery he had soon run it up to eighty dollars. Then he called for his money and was told by the dealer that his "pardner" who carried the money was out,

[6] John Morris: *Wanderings of a Vagabond* (New York, 1873), pp. 354–5, 366.

but would soon be back. The old man growled at this way of doing business and held aloof from any further participation in the game. Shortly afterward the dealer began to feel that his absence would be most conducive to his health. He called an onlooker and asked him to deal for him while he went to see what had become of his partner. When he got to the door he found it blocked by the massive form of the old Kentuckian. "Look here, stranger!" he warned, "you can't pass here till I gets my money back nohow," emphasizing his words with the shake of his big fist under the gambler's nose. All attempts on the part of the gambler and his friends to argue the old woodsman out of his determination were of no avail. He would allow no one to leave until he got his money. The gambler then landed a blow with his clenched fist on the old man's face, but he felled the sharper with one blow. When the latter's companions then joined in the fray, he made short work of them. A blow from his hammerlike fist or a kick from his cowhide boots sent them "to grass" in every direction. They soon picked themselves up and slunk away. The old Kentuckian, finding himself alone, stepped onto the street, hailed a passing dray, and proceeded to load up the gambling equipment and all other valuables. Just as they were ready to drive to the auction rooms, a stranger appeared, representing himself to be the owner of the property. He said that the dealer had spoken the truth when he said his partner was absent, for he was the partner and had been delayed much longer than he had anticipated, but was ready to settle all claims against the bank. "Then shell out now!" roared the straight-shooting old Kentuckian. He was finally coaxed back into the gambling room—much to the indignation of the crowd that had assembled—and received his money without creating any further disturbance.[7]

Card gamblers traveled in small companies. The steamboat was an especially advantageous place for gamblers. Since

[7] Ibid., pp. 369-72.

they dealt with transients, no one knew them, and if their dishonesty created too much criticism, they could drop off at the next stop. Their game was to circulate among the passengers and induce one or two "gulls" to join them in a small game for amusement. This would lead on into gambling for ever larger stakes. If the sharpers could not beat their victims by the more common, obvious means, confederates would seat themselves in such a position that they could see the cards of their prey, and by means of signals "item" the strength of their hands. This was done by means of fingers, puffs of smoke skillfully blown from a cigar, the twirling of a cane, or other means.

Three-card monte was a simple game, in which the sharper took, we will say, two red cards and one black one between the fingers of his hand. He showed these to the crowd and threw them down, back up, on the table, saying: "I'll bet ten dollars [or twenty or fifty, as the case might be] that no one here can pick up the black card." When played fair, this game was two to one in favor of the man throwing the cards. He handled the cards with such dexterity that he confused the sight of the spectator. He enticed "green uns" into the game, however, by making them think that they could be sure winners. Often those with conscientious objections to gambling would find their scruples vanish like dew before the summer sun when they saw a sure chance to win. Five or six "cappers" would make sham bets and entice the unwary into the game. While the gamester was tossing his cards about, a "capper" would attract his attention in some way. While he looked away momentarily, a second "capper" would bend a corner of the appropriate card perceptibly. Then the gambler turned his attention once more to his playing, never noticing the condition of the card, and, unsuspecting soul that he was, threw the cards on the table, offering to bet that no one could pick out the winning card. He threw the three cards, among them the same black card face up on the table so that all could see the bent corner. Then he gave them a final shuffle, deftly and imperceptibly straightening the bent corner and bending the corner of another. Then, throwing them on the table, he would take bets up to any amount. So certain did the chance of winning seem that a gull was sure to bet. If he was cautious and wanted to bet only a small amount, the gambler would suddenly decide that he would not take a bet of less than a certain amount. If the "gull" did not have enough money, a "capper" would lend him enough to make up the amount. Thus at one play the unsuspecting backwoodsman became wise to the ways of the world, but at the cost of his hard-earned cash.

Some very heavy gambling took place on the river boats. In 1833 on a steamer on the Alabama River a group of gamblers enticed a non-professional named Brown into a game. He was known to have a quantity of money. The agreement was made that if anyone was caught cheating, he was to forfeit the stakes and be put off the steamer at the nearest land. Brown won consistently at cards and a gambler challenged him to give him a chance to win back the money with dice. Brown then lost every time. Finally Brown went to his stateroom and brought out thirty thousand dollars and threw it on the table. The gambler raked enough together from among his fellow gamblers to cover it. Sixty thousand dollars was to be lost or won at a single throw. Then Brown caught the gambler slipping the dice up his sleeve and substituting loaded dice. Brown claimed the money and was backed up by the passengers with drawn pistols. The gambler was loaded into a boat and taken to a low sandbank entirely surrounded by rising water. Long after they had lost sight of him they heard his piteous appeals, denunciations, and wild cries through the dark night as the angry waters of the swollen stream rose higher and higher. Finally his despairing appeals were drowned out by the roar of the wheels in the surging current. But the passengers could not forget the cries of the doomed man, for no swimmer could have stemmed that fearful current. There was no more gambling on board that night, and the next day many of the passengers left the boat, fleeing as if from an accursed place.

XVI

Schools

THERE are indications that the first generation of settlers who crossed the Allegheny Mountains were more literate than the second and third generations. Limited schooling opportunities during the early conquest of the Indians and the wilderness produced an illiterate second generation, which in turn, moving farther out on the frontier, lacked appreciation of schooling and produced another generation similar to or even worse than itself. As a result, a very large percentage of the people were unable to read or write, were suspicious and superstitious. They were narrow and provincial and easy marks for the fortune-teller and the itinerant magician. Many were crude and uncouth in their habits. Most men who carved out a successful career did so with almost no schooling.

David Crockett when grown began to feel that his lack of success in securing a certain girl for a wife was due to his lack of education and decided to go to school. He agreed to work for a married teacher two days a week if he would teach him the other four days and give him board and room. Crockett said:

At it I went, learning and working back and forwards, until I had been with him nigh on to six months. In this time I learned to read a little in my primer, to write my own name, and to cypher some in the three first rules in figures. And this was all the schooling I ever had in my life, up to this day.[1]

Thus spoke the man who later took his place in Congress and commanded the acclaim of the country.

The frontier school even more than others centered in the teacher, who was always called "the master." This title corresponded in that backwoods world to ours of teacher, professor, principal, president, or superintendent. The early teacher was likely to be a Yankee educated in the New England schools or an Irishman. He was expected not only to be able to hear the pupils read, teach them to spell and write, and direct a few simple operations in ciphering, but to supervise also the making of ink, shaping goose quills into pens, and ruling paper for copybooks. The better teachers even made the arithmetic books.

When public schools began to function in Missouri, the trustees were called to examine a candidate for his fitness for teaching. One asked: "Mr. Jones, is the world round or flat?" The prospective teacher answered: "I do not know for sure, but I am prepared to teach it either way." The board hired him and decided that he should teach it flat.

The earliest attempts at education, however, were in private schools. When Albert Pike asked how he was to get a school to teach, a settler told him to prepare articles of agreement stating the tuition he wished to charge, the length of the term, and other conditions. He was then to get enough signers to guarantee a school. He was told there was to be a shooting match on the morrow and that he should be there. The next day he was introduced to the gathering and also took part in the shooting match. No doubt his skill in shooting commended him more forcefully to the assembled settlers than did his articles. Whatever the reason,

[1] David Crockett: *A Narrative of the Life of David Crockett* (Philadelphia, 1834), p. 49.

he soon had twenty "scholars," as they were called, signed up. A small tuition charge was made.

When Sam Houston taught at Maryville, Tennessee, in 1811, he received eight dollars per term per pupil. This was paid equally in corn, cash, and cotton goods.

If there was a schoolhouse in the settlement, all was ready for school to open, but if not, the community had "a chopping" and "a raising" and in two or three days the schoolhouse was ready. Located at the edge of the forest, the schools were often called "forest schools." Others, located on worn-out cultivated areas, were called "old field" schools.

If the teacher was married, the community built him a cabin near the school, but if he was single he "boarded round" for part of his salary. This had its drawbacks and its compensations. The master was a guest and the family tried to have the best food and entertainment for him. On the other hand, the cabins were crowded and the beds were few. The boys vied with one another for the honor of sleeping with "the master," a joy not reciprocated by "the master," for the children often carried food to bed with them and left crumbs in the bed.

The schoolhouse was the usual log cabin. For windows two logs were cut out, one on each side. Beneath these openings holes were bored in the logs and broad boards were securely fastened at an angle so that the light would fall on them. These served as desks. Other such boards formed shutters to close the drafty openings. The benches were of split logs with the faces smoothed. They were supported by four legs driven into holes on the under side. They were usually of the same height, made for nearly grown children, and the legs of the little children dangled. A small youngster in mounting the bench placed his hands on the top and, hooking his big toe and the one next to it around one of the legs, climbed up. The floors were often earth from which the roots of the brush had not even been grubbed.

Just as there are well-defined groups today such as freshmen, sophomores, and upperclassmen, there were likewise the groups: "big boys," "little boys," and "the girls."

In his "articles" the teacher often reserved for himself a court day in each month, a week for Christmas, ten days for harvest, and certain other days. Indeed, many schools ran for only a few weeks in the winter or for a short period in the summer after corn was "laid by" and before "fodder-pulling."

It was a day of harsh discipline. Frontier conditions did not soften the temper of the times. As suggestive of the merits attributed to corporal punishment, one of the first schools in Tuscaloosa, Alabama, was named "the Thrashing Machine." Certainly if the children were spoiled, it was not as a result of sparing the rod. A brace of beech or bois d'arc (Osage orange) switches, well seasoned, graced the corner of the room. These were not merely for ornamental purposes. It was thought there was nothing like the rod to stimulate learning, nor abusive reproof to encourage industry.

Other severe and interesting punishments were administered. One attendant at a frontier school remembered seeing a teacher take off his suspenders and hang a little boy until he was nearly strangled before he was let down to sin no more. A youngster was made to remain in a kneeling position or stand on one foot like a rooster on a cake of ice. The "laugh-block" was also used to work reformation by ridicule.

When the teacher stormed out: "Mind your books," the pupils struck up a loud blatant confusion of tongues that one observer said beat anything he had ever heard before. When the visitor came in sight of the building, he heard the pupils spelling and reading at the top of their voices, a perfect babel, confusion of tongues. There was a pause when the visitor arrived and then at a command everyone as before began at the top of his voice. What they lacked in brains they made up in noise, testified a student of such a school. The classroom procedure earned such an institution the title of a "blab school."

Philip Gosse found that the young sons of planters in his school were as rude as his dirt-floored schoolhouse. They were real hunters who handled the long rifle with more ease and dexterity than they did a goose quill, and were incomparably more at home in "twisting a rabbit" out of a hole or "treeing a possum" than in conjugating a verb. Sometimes if the school was at a station, the big boys were sent in "Indian times" to keep the children from wandering about where the Indians could catch them.

Gideon Lincecum found in his border school in the ranching area of western Georgia some of the coarsest specimens of the human family he had ever seen. During the first day they had half a dozen fights right in the schoolhouse. A number were young married men, who gleefully participated in the deviltry along with the youngsters. Nevertheless he gained their goodwill and they thought he was doing wonders for the community. One of these married men, enthusiastic over his program, addressed a group including his teacher in this informal frontier fashion: "I tell you what, folks, this is a big thing. We never had such sort of doings afore in these diggings. What next, Old Hoss?"

The teachers did attempt to teach manners, however. Dr. Drake said that in his school days after the master had taken his seat, the boys were required on entering the door to take off their hats and bow and the girls to curtsy. In some schools the same was required in the evening. The children were furthermore taught to take off their hats and bow and curtsy to all whom they met, either coming or going. During play hours when someone went by, play was stopped and the children ran to the road and gave the salute. When someone met them on the way to or from school, the children stepped to one side in a row, took off their hats, and made their bows as nearly at the same time as possible.

School hours were long—from "an hour by sun" in the

morning to "an hour by sun" in the evening. The pupils brought their lunches, and during the "dinner spell" they gathered in congenial groups indoors on the benches in bad weather and on logs in the forest in pleasant seasons.

An observer in Louisiana mentioned that they sang their geography lessons and called z "zu." In east Tennessee pupils were taught the sound of the vowels by the following saying: "A for ablesome, fa; E for eblesome, fe; I for iblesome, fi; O, oblesome, fo; U, ublesome, fu; Y, yblesome, fy." Z was also called "izzard" or "zed." The spelling of Aaron was orally given as "great A, wee a, r, o, n." Getting an arithmetic lesson was called "working sums."

Equipment and books were scarce, but the general store handled a few books, slates, foolscap paper, and pencils. Youngsters used a "hornbook" to learn their letters. This was a paddle with big letters on one side and small letters on the other, covered with horn scraped thin to transparency.

In some places the first pupil at school recited first. After the master took his place he immediately called out: "Come, First!" and the first comer advanced to recite.

The last thirty minutes in the evening were given over to spelling. When time for "letting out" approached, the whole school was summoned to line up and spell for "head marks," the one who could spell a word going ahead of those who missed it. When the word for dismissal came, the crowd like a herd of wild cattle rushed out, running, skipping, jumping, and yelling at the top of their voices.

Amusements tended toward the forest life of which they were a part: swinging by grapevines, hunting nuts, picking persimmons, eating pawpaws, climbing trees, hunting for birds' nests, throwing at squirrels, shooting with the bow and arrow, making whistles in the spring, and indulging in many common athletic sports.

Very few girls went to school. There is abundant proof in the county records of the times that very few of the women could even sign their own names. Both sexes played together. Two favorite games were "prisoner's base" and "shuffling the brogue," a game probably brought from Ireland by the Scotch Irish. It consisted in the players' forming a ring by standing close together facing inward and passing a mitten around the circle behind them. One appointed to be "it" stood in the center and tried to discover who had the brogue. When one was caught with it, he had to be "it." Kissing games were also popular.

The favorite sport and event of the year was "barring out" or "turning out" the master. This performance, peculiar to the Southern area, was not practiced from the central portion of the Old Northwest northward. The ceremony was intended to secure a holiday, usually Christmas, without having to make up the time. It took the form of the pupils' compelling the teacher to dismiss school. In reality it was a scheme against the parents, for the teacher was glad to co-operate, but made a show of resistance so that he might not have to make up the lost time.

The farce would begin with a petition from the pupils asking for a week's vacation and a treat. This was peremptorily refused. That night the big boys would take possession of the schoolhouse. The whole night was given over to a frolic, the roasting of game, and fiddling. Some grown-ups in on the secret were admitted. When daylight came, the outsiders left and the boys barricaded the doors and windows with logs and held the fort. They then awaited with real anxiety the coming of the master. Ordinarily he put up a mere show of resistance, but sometimes he actually broke into the schoolroom and thrashed some of the more belligerent. Sometimes the teacher's obstinacy was cured by ducking him in the cool December creek water. The master then sent for apples and cider and sometimes more stimulating refreshments. Over the refreshments general merriment ensued, in which victors and vanquished united in reciting in friendly spirit both tragic and comic sides of the siege. Then there were good wishes and a week of amusements and good times. At its close all bad feeling between the master and the boys had been wiped out and when "Books!" was called, each pupil quietly recognized the legitimate overlordship of the master and gave loyal obedience until the next holiday season.

At the conclusion of the term a public examination was often held. At Columbia, Missouri, the female school closed during the May court week in 1836 and the judges and lawyers attended the examination. One little girl, the daughter of a planter, nearly collapsed before that assembly of dignitaries, but took a pull at her hartshorn (a common smelling salt of the time) and bravely read her composition, entitled: "Life Compared to a Rose."

In addition to the backwoods subscription school, other kinds of institutions of learning were the home tutoring system and the private academy, giving a kind of higher learning. The planter often employed a clerk who spent part of his time in teaching the white children on the plantation.

The subscription school in the village began to extend the courses offered and teach a select few who were prepared higher mathematics, ancient languages, and other subjects now falling in the high-school curriculum. Such schools were called academies. Some of the earliest of such enterprises were nurtured by the clergy. Wherever ministers went they sowed the seed for educational institutions. Samuel Doak, a Presbyterian minister, pastor of an early church in the Holston settlements in Tennessee, started such a log academy, called Martin Academy. It was chartered in 1779 by North Carolina and was the first English-speaking institution if its kind in the Mississippi Valley. This grew into Washington College. Almost all higher education was in the hands of the clergy.

The academies and even the colleges were often one-room log buildings with or without glass windows and with rough puncheon furniture. The college library consisted of a few copies of Latin and Greek classics, a few tattered grammars, and dog-eared dictionaries. A surveyor's compass and chain were sometimes the sum total of the laboratory equipment.

Transylvania College, at Lexington, Kentucky, claims the honor of being the oldest college west of the Allegheny Mountains. Before 1800 it had taken the title of Transylvania University. The program was rigorous. The students were required to be up and at their books by eight a.m., and from then until eight at night they were required to be in their rooms unless called out for recitations or given special permission to be absent, with the exception of an hour and a half at noon and one hour for supper. There was a half holiday on Saturday afternoon. The rules required that at the completion of a course the student "shall be strictly examined" in the presence of the board of trustees and "gentlemen of learning." All students were required to attend prayers every evening at the conclusion of recitations and to attend church on Sunday. In spite of its definite religious background there was no hesitation or horror felt about using a lottery to raise five hundred pounds for a new building in 1791. By 1827 Transylvania had grown almost out of its pioneer status, but even then the students had plain dessert only once a week at the refectory and ate corn-meal mush for supper.

Admission requirements were high. Cumberland College would admit no one who had ever fought a duel or had ever taken any part in one. Any student who became involved in such an affair of honor after matriculation was to be expelled at once. At La Grange College the rules required that the one in charge visit the students' rooms "regularly" "both day and night." Every absence from prayers, room, or recitation was noted, and delinquents had their offenses read before the student body weekly.

The South did not take kindly to coeducation. Even in

academies the boys and girls, although sometimes admitted to the same school, were taught in separate rooms.

The churches also began to give attention to the education of women. At Judson College, one of the oldest colleges for women west of the Alleghenies, the girls lived in a dormitory, four in a room. They were required to wear a uniform daily. For winter it was green merino and for summer pink calico. On Sabbaths they wore white muslin and a straw hood trimmed with green in winter and with pink in summer. The girls who boarded with the teachers were required to converse in French with Parisian accent, according to an advertisement. No jewelry was permitted. The girls were allowed to go to town only once a month, and then all purchases had to be approved by a chaperon accompanying them. Only fifty cents a month was allowed for spending money. When the girls went out, they marched in a group. Their president walked in front of the procession carrying his gold-headed cane and seated himself with them.

Now and then an itinerant offered a series of lessons in stenography, a sort of roving business college. Such a business course was offered at Tuscumbia, Alabama, in 1825. The terms were five dollars per pupil.

In the plantation region, after a pupil had been prepared by a tutor, he was sent to the East or North to college. So general was this practice that on the eve of the Civil War the percentage of college-trained men was much higher in that area than in the North. An example of this was A. O. P. Nicholson of Maury County, Tennessee. When at the age of fourteen he finished the local school, he was sent to the University of North Carolina at Chapel Hill. He remained there four years without going home or seeing a member of his family. Upon graduation he made his way home and surprised his mother, whom he met at the door of the old home before noon one summer's day. His mother, overjoyed to see her son, took down the dinner horn and called all the colored folk in from the field to rejoice and have a family holiday.

Louisiana as early as 1805 passed an exceedingly forward-looking educational law. It provided for a university at New Orleans and academies in every parish. The parish judge was to appoint a committee of from twelve to twenty to make arrangements for the academy, five from this committee to constitute a school board.

XVII

Religion on the Frontier

VARIOUS causes operated to promote an unreligious atmosphere on the frontier. Often the less pious moved west. The lack of women had a tendency to remove the steadying influence normally present. Very rude surroundings, with an intense struggle for existence, tended to promote ungodliness.

Contemporary writers in early Kentucky noted with amazement the lack of piety in the country. A most liberal estimate of the number of church members in 1792 still left two thirds of the population outside the fold of the church.

In some instances in Alabama preachers were driven off. There is a tradition that at St. Stephens a Baptist minister was rowed across the river and told that if he ever returned he would be tarred and feathered. A minister by the name of Sturdevant labored a year without organizing a "society" or enrolling a member.

Timothy Flint complained that in Arkansas in 1819 part of the audience listened for a time to his sermon and then returned to the billiard room. Another part went directly from services to a ball. At St. Charles, Missouri, in 1817, although there was an average of a hundred people daily coming to the town or passing through nearby points, not one family in fifty had a Bible, Flint said. At about the same time John Mason Peck estimated that at least half of the American inhabitants of St. Louis were infidels of low and indecent grade. They were vulgarly profane and mocked religion, even going so far as to burn the Bible. It was their boast, often made, that the Sabbath had never crossed and never should cross the Mississippi.

The Baptists were the pioneers in religion in Kentucky and the most numerous body of Christians in the early settlement of the state. The first Methodist conference west of the Alleghenies was established by Bishop Asbury in the state of Franklin (now eastern Tennessee). He wrote of the work in Kentucky that "the Methodists do but little here, others lead the way." Despite slow growth in early years the Methodists became the leading denomination throughout the southern and southwestern frontiers. The Baptist church was next in size and influence.

In 1787 there were about fifty families in Pottinger's Creek settlement when Father M. Whelan was sent as the first missionary priest into Kentucky. Under the leadership of Samuel Doak, the Presbyterians early possessed the field in eastern Tennessee. Educated at Princeton, he walked through Maryland and Virginia, driving before him a "flea-bitten gray horse loaded with a sack full of books." The Presbyterian belief was rigid, formal, and austere. The doctrine of predestination was not so popular on the frontier as the free-will doctrine of the Baptists and Methodists. As a result of the revival of 1800, however, a free-will branch of the Presbyterians, known as the New Lights, grew up.

When there were enough people in a neighborhood to support a church, all hands turned out and raised the walls for a meeting house. These churches were log cabins without floors and in the lower South were without any heating apparatus. Of these churches John Poage Campbell said:

> Numbers of them were open to everything and more like hog pens and stables, than places where men can worship

God. . . . A pane of glass to let in the light and keep out the wind and rain is scarcely seen, a pew or decent seat about as rare.[1]

Sometimes a graveyard was started in a little clearing and later a church was erected near by. In some places for years services were held out of doors and at other times the school house was used for worship. In the towns lotteries were often the means of erecting a church, and at Lexington, Kentucky, those who subscribed thought nothing of pledging whisky to pay for the meeting house.

Preaching appointments were happy occasions. The people lived far apart, and there was preaching only as often as the itinerant came to the neighborhood, which usually was only once a month. It was a day of social communion as well as spiritual uplift. When the minister arrived he saw the fence and the yard around the building crowded with men, women, and children. Numerous guns leaned against the log cabin, with strings of squirrels, a few opossums, and numbers of partridges. In Indian days every man took his place on a bench wearing his shot-pouch, tomahawk, and scalping knife, and with his gun in his hand. Most of the congregation had on neither shoes nor stockings and were clad in apparel that was unlike that worn in more civilized areas.[2] Every man brought his dogs. In that period an average congregation would consist of perhaps fifteen families. Each couple had an average of five children, two of whom were infants and a third was too small to keep quiet during services. It would be conservative to estimate five dogs to a family. As one minister facetiously remarked, there were in a congregation "forty-five babies and seventy-five dogs, with only sixty adults to police the mob.[3] The preacher had his

[1] Charles R. Staples: "Pioneer Kentucky Preachers and Pulpits," *Filson Club History Quarterly*, IX, 153, 157.
[2] *Brother Mason, the Circuit Rider* (Cincinnati, 1856), pp. 71–2; J. W. M. Breazeale: *Life As It Is* (Knoxville, 1842), p. 108.
[3] Srygley: *Seventy Years in Dixie*, p. 66.

hands full to compete with quarreling dogs without and squalling children within.

There was much handshaking in the yard before meeting and much visiting there afterward. To smoke in church was not considered impious or out of order. On a hot summer day a new minister noticed a boy on his way to church swinging a firebrand to keep it burning. He was at a loss to know why fire was needed in summer. When he arrived in the yard after caring for his horses, he found the fire had been placed in a large stump and was burning freely. Old and young took out their pipes and, drawing from their roomy pockets home-cured tobacco, lighted their pipes at the stump and sat down to enjoy a smoke and visit before going in to the service. During the sermon he noticed a woman but a few feet in front of him nudge the one next to her, who nudged the one next to her, and the nudge was carried on down the bench. During this time every eye was fixed on the speaker. Soon the signal was repeated. Then all rose from the bench with almost military precision, quietly moved to the burning stump, lighted their pipes, and sat on the ground near by, smoking. During all this time they paid perfect attention, apparently never missing a word.[4]

The people were fixed in their ideas of worship, anxious that the program be carried out in the old way, and informal and democratic enough to speak out if the minister forgot anything. When a new minister attempted to dismiss a service, a brother rose and in a loud voice drawled: "Ain't you goin' to give out no app'intment for the nixt round?" "Yes, brother," replied the preacher, "my colleague will be here in four weeks." Another brother called: "Give out the class meetin' for nixt Sunday." "At what hour?" "Three o'clock," was the reply. The minister then announced: "Let us be dismissed!" "Not yet! Not yet," implored a man with a red bandanna over his head. All was silence. "Ain't you goin' to

4 Pierson: *In the Brush*, pp. 174-7.

give out prayer meetin' for next Thursday night?" "Yes; there will be prayer meeting in this house next Thursday evening." Someone offered: "Not in this house, brother; it will be at Brother M.'s, in the lower end of town." Finally the congregation was dismissed.[5]

When the itinerant did not arrive at the announced time, the crowd would patiently await his coming for hours. John Mason Peck got lost while on his way to an appointment in 1818. He arrived at the clearing just at sunset and found more than twenty people who had waited since noon to hear the strange preacher. Often at church service business announcements, notices of lost stock, and other secular matters were "given out."

Although there were the beginnings of class distinction in social life, religion was one common plane upon which all classes met. The plantation-owners, their slaves, and "poor white trash" all worshiped together. The names of the slaves appear on the same church records as those of their masters and they were baptized together. As time passed, however, there was a tendency to hold a morning meeting for the whites and an afternoon session for the servants, although this was not a clear-cut rule. Negroes were often allowed to attend the morning sermon. In some instances a colored minister even preached to mixed congregations. Many Negro preachers could not read, of course, and it was necessary for them to get someone in the big house to read the Bible to them until a text was struck that suited them. Then they memorized it and other Scripture, and by means of homely but often apt illustrations they built up their sermon.

One Calvinistic Baptist Negro preacher who was endeavoring to explain to his congregation the superiority of predestination over the free-will doctrine of the Methodists shouted:

[5] *Brother Mason*, pp. 20–1.

De Methodiss, my bruddren, is like de grasshopper—hoppin', all de time hoppin'—hop into heaven, hop out, hop into heaven, hop out. But, my bruddren, de Baptiss, when he get to heaven, *he's dar!* De Baptiss is like de 'possum. Hunter get after him, he climb de tree; he shake de limb, one foot gone; he shake de limb, anudder foot gone; he shake de limb, ebbery foot gone; but tink you, my bruddren, *'possum fall?* You know, my bruddren—you cotch too many—you know *'possum hang on by de tail,* and de berry debbil can't shake him off!

At the conclusion of the service the Negroes could not separate without the breaking exercises, so called from breaking up the meeting. One who attended such an exercise said they sang the grandest, wildest, most beautiful African music he had ever heard. They began to sing and move in a procession by the pulpit, shaking hands with the minister as they passed. As the long column filed by, faces shone with delight as the music rose wilder and more exciting. Finally the handshaking ended, the meeting "broke," and the service was over.

The duties of church membership were taken seriously. If a man did not live up to his profession he was summoned to answer for his conduct. The Baptists held a monthly business meeting and the Methodists held one quarterly on Saturday. On these occasions the private lives of the members came up for review. Those whose conduct was deserving received a ticket admitting them to the communion the next day, and the black sheep were disciplined. These tickets were taken up by a sentinel at the door.

The observance of the Lord's Supper by the Presbyterians took place only once or twice a year and was called "sacramental solemnities." The members were given an examination before the occasion and issued pewter or lead tokens similar to street-car tokens. These were taken up at the communion table.

The rules adopted by the Buffalo Lick Baptist Church of

Kentucky provided for a moderator and efficient sensible rules of order covering all conceivable cases. Church trials were held regularly at these meetings. Witnesses were summoned and sworn in, they gave their testimony, and judgment was rendered by a vote of the church. Sometimes the offenses were church cases and warranted discipline by the church. Some, however, were of the nature of lawsuits or trials between individuals and were settled without cost or fees. Some of the cases that came before the Cooper Run Baptist Church in Bourbon County, Kentucky, for discipline were: neglecting to attend worship, chastising a slave too severely, playing the fiddle for dancing, horse-racing, telling a lie, committing adultery, forging the father-in-law's name on a marriage permit in order to get the girl, permitting gambling in one's house. The women were disciplined for slander, tale-bearing, whispering, and quarreling; one married woman was hailed before the brethren for "unjustifiable familiarity with a young man in permitting him to kiss her three times." At the Bent Creek Church, Lucy Clark was excluded for adulterating beeswax with tallow. James Carter was suspended for not settling a personal debt where he came from.[6]

The churches apparently regarded dancing as a sin and sufficient cause for excommunication, while placing their endorsement on distilling whisky. In 1795 a Kentucky church minute book recorded the fact that a certain woman was summoned to answer before the church for her disrespectful remarks about the distilling business. At the second meeting thereafter the same woman was excluded from membership for permitting dancing in her home.

Sectarianism arose after the Great Revival, and members were disciplined for hospitality to ministers of other churches. On a Mercer County, Kentucky, church minute book appear charges against a brother "for having Barton Stone

---

[6] Bent Creek Church Records, McClung Collection, Lawson-McGee Library, Knoxville, pp. 17, 33.

preach his wife's funeral within the bounds of the church." His plea was that "it was done at his wife's dying request, but would a like occasion arise again, he would be more circumspect.[7]

Ministers, the Methodists in particular, were against the wearing of jewelry, ornaments, and fine apparel, which were considered an indication of pride. The Reverend Silas Drake pronounced earrings the devil's stirrups. One day at a meeting he saw a woman with large bows of ribbon on her hat and reproved her publicly, charging that her bows were of absolutely no use. She countered by charging that the buttons on his sleeves and the back of his coat were just as useless. He immediately pulled off his coat, cut off the buttons, and never wore them again.[8]

The question whether a master could whip a black brother instead of taking the gospel steps was raised in one church and settled in favor of whipping. The marital status of slaves who had been married and separated from their spouses by sale and then married again came up at the Tick Creek Church in Kentucky. It was voted that the slave brethren were not guilty of adultery, but the masters were out of order in separating husbands and wives.

The Buffalo Lick Church, in Kentucky, voted to treat slaves the same as any other brother in the church in settling differences; that is, masters should settle a grievance with them as they would with a free brother.

Since drinking was almost as common as eating, it is not surprising that nearly all good church people drank. One never thought of entertaining without liquor in some form. A minister reported a conversation between two prominent church members who had been to market to lay in supplies for the annual revival. One asked the other: "How much 'sperits' did you git?" "Ten gallons," his brother replied.

[7] Staples: "Pioneer Kentucky Preachers," *Filson Club History Quarterly*, IX, 155.
[8] Otto A. Rothert: *A History of Muhlenberg County* (Louisville, 1913), p. 130.

The other retorted: "Jest sech stinginess as that will spile the meetin' and kill the church. I got twenty gallons myself an' you are jest as able to support the gospil as I am, if you wuzn't so dog stingy." Ministers regularly took their morning eye-opener and their nightcap in the evening. Some even made whisky or trafficked in it.

By 1825 a consciousness of the evils of liquor began to arise. The Methodist church was the outstanding denomination in its advocacy of temperance and teetotal abstinence. In other churches the discussion over the use of liquor grew so heated that it was a red-hot issue for years, causing wrangling and ill feeling. St. Paul's admonition to Timothy to take a little wine for his stomach's sake was a tower of strength to those who liked their toddy. Disputes over one thing and another grew so spirited that churches were split.

Among other fruitful causes of quarrels was the music. There were disagreements on whether to have a choir and whether to have an instrument. One or two headstrong or selfish members could keep a church in turmoil for years.

The minister usually lined or "passeled out" the hymn; that is, he read the first two lines, after which they were sung; then the next two were read. In this manner—piecemeal—the song was sung. The minister usually not only lined the hymn but "histed it"; that is, pitched it for the congregation. In some songs the words with the exception of one or two were alike in each stanza, and these were soon committed to memory.

To denote the receiving of the offering, it was announced that the collection would be "lifted."

Worship was extremely informal. Loud shouts of "Hallelujah!" "Amen!" "Glory!" and other exclamations of praise and joy in Christ arose spontaneously. At a "love feast" of the Cumberland Presbyterians, a minister present said the procedure was for a man to rise, give his testimony, and then start out shaking hands with everyone in the church, continuing his remarks and ejaculations. A sister would rise, speak of the love of God, and then start out to embrace the other sisters. Before long almost the entire church was shaking hands and embracing, keeping time in their movements with a wild Western melody they were singing. Handshaking or kissing was very cordial when someone was converted, or "came through," as they called it.

The Old Presbyterians attempted to provide an educated ministry. The Baptists, congregational in organization, chose from a congregation certain men, often almost as ignorant as the rest of the church, to be ministers. Sometimes the license for such a man to preach stated that the candidate was "tolerated to make use of his gift as he feels God has called him." Not until 1816 did the Methodists prescribe any educational requirements for the ministry. Then a course of studies was prescribed which was to be pursued while the novice was "on trial," and he was to pass the required examination before being admitted to "full connection" in the ministry. This course, about 1840, consisted of English grammar, geography, and Wesley's *Account of Christian Perfection*, together with another book on theology. One minister mentioned that in his case, which was probably typical, he came up to the examination with great fear and trembling. He had been riding the circuit day after day and had been unable to prepare very well. But a committee of two unlearned men was appointed to examine him. They freely admitted they knew nothing of grammar or geography, and with a few plain questions on the Bible the dreaded examination was over.

Indeed, a "call to preach" was thought to exceed, by far, any preparation that might be made in the matter of education. There was a prejudice even against preparation for a particular sermon. A parishioner in visiting with a circuit rider remarked that since the minister had only one appointment a day and two on Sunday, he would have plenty of time to visit the homes of the people, and that if he did not "the sisters would be down on him." "But," replied the young minister, "I must have some time for rest and study." "As to study," replied the good brother, "I don't believe in it any way. It's no use; just get up, and look to God, and fire away."

A representative of the American Bible Society said that the deeper he got into the brush and the denser the ignorance of the people, the greater was the number of preachers. Some of them could not read at all and many mispronounced a large number of the longer words. An Indian man said that one of these inspired clergy, standing before the congregation, would recite this homiletic creed:

Yes, bless the Lord, I am a poor, humble man—and I doesn't know a single letter in the A B C's, and couldn't read a chapter in the Bible no how you could fix it, bless the Lord! —I jist preach like old Peter and Poll, by the Sperit. Yes, we don't ax pay in cash nor trade nither for the Gospel, and arn't no hirelins like them high-flow'd college-larned sheepskins—but as the Lord freely give us, we freely give our fellow critturs.[9]

A correspondent of the *Christian Repository* wrote that whenever one of these preachers rose to address the people, he usually "threw the reins upon the neck of feeling and let her run full speed." The backwoods preacher drawled out his message in a singsong tone from beginning to end. He ran his voice up and sustained it at such a high pitch that he could make very little variation upward. He ran out of breath and at the close of each sentence would catch his breath with an "ah." Often the preacher had no idea what he would say from one "ah" to the next. This "holy tone" had charms for the audience and they preferred such a sermon to that by a learned college president.

The mispronunciation of words and ignorance of their meaning often led the backwoods preacher into the most fantastic interpretations. One word, wrongly interpreted,

[9] James A. Woodburn (ed.): Baynard Rush Hall: *A New Purchase* (Princeton, 1916), p. 121.

often served as material for a whole sermon. One pious minister took for his text: "Wherefore, gird up the loins of your mind. . . ." He confused the word "loins" for "lines" and dwelt at length on the different kinds of lines: lines by which carpenters carried on their work, lines to divide land, stage lines for travelers, and lines with which to drive horses. In all these uses of the word he unfolded a deep mystery, to the delight of his hearers.[10]

A preacher was explaining the reference in Ecclesiastes xii, 6: "Or ever the silver cord be loosed. . . ."

"The doctors say that there is a cord that runs from the nape of the neck, down the backbone, through the small of the back, into the heart, right thar; and that when a man dies that cord always snaps: That is the silver cord loosed."

"Ah," said a sister, her face radiant with delight, "Brother P— has studied *that*."

The delivery of a written sermon was little short of a disgrace. Old Peter Cartwright said that "it made him think of a gosling that had got the straddles by wading in the dew." Some of the ministers of the Disciples of Christ were alarmed because they felt their brethren studied the Bible too much. One of these Bible students on his way to meeting was joined by one of the fearful, who told him he hated to see him take the Bible to church. When asked why, he said he was afraid someone would think he was going to preach from it.

Strong lungs, vigorous gestures, copious tears, a ready flow of language, and an ability to describe in picturesque language the horrors of a literal, eternal, burning hell and the joys and bliss of a home in the Heavenly Canaan were the chief stores of ordnance in the backwoods minister's arsenal. And yet his message was powerful. He spoke in the common language of the people and seasoned it with illustrations familiar to all.

[10] Walter B. Posey: "The Frontier Baptist Ministry," East Tennessee Historical Society's *Publications*, No. 14, pp. 5–6.

The itinerants rode good horses. Some whispered that they could even hold their own in a horse trade. A sheep-skin blanket hung down on the horse, and across the saddle were hung the saddlebags, containing the preacher's library, study, writing materials, wardrobe, laundry, and barber shop. Behind him was strapped a blanket for a bed and an umbrella for sun or rain. The stirrups were faced around and lined with sheepskin to keep his feet warm.[11] He wore a cheap cloth cap or hat, a coat of coarse material, hip trousers of colored jeans, and a rough coarse shirt. Leggings and an overcoat protected him from the cold and the splattering mud of the bottomless roads. When these men went to attend conference, however, they dressed up in white shirts and clerical suits of black.

During a sermon, when the preacher warmed up to his subject he took off his long coat and hung it on a peg behind the pulpit, rolled up his sleeves, spit in his hands, rubbed them together, and clapped them until the woods rang. At the height of his effort he often unbuttoned the collar of his shirt.

In season and out the itinerant had his schedule to make even though it was too stormy for ordinary folk to be out. Rarely did he fail to meet an appointment. There was a saying when it was very sleety or stormy: "This is circuit rider's weather."

When Bishop Asbury traveled to Kentucky, the old general got a taste of the lot of the rank and file of his army. He wrote in his journal that among other trials he had "taken the itch; and considering the filthy houses and filthy beds . . . it is perhaps strange I have not caught it twenty times." Later he wrote: "Oh, the rocks, hills, ruts and stumps! My bones, my bones!"

The route of the itinerant was often through uninhabited country and he spread his blanket on the moss at the foot

[11] Emmie Martin Hunt: "Old Clay Bank Church," *Alabama History Quarterly*, I, 433.

of a tree, arranged his saddle for a pillow, and slept beneath the stars. At four he was stirring. First he knelt in prayer, then rubbed down his horse. As soon as it was light enough, he took the Bible from his saddlebags and studied it before starting. By noon perhaps he reached his appointment.

Sometimes an Indian arrow or tomahawk laid low the man of God. In 1794 on the road from Kentucky to Tennessee two Baptists ministers were ambushed by the Indians and killed while traveling with a group.

Singular as were these "brush preachers," they did not quail at the duty of thundering out against sin in its various forms. They blasted dueling, drunkenness, dishonesty, immorality, and worldliness in general. Their lives of sacrifice bore fruit in the experiences of their congregations, who appreciated their labors.

XVIII

The Great Revival

THE Great Revival of 1800 and its attendant institution, the camp-meeting, were pure products of the frontier of the Old Southwest. Although accounts vary, camp-meetings seem to have been started two or three years previously in various places in a small way. In the summer of 1800 in the Cumberland country of southwestern Kentucky they appeared in full bloom.

At the sacramental solemnities of a Presbyterian church on the circuit of the Reverend James M'Gready, two brothers named John and William McGee, one a Methodist and the other a Presbyterian minister, were in attendance. The two brothers preached, and such a stirring experience followed that when the time came for the next meeting the ministers appointed to preach were unable to do so. There were cries and sobs all over the house and excitement indescribable. The inhabitants round about, on hearing of the stirring times, flocked in in such numbers that the church house was unable to accommodate the crowd. The people were so anxious about their salvation that these woodsmen soon cleared out the underbrush, felled the pine trees for pews, improvised a platform of poles, and erected an altar in the forest. After enjoying the spiritual refreshing, the people did not want to go home, and while some went foraging for provisions, others began the erection of temporary abodes made of poles and boughs. Such bedding as had been brought was used to improvise tents. Near-by farms were visited to secure straw for beds. This gave the meeting a new impulse; others flocked in bringing camp equipage. People came fifty to one hundred miles in carriages and wagons and on horseback. The meeting lasted several days in spite of the fact that it was harvest time. The movement soon swept beyond the borders of Kentucky into the neighboring states. These camp-meetings during the Great Revival were interdenominational, with the Presbyterians, Methodists, and Baptists taking the lead. Sectarianism was wiped away. Later the Presbyterians dropped the camp-meeting plan, leaving it to the Methodists and Baptists.

For some years previous to this, certain strange religious phenomena had cropped out at times. Now, with the gathering of great crowds and a general revival sweeping the whole region, these spiritual "exercises" burst into full flower. The "falling exercise" appeared at the McGee meeting mentioned above.[1] In this experience the individual felt the constriction of the large blood vessels, a shortness of breath, an acceleration of breathing, and dropped prostrate. The hands and feet were cold. He lay from one to twenty-four hours. Upon returning to normal he was sometimes in a state of despair and felt he was such a sinner he could never be saved. More often he rejoiced that his sins were forgiven and immediately began to exhort others to give their lives to Christ. Timid people without apparent talent often showed great ability in praying and exhorting at that time. Scoffers and unbelievers as well as those seeking salvation were "struck down." Whole families at home, individuals in bed asleep, on the road, or plowing in the field, were stricken. Children at school where there were no religious exercises were seized. John McGee in speaking of it said: "The people

[1] Lawrence Edwards: "History of the Baptists of Tennessee with Particular Attention to the Primitive Baptists of East Tennessee," MS. (Master's thesis, University of Tennessee, 1941), p. 34.

fall before the word like corn before a storm of wind; and many rose from the dust with Divine glory shining in their countenances. . . ."

The next most common phenomenon was known as "the jerks." It was similar to the falling exercise in affecting all kinds of people everywhere. Like the falling exercise, it frequently fell upon people at meetings, but those far from the meetings were stricken. Elder Jacob Young said he had often seen ladies take it at the breakfast table as they were pouring tea or coffee. They would throw the whole up toward the ceiling, sometimes breaking both cup and saucer. As they left the table their heads would be so violently jerked that their braided hair, hanging down their backs, would crack like a whip. Witnesses say that some were taken up in the air, whirled over on their heads, coiled up so as to spin about like a cartwheel. They endeavored to grasp trees or saplings, but were carried headlong and helplessly on. J. B. Finley said that as many as five hundred of these subjects might be seen in one congregation in west Tennessee, bending the whole body first backward and then forward, the head nearly touching the ground forward and back alternately.

The Reverend Samuel Doak, an educated conservative Presbyterian of east Tennessee, went north on a visit about 1804, and when he returned was welcomed by a large assemblage to hear him preach. In the midst of a moving sermon, he was seized with a strange convulsion that made his limbs jerk and twist. He soon began to jump and finally went jerking and rolling off the platform down the hill while his congregation stood awe-stricken. After a while he finished his sermon, but he continued to jerk more or less for some time.

Lorenzo Dow had heard of the strange doings in Tennessee and said that he, like the Queen of Sheba, went to see for himself and found it was the real thing. Large numbers in his audience had the jerks. He said he had seen Presbyterians, Methodists, Quakers, Baptists, Church of England members, and Independents, black and white, rich and poor, aged and young, affected. As Elder Dow passed a camp-meeting site he noticed from fifty to one hundred saplings cut off about breast-high. This seemed a slovenly way to clear an area and he asked the cause. When informed that they were left for people to jerk on, he went to see and found the people had laid hold and jerked so powerfully that they had kicked up the earth like a horse stamping flies.[2]

In the "barking exercise" the victim would bark like a dog as he chased the devil. One who saw this said the person affected jerked, foamed at the mouth, rolled into a hog wallow, and then rose and with arms uplifted began to bark as he took the trail through the woods. Half a mile off he found a creek and, still barking, stopped at a tree, placed his hands on it, and looking up exclaimed: "I have treed the devil."

Sometimes a whole congregation would be thrown into side-splitting convulsions of laughter. When it got started in an audience, everybody would be seized with hearty natural laughter. It would last for hours sometimes. This was known as the "holy laugh." The "holy dance" was probably a variation of "the jerks" and was ungovernable until it ran its course.[3]

In some instances children ten years of age mounted a log and preached with eloquence and the wisdom of the learned.

Some, while lying on the ground as a result of the exercises, had visions and, on regaining their normal composure, told of having been taken to heaven, of the delightful scenes there and whom they saw. Others brought back reports of a trip to hell with its horrors. While in this supernatural state

[2] Lorenzo Dow: *History of Cosmopolite* (place of publication not given, 1848), pp. 181–4.
[3] Srygley: *Seventy Years in Dixie*, pp. 219–22; Moore: *History of Alabama*, pp. 153–4.

they were able to do astonishing feats. Many of these phenomena kept popping up on the frontier for the next third of a century and were carried into the new territories and states. The "holy dance" and other ecstasies appeared among both white and black worshippers in Alabama and Mississippi as late as 1835.

As a frontier institution the camp-meeting developed a standard pattern during the first few years of the nineteenth century. A forest area was selected near a sparkling stream with plenty of shade and grass for the hundreds of horses. A large square clearing was made and over this was constructed an immense brush arbor or, as a camp-ground became permanent, a long shed covered with clapboards. The logs were laid end to end in rows lengthwise, and rough slabs, split from other logs with wedges, were laid across these in tiers the full length of the arbor. At one end was a high platform, known as "the pulpit-stand," made of poles or poles and slabs. At the foot of the stand was a straw-floored enclosure about thirty feet square, known as "the altar" or "penitent's pen." A rail fence was built down the center of the arbor to separate the men from the women.

Forming a quadrangle or large ellipse of about two acres including the arbor, and some distance from it, were the dwelling-places of the worshippers. These were called "the tents," although in a permanent camp they were often pole pens covered with clapboards. Many, however, were tents made of tow, or improvised tents made by stretching quilts, sheets, and counterpanes around and over crude pole frames. On the fourth side of the quadrangle, behind the pulpit-stand, were the dwelling-places of the ministers. The women cooked with Dutch ovens, pots, and skillets around fires in the open air and served the meals on long clapboard scaffolds. At night the grounds were lighted by pine-knot fires built on wooden altars covered with dirt or flat rocks. As roads were improved enough to permit vehicles, many people came in covered wagons, which were their home for the following few days. The underbrush was cleared for a great area around, permitting retirement for secret prayer. The men went one way and the women in the opposite direction.

Hundreds of horses fed in the area adjacent to the camp, and long rows of light vehicles were collected. At night ladies were not allowed to go beyond the lighted area of the camp.

The day's program was regulated by the blowing of a cow's horn or tin trumpet. There were prayers at the general assembly before breakfast. After breakfast there ensued an hour of secret prayer in the woods. At ten and two were general meetings. At four came another hour of secret prayer in the woods. The big meeting of the day was at candle-lighting time in the arbor. It did not often adjourn until after midnight and during stirring times lasted until broad daylight.

The night meeting was picturesque, with the deep shadows of the primeval forest lighted up by lurid flames which cast a glare on the earnest ministers and their vast congregation. This scene, with its background of the majestic forest, presented an imposing effect. In this setting the great throng worshipped in a primitive way.

The meeting in the early evening proceeded with a good degree of decorum, but as the night progressed, wilder and wilder became the disorder. As the minister began to warm up to his subject, which itself was often a hot one—an eternal burning hell in which the wicked were suffering—people began to respond. So realistically was the destiny of sinners portrayed that the listeners could fairly feel its scorching breath and smell its brimstone.

In 1820 James Flint listened at a distance to a meeting and noted that female voices mournfully predominated. His imagination pictured to him a multitude of mothers, widows, and sisters giving the first vent to their grief in bewailing the loss of a male population by shipwreck, war, or some other great catastrophe. When the call for penitents was made, sinners pushed forward until the pen was filled with those seeking forgiveness. Then ensued in that enclosure the greatest confusion—shouting, screaming, leaping, jerking, clapping of hands, falling, and swooning away. Ministers and other workers stood by and urged those under conviction to "come through." Flint stood close by the fence in an effort to discern the words spoken by those *exercised* in the pen, but out of the confusion could catch only a word now and then: "Glory! Glory! Power," "Jesus Christ," and other groans and exclamations.[4] Thus the wild confusion continued, many times until daybreak. Between meetings in the large assembly the same sort of work for sinners and the same sort of exercises took place in the living-quarters.

So popular was the movement that everybody came. Although the primary objective was religious, the curious were there too. The ambitious and influential attended, for public opinion was all-powerful on the frontier and their presence was demanded in order for them to hold and extend their influence. Aspirants for office were there to gain popularity and electioneer in a quiet way. Young ladies were there to show themselves and their costumes. The young men went to see the girls and frolic in a quiet way. Couples promenaded about the camp-ground between meetings. It was an enjoyable social season as the long isolated frontiersmen met together for a time in the warmth of Christian fellowship.

Unfortunately some unconverted ones almost always caused trouble for the campers. These "rowdies," as they were termed, would fortify themselves with whisky illicitly obtained somewhere near by. They engaged in all sorts of devilment, from pranks down to riotous conduct and stealing horses and rigs. It was necessary to post a line of sentries around the quadrangle and sometimes the ministers slept on their arms, so to speak, by keeping clubs at hand in order to be able to rush out in the night as a sort of auxiliary police

[4] James Flint: *Letters from America* (Edinburgh, 1822), p. 231.

force to assist in clearing the grounds of evil-doers. Peter Cartwright had many an adventure with rowdies. Once he captured the whisky that they were drinking and thus dried up the mischief at its source. Another time he gained the victory by strategy. He appointed the leader of the rowdies captain of the camp guard. On still another occasion, when a timid officer feared to arrest a whisky-seller, Cartwright got the sheriff to appoint him and four other preachers as bold as himself a posse to arrest the trouble-makers. They took the culprit and never left him until he had paid a fine and costs. When the rowdies in retaliation attempted to rout the preachers from their quarters at night, he drove off one of their leaders by hitting him a violent blow with a "chunk of fire" and another a blow on the head that drove out his "dispensation of mischief." One rowdy leader was "struck down" by an unseen hand just as he came up quietly to hang a necklace of frogs around a preacher's neck, and he got up a converted man.[5]

The Great Revival reached its crest with the tremendous camp-meeting at Cane Ridge in Bourbon County, Kentucky. A vast crowd variously estimated at from twelve to twenty-five thousand gathered. That vast sea of human beings seemed agitated as by a storm. The noise was like that of a giant waterfall. Hundreds were swept down in a moment as though batteries had swept the crowd with grape-shot, and then followed shrieks and shouts that fairly rent the very heavens. It was estimated that three thousand fell at that meeting. The congregation was so large that it had to be split up, and twenty-six ministers occupied various improvised pulpits such as stumps, fallen trees, and wagons as they each preached to good-sized groups.[6]

The Cane Ridge meeting lasted seventeen days. Later

[5] William Henry Milburn: *The Pioneers, Preachers and People of the Mississippi Valley* (New York, 1860), pp. 383-4.
[6] Staples: "Pioneer Kentucky Preachers and Pulpits," *Filson Club History Quarterly*, IX, 154; W. P. Strickland (ed.): *The Backwoods Preacher, an Autobiography of Peter Cartwright* (London, 1858), p. 9.

camp-meetings usually lasted from four to ten days. At the close of the meeting it was customary to gather for a final blessing where so many had been enjoyed. Then with tears, benedictions, hearty handshakes, and fond embraces the worshippers took their way homeward.

There was a wide difference of opinion as to the Great Revival and camp-meetings that sprang from it. Many felt that the meetings and the exercises that accompanied them were of the devil. As an overview from the vantage point of several years' observation, perhaps the evaluation of Timothy Flint sums up the situation as well as any. Flint, a Harvard graduate, had little sympathy for camp-meetings on principle at first, but said of them:

> Notwithstanding all that has been said in derision of these spectacles so common in this region, it cannot be denied, that their influence, on the whole, is salutary, and the general bearing upon the great interests of the community, good. . . . Whatever be the cause, the effect is certain, that . . . these excitements have produced a palpable change in the manners and habits of the people.[7]

Protracted meetings were another form of meeting that became especially popular in Alabama and Mississippi in the thirties. These lasted from three to thirty evenings and were attended by black and white alike. Often among the Baptists several ministers in a given region would club together and help each other in their meetings, itinerating to the various churches and holding the meetings in a group.

The basket meeting was a week-end meeting similar in some ways to the camp-meeting. A stand and seats were arranged in the forest. The minister hung his saddlebags across the board used as a pulpit and preached from this piece of crude wilderness furniture. After meeting, the baskets were opened and the congregation ate in relays. That evening the near-by cabins arranged to keep the guests overnight.

[7] James Stuart: *Three Years in North America* (New York, 1833), II, 176.

XIX

Travel and Accommodations

FOR the first few years the narrow traces were mere aisles through the forest, with here and there forks that would have misled the traveler had the trace not been blazed by chopping certain marks on every fifth or sixth tree. Such roads, of course, were fit only for foot or horseback travel. The most famous of these trails were the Wilderness Trail, beginning in northeastern Tennessee and running through Cumberland Gap out onto the blue-grass area of Kentucky; the Cumberland Road, from the eastern Tennessee settlements to the bend of the Cumberland River at Nashville; the Federal Road, running from Georgia to Natchez, Mississippi; [1] the Natchez Trace, from Natchez to Nashville; and the Military Road, from Memphis to Fort Smith.

Some of these traces were used for years as mere horseback trails. For example, not a wagon passed over the Wilderness Road for twenty years after Daniel Boone laid it out. So wild and dangerous was this road that travelers did not dare travel alone. The following advertisement in the *Kentucky Gazette* explains the method of rendezvous for those going east over the road:

[1] This was popularly known as the three-chopped way, from the triple blaze the surveyors used in marking the trees.

A large company will meet at the Crab Orchard the 24th of November . . . in order to start early the next day through the Wilderness. As it is very dangerous on account of the Indians, it is hoped each person will go well armed.[2]

Sometimes notices were posted on trees on various trails instead of being printed in newspapers.

Transportation on these traces was limited to pack-horse trains and express riders. The only mail system was by private carriage of letters or by special messengers, known as express riders, carrying government dispatches. Those who wished to send a letter sent it by someone going east; arrivals at the stations brought letters from friends in the East. It was customary for one who received a letter to carry to give a receipt promising to deliver it for a certain sum. Neighbors carried missives free.

The danger to express riders was great. Governor Blount of Tennessee wrote to James Robertson on March 8, 1794 that his last letter had been received stained with the blood of James Russell, who was attacked by Indians eighteen miles from Southwest Point. Governor Blount well remarked that his fifty dollars for carrying the message from Nashville to Knoxville had been dearly earned. The next letter was delayed four days by the express rider's losing his horse at the Cumberland River.

By 1800 the mail was carried by horseback over the Natchez Trace. John Lee Swaney, who carried the mail, left Nashville Saturday night at eight and in ten days and four hours the mail was due in Natchez, 550 miles away.[3] He rode a big horse, carried half a bushel of corn for his horse, provisions for himself, an overcoat and blanket, and a tin trumpet to blow at the way stations. Friendly Indians kept places of accommodation along the trace where he could stay except for one night when he had to lie out in the woods.

[2] *Kentucky Gazette*, November 8, 1788.
[3] The distance was shortened as the road was improved.

There was always much complaint about the slowness of the mail. Boatmen traveling on foot from Natchez to Nashville wagered they could beat the post to the end of the line. On some lines there was so much mail the rider had to lead a pack horse in order to carry all of it. The editor of the *Arkansas Gazette* in the issue of February 5, 1820 complained that no mail had been received at Little Rock for nearly five weeks, although fortnightly mail had been promised in place of the previous monthly post. In Arkansas when the water was low in summer, the beds of streams were often used as roads.

As the amount of mail increased, it became necessary to carry it in vehicles. This necessitated improved roads. They were widened and bridges or ferries put in. Even these were not very good, although perhaps the main roads were not so primitive as the contract for a road from Potosi to Osage, Missouri, would indicate. This road was to be cut twelve feet wide, with no stumps left over eight inches high! The frequency with which a vehicle got hung up on a stump gave rise to the expression: "I'm stumped," meaning nonplussed.

Earlier vehicles had four benches on a level, no back support, and the entrance in front as in a railway coach. The passengers on the back bench had to crawl over three to get to their places.

Later vehicles were the familiar Concord coaches, for which Concord, New Hampshire, in renowned. There were three benches inside. The middle one was provided with a broad strap as a back support. The passengers on the front and back seats had more comfortable back rests. They faced in and leaned against the front and back of the vehicle. The center seat was most uncomfortable. Three passengers rode on each of the inside seats, and occasionally an outside passenger rode with the driver on an elevated seat on the front of the coach. The good seat was given to a lady passenger, and her husband was given the place beside her. Three large leather curtains suspended from the roof could be rolled up or lowered at the pleasure of the passengers. There was no place for baggage. Each person was expected to stow away his things any way he could under his legs or his seat. In riding over a rough road, owing to stumps or chuckholes, the passengers were often obliged to throw all their weight toward one side or the other to balance the vehicle and keep it upright. Sometimes, even on a dark, rainy night, the men were obliged to get out and walk long distances through mud and water.

In 1834 Tyrone Power took a trip from Georgia to Montgomery, Alabama. On the last stretch of the journey he was almost constantly on foot from midnight until daylight. The driver in one or two instances refused to go on until even the one woman passenger got out and waded through the mud, which was frequently over knee-deep. They arrived at Montgomery at six in the morning, having completed a journey of ninety miles in thirty-two hours, and Power felt he had paid well to be permitted to help get the mail bags through roads that for the next few days, he said, were utterly impassable.[4]

James Davidson gloomily wrote in his diary as he started on his journey from Alabama back to his home in old Virginia:

> But I am now to venture upon the perils of stage travelling —cracked skulls—broken bones—dislocated shoulders . . . loss of sleep—hard jolts—rough fare—upset stages—mud —wind and cold are to be my portion for the next ten days.[5]

Charles Dickens said of riding across the country north of the Ohio River:

> As night came on, the track grew narrower and narrower, until at last it so lost itself among the trees, that the driver

[4] Tyrone Power: *Impressions of America* (Philadelphia, 1836), pp. 99–100.

[5] "Diary of James D. Davidson," November 30, 1836, *Journal of Southern History*, I, 370.

seemed to find his way by instinct. . . . Every now and then the wheel would strike against an unseen stump and with such a jerk, that he was fain to hold on pretty tight and pretty quick, to keep himself upon the box.

At times it was so muddy, as an Arkansawyer put it, that "a buzzard would mire down in its own shadow." In Mississippi when the mud got so deep it was impossible for coaches to move, the driver, who was duty bound to see that the mail went through, fastened a big deep box on the axle of the front wheels of a wagon running-gear, put the mail in the box, and stood in it himself while he drove four big horses.

The stagecoach got its name from the fact that a change of horses was made at regular distances. The drive of one team was known as a stage.

The coach-driver was a grand figure, a hero to all the boys and girls, for did not he fly out of the domain of their common everyday surroundings and into the enchanted land where only their imagination could wander? He was known by everyone, old and young. He was the radio and newspaper of his time, collecting news at all the stations along the line and broadcasting it at all of them. Some observers described him as a cocky, cursing individual, not very sympathetic to foreigners. Others called him obliging, accommodating, light-hearted, rollicking, but given to quips and jokes on a fit subject among his passengers.

A writer in mentioning the arrival of the stage at New Albany, Mississippi, described the driver as sitting on the front boot of the coach with four lines in his left hand and his whip with a twelve-foot lash in his right. He came every other day at noon. As the blast of his musical trumpet sounded at some distance, "the hands" would be seen coming from every direction to the little post office in a corner of the general store. Large numbers of others had gathered. With this inspiring surrounding of spectators, the driver-actor was at his best. Some fifty yards before reaching the post office, with a flourish of the whip, he began his triumphal entry and, dashing up, suddenly drew on the reins, put on the brakes, locked the hind wheels, and the huge vehicle slid in to a stop. Everyone deemed it an honor to claim acquaintance with that great person. Some shook his hand, exchanged a jocular remark with him, or escorted him to the tavern for a drink. Other spectators, not so fortunate, stood agape or gathered about the coach and horses, passing judgment on the equipment. When a new coach, painted shining red or yellow, was put on the line, it was a topic of conversation until all had inspected it. After a ten-minute stop while fresh horses replaced his jaded ones, the hero of the lines mounted his throne, flourished his whip, and sped on his way.

About 1840 an "express mail" was established between New York and New Orleans. Letters, printed clippings of news, prices of goods, and other things of sufficient importance to warrant the extra expense were sent by this method. It was the forerunner of the later more famous pony express across the plains to California. A relay of horses was posted all the way at intervals of four miles. Five hundred horses were kept in readiness or were on the road constantly. Each boy rode twenty-four miles, twelve each way. He galloped the whole way and made a speed of fifteen miles per hour, including all stops.

Only along the mail routes and in the cities and towns were houses of entertainment to be found. Before 1800 such a house was known as an "ordinary," inn, or tavern. Gradually the first two terms were dropped, and by 1825 the last was beginning to pass into oblivion. In time, particularly in the cities, the term "hotel" or "house" came in. Usually when the latter term was used, the keeper's name was prefixed. Now and then more originality was shown. The first tavern in Pacific, Missouri, was called Buzzard's Roost. The term "stand" was also used for a tavern along the stage lines. In earlier years the larger taverns had a tall post with a sign giving the name of the place swinging from a crossarm. A bell on a post was rung at meal time, and a mounting block enabled travelers to get on their horses more readily.

When the traveler had given his horse to the slave who cared for the horses, he went to the well in the back yard, where another servant was in attendance. Here water was poured either from a gourd over his hands or into a basin for his use. Sometimes a dozen guests used the same towel. In Harrisonville, Illinois, in 1818, a typical tavern was offered for sale. It was advertised as consisting of "the house containing Four commodious Rooms, a Kitchen, Smoke-House, Corncrib and a stable, and a garden. . . ." Of these four rooms, one was the dining-room, a second the barroom, and the other two bedrooms. A minister upon entering the dining-room of such a tavern at Alton found that the table was made of rough, newly sawed boards resting on forked posts driven into the ground. An old cloth, filthy like the rest of the establishment, covered part of the table. The other part was occupied by three men who were playing with dirty cards.

At Louisville, Kentucky, a visitor found that in the barroom about six men had gathered around the fireplace and shut all others away from its warmth. Others paced the floor like a commodore walking the deck at sea. The men smoked cigars at every hour of the day, and spirited discussions of politics took place. In Alabama a visitor noted that the men leaned back in their chairs, placed their feet against the sides of the fireplace at a point as high as their heads, and amused themselves by spitting into the fire incessantly. In Louisville there was a large tub of water on the bar with a ladle in it. When a customer wanted a drink of water he helped himself. If he wanted a stronger draught he called for spirits, and a decanter and a small glass were placed on the bar. The customer would then pour out what he wanted, drink it, and wash the spirits down with a ladle of water. He was charged half a bit each time he served himself, no matter how little or how much. The barkeeper watched to see how many times he helped himself.

Bath and toilet facilities were almost nonexistent. Frederick Law Olmsted, finding no toilet facilities at the "principal hotel" in Jackson, Mississippi, in 1856, on inquiring was advised by the landlord himself to go to a cypress swamp perhaps a quarter of a mile distant.

The guest rarely found more than one sheet on his bed, and it was soiled unless he happened to arrive at the first of the week. Fortunately sheets were often made of checked blue cotton goods and did not show the dirt so much as bleached muslin. Olmsted bribed a servant to change the soiled sheets and greasy pillow on his bed, but noticed a little later that a gentleman with embroidered waistcoat took the next bed, soiled as it was, with no reluctance.[6]

At this time such a thing as a nightshirt was unheard of on the frontier. Men slipped off their trousers and boots and retired—very much as they slept around the campfire—without removing their shirts. Neither innkeeper nor traveler knew of any other custom. Just before James Whitcomb was elected Governor of Indiana he with a group of fellow lawyers stayed overnight at a tavern kept by Captain Berry of Andersontown, Indiana. Berry was inordinately proud of the cleanliness of his establishment. Whitcomb had somewhere learned of the refinements of a nightshirt and used one even on his travels. His rollicking friends of the bar slyly poked fun at his odd ideas and decided to play a trick on the tavern-keeper, using Whitcomb's idiosyncrasy as its basis. They accordingly approached the doughty landlord and whispered to him that Whitcomb on a prior visit had formed a very poor impression of the cleanliness of the sheets on the beds of Berry's hostel. They further let him in

[6] Frederick Law Olmsted: *A Journey in the Back Country* (New York, 1860), p. 17.

on the secret that their comrade had brought with him a special shirt that he planned to wear to bed to keep from soiling his shirt.

Berry refused to believe that his guest could be so rude and unappreciative, but the rogues insisted it was true and suggested that he watch Whitcomb prepare for bed. When Whitcomb went to the bedroom the landlord spied on him. Sure enough, his guest actually took off his shirt and put on a longer one, as though to protect himself from the bed. The impossible story, then, was true! In a fury the captain burst into the room, sprang upon Whitcomb, bore him to the floor, and was about to inflict dire punishment on the rascal who dared cast such undeserved reflection on his institution. The pranksters waiting around the corner rushed up to prevent injury to their fellow traveler and, amid roars of laughter, confessed that the whole story was a hoax.

Of all the faults European travelers found with America, one of the most displeasing was the lack of privacy in sleeping-arrangements. The bedrooms had from four to a dozen double beds in them. When a guest asked for accommodations he was charged for a night's lodging and not for a room or even a bed. When he retired, there might not be another person in the room, but perhaps several times during the night guests arrived and noisily went to bed in the room where he was attempting to sleep. If he was not too light a sleeper he might wake up in the morning to find an utter stranger in bed with him. Sir Charles Lyell on a visit to America one time coaxed the host to allow him to sleep by himself. He felt almost ashamed to see before morning three men crowd into the bed next to him. When Francis Bailey complained of a stranger's being put to bed with him at the best tavern in Nashville, in 1797, he was immediately silenced by the all-powerful argument that it was the custom of the country and that there was no way to remedy it.

Sometimes tipsy or dishonest people went into one of these establishments and went to bed without paying. In order to check this, David Rorer, of Arkansas, made a practice of going around the big guest room and jerking the covers from off the faces of the sleepers to see who they were. Women especially objected to this.

As a result of frontier tavern practices bedbugs, lice, and the itch multiplied and spread to an alarming extent.

When the dinner bell rang, there was a general rush into the dining-room, where with the greatest haste and without a semblance of table etiquette or conversation the crowd bolted their food, licked their knives, and without excusing themselves retired to the barroom to smoke and spit tobacco juice.

Mrs. Basil Hall upon eating at a St. Louis tavern, in 1828, wrote:

> An American breakfast or dinner never fails to remind me of the directions given of old for the eating of the passover, "With your loins girded, your shoes on your feet, and your staff in your hand; and ye shall eat it in haste"; and truly if the Israelites obeyed the command with a strictness equalling American speed it must have been a strange scene.[7]

Captain J. E. Alexander made a similar observation, in 1831, after eating at the principal inn at Nashville. When the bell rang, he said, the crowd rushed into a long hall like a squadron of cavalry charging the enemy. They found the tables covered with good things, and down the company sat in a hurry—noses were blown to one side, handkerchieves were spread on the knees, cuffs turned back, and then commenced "the crash of the crockery and the clash of the steel." No ceremony was used; each man helped himself with his own knife and fork, and reached across his neighbor to secure a fancied *morceau.* Bones were picked with both hands; knives were drawn through the teeth with the edge to the lips. Some rushed through and, wiping their mouths with the heels of their hands, got up and left without

[7] Mrs. Basil Hall: *The Aristocratic Journey* (New York, 1931), p. 275.

excusing themselves. The rest continued to choke the food down as if it were their last meal. On going into the barroom after they had finished, Captain Alexander found those who had been in such a hurry lounging about with their hands in their pockets.[8]

Charles Dickens ordered "wheat-bread and chicken fixings" in preference to "corn-bread and common doings." The latter included only pork and bacon while the former included hams, veal cutlets, sausages, steaks, and other savory foods to accompany the fried chicken.

The traveler was at liberty to do his own baking or cooking at a tavern instead of eating his meals at the tavern table. If a traveler did his own cooking, the price of lodging was only six to ten cents, according to a German immigrant in Missouri. The price of each meal was twenty-five cents.

[8] Captain J. E. Alexander: *Trans-Atlantic Sketches* (London, 1833), p. 269.

XX

Sickness and Death

THE frontiersman, because of his frugal diet and his outdoor life with its exercise and fresh air, escaped many of the ailments that accompany the more modern and less natural life. These very conditions, however, together with the lack of knowledge of hygiene and the primitive state of medical science, brought about a great many ills and diseases that are almost unknown or easily controlled today. In spite of the claims of people who looked back from the comfortable circumstances of old age into a dimming but ever more glowing, rosy past, it can safely be asserted that the health of the pioneers was far below that of their great-great-grandchildren of a century later. To a large degree the picture of the pioneer as a sturdy, robust character must be exchanged for that of an emaciated one often sick, and dying before old age as a result of early privations.

In the earliest days there were few doctors on the frontier. The settlers doctored themselves or sometimes secured the services of Indian doctors. Women were the first medical practitioners. In every community there was an old woman who doctored with the aid of herbs (pronounced *yarbs* in the lower South), poultices, roots, and other simple remedies that she had acquired personally or that were a part of her racial tradition. In some instances conjurers were called in to drive out the evil causing the illness. Hardly a practitioner was a doctor among the very earliest transmontane settlers. Even afterward people doctored themselves until they saw the situation was entirely beyond their control. When a physician was called, the case was thought to be serious. When the patient was confined to his bed the neighbors came, inquired about the sick one, and offered their help. When he became worse, "watchers" stayed with him day and night. There was never lack of neighbors to relieve one another. Thus the nursing was taken care of without cost to the family. Rough awkward woodsmen under such circumstances showed every consideration and the utmost patience. This practical sympathy, although very comforting to the relatives, was often carried to extremes and was harmful to the patient. Visitors frequently went in and out the whole livelong day inquiring, expressing best wishes, and showing sympathy. This closing and opening of doors, whispering, and tiptoeing kept up a ceaseless confusion in the little log cabin, which deprived the patient of life-giving quiet and rest.

At the siege of Boonesborough Squire Boone received a bullet in the shoulder. His wife examined him, pronounced it a minor wound, and he went back to his porthole. The painfulness of the festering wound, however, forced him to his bed, beside which he placed his favorite broadax in readiness for what he termed "the last action," should it be needed. At this time there came a short lull in the fighting and Daniel hastened to his brother's aid. He opened the wound with his hunting knife and took out the bullet, which had lodged against the shoulder bone. Squire courageously withstood the ordeal with no other anesthetic than a fighting heart and a courageous spirit.[1] Three years later Squire was wounded three times in an Indian attack and suffered a

[1] Willard Rouse Jillson: "Squire Boone," *Filson Club History Quarterly*, XVI, 154.

broken arm. Roughly set by amateurs, when it was healed the arm was an inch and a half shorter than the other.

When James Smith was out on an exploring expedition to Kentucky in 1766 he stabbed his foot on a sharp cane stub. The cane remained in his foot, causing his whole leg to swell. There he was, hundreds of miles from any medical aid, attended only by a mulatto servant. He determined to take the snag out. He had no instruments except a moccasin awl, a bullet mold, and his hunting knife. He stuck the awl in the skin and with his hunting knife cut around the cane. The servant then pulled it out with the bullet molds. He then directed the black boy to get bark from the root of a lynn tree, beat it on a stone with a tomahawk, and boil it. He soaked his foot in this ooze and, in the absence of bandages, placed moss over the wound and wrapped it round with elm bark. The swelling abated and he and Jamie returned safely to old Virginia.

A home doctor book found in one or more homes in many frontier communities was Gunn's *Domestic Medicine*. This volume stated that any man, unless he was a fool or an idiot, could amputate an arm or leg, provided he had half a dozen men to hold the victim down.

Nearly everybody believed in the mad stone. One of these at Huntsville, Alabama, was described as about the size of a walnut and porous like a honeycomb. When a person was bit by a mad dog, he was immediately taken to the precious stone, which stuck fast when applied to the bite. When the pores became full of poison, so the belief ran, it dropped off. When washed in warm milk and water, the poison was leeched out and the stone would stick on the wound again until all the poison was extracted. Then it would drop off.

Some home remedies were novel indeed. John Sevier wrote down many cures that he learned from various sources. Hunters were often afflicted with rheumatism, which was thought to be a result of exposure. One of Sevier's remedies for this ailment read:

Take a handful of the inside bark of prickly ash about six inches long, the same quantity of red earth-worms, and about the same quantity of both those articles of the oil of hog's feet and stew all together until the worms are desolved [sic]. Strain out the sediment and anoint with the oil for rheumatism.

A simpler remedy was one composed of one part pokeberry juice and three parts whisky. No doubt this was intended to be taken internally.

Traveling on foot long hours in wet, muddy weather often caused scalded feet. Daniel Boone soaked his feet in an ooze made of oak bark as a remedy for this ailment.

The great scarcity of doctors in early times brought fortunes to the few practitioners. This encouraged a great influx of doctors and led many young men to choose the medical profession. By 1820 the field was crowded. Anne Royall reported that there had been fourteen doctors in Florence, Alabama, but that half of them left for lack of room. The same general situation obtained in that whole area, she said. Not only was the field crowded, but each practicing physician had three or four students, she asserted. While this may be somewhat overdrawn, the ease with which a man could become a doctor tended to overcrowd the profession.

In most states no license was necessary to practice and consequently no examination was required. The preceptoral system of training doctors was the regular procedure at that time. A young man served an apprenticeship under a practicing physician. He lived in the doctor's home, helped him with his medicines, went with him on calls, and at odd times was presumed to read medicine from his mentor's library. After this had gone on for an unspecified length of time, his preceptor gave him a letter of recommendation, stating that he felt his student was qualified to practice medicine. This was his diploma.

The famous Dr. Daniel Drake, without any more education than was to be secured in the village school, at the age of fifteen began his apprenticeship. He was nominally a student less than four years, and three of these it was his job to put up and deliver medicines over the village. These were compounded in the doctor's shop, corresponding to a pharmacy. At eighteen he began to practice. Later he took some lectures in the East by way of a postgraduate course.

Many took a short cut and, securing a doctor book or two, read up on the subject independent of a teacher. Gideon Lincecum, who was fourteen years old before he ever saw a school, attended a log school for only five months, learned to read, write, and spell, taught the same kind of school for one year, and within three years began to study medicine independently. Successively he was a store clerk, proprietor of a store, pioneer farmer, and town boomer. He finally became bankrupt while in the store business, got up a troupe of Indians, and exhibited them over the country, with no financial gain. Having continued to study medicine more or less independently for several years while in other business, he borrowed a hundred dollars, bought eighty dollars' worth of medicines, and began the practice of allopathic medicine. He began in August and by Christmas had repaid the hundred dollars and had three hundred dollars of good accounts on his books. The neighborhood pronounced it the biggest drug setup in the country and said that he must be a good doctor to know how to handle all that medicine. Eighteen months after starting practice he had collected two thousand dollars, a tidy sum in those days. Then he went and learned herb remedies from an Indian doctor and the steam system from a Thompsonian doctor. During seven years' practice in Columbus, Mississippi, ending in 1847, he "booked" fifty-one thousand dollars besides cash fees.

H. V. Wooten, educated in an Eastern college, found six doctors in Lowndesboro, Alabama, when he began to practice. At first he was nearly starved out, but at the end of a few years only two doctors were left. For the year 1840 his business amounted to four thousand dollars.

After a few years the more progressive doctors began to attend a few series of lectures. These were given by medical colleges and ran for a term of from twelve to sixteen weeks during the winter. After attending a series of these and passing a final oral examination, the candidate received an M.D. degree. The right to use those magic letters after one's name was for years the only differentiation between the poorer-trained and the better-trained practitioners. As early as 1799 Transylvania University started the first medical school west of the Appalachian Mountains.

Naturally, it was easy for quacks to arise. And it was difficult for conscientious untrained practitioners to know which system to follow. Gideon Lincecum carried in one saddlebag allopathic or old-school remedies and in the other Thompsonian. He treated his patients by whichever system they chose.

In line with all medical practice, frontier medicine was just emerging from the barbarous superstitions of the past. Bleeding was a popular remedy up to almost the middle of the nineteenth century. On August 23, 1806 John Shaw, a well-digger at Knoblick, Kentucky, was "blown up" as a result of a premature powder discharge in a well. The man sent down in the well to assist him saw his brain oozing out and called up that it was not worth while to take him out, for he was dead. His skull was fractured, and several small pieces of bone were lifted out and removed, his right shin bone was battered, his left arm fractured in one place, his right in two places, two fingers were blown off, the skin on his face and chest was cut and bruised, and his eye cut. His torn face was so covered with powder, dirt, and blood that it was impossible to recognize him. The doctor said that he was mangled beyond anyone he had ever seen, but in spite of this the doctor, who according to Shaw was a skilled physician, bled him sixteen times in ten hours. The patient must have had an iron constitution, for in spite of this treatment he was on the road to recovery shortly.[2]

The most universal and ever present disease, which is now known as malaria, was called intermittent fever, congestive fever, the ague, or bilious fever. It began with a chill, which called for every blanket obtainable. An hour or two of teeth-chattering chills was succeeded by fever, a terrible headache, and delirium of some hours. A devitalizing sweat followed. The patient then enjoyed a temporary recovery, only to have the experience repeated on the first, second, or third day following. It was said that in some sections when a person was invited out to dinner on a particular day, Wednesday for example, it was not uncommon for him to start reckoning: "Monday, Tuesday, Wednesday—no; I cannot come Wednesday, for that is my fever day."

In certain areas almost every person had a sallow or pale-yellow complexion without the slightest tint of healthful bloom. The common treatment consisted in completely depleting the body by copious bleeding, sweating, vomiting by powerful emetic, purging with calomel and other drastic cathartic drugs. Then when the fever abated (called an intermission), the doctor gave what we now know to be the best treatment for the disease—quinine. In addition to the other remedies some practitioners blistered the neck and the feet with mustard. A Louisiana physician wrote to Dr. Drake that in a certain epidemic he had drawn "blood enough to float and given calomel enough to freight the steamboat *General Jackson*." [3]

The sheer ignorance of many practitioners is illustrated by the Missouri physician who treated a certain child. It was evident that the child was dying. The doctor was at his wits'

[2] John Robert Shaw: *A Narrative of the Life and Travels of John Robert Shaw* (Louisville, 1930), pp. 190, 198–200.
[3] Daniel Drake: *A Systematic Treatise, Historical Etiological, and Practical, on the Principal Diseases of the Interior Valley of North America*, etc. (Cincinnati, 1850), pp. 804–5.

end and, suddenly grabbing his little patient, he ran up and down the room, shaking it in the most merciless manner. When the mother remonstrated, asking him what he meant by such treatment, he said he "just wanted to make a final effort to put the blood in circulation again."

On the other side of the picture, there were a few frontier doctors, educated in the East or in Europe, who were progressive and made a contribution to the advance of medical science. As early as 1802 Dr. Samuel Brown, of Transylvania, vaccinated five hundred persons. Vaccination was being very generally adopted in Indiana by 1817.

In 1809 Dr. Ephraim McDowell, of Danville, Kentucky, first removed a tumor from the ovary of a woman. The operation, performed without anesthetic or antiseptics, was successful. Dr. McDowell also early performed operations removing stones from the bladder. In twenty-eight operations he did not lose a patient. One of these cases was James K. Polk, later President of the United States.

As early as 1776 Dr. Patrick Vance discovered a treatment to restore the scalp when a person had been scalped. His treatment consisted in boring holes about an inch apart through the bare bone of the pate with an awl. Reddish fluid appeared, and this was said to start healing. In about two years, it was said, skin covered the top of the skull.

When a person died, the neighbors "laid him out"; that is, washed and dressed the body in preparation for burial. Women cared for the bodies of their own sex. Friends sat up with the body if it was kept overnight. Bodies were not embalmed and burial took place within twenty-four hours after death.

While the body was being prepared for burial, other friends dug the grave. Often interment took place in a private burial plot on the family property. There were also community and church burial grounds.

In digging a grave a hole much larger than the coffin was made. When a depth of four feet was reached, the bottom was smoothed and leveled. Then a depression the exact size of the coffin, called a vault, was dug. Two pieces of wood were laid at the bottom of the vault, and as the casket was lowered, two men jumped down into the grave and guided it to its place. Then boards were laid over it and the dirt quietly thrown in.

The casket was made of cherry or walnut if boards were available. If not, among primitive settlements a log was sometimes hollowed out for a coffin and covered with clapboards.

An observer noted that at a Kentucky funeral the casket was carried on two rudely hewn sticks by four bearers. Then followed four or five relatives abreast. The bereaved widow followed on horseback, and after her the assembled crowd, twelve or fifteen abreast. The procession moved into a grove, forded a stream, and followed a path that turned into a cornfield. There on an eminence in the center of the field was the open grave. In the early days, especially among the hill people, a grave house was constructed over the grave to protect it from the elements and the grave robber. It was made of logs covered with shakes.[4]

The burial was accompanied by little ceremony, perhaps simply a prayer by a layman. The funeral took place several weeks or perhaps even a year afterward. The social code prohibited the bereaved from courting during the period between the burial and the funeral. Sometimes the exigencies of frontier life made it impossible to postpone a marriage over the long period occasioned by a long-delayed funeral. One woman married a second time one year after her first husband died. At the funeral of her first husband, some months after her second marriage, she was puzzled about what to wear. She could not bring herself to don mourning again and finally decided to wear the new black silk dress her second husband gave her for a wedding present. To make her costume fit the occasion she took the buttercups

[4] Clark: *The Kentucky*, p. 196.

off her bonnet and sewed on black strings from her mourning bonnet.

The funeral appointment was made with the itinerant minister and the whole countryside was notified. Often the deceased had made full plans for the funeral. Indeed, sometimes a choral group would practice funeral songs under the direction of the deceased-to-be.[5] A man often left messages for his friends that were to be used in the funeral sermon. The skillful minister could bring a powerful message appealing for a reformation in the lives of the listeners. Many attended a funeral simply to learn about the life of the deceased and to hear his communication to others. It took a skillful minister to keep from offending someone in preaching a funeral sermon. As Professor Albert Burton Moore well said, to say that a man was in hell offended his relatives and to say he was in heaven surprised his enemies, to say the least.

Necessary as a funeral was as a spiritual institution, it grew to be a great business event also. An old minister, clad in rough clothes, who had walked a long distance through the dust and heat, was asked by the minister in charge to sit on the platform and open the meeting. Before he "gave out the hymn" he paused to remark: "But while I'm before you, I want to say as how my main business over here is a huntin' of sum seed peas, an' if anybody here has got any to spar', I'd like to know it after meetin'."

Everybody came to a funeral—men, women, girls, boys, babies, and the dogs. Jockeys went to funerals to swap or run horses, sheriffs to summon jurors, serve warrants, or subpœna witnesses, the politician to electioneer, the road overseer to "warn hands," schoolteachers to "circulate articles" and organize schools, and others to advertise a log-rolling, corn-shucking, or house-raising.

[5] Srygley: *Seventy Years in Dixie*, pp. 202–3.

XXI

Frontier Justice

AN Alabama newspaper in castigating the fights and shameful barbarous deeds committed there boldly expressed the opinion that there were too many in the town who had left older and better-regulated states to escape the penitentiary and the gallows. The frontier habitually received more than its quota of undesirable citizens, who escaped to a land where the hand of the law was feeble. In addition to this was the fact that settlement proceeded far ahead of organized government. Then, too, there were few women and many men—a condition tending to promote a wild society, since it lacked the refining touch of womanhood.

The early Kentucky settlements were five hundred miles from the courts of the mother state, Virginia. In time, however, three counties were laid out and organized into a judicial district. At the first circuit-court term in Kentucky there were nine cases of persons selling liquor without a license and eight cases of adultery and fornication. Most of the early cases, however, were for debt or assault and battery.[1]

In the later part of the eighteenth century the cruel colonial punishments crossed the mountains with the settlers. A

[1] Circuit Court Order Book I, Pulaski County, Kentucky.

typical case in the eighties was that of James Fulsome and John Wilson at Jonesborough, Tennessee. Convicted of horse-thievery, they were sentenced to be confined in the public pillory for one hour, to have both their ears nailed to the pillory and severed from their heads, and to receive thirty-nine lashes upon their "bair" backs, well laid on. Each was to be branded upon his right cheek with an *H* and on the left with a *T*, and the sentence was to be carried out "this afternoon." [2]

As jails were built, these barbarous punishments disappeared. In fact, from the beginning the criminal laws were less severe west of the mountains than in the East. Whipping and hanging continued as common punishments, owing to the fact that the absence of jails made it impossible to incarcerate the criminal. Whipping was in vogue on the frontier as late as 1823. The scientist Nuttall noted that in 1819 the penalty for rape in Arkansas and Missouri was castration. People would come many miles to witness a hanging. Men, women, and children, whites and Negroes, enjoyed the gruesome spectacle just as they would a picnic or a barbecue.

On the raw frontier there was a decided tendency to settle cases by what was felt to be common sense and fairness without regard to law. For example, when a man returned after years of absence and found that his wife, believing him dead, had married another, the wife was allowed to choose between them. This was done without any thought that the decision was not in harmony with the law.

In an area where desperate characters abounded, only the most resolute could enforce the laws. In the country clerk's records at Paris, Kentucky, is to be seen a writ endorsed on the back: "Executed on Thos. Theobold, and he has not give security, because he run in a house and armed himself with a shot gun after the writ was served. George Mount-

[2] Miriam Fink: "Some Phases of the Social and Economic History of Jonesboro, Tennessee, Prior to the Civil War," MS. (Master's thesis, University of Tennessee, 1934), p. 17.

joy." The above endorsement is crossed out and beneath it is written: "Executed and broke custidy. George Mount-joy." [3]

But a region that produces desperate men fortunately bears also men of courage and action who do not flinch to do their duty. For some time after Parish Judge George S. Guion took over his duties in Concordia Parish, Louisiana, he felt obliged to go constantly armed on account of the turbulent times and lawless element infesting the region. By vigorous measures the lawless element was in time subdued.

When Andrew Jackson was sitting as a circuit judge at Jonesborough, Tennessee, Russell Bean, the first white man born in Tennessee, a lawless individual, had assaulted and beaten a man unmercifully. He had been indicted, but at the time the court met, the officers had been unable to arrest him. It was reported to the judge in open court that the offender was sitting in the door of his home with a rifle at his side and a brace of pistols in his lap, defying arrest and threatening to kill the first man who approached his house. Jackson immediately ordered the sheriff to bring Bean in dead or alive if he had to summon every man in the courthouse. The sheriff in an effort to turn the tables, responded: "Then I summon your honor first!" Jackson, with characteristic energy, jumped down from the bench, exclaiming: "By the Eternal, I'll bring him." With pistol in hand and the crowd at his heels, the fearless judge did bring the cowed prisoner in, and in a trice he transformed himself from sheriff to judge and fined the culprit heavily.

Even after arrest it was almost impossible to hold a prisoner until he was convicted. He had to be placed on horseback and guarded perhaps several days' journey to the seat of justice. Traveling along narrow traces and camping at night along the trail presented favorable opportunities for escape. And when they arrived at court there was often no

[3] William Henry Perrin: *The Pioneer Press of Kentucky* (Louisville, 1888), p. 36.

jail or the poorest excuse for one. In a western Georgia county there was no jail for twelve years. When a number of drunken men threatened the dignity of the court, these trouble-makers were thrown on the ground and a wagon box inverted over them until they had cooled off sufficiently to allow business to proceed. Behind the crude log court-house was usually a big rail stray pen and drunks were sometimes put into these pens to sober up. When one prisoner kept climbing out, the sheriff put the culprit's head between the top two rails and sat on the top one, forming an improvised pillory. Not until eight years after the first settlement was the first Kentucky jail built. At that time the population of the commonwealth was between twelve and fifteen thousand.

It was hard to find punishments to fit the crime. Jail sentences were difficult to carry out when there were no jails. In Indiana in order to execute a jail sentence the sheriff pried up the corner of a heavy rail fence, using a bee gum for a fulcrum and a rail for the lever. Two or three rails above the ground he made a crack. The prisoner's head was thrust through this and the fence lowered. In that manner the prisoner lay yelling and complaining while he served a three-hour jail sentence for flogging his wife.

The first courthouse in Conechu County, Alabama, was a typical seat of justice. It was a primitive log cabin with dirt floor. Across one end was a rough table, behind which sat the wearer of the ermine in all his democratic glory. The prisoners were kept in a jail thirty-five miles away and during the court session had to be guarded under the mighty trees of the forest. The members of the jury had to retire to the forest fastness under the watchful eye of the baliff, and there they could be seen sitting on logs whittling while coming to a decision on some weighty case.

Frontier court scenes gave the European a very unfavorable impression of democratic order. The judge sat on a rough platform, often balanced himself on the hind legs of an ordinary chair, with his head supported against the wall behind him. The lawyers were seated around a common table, most of them with their feet on it. They wrangled and disputed among themselves within the bar, the witnesses were impudent and contemptuous, the spectators—some sober and others drunk—took sides and laughed, talked, shouted, and not infrequently brawled and fought in the presence of the court. The whole scene was picturesque, and burlesque to one accustomed to Old World dignity and decorum.

One contemporary description pictured a court scene in which the witness on the stand, having been asked a question, said: "I say, mister, if you'll just hand me that there pitcher I'll take a drink, and then answer the man's question." The pitcher was passed across three or four pairs of legs; the witness took a long draught from it, cleared his throat two or three times, spat on the floor as many, and then answered the question.

Another observer noted that the judge shook hands with the prisoner and wished him well through his unpleasantness. It was well known that a jury would not convict a neighbor of murder if they considered him a better citizen than his victim. The judge was anything but professional. Reliable observers note that it was common for judges to become so drunk while presiding that they were almost "unable to sit erect or get through the customary formalities of judicial proceeding without some grotesque and unseemly exhibition which was exceedingly painful to witness." [4] Joseph G. Baldwin said he knew a judge to adjourn two courts to attend horse-races at which he officiated, and with more appropriateness than on the bench.

These judges were often almost entirely innocent of legal learning. One such Mississippi judge became very sensitive to lawyers' insisting on arguing points after he had decided

[4] Henry S. Foote: *Casket of Reminiscences* (Washington, D.C., 1874), pp. 21–2, 265.

them. A clever Irish lawyer clashed with the judge. The Irishman knew too much law and the judge too little for an equal struggle. On one occasion when the judge had made a ridiculous decision, the lawyer rose with open book, but was interrupted and reminded by the judge that the question was settled. The Irishman very apologetically remarked:

> If your honor plase! far be it from *me* to impugn in the slightest degray, the wusdom and proprietay of your honor's decision! I marely designed to rade a few lines from the volume I hold in my hand, that your honor might persave how profoundly aignorant Sir William Blackstone was upon this subject.[5]

The judicial circuit was an immense area, over which the judge and lawyers, each accompanied by his valet, made semiannual trips on horseback. By the time they had made the rounds, it was almost time to start again. In early Tennessee the lawyers always took their branding irons. Since the circulating medium was largely livestock—calves, steers, and milk cows—the fees were often paid in cattle. The lawyer branded his animal and turned it loose on the range under the care of a local herder. The whole troop rode horseback, and a jollier, more sociable crowd cannot be imagined. They told stories, played pranks, and had a rollicking time generally. They often took a lunch along and ate by some cool spring in the woods. On their arrival in a court seat they often met their clients and were introduced to their cases for the first time. This meant study and work in preparing the cases. Once the session began, many of the lawyers spent late hours roystering in the tavern.

Court days brought together crowds from the entire region. They sat for hours listening to legal speeches. It was almost their sole entertainment, corresponding to a movie among rural people today. Lawyers were called "gentlemen

[5] Blackstone was, of course, an outstanding authority on legal proceedings, the author of the lawyer's "blue book." This joke became a classic. Joseph G. Baldwin: *The Flush Times of Alabama and Mississippi* (New York, 1854), pp. 316–17.

of the green bag," no doubt because they carried their belongings around the circuit in a green bag.

The legal profession was as easily entered as others on the frontier. So superficial were the professional requirements that Reuben Davis, of Alabama, "read medicine" with a doctor, began to practice medicine, after a year or two decided to change to law, began to read law, was admitted to the bar at nineteen, and by the time he was twenty-three had saved up twenty thousand dollars. This is not to be wondered at. One lawyer wrote to his friends in the East that "lawyers live in clover in Mississippi; the most ordinary make two or three thousand dollars a year and some of them five, six and seven." [6]

When J. C. Guild read law with a Nashville firm in 1821, there were five young men reading with that one firm. It was his duty to bring water from the spring, make a fire, sweep the office, carry the mail, copy letters in the letter books, and file letters away. After he had been there for a while he learned to draw up legal forms and do other work about the office. There was much good-fellowship and rollicking fun among the boys, and at certain times all the law readers in town assembled and conducted a moot court, which was of real educational value.

When Guild went to Judge John Haywood, of the supreme bench of Tennessee, to be examined for admittance to the bar, he found the judge lounging on a bull's hide in the shade of a large oak in his yard. He turned on his side and asked what the stripling desired. On being informed, the judge then called two Negro servants and had them bring a chair for the visitor. Since the sun was encroaching on his shady preserve, he directed his black boys to take hold of the bull's tail and pull him into the shade. Guild then sat down and the justice examined him in the intricacies of law.

---

[6] Reuben Davis: *Recollections of Mississippi and Mississippians* (Boston and New York, 1891), pp. 30–6.

In his *Flush Times of Mississippi*, Joseph Baldwin pictured the thirty or forty young lawyers on his circuit as a crowd of sham lawyers who had got their fresh licenses gratuitously, and with a plentiful stock of brass went forth to prey on the citizens. The only consolation, he reflected, lay in the fact that the cases were generally as sham as the counselors. Their work, it would seem, was to thwart justice. Their only skill was in getting the right sort of jury, a thing that could be ascertained from the defendant, who had usually been out on bail until the time for the trial. Every technicality imaginable was taken advantage of to short-circuit justice. Attachments were very popular at this time (1836) when a new crop of frontiersmen were leaving for Texas. It was then to the interest of debtors, their securities, and rival creditors to quash or throw out of court such cases by means of technicalities of one kind or another. On the records of one Mississippi county opposite nearly every attachment case was the brief notation: "Quashed for lack of form." In one court bonds to the amount of some hundreds of thousands of dollars, held by foreign creditors, were quashed because in the execution was written "State of Mississippi" instead of "*the* State of Mississippi."

Lawyers worked up cases where people did not even know they had a case. Some won cases by arranging for officials to file papers in improper places or carelessly neglecting to fill in certain forms. Often cases were settled by public opinion as expressed in the judge and jury rather than by law. Some shrewd lawyers were able, before the case came to court, to form such public opinion. If one of his jurors should be challenged, he was careful to see that his place was taken by "a man good and true." In criminal cases almost anything was made out to be self-defense. A threat, a quarrel, an insult, going armed, shooting from behind a corner or from behind a door—it was all self-defense. In a time when killing Indians was a normal thing the murder of whites did not seem so serious. In fact, horse-stealing,

owing to frontier conditions, was much more often prose-
cuted and more severely punished than murder. But after
the Indian hostilities ceased, murder became more conspicu-
ous. Even so, though a man was murdered from behind his
back, a jury of *his peers* usually acquitted the murderer. As a
result of the failure of justice to triumph in the courts, or
where settlement ran far ahead of organized government,
there were almost certain to arise spontaneously organizations for the purpose of rectifying the miscarriage of justice.
Thus came into being the Regulator or other extralegal organization, which appeared in every section.

At Natchez a young man in a passion flogged his wife to
death. As there were no witnesses but Negroes and their
evidence was not admissable against a white man, he was
acquitted. The public did not stand for it, however. He was
tarred and feathered, scalped, and turned adrift in a canoe
without paddles. A young Yankee was caught stealing
Negroes, but as the indictment was not worded properly, he
knew the case would be dismissed and cockily boasted of it.
"I told you so," he triumphantly called as he left the court
on acquittal. The crowd, which had been awaiting the out-
come, answered in effect: "Yes, it is true that you have been
released by Judge Smith, but you have not yet been tried by
Judge Lynch." He was tied up, cowhided until he was
nearly dead, and then sent down the river in a dugout in the
usual way.

Next to horse- and slave-thievery counterfeiting was the
most hated crime. When barter gave way to money economy, bands of counterfeiters appeared on almost every
frontier. The multiplicity of paper money made counterfeiting easy. At Tuscaloosa, Alabama, a gang of counterfeiters passed several bogus fifty-dollar bills. A spontaneous
posse was raised and, disguised as hunters, started to ferret
them out. After traveling a long distance into the back
country, they found smoke coming out of a hill. As they
lingered in the vicinity, a little girl, going to warn the gang

of its danger, was followed. She went behind a waterfall and into a cavern. The leaders of the posse, unnoticed, followed and waited there outside the entrance to the gang's stronghold. As the door opened to let her out, they seized the counterfeiters, took them back to Tuscaloosa, and meted out summary punishment to the gang.

During the eighteenth century these self-appointed companies of law-enforcers were called Regulators. About the beginning of the nineteenth century such law-enforcement was known as lynching, and still later such an extralegal police organization came to be known as Captain Slick's Company.

In a northern Alabama town a system of giving culprits a ride in a "coach" originated. The coach was a hogshead. Pegs were driven through the side to add to the enjoyment of the passenger. The victim was placed in the big barrel and the head fastened on. It was then rolled down a hill. The culprit was required to walk back up and he was given as many rides as Captain Slick's Company deemed the offense merited. A thief caught taking money out of a merchant's cash drawer was given several rides in the coach, carried about on a sharp rail, and thrown into a mud pool to repent. In Missouri in the thirties occurred the "Slicker War," in which a large number of citizens known as "Slickers" cleared out a nest of counterfeiters. This name no doubt was a variation of the name Captain Slick's Company.

The danger in allowing such organizations to function became evident in 1835 in Mississippi. In the central counties of the state a slave-insurrection panic swept over the country. It was thought that the Thompsonian doctors were involved in plotting an indescribable reign of devastation and bloodshed. On a certain day at midnight it was thought the slaughter was to begin. The plan, it was believed, was for the slaves first to kill their masters and then burn towns and lay the whole region waste in a general simultaneous uprising. Although the whole thing was false, so great was the panic that night after night the women and children were assembled at a central place while the males guarded them. Excitement increased hourly. Suspected blacks and whites were arrested everywhere. Some were given a farcical trial before the mobs. Others were hanged without ceremony by the roadside. In time, after many lives had been sacrificed, this great unreasoning fear died out as suddenly as it arose.[7]

[7] Foote: *Casket of Reminiscences,* pp. 247–61.

XXII

Politics and Elections

THE spirit of political independence and genius for self-government of the early settlers west of the mountains showed itself immediately upon their removal across the mountains. The Watauga Association, the attempt to set up a new state of Franklin, the Transylvania Colony, and the Nashboro compact, all were the beginnings, under the crudest of circumstances, of state government.

In the state of Franklin, for example, the lower house of the legislature met in a log courthouse of unhewn logs without windows, the light coming through the cracks between the logs and at the door. The new state, which was acclaimed with enthusiasm in an attempt of the settlers to free themselves from the government of North Carolina, was not too popular when taxes were levied and an attempt was made to collect them among the backwoods people.

These governments, all of them in Kentucky and Tennessee, were spontaneous and organized without the aid and supervision of the central government. From time to time petitions were made to the central government to allow Western people to form new states and come into the Union.

In 1790, however, Congress passed an Act for the Government of the Territory South of the River Ohio, which provided for the governing of that region in a manner almost identical with that of the Old Northwest, except that north of the Ohio slavery was forbidden. The area was to be divided up into territories, which were to be governed in an almost autocratic manner by the central government. By easy stages, however, a territory was to become more self-governing, until it was to be admitted to the Union on the same basis as the older states.

All of the Southern states west of the Alleghenies except Kentucky passed through the various stages of territorial government. Newly organized territories selected laws from older territories or states to be used in governing them.

When Arkansas began her existence as a territory, in 1819, a statute was passed that enacted as law "all the laws and parts of laws now in existence in the territory of Missouri, which are of a general and not of a local nature, and which are not repugnant to the provisions of the original law of this territory."

The legislatures were crude and lacking in the fine arts of statesmanship. Many of their members were unlearned backwoodsmen hardly above the constituents they represented. When David Crockett first ran for the state legislature of Tennessee he had never read a newspaper in his life and was completely ignorant of governmental affairs. Not a few members attended the legislature arrayed in hunting shirts and armed with dirks and pistols.

Simon Cockrell appeared at the first election held at Liberty, Missouri, in August 1822, wearing tow-linen trousers and shirt, brogan shoes, and a hat made of wheat straw. He had raised the raw material and his wife manufactured the articles of his dress. That day he was elected to the legislature. He borrowed a horse to ride, made a saddle of corn shucks, a bridle of strings, and in due time rode to the capital to take up his work as the first lawmaker from Clay County.

Local government was in the hands of what was known

in some of the states as the county court. This was a body comprising the assembled justices of the peace in the county. Roughly it combined the work of the county board, or board of county commissioners where county government obtains today, and that of the county or probate judge. It met every other month or once a quarter and authorized the sheriff to collect the taxes, laid out new roads, gave permission for the establishment of mills and ferryboats, ordered the payment of bounty on wolf scalps, appointed constables, took charge of probate matters, gave ministers (on bond) permission to marry couples, set rates to be charged by taverns for liquor, meals, and so on, for the year, registered ear-marks and brands of stock, recommended militia officers to the governor, and acted as a sort of grand jury for returning indictments for crimes and misdemeanors. It also tried cases too insignificant to go to the circuit court.

In a general way this sort of local government obtained along the Southern frontier. There were, of course, certain exceptions. In Louisiana, for example, the county was (and still is) known as a parish and the body corresponding to the county court was (and still is) known as the parish police jury.

An early problem of the county court was the selection of a county seat. Very often a town near the center of population became the seat of government without much difficulty, but if there was any question, the county seat was frequently located as near the center of the county as possible, even if that were in the heart of the wilderness. A contract was then given for the building of a crude courthouse. In Izard County, Arkansas, a heated discussion took place over the type of chimney to be built. Some favored a stone chimney, which would look better and last forever, but old Jim Creswell took a decided stand against such extravagance. He declared he was not in favor of grinding the people to death with taxes, and stated that he was in favor of honoring the old landmarks and building a chimney of mud and sticks such as all were used to and which would be much cheaper. His argument was too powerful for the "extravagant" wing and a stick chimney was built.

In some instances at least, the tax-collector itinerated over the county, remaining a day or two at each of several centers. In this way people in large counties—at one time there were only three in all of Kentucky—did not have to travel so far in order to pay their taxes. Many early taxes were paid in skins or other frontier products. This gave the office-seekers a chance to travel with the tax-collector and meet the people when they came to pay taxes.

It seems that before the War of 1812 it was not considered good form for a candidate to traverse the country seeking election. A sort of supposed modesty forbade his acting as if he wanted the office. The office was supposed to seek the man. This false modesty disappeared in due time and backwoods politicians became expert at electioneering.

Speakers of opposing sides arranged to appear at the same place, divide the time, and give each other an equal chance to win popular approval. They each spoke an hour by the clock.

Political campaigns and elections were educational and social institutions. People would gather from miles around to hear the "promising" candidates speak from a stump in a clearing; hence the term "stump" speech. This was a real educational experience. The people often learned considerable of the affairs of the nation at one of these gatherings, particularly if the speaker was a candidate for re-election.

Many candidates, however, knew very little about the merits of the issues. When Davy Crockett began his first campaign for the legislature of Tennessee he was so totally ignorant of government that he had to confess his ignorance and tell bear stories and other amusing backwoods anecdotes, to the great satisfaction of the crowd. His opponents, men experienced in the ways of politics and public life, were to speak next, but Crockett took the crowd to the refreshment stands for a treat, continued his stories there, and left his politically wise opponents to parade their wisdom to the trees. Crockett was perhaps a bit more frank than some of his successors in the political arena. He said that he was as sly as a fox, did not commit himself on certain controversial issues, and got the votes by telling stories, joking, and being a good fellow generally.

In speaking of his ignorance when first elected, Crockett said that Colonel Polk, a member of Congress, addressed him thus:

> "Well, Colonel, I suppose we shall have a radical change of the judiciary at the next session of the legislature." "Very likely, Sir," says I, and I put out quick, for I was afraid some one would ask me what the judiciary was: and if I knowed, I wish I may be shot. I don't indeed believe I had ever before heard that there was any such thing in all nature; but still I was not willing that the people there should know how ignorant I was about it.

And yet it was not very long before he became an astute politician, a member of Congress, and eventually a statesman of no mean proportions.

Andrew Johnson, later President of the United States, was a master at gaining the support of the mountaineers. At a barbecue he attended, the current of public opinion was running decidedly against him, but he knew how to win the old settlers. "Fellow citizens," he began, "the first time I ever saw this country, I cut my way through the cane-brake with a large hunting-knife near the spot on which I now stand." The old hunters gave a yell of approval that reverberated half a mile through the forest. That opening sentence went straight to the hearts of his listeners and completely turned popular feeling to him.

All candidates were compelled to furnish the crowd with whisky at such a gathering. The people helped themselves from the jug, which was passed from person to person.[1] A

[1] Foote: *Casket of Reminiscences*, pp. 265–7.

barbecue with its accompaniment of whisky was so general that the people always expected "shoat and whisky" at a political campaign gathering.

Some backwoods politicians were perennial candidates. A minister reported this speech which he heard "in the brush":

"My fellow-citizens, when I look back over the twelve years since I became a candidate for this office, I feel encouraged. When I look back and think of the very few that for years gave me any encouragement, and compare them with the numbers that now promise me their votes, I am proud of my success. I begin to feel that my hopes are about to be realized—that a majority of my fellow-citizens will honor me with their suffrages, and that I shall proudly go up to the Capitol and take my seat among the legislators of the State. But, fellow-citizens, if, unfortunately, I should fail in this election, *I take the present opportunity to announce myself as a candidate in the next race.*" [2]

Sometimes a candidate who was at a disadvantage in speechmaking slipped off and went on "a still hunt"; that is, he visited the people house-to-house and attended small gatherings unheralded. The name for this sort of campaigning came from the hunt. Sometimes large parties took part in neighborhood hunts, but more often a lone hunter went into the forest on his own—a still hunt.

A Bible agent said that when he rode up to a cabin and did not make his business known, he was frequently greeted with: "Howdy, sir? I reckon you are a candidate, stranger!" An Englishman was astonished to find that more than once a "half-horse and half-alligator" possessed accurate information on politics and government. Politics, he said, were discussed in the remotest hut in the woods.

Lynn Boyd, who was speaker of the U.S. House of Representatives from 1851 to 1855, was an excellent example of what could be done in the still hunt. When he first ran for

[2] Pierson: *In the Brush*, p. 34.

Congress, he carried his fiddle and visited among the people. Although he made very mediocre speeches in the daytime, he gained the great admiration of the people by his fiddling for their dances at night. He had a very indifferent education, no knowledge of grammar, and no real preparation for a career in Congress, but his fiddling, dancing, fine·personal appearance, and wonderful skill in mingling with the people won him personal favor and admiration. On taking office he grew in ability with his responsibilities and became a recognized leader of his party.

The hero of Indian warfare was always possessor of great political capital if he cared to use it. One pioneer in speaking to this point said: "Old Michael Cassidy had no earthly claims to office; was a man of no talents. But was elected to the legislature several times, alone because he was not killed that night when Burnet & Spohn were killed." [3]

"Election day" was, in some places at least, an irregular period covering two or three days. James Flint, who visited the West in 1820, said that at Louisville the polls were kept open for three days.[4] The vote was made orally before the judges and the crowd. The local candidate sat near by to thank partisans for their support, and on learning of victory partisans carried their candidate about on their shoulders.

The states north of the Ohio River voted by ballot, those south viva voce. This was productive of many fights. Flint saw three in the course of an hour, he said. Whisky flowed freely, adding provocation to the primary cause of strife. It was quite customary for someone to carry a bucket about, asking people to "throw in" for a general treat. When sufficient funds had been thrown in, the solicitor returned with the bucket filled with liquor and bearing a gourd dipper. A general treat put life into an election.

In Alabama and Mississippi the divisions of the county

[3] Draper MSS. 11CC79, Wisconsin State Historical Library.
[4] In many places the polls were open from eleven a.m. until two p.m. the following day.

used for election purposes were called beats. These originated with the assignment of military companies of the militia to protect or patrol certain areas. Indeed, certain local officers such as justices and constables were elected at the muster under the direction of the captain of the company.

XXIII

Frontier Manufactures

THE manufactured goods needed most were salt and ammunition. Without ammunition there was no meat and without salt the meat was unpalatable and could not be preserved. Technical difficulties discouraged the production of gunpowder, and salt became the first manufactured product.

As early as 1778 Daniel Boone led a party of thirty men with salt kettles, on pack horses, to the Blue Licks to boil salt. The kettles had been sent out as a gift from the Virginia government. The salt-makers were to camp at the licks a month, when they would be relieved by a new party. The reliefs were to succeed one another until a year's supply had been sent to the station. Two bushels of salt with a few light articles was the usual load for one pack horse.

In the 1790's in the Ohio Valley it took eight hundred gallons of water to make one bushel of salt. (The amount differed at the various salines.) It was customary at that time to trade a load of hay—all that two horses could haul—for one bushel of salt.

Winter was the best time to make salt. Usually the Indians kept close to their villages at that season. Then, too, it was hot work at the best.

In early times salt-boiling was fairly simple. The brackish

water was taken from surface pits. By 1779 the earth had been excavated twelve or fourteen feet over an area of many acres. As men dug deeper, they found the water boiled up deeper and stronger. The water was caught in large troughs made of logs hollowed out. A long ditch was dug just wide enough so the edges of the bottoms of the kettles would rest on the edges of the trench. A battery of ten or twelve of these huge brass kettles, each of which held twenty-five gallons of water, were set side by side. All spaces around the kettles were chinked with handfuls of white clay. The trench was ten feet deep at the mouth of the furnace and made a gradual ascent to a depth of four feet at the chimney end. Cordwood in sticks three feet long was fed into the mouth, and the flames ran under the line of kettles.

The water was run from the storage trough into the kettle at the end. As the water evaporated there, the residue was ladled into the ones near the chimney and the empty ones were then refilled. The kettles near the chimney were, by this arrangement, in a constant state of crystallization. Pack horses were driven to the salt works laden with lime and the blood of pigs and beef cattle. These things were always placed in the kettles where the brine was being finished to ensure the proper texture and whiteness of the product. Sometimes tallow and corn meal were used to promote crystallization.

Each man had his work to do. Three were kept busy scouting. One or two managed the brine. One fired the furnace. By far the largest number were engaged in cutting and drawing up wood.

Later at certain points wells from forty to one hundred feet deep were dug. At other places wells were drilled. A long pole was cut and firmly fastened to the ground at the butt end. The middle rested on a fork, and the heavy drill was tied to the switch end of the pole. Two or more men, with the aid of the spring in the pole, lifted the drill and let it fall in the hole.

By 1802 Kentucky was exporting salt. During the first half of that year 2,385 barrels were exported, and this industry made possible the curing and exporting of 72,000 barrels of pork.[1]

Daniel Boone took the lead in salt-manufacture in Missouri, also. He discovered Boone's Lick and his sons and he began boiling in 1807. At Natchitoches, Louisiana, in the Red River Parish, a salt works operated for years before American occupation and continued after the Americans came.

The national government, various territories, and states attempted to preserve the salt springs for the use of the public instead of allowing them to fall into the hands of individuals who might take advantage of the natural monopoly to enrich themselves at the expense of the public.

Almost contemporaneous with salt-manufacture came the making of gunpowder. Saltpeter or niter, sulphur, and charcoal were the ingredients. How he learned the art is not known, but Daniel Boone made some when the settlement ran out. The slave Monk also made it. The ingredient hardest to secure was saltpeter. It was found in the many caves in the hill country. Wood ashes were mixed with the dirt in the bottom of the cave, and this combination was leached similar to the way in which lye was leached from wood ashes. The liquid thus obtained was boiled and crystallized. In Mammoth Cave the old niter-making plant used about 1812 is still to be seen and is one of the primary points of interest. Sulphur was obtained in the East and willows were burned to make the finest quality of charcoal.

Schoolcraft in an exploratory trip through the hills of Missouri and Arkansas noted that on November 12, 1818 he had visited seven caves that day, all of which afforded saltpeter. In the largest one Colonel Ashley of the Mine a'Burton gathered it for his powder factory. By 1810 there were

[1] Hazel Yearsley Shaw: "The Ohio River Trade, 1788–1830," MS. (Master's thesis, University of Illinois, 1908), p. 17.

sixty-three gunpowder mills operating in Kentucky. Big Bone Cave in that state by 1814 was yielding five hundred pounds of saltpeter a day for the raw material. Powder was made in the same way in Alabama, Tennessee, and elsewhere.

In eastern Missouri a little below St. Louis were the famous lead mines. These were opened up by the Spanish and French and came to peak production about 1820. Large log furnaces smelted the metal and shot-towers were used to produce shot.[2]

The presence of large numbers of hard or sugar maple trees and the need for sweetening early induced the settlers to make maple sugar. These trees grew in clumps, and a clump numbering from one hundred to three hundred trees was chosen for the operation. Such a clump came to be called a sugar grove. Each large tree was tapped; that is, a boxlike cavity was cut in the tree with the bottom sloping down in, about two or three inches. This box would hold about half a pint of sap. A hole was then bored in the tree below the box, upward into its bottom, to drain off the accumulating fluid. A tube made of alder or a quill inserted in this hole carried the juice clear of the tree and into sap troughs. These were made of short lengths of logs split in half and hollowed out. Sometimes, to increase the flow, gutters were cut on each side of the box leading down to it. The older trees produced the most and best sap. The best quality flowed during the early part of the season, which began just at the close of winter and lasted about six weeks. Toward the end of the period the juice got too thin to make sugar, and it was then made into syrup, spirits, and table beer.

The family usually made a temporary dwelling in the forest, took their stock, and camped there during the sugaring season. The chickens provided a very necessary element,

[2] See Everett Dick: *Vanguards of the Frontier*, pp. 145-55, for a description of the activity in the lead mines.

for the whites of eggs were used to help crystallize the sugar. The women and children did most of the actual sugaring although the men tapped the trees and cut the wood. Boiling the sap was not very different from boiling salt, except that it was a home process, while the latter was more of a factory process. Only two or three kettles were necessary, since only eight gallons were required to make a pound of sugar, whereas it usually took sixteen gallons of brine to make one pound of salt. A family with four children could make fifteen hundred pounds of maple sugar. Around Jonesborough, Tennessee, families regularly made a thousand pounds. A family generally used two or three hundred pounds a year.

Closely akin to making maple syrup was molasses-making. The early mills were built of wood. Three wooden rollers about two feet long and eighteen inches in diameter formed the mill. These were set vertically side by side on a solid bench. Wooden cogs or spurs were attached to the top of the rollers and a sweep fastened to the top of the middle one. A horse hooked to the outer end of the sweep traveled in a circle. It took four people to run this mill. One drove the horse, one "toted" up the cane, one in the front of the mill fed the stalks in between two of the rollers, and another on the other side fed them back between the other two. In speaking of these primitive mills in Louisiana, one man said that he could hear the wooden cogs squeaking a mile away.

The bagasse or crushed cane came out in front of the mill. The juice dripped down into a barrel or into a large trough made from half of a log dug out. From this it was carried to a big kettle for boiling. This required the labors of a fifth man. By working from four in the morning to nine or ten at night the crew could make from five to ten gallons of molasses in a day.

Cane molasses was made in the lower South where sugar cane grew. The children delighted in making molasses. They had tiresome tasks, but they chewed cane, drank juice, and sometimes licked the stirring stick. If the molasses-making lasted long enough, they got as fat as pigs. They would get the sticky cane juice all over their hands and faces; the smoke from the fire would settle on this and their eyes would shine out through the soot like coals of fire on a dark night. At the close of the season the trousers of the man who cared for the boiling were so stiff they would stand alone. Sorghum cane was introduced into America about 1840 and was used to make sorghum molasses in the late frontier years of Missouri and Arkansas.

Before there were any mills, the pioneers used various devices to grind grain. The earliest and crudest mill was the hominy block. This was a mortar and pestle made by cutting a section of a large hardwood tree and setting this on end something like a meat block. An excavation was burned in the end, a little larger at the top than at the bottom, for the mortar. The pestle, also made of hardwood, crushed some of the corn and pushed other grains up the sides, where it continually dropped down under the pestle. It was most effective in the fall, when the corn was soft.

When corn grew harder, the work was tedious. A sweep was often used to lighten the toil. The butt end of the sapling was placed under the side of the house, and the center was supported by a forked stick, leaving the springy end fifteen feet from the ground. The pestle was fastened to the pole and had a handle driven through it so two persons could unite in forcing it into the mortar. Such a device was called an "Armstrong mill" in Alabama. By means of a crude homemade sifter the coarse material, called grits, was separated from the fine and then boiled for hominy. The powdered matter was used for flour. Rock mortars and pestles were also used.

Where there was opportunity these sweep mortars were run by water power. It was so arranged that when a receptacle ran full of water, the sweep lifted the pestle. This poured the water out, allowing the pestle to fall down upon the corn. Then the receptacle began to fill and the process was repeated. It was called a hominy-pounder or "slow john." One such hominy-pounder in Tennessee was run by a crude water wheel with cow horns attached to it, which filled and emptied as the wheel revolved.

Hand mills were sometimes used, succeeding hominy blocks. They consisted of two circular flat stones. The lower was called the bed stone, and the upper the runner. Corn was fed in through a hole in the runner. By means of a handle two people turned the runner, and the corn meal ran out of a spout on the side of the bed stone. In later times a small steel mill was used.

Some of the first water-power mills were "floating mills." These were built on two large dugout canoes. An undershot wheel was placed between them. It was anchored in the strongest possible current. This turned the wheel, which transmitted its power to the stones above. It had the big advantage of movement, as it could be floated from one station to another. Instead of going to the mill, the settler had the mill come to him if he lived along the river bank or in a settlement.

In the hill country a mill could often be built without constructing a dam. One of the first in Tennessee was six miles southwest of Jonesborough. The small building was made of logs. The water was taken from a swift-flowing creek several hundred feet above the mill and led down to the wheel in a race made of hollowed-out halves of logs. As it shot over the wheel and turned it, crude cogs of wooden pegs on the other end of the shaft meshed with similar cogs in the upper stone and did the grinding.

Where there was no water, crude ox or horse mills were often built. Sometimes the power was furnished by a treadmill arrangement. The animals were driven up a slight incline, but their weight continually kept them at the bottom. The platform on which they walked kept turning and the power was applied to the mill. Sometimes they were hitched by means of a sweep to a vertical shaft. A belt from the upper end of the shaft turned the stone above.

The miller was required to grind the grain as it came. His compensation varied from one twelfth to one eighth of the meal at various times and places. The mill ground exceedingly slow. An old story pictured a witty boy who impatiently watched the miller. After silently regarding the tiny little stream of meal dribbling out, he disparagingly remarked: "I could eat the meal as fast as this mill can grind it." "How long could you eat it?" asked the miller. "Until I starved to death," replied the boy.

Often it was necessary to stay a day and a night or perhaps two to get the work done. With numbers of men waiting for their grist, the mill became a social center of the entire region for the male inhabitants.

When population and wealth increased, more efficient water mills were made by damming up streams. Great difficulty was encountered in this, however, for a freshet would destroy the dam and often even ruin the mill proper. Davy Crockett lost his fortune in this way in western Tennessee.

These mills often housed the machinery for sawing lumber and for carding. The first boards were split. Next the whipsaw was used. In this process a log was placed on a high scaffold or, if sawed on the level, a pit was dug underneath the log. One man stood below and a second stood on top of the saw-log. The log was first hewed to a square with broadaxes and lined. The sawyers sawed down the line. Two men could saw as much as two hundred feet of lumber in a day. With the coming of the water mill, the log was fastened on a moving frame that slowly fed the log to the circular saw and cut the boards the desired thickness.

The clothing that the first settlers brought to Kentucky was soon worn out, and in an effort to replace fabrics the settlers gathered nettles in the spring. The frost and snow had rotted the centers of the stems, and the bark was processed and made good thread. This, when woven, made a fabric coarser than hemp. It was customary, however, to utilize also the long buffalo hair taken from an animal shot in the spring. This, when carded and spun, was used for the woof, and nettle thread was used for the warp. Buffalo wool was made into felt hats also. Hemp was woven, too. It was first rotted by placing it in water and then was broken, spun, and woven on the hand loom in the house. At first the sinews of the buffalo were split and used for thread, but in time flax and cotton thread took its place even for sewing skin clothes. When sheep came into the country in numbers, wool was used largely for weaving. Cotton was not in common use until about 1815. Often linen and woolen thread were woven together to form the famous linsey-woolsey. On the ordinary cabin wall was to be seen, suspended from pegs, festoons or bunches, called hanks, of homespun. These, spun on the spinning-wheel, were woven on the crude loom by the womenfolk. The cloth was dyed by using the bark of various forest trees, as well as copperas, indigo, and madder purchased at the general store.

The first improvement over taking the seeds from cotton by hand was a machine made of two wooden rollers, one above the other, turned by cogwheels attached to a crank. Three persons ran the device. One turned the crank, one put a ball of cotton in at a time, and a third pulled the lint through from the other side. Squatters continued to use these for cleaning seeds from cotton for home use, but for commercial use some form of the machine invented by Eli Whitney was used. The gin (a corruption of the word "engine") was run by horsepower. Gradually gins came to be specialized institutions. The larger planters owned them and ginned cotton for all their surrounding neighbors. Going to the gin was sometimes several days' journey away, and since ginning was a slow process and a man might have to wait some time for his turn, the owners of gins got into the habit of giving receipts for cotton. These were sometimes used as a medium of exchange. The toll for ginning was ten pounds for every hundred. The capacity was about two or three bales a day. The seeds were taken out in the lint house and carried in baskets to the press box. The heaviest Negro on the plantation was placed in the box to tramp. In finishing the bale, a screw pulled by an old mule screeched as it pressed the bale.

Skins were tanned at home at first. The Indian method was used to dress deerskins. They were soaked in water overnight, placed on a smooth board, and the hair scraped off next morning. The brains, mixed with an equal amount of water, were boiled and the mixture rubbed into the skin, which was kneaded until it was thoroughly saturated. It was then pulled across a sharp board until it was dry. At this time it was pliable, as white as snow, and as soft as velvet. If such a skin were to get wet, however, it would become as hard as stone. To prevent that, two skins were fastened together, forming a sort of sack. This sack was placed over a fire and thoroughly smoked. Then the sack was turned and the other side smoked. It was then a yellowish brown in color and was ready to be made into clothes for man or woman. Other skins were tanned in a tan vat made of a large tree hollowed out and sunk to the upper edge in the ground. The hides were soaked in a strong solution of ashes and water to take the hair off. The surplus flesh was then scraped off. The hide was now soaked in a strong tan ooze made by shaving and pounding dry oak bark on a block until it was well powdered and then mixing it with water. Bear's oil and lard were used to soften the leather. If the leather was to be black, soot was mixed with the grease. Before long, tanning became a specialized business. Skins were often tanned on the share.

Iron was badly needed on the frontier, but there was little manufactured. So critical was the need in ironwork that the blacksmith was excused from military service. Around Kingsport, in eastern Tennessee, and also on the Licking River in Kentucky, ironworks were early in operation.

Production of iron from ore followed two methods. The simplest and most widely used was the forge or bloomery. The ore was heated in a charcoal fire to white heat and then beaten under the blows of a large trip hammer run by water power until the impurities were beaten out. This wrought iron was very serviceable, considering the conditions under which it was made. The second and more efficient method was the furnace. It was made of stone twelve to twenty feet high and six to eight feet in diameter. The raw ore was mixed with limestone and charcoal, the mass ignited, and cold air was driven into the furnace by huge bellows driven by water power. When the iron melted, it was run into cast-iron pigs. A further process at a refinery forge consisted in heating and pounding the pigs into wrought iron. The latter product was superior to that produced in the bloomery. Since water power was essential to this early iron-manufacture, these ironworks were located on streams and the ore hauled to them.

Distilling began early, particularly in the non-cotton-producing region. Corn was the chief grain, and when a surplus was raised, there was no ready market for it. To pack it east across the mountains on horses was impossible because of the bulk. A horse could not even carry enough corn to feed himself on such a journey, not to mention transporting enough to make a profit. Consequently it was profitable to reduce the weight and at the same time increase the value. A bushel of good corn valued at fifty cents would make three to five gallons of whisky valued at from one to two dollars a gallon. At the same time the value increased, the bulk decreased. Thus originated a business peculiarly fitted to the frontier. The equipment for a small distillery consisted of a building about twice the size of the ordinary log house with two stills—one of a hundred and ten gallons and the other of seventy gallons—eighteen tubs and a number of casks, barrels, piggins, and buckets. The corn meal was cooked, yeast and malt were added, and in four days the beer was ready to distill. A famous primitive distillery was the Red Heifer, erected at Nashville in 1784.

Fine apples and peaches were grown in Kentucky and Tennessee. The Kentuckians particularly liked peaches. Quantities of peach brandy were made and drunk locally and some was exported. The neighborhood distillery processed the peaches for a certain toll of the product.

Meat scraps of all kinds were saved religiously all during the year to be used in the spring for soap-making. Lye to be used in this process was got by leaching ashes. A hopper made of boards about four feet long and forming a V-shaped receptacle with a crack at the bottom was used to store the hardwood ashes during the winter. Running lengthwise beneath the apex was a trough. When it was time to make soap, the women and children carried water and poured it over the ashes. One man remembered that as a boy he helped carry bucket after bucket of water to soak the potash out of a hopper of ashes. The water dripped through the ashes and down into the trough, soaking the alkali from the ashes. This brown liquid, when stout enough to float an egg, was strong enough to make soap. The liquid was poured over the grease and gently boiled until it reached a ropey consistency. This was known as soft soap. By adding salt it was hardened into cakes. If soap was made in the time of a waning moon, it was said the soap would not boil over so readily. When towns reached some size and slaughter houses were established, soap-manufacture assumed the status of factory production.

XXIV

Whites and Indians

THE first white men who crossed the Cumberland Mountains found the Indians friendly. When Thomas Walker went into Kentucky in 1750 on his exploring expedition the party did not try to evade the Indians.

When Daniel Boone and a companion were captured while trapping in 1769, their peltry was taken from them, but they were released unhurt. The Indians regarded the pelts as legitimately their own, since the white men had taken them in Indian territory illegally. When the Indians released the men, they gave them moccasins, a gun, and bullets to kill food for themselves on the way to the settlements, but warned them to go home and not return, for if they did they could be sure the wasps and yellow-jackets would sting them. This action of these hunters was merely a forerunner and true type of the procedure of the white man from that day until the frontier era closed. No matter how sacred the treaty between the Indian and the white man, reserving certain land to the Indian, venturesome, spoils-hungry, white men were sure to intrude on the rights of the Indians. Such incidents were among the chief points of friction between the two races.

When unruly or undisciplined individuals from either race committed admittedly illegal and even criminal acts, there was a strong tendency for each race to protect its wrongdoer. Among both Indians and frontiersmen a democratic, undisciplined, lawless regime held sway. No strong central authority existed among either race. Often when called to account, the old chiefs explained that the offenses had been committed by their "bad young men," whom they had no power to restrain. These overt acts were often in retaliation for some like offense committed by lawless white men, who went unpunished because of public sentiment and lack of ability to enforce the laws in such a case.

Beginning with the Revolutionary War came a twenty-year period of warfare, and many frontiersmen, even after that, held a deadly hatred for the Indians. To their minds there was no good Indian but a dead one. William Newnham Blane stated that when he made his excursion on the frontier in 1882, many with whom he hunted would feel no more compunction at shooting an Indian than they would at shooting a deer or a bear.[1] These, no doubt, were like Colonel James Hubbard, who lived on the French Broad River in eastern Tennessee. He challenged an Indian to shoot at a mark. When the Indian shot, Hubbard shot the Indian. When Hubbard was sent to North Carolina for trial, a witness swore the Indian shot first and the Indian-hater was acquitted. At another time he saw an Indian on the river bank fishing, shot him, and said he "guessed" the Indian saw a fish and in his eagerness for it dove down and never came up again. An Indian on a platform at a lick, waiting to shoot at game, was shot by Hubbard, who presumed that the red man had got dizzy, tumbled down, and dashed his brains out.

John Johnston, long-time Indian agent, in a letter dated September 24, 1840, stated:

That the whole race within the U. S. must perish in the course of time is certain. They cannot be protected under a

[1] William Newnham Blane: *An Excursion through the United States and Canada, during the Years 1822–23* (London, 1824), p. 301.

popular government. Nothing short of the iron hand of
absolute power can restrain the avarice, cupidity, over-
reaching and frauds of the white man.

On the headwaters of the Wapetonmace in the 1770's three
Indians belonging to a tribe at peace with the whites, were
killed while on a peaceful journey into the settlements. The
white murderers were arrested and remanded to jail, but
their neighbors raised a party, rescued the prisoners, and set
them at liberty. They were never even brought to trial for
the offense.

In warfare, at first, the Indians did not disfigure their
fallen foes. By 1788, however, they had begun to take not
only a small patch of the skin off the head as a scalp, but to
take the skin and hair off the whole head, and then to "chop"
the victim. Of such a person's demise, the frontiersman's remark was that they "chopped him," "made wolf meat of
him," or "made mince meat of him." If he were shot several
times, he was said to be "riddled" or "as full of arrows as a
porcupine is of quills."

The whites never scrupled at taking scalps and, on occasion at least, disfigured the bodies of the slain otherwise.
Blane mentions two Indians who were skinned and their hides
used to make drumheads. When Tecumseh was killed, the
Western militia cut razor strops from his skin.

The Kentuckians rarely took an Indian prisoner. They did
not want to run the risk of prisoners' escaping and carrying
back to the British and Indians the secrets of the defense of
their stations. The Tennesseans, on the other hand, regularly
took prisoners, and at times an exchange was effected similar
to that under the laws of war among nations. Perhaps this was
a hang-over from colonial days when the Southern whites
captured and enslaved Indians.

Both Northern and Southern Indians took prisoners. Sometimes they were tortured to death by the Northern Indians,
almost never by the Southern. Many times the Indians north

of the Ohio attempted to replace the loss of one of their number by adopting a prisoner into the family and tribe. When the prisoner reached the Indian town, he was sometimes given a chance for his life. An ordeal known as running the gantlet was held. In this ceremony all the Indians in one or more villages turned out for the sport. From one to three hundred Indians formed two lines a few feet apart and terminating about fifty yards from the council house. The victim was stripped and compelled to run the length of the line. If he reached the council house, he was safe from attack. Each Indian in the line attempted to strike him with some weapon—a switch, rod, club, paddle, or sometimes even a knife. Not many ever reached the council house. Those who did were usually bloody and lacerated.

Simon Kenton succeeded in surviving this form of torture at three different towns when he was a prisoner. Daniel Boone was so clever he passed through the gantlet without injury. He ran so close to one line that the warriors could not strike him and he was too far away for those on the other side to reach him.

Whites who had been in captivity for a time and adopted into a family were loved by their Indian relatives and in turn had a warm affection for their Indian parents and brothers. Often years later they were able to do a good turn for their Indian kinfolk.

Many women were taken prisoner by the Indians. Although they were subjected to cruel treatment, privation, and the hardships of travel back to the Indian country, their chastity was never violated by the Indians. When they decided to save a woman's life, they also saved her virtue and honor. They believed that to take a dishonorable advantage of a female would be unworthy of a warrior and would disgrace him in the eyes of his companions.

Often a captive was fortunate enough to escape before reaching the Indian towns. Israel Donaldson, a Kentucky schoolteacher, was captured while surveying. He escaped one night by gnawing and picking in two the bark rope that crossed his body and on which an Indian lay on each side of him. Having no weapon, he was obliged to live on turkey eggs and such other food as he could pick up. Finally, with his bare feet full of thorns and briers, he made his way back to a station, eventually reached home, and received a royal welcome from his pupils and friends.

With the exception of certain periods of war, relations between the races were often very amicable. Sometimes the whites would buy land from the Indians if they settled before the Indian title had been extinguished. At other times some of the Indians would remain on their ancestral domain after the area had been ceded to the whites and was being settled by them. This was particularly true of the Choctaw and Chickasaw tribes. They helped the planters pick cotton in the fall and in other ways proved a real benefit to settlers because they were a source of cheap labor to them. The Indians would bring game, wild fruit, and other things desired by the whites and trade them for a pretty red dress or other colorful things that they wanted. Not infrequently a settler would lend his gun, shot-flask, and powder horn to a trusted Indian, who would bring back something desired by the settler in return.

In Henry County, Missouri, just before the removal the Indians who were semicivilized became fairly expert traders. They still went on hunts through the country and drew an annuity of lead and powder from the government. When the settlers did not have enough furs to take to the trading post, they traded them to the Indians for powder and lead. The Indians marketed the furs at the post. The Indians shared their medical secrets, their knowledge of plants, animals, and other woodlore, with their white dispossessors.

In 1836 on the banks of the Ouachita in Clark County, Arkansas, a little boy wandered from his home into the dense woods and canebrakes. His parents, terribly distressed, feared that the child would be torn to pieces by wild animals, bitten by poisonous snakes, or drowned in the deep water of the river. All that day the whole neighborhood hunted for the lad. The father thought of Wauhachie, a Delaware brave who had refused to leave the haunts of his people when they went west, and sought his aid. But the brave had gone off in his canoe for the day. Remembering his uncanny ability to trail, the father searched until he finally found him. The Indian asked to be shown the spot where the child was last seen and then followed the trail like a bloodhound through the jungle to the river bank. At last he found the little boy and carried him, frightened and worn out by his long tramp, but unhurt, to his parents.

The Indians had a keen sense of humor and at times would stage a mock attack in order to scare the jumpy whites. On one occasion in Clark County, Arkansas, they chased the timid children as they went home from school. Sometimes these Indians became a great nuisance to the whites. They came around the settlements and, used to Indian ways, walked right into the cabins without knocking, helped themselves to the food, or in other ways made themselves at home as they did upon entering a neighbor's tepee. They picked up strange articles of clothing and tried them on, examined other unfamiliar articles, inquired their use, and tested them. If the cabin was closed, they peeped in at the windows and in general pried into the affairs of the whites. Then, too, when they had been dispossessed and their old way of life disrupted, they often became beggars and were a nuisance to their white neighbors.

Interestingly enough, when this time was reached and there was no longer any danger from the Indians, some of the old Indian-slayers became the most staunch friends of the red men, extolling their courage, their love of their old homes, their tenderness to their children, and their respect for their dead. Often the remnant of a once proud tribe was seen camped around the plantation of such an old pioneer, subsisting on his benevolence.

XXV

Frontier Military Life

A MILITARY organization was of first importance in the early frontier community. The Virginia militia system was carried into Tennessee and Kentucky and, with minor changes, from these states into adjoining areas. Allowing for minor variations among the various territories and states, the system was this: Every qualified male inhabitant between the ages of eighteen and fifty was a part of the organization. The county was the local territorial unit. A county lieutenant with a rank of lieutenant colonel or colonel—in any case called a colonel—was in command. It was expected that there would be enough men in the county to form a regiment or legion [1] of two or more battalions. Each battalion was commanded by a major, one of whom was designated a first or senior major. Two to five companies in each battalion were each commanded by a captain. Each company had from forty to sixty men and besides the captain had as commissioned officers a lieutenant and an ensign. The noncommissioned officers consisted of four sergeants, four corporals, and two musicians. Officers of the rank of captain and below were elected by the men of their command. Those above that rank were elected by the commissioned officers of their

[1] This term was used for a while following the Revolutionary War.

respective commands. After about 1830 all commissioned officers were elected by the members of their command. A number of regiments were combined to form a brigade under a brigadier general, and a number of these to form a division commanded by a major general. As a matter of actual practice, in the early years, each station organized itself into a company under a captain of its own choice. Sometimes not over half a dozen men could be raised to a company.

At times it was necessary to make up a detail of men to guard those who were farming, go to the relief of a certain station, proceed to a certain point to secure ammunition, or go on a scouting mission. In such a case the entire number of available militiamen was mustered and the required number was then drafted. Often such service was very irksome because it involved leaving one's work and family for a month —that was the customary tour of duty—to go to some distant place, abandoning one's family to the care of others and allowing one's farming to drift, perhaps at the very busiest season of the year. Sometimes before the names were drawn, a number of men would arrive at an agreement by which each of those who were not drawn would pay the unlucky one a certain amount.

In the earlier years militia service was not required by law, but a desperate common need inspired a public opinion that was almost as effective as law-made compulsion. Whoever made thin excuses and attempted to avoid service when called could not "hold up his head" among faithful brave men. Good excuses were at times given and accepted, but false or feigned ones branded a man as "slack twisted" by those whom "it would do to tie to." The slacker was known to the reliable, public-spirited, patriotic man as one who "could not come it," and he was treated with contempt and scorn. So hot did public disapproval wax that he felt it more comfortable to leave the country. In such a case he was said to have been "hated out." Sometimes reckless, impetuous borderers chose a more summary fashion to rid the community of such an unworthy person.

In the Revolutionary War days and for some time thereafter the hunting shirt was the militia uniform. In 1790 Colonel Jarman, of Tennessee, with his command, prepared to give General Johnson a salute when he arrived with his brigade. It failed completely because when the general arrived, there were no spectacular insignia of rank nor flashy uniform; there was nothing whatever to distinguish the general from the plain soldiers of his command. A hunting shirt and a tin cup hanging by his side were his simple garb and equipment. By 1830 the militia officers, in particular, were wearing highly colored and ornamented uniforms. An observer in Alabama wrote:

"I do not recollect in all my travels ever having seen so many long white plumes floating in the air; as many scarlet sashes; and war-horses so richly caparisoned, as I used to see at the brigade musters in Moulton in early times."

A writer in describing an inspection of the militia by the Governor of Mississippi observed that the Governor as commander-in-chief, and his staff were gorgeously dressed in blue and buff, with surprisingly rich plumes, and that they rode between the lines on high-spirited horses, which pranced and reared all during the review.

From the seventeenth century on, paid soldiers known as Rangers had served on the fringes of the frontier. Some of these were regulars, but others were militiamen serving tours of duty. They ranged out from their established headquarters along the frontier to protect the settlers.

In the trans-Appalachian region, since settlement advanced before government, military protection was almost entirely in the hands of the militia or volunteer soldiers. Sometimes a detail of scouts was sent out to range the woods in all directions from whence danger was expected. It was customary when on the march to keep some active experienced woodsmen on the right, left, front, and rear even to the distance of a mile to guard against surprise or an ambush. In camp, likewise, a number of sentinels were posted strategically about the camp. It was difficult to keep undisciplined militia at their posts, however. The punishment meted out to a Missouri guard for sleeping on sentry duty was to grind a peck of meal for each of the seven widows in the settlement.

Often solitary scouts were sent out. These were usually the most experienced Indian-fighters and the best woodsmen. Since, because they needed to be skilled in woodcraft, it was impossible to draw them by draft from the ordinary citizen soldiers, volunteers were used for this purpose. They were kept out much of the time and were paid a fixed wage. In Tennessee in the 1780's their wages were seventy-five bushels of corn per month. These were the first "regulars," although paid by the local settlements. They were called "spies," or less often scouts. Two of the most famous of these spies were Simon Kenton, of Kentucky, and Abe Castleman, of Tennessee. It was the duty of Kentucky spies, for example, to range along the Ohio River and pick up any traces of Indians on the way from the savage lair to the white settlements. To facilitate recognition of Indian signs and in order that moccasin tracks might be a final proof of the presence of Indians, a law was made forbidding any white man to wear moccasins. White people who came down the Ohio River in the seventies were required to sink their boats in order to keep Indians from taking and using them.

In the wooded sections of Kentucky and Tennessee cane, weeds, and small bushes grew up in such profusion that two or three men even on foot could not pass through without leaving a trace. Out on the barrens the grass and nettles revealed to the discerning woodsman the route of those passing. Unpracticed persons could cross and recross such a trace without detecting it, while Indians and woodsmen would discover it even "when on a running trot." They could take up such a trail and follow it like their hounds. Their horses as well as their dogs would "snuff an Indian or an Indian's footprint."

In hundreds of instances spies gave credit to their dogs and horses for timely warning and safe deliverance from Indians. A favorite pastime of these spies was to tell stories of their narrow escapes. Often they related these hairbreadth experiences while patting the faithful dog on the head or smoothing the mane of the loyal steed. It was easy to imagine that these steadfast companions in danger could understand the narrative and appreciate the compliments showered on them.[2]

The spy was dependent upon his skill for his very life. He walked slowly and noiselessly without betraying his presence. He walked carefully on dry leaves, took care not to leave any trace of his passing by breaking a twig or bush or moving a log or stone. He saw every animal, falling leaf, and disturbed branch. Silent himself, he heard every sound. Any movement in the vista of the forest instantly caught his eye and froze him into a statue until he could scarcely be discerned from the objects around him. Lest he leave a "sign," he allowed the choicest game to pass unnoticed, went hungry, and forewent, as a rule, the comfort of a fire to cook his food and warm himself.[3] When he did take this risk, he made a pit, built a charcoal fire, hovered over it, and, drawing his blanket over his head, was soon comfortable although he was invisible a few feet away. Often these spies were able to sleep in a rock house or in a hollow sycamore tree in inclement weather. Every circumstance was utilized by the spy in drawing his conclusions. By "signs" he could tell whether the enemy was far off or near at hand. If the water was muddy or the horse dung warm, the sign was fresh and the enemy near.

[2] A. W. Putnam: *History of Middle Tennessee* (Nashville, 1859), p. 340.
[3] John W. Monette: *History of the Discovery and Settlement of the Valley of the Mississippi* (New York, 1846), II, 44.

As a result of the work of spies, usually warning was given of an attack by any considerable number of Indians. In 1792, when Buchanan's Station, in Tennessee, was attacked, owing to the effective work of the able, faithful scout Abe Castleman, the people had gone inside the fort and were prepared for the attack. He had based his warning on numerous signs, chief among which was this: An old Indian hunter named Black Fox often came to the settlement to trade furs and venison. Castleman went to visit his camp and found it deserted although the fall hunting season was not half over. This season normally reached its climax with the hunter's moon, the full moon, in October. Then the weather was cool enough to cure meat without difficulty and yet game was fat. Abandonment of the hunting camp in mid-season put the finishing touches on an almost complete picture painted by other signs, and Castleman warned the pioneers to "fort."

If two spies were scouting together, when they sat down they sat back to back, or if there were several, they sat in a circle facing outward in order to be on guard constantly.

The spy's accouterment consisted of a blanket tied behind his saddle, a wallet of parched corn and other food, a sack of charcoal, a long rifle, and a hunting knife. Spies were called "the eyes and the ears" and "the watchdogs" of the settlements by the Indians and were considered in a distinct class by them. So fierce did the Indians' anger rise against them that special vengeance was wreaked on them. The Indians cut off their ears, plucked out their eyes, and sometimes even cut off their heads and arms and legs. Such military personnel as these were sent by George Rogers Clark to Kaskaskia long before he went to Richmond for aid for his project of the conquest of the Northwest. They returned to Harrodsburg with all the information he "could reasonably have expected."

Such training enabled James Robertson to make fourteen round trips from Nashville to North Carolina accompanied only by his Negro servant when Indian hostilities were at their height, crossing and recrossing the numerous war trails. Besides he took several trips into Kentucky and Illinois. He often rode up the beds of small streams, leaving no trail. Again he made false or misleading trails and camped in hidden spots.[4] Spies often left messages for one another or for others by means of marks on trees, certain sticks of different sizes with marks on them, or bent or broken twigs.

In order to keep the militia in military form, a company muster was held each quarter, a battalion muster in the late spring, and a regimental muster in early autumn. Attendance with arms was compulsory at these musters. The order book of the Sixth Regiment Kentucky militia shows that in 1803 at a court martial a man was fined one dollar for absenting himself from battalion muster, and another fifty cents for failure to appear with arms. Various ones were excused from military service because of physical disabilities.

The officers, commissioned and noncommissioned, sometimes met the day before the general muster to learn their duties, commands, and evolutions under the tutelage of the field officers. In that school all officers and noncoms from the rank of captain down were drilled.

During the few years following the wars with Great Britain or an Indian war these militia musters were fairly effective and a martial spirit was maintained, but as the years passed with no motivating element, the militia muster became a legal formality from which the spirit had largely fled. A printer on the *Arkansas Gazette* wrote that he had been warned repeatedly to attend muster, but had never performed military duty and had never paid a fine.

A muster in 1825 was described as presenting every kind of firearm from rifles, muskets, and shotguns to horse pistols. Those who had no firearms to bring, or who had forgotten them, carried a trimmed sapling or cornstalk. This gave the

[4] Maxine Mathews: "Old Inns of East Tennessee," East Tennessee Historical Society *Publications*, No. 2, pp. 22–3.

organization the title of cornstalk militia. When the captain was ready to drill his company, he mounted a stump or barrel and called out: "Oh, yes! Oh, yes! Oh, yes! All you who belong to Captain So-and-So's company" (giving his name) "fall into ranks and parade!" The "Oh, yes!" was from the French "*Oyez*," ("hear ye"). It was a form of address used to open court or other formal occasions. If this call failed to move his men, he would call out: "Everybody in my company, off the fence there and fall into line! Now come on, men, come on, everybody, and let's get started with our revolutions [evolutions]!" The order "Right dress" was lengthened into "Look to the right and dress!" The command "Halt!" was mangled into "Stop!" or "Hold!" At parade some kept step and others followed along, forming a wavering reluctant line.

An observer in Franklin County, Missouri, reported that as the company was marching past a spring the drummer suddenly placed his drum on the ground and called out to the company: "Hold on, boys, I am dry." The fifer and a large number of the men dropped out and went to the spring. The company commander stood patiently through this interruption and took out his knife and a plug of tobacco. Since his saber was in his way he, in a very unmilitary manner, held the saber between his legs while he cut off a slice and began to chew. When the battalion muster was called, a general was present to review the troops. After the unit had fallen in, two officers rode along counting the men in order to divide them into even-sized platoons. The two officers got a different talley and, when they counted again, found a still smaller number. Upon investigation it was discovered there were now great gaps in the line. Far and wide these absent, independent citizens were crouched or lying among the hazel brush picking the wild strawberries that flourished there. The colonel was by no means angry, but laughed and called to the adjutant: "Go and drive up these strawberry hunters." When the recalcitrant ones returned, the colonel merely said: "Now, boys, behave yourselves, else we won't get through with our exercise."

At a muster at Little Rock, Arkansas, about 1829, some carried parasols in lieu of guns. The Governor was to review the troops. One company was composed of the elite of Little Rock. The rest were the rural residents of the county. Just as the Governor was passing along the lines, rain came down in torrents. The whole regiment with the exception of the Little Rock company and a few others here and there broke ranks and precipitately sought shelter in the neighboring houses. The colonel in water-soaked uniform and with a bedraggled plume sought unsuccessfully to rally his scattering host while those armed with umbrellas stood in the now almost entirely deserted ranks, using their arms to shelter them from the torrential downpour.

The colonel was so mortified at this shabby behavior before the Governor that he ordered a court martial to try those absent without leave. Each man who had left ranks was fined five dollars. This ended the colonel's career as an officer, for at the next election he was relegated to the ranks by the sovereign citizens who made up his command. There is little wonder that discipline was practically nil when an officer was so easily deposed for doing his duty.

Many soldiers lined up for drill barefoot. As for a uniform, there was none. There were fur hats, wool hats, caps, and no headdress at all; cloth coats, calico, jeans, linsey, and no coats at all; moccasins, boots, shoes, and no shoes; white pants, black pants, buckskin pants, and no pants at all; ruffled shirts and unruffled shirts, buckskin hunting shirts, cotton and linen shirts, black, green, gray shirts, and no shirts at all.[5] This ununiformed motley array marched with their leaders calling out to their men to get into step. As they marched, those with umbrellas put them up, and many smoked. The officers were equally unmilitary. Some smoked

[5] Rothert: *History of Muhlenberg County*, pp. 167-8, 170-2.

corncob pipes, some were adorned with scarlet sashes, pewter buttons, and plumes. Others wore plain hunting shirts.

The outstanding movement in the parade and ceremonies was the forming of the hollow square just prior to dismissal for the day. When this maneuver was accomplished, the command "Parade rest" was given, and opportunity was offered to the command to advertise. Farms were offered for sale or rent, stock and seed for sale, estrays inquired about, and house-raising announced. After two or three hours of drill the pseudo-soldiers were dismissed.

Then came the real reason for the gathering of the whole countryside. Generals and other officers became common folk in the twinkling of an eye and all mingled in one grand assemblage. Many stands, often run by slaves, offered ginger cake, whisky, cider, apples, and other treats. Sometimes a barbecue or family lunches were eaten. Shooting matches, cockfighting, horse-swapping, and other amusements dominated the activities. At these gatherings the itinerant blacksmith came to shoe horses, the candidate for office to address his public, and the gunsmith to ply his trade.

As has been intimated, there was only the vaguest control exercised by the officers of the militia and of the volunteer troops. And yet in spite of the intense individualism, they made a formidable fighting force. The individuals were excellent shots with their deadly long rifles and were the hardiest of woodsmen. In the face of danger they turned to their natural leaders, disregarding rank and office almost completely and following their own neighborhood chiefs. These troops were extremely efficient on short expeditions in defense of points near home and in small-scale bushwhacking actions. They were ready to march on a few hours' warning. Their preparations consisted in examining their guns, filling their powder horns, running a supply of bullets, parching a half-gallon of corn, filling a knapsack with pounded corn, and stowing away some jerked meat. On the Cold Water expedition of 1787 Colonel James Robertson took along a few collapsible rawhide boats for the movement of arms and indifferent swimmers over the Tennessee River. When they reached the river they plunged in, some on horseback, some swimming beside their steeds, and the leather boats were pushed over by swimmers. When they reached the enemy country, the clothes of most of the men were completely wet. When they landed they made their breakfast of parched corn and venison and hung their wet clothes on the bushes to dry. There they were—a nudist army in the enemy country within six miles of the enemy's stronghold—a laughable sight indeed. At the command "Prepare to mount," they "donned their duds" and in no time were away upon the mission of destroying the enemy.

In George Rogers Clark's campaign of 1780 from Kentucky to Piqua, Ohio, most of the thousand Kentuckians had no other provision for twenty-five days than six quarts of corn and a gill of salt, except what they captured from the Indians when they burned their town. Some of the best fighting was done by those who knew almost nothing about formal drill and military commands but, by long years of contact with the Indians, knew almost by instinct how to move. In an attack they advanced from tree to tree, taking care never to let the enemy get behind them. There were times when hostile whites and Indians clashed without firing a gun, the Indians retreating from tree to tree and the whites advancing in the same way.

When the fighters found or captured any Indian loot, they cast lots for it or divided it in any other amicable manner.

Some very remarkable victories were gained by these border warriors and some real disasters were suffered. The Battle of King's Mountain is an example of the former, and the annihilation of the second escort of military supplies procured by the Americans from New Orleans during the Revolutionary War in the spring of 1779 is an example of the latter. In this action there were about one hundred men and two keelboats. On just about the site of present-day Cincinnati they fought a battle with the Indians on a sand-bar. There is no bloodier nor more disastrous page in the annals of border warfare. One boat with two men got away and drifted down to Louisville. Not more than ten men ever reached their homes.[6]

[6] Mann Butler: *A History of the Commonwealth of Kentucky* (Louisville, 1834), pp. 105–7.

XXVI

The Frontier Woman

THE pioneer woman, much like her sisters the world over, followed her husband wherever he went, stood beside him in every hardship and difficulty, and bore and reared his numerous progeny. Some timid maidens, reared in the midst of plenty and thrown into circumstances of hardship, rose to the occasion and resolutely conquered the savage environment. Others, with clinging-vine characteristics, pined away and were a distinct liability to their husbands and the community in which they lived. The typical frontier women, however, had come from a country a little way to the east that was just emerging from the primitive. Fashioned in a frontier mold, they ably stood by their husbands in the conquest of the wilds. Such a woman was Rebeccah Boone, the wife of Daniel Boone, and the first white woman in Kentucky. Many of these women, before they came west, never would have thought they could do some of the heroic deeds that they performed when circumstances demanded action.

On the road there were many hardships. When J. Luckey came to Kentucky, about 1790, his father took a bedtick, made an opening at the two ends, put one child in each end, and slung it over a horse. A third, a little larger, rode a horse, and a baby was carried in front of its mother. Thus did many a mother bring her flock over the mountains to the land of milk and honey.

It was not an unheard-of thing for the company to stop a day while one of the women was confined. More than likely the new mother was up and on the trail with the group the next day or the following one.

In the midst of disaster under circumstances that called for quick action, often a courageous woman would take the lead and save the day. In April 1780 a group of settlers moved from farther east in Kentucky to Fort Jefferson, nineteen miles below the mouth of the Ohio River. The Indians attacked them three times, killed a number of people and all the cattle, and cut down all the corn which was in roasting ears. The group decided to go to Natchez for the winter since they were nearly destitute and could not get through the cold season. They left in seven boats, but one boat, in which were nineteen persons, failed to keep up with the others. Among the number were a Mrs. Pears and her husband and another man and his wife. The boat was grounded on a sandbar for three weeks. Pears and one woman died. The rest of the party, although very weak, finally got the boat afloat. By this time all the provisions were gone except a peck of flax seed. They parched that, beat it to a meal in a pot, and made soup to save their lives. They had nothing to live on for three weeks except what they were able to gather along the shore, such as grapes, honey-locust pods, wild peas, and tongue grass.

They burned the hair off a few skins that they had and then roasted them so they could grind them to powder between their teeth. The one remaining man on board went to pieces, lost his courage completely, and would not hunt or allow the two boys on board to hunt. Once the Indians gave them a supply of meat, but took all their clothes, bedclothes, pewter, and other plunder. When five hundred and fifty miles from Natchez, they met a white man and tried to get him to take them to Ozark. He could not, but gave them some supplies and advised them to hurry and catch a boat ahead of them. It took them fourteen days to catch this boat. The dauntless Mrs. Pears safely led the survivors of that terrible journey through the many dangers. They lost track of the days. When they arrived at Natchez, the settlers there were astonished and thought the survivors could not possibly recover. Mrs. Pears was so weak she could not turn her head on her pillow except with her hands. She could not rise, but, once up, could walk around. On the horrifying journey she had lost her husband, a sister, a daughter, and other relatives, most of whom she had buried with her own hands.

In 1784 when a party floated down the Ohio River on the way to ascend a tributary of that river and settle in the interior of Kentucky, the Indians on the Ohio shore gave chase. The two flatboats were lashed together and the seven men placed at vantage points for an attack. The Indians, a large party, approached within one hundred yards, and the party expected an attack at any moment. Just at this critical point the mother of the family coolly rose from her seat, collected the axes, and placing one by the side of each man as he stood at his post, leaned the handle against his knee that he might know it was there. Keeping a hatchet for herself, she returned to her seat. This pioneer mother did not go into hysteria in the face of danger. Coolly she showed her expectation that the boat would be defended against all odds and thus instilled courage into the men. Afterwards she remarked calmly and simply that they had had a providential escape and that they ought to be grateful.

About 1790 a party of travelers was attacked near Mayslick, Kentucky. They were sitting around their campfire when the Indians sneaked up and shot one man. All was confusion, and but for the presence of mind and the heroic action of a woman, who with an ax broke open a chest in one of the wagons, handed out ammunition, and called upon the men to fight, all would have been lost. This, together with the extinction of the campfire, which left the whole area in the dark and caused the Indians to retreat, saved the day.

Life within the station was in many ways pleasant. There was the companionship of other people and especially other women. There were the usual activities of a small community where everyone knows every other one's business—coquetting, courting, jealousies, and petty talebearing. There were even marriages while the people were confined in a fort expecting every moment an attack.

In an attack many pioneer women showed as much resourcefulness and bravery as their husbands. The night attack on Buchanan's Station near present-day Nashville was so sudden that the defenders took no time to put on their clothes, but commenced the fight dressed only in their underclothing. It was found that a party which had left the station had taken nearly all the bullets. Sally Buchanan, wife of the commander, undertook the job of molding bullets at the kitchen fire. It was later reported that when a batch was ready, she would run out and distribute them with the injunction not to fire them until they would account for some of the red devils. Seeing a man shirking his duty, she approached him and asked what he was doing there, why he was not fighting. Then she told him that she would rather die fighting like a man than be cowering in a corner. She admonished him for the sake of his own credit to get to his post at once. He responded to this appeal.

A woman fearful of capture, and believing the women and children would be carried off, wanted to appear well and went to her cabin, dressed herself and her children, and started for the gate of the fort. Mrs. Buchanan, seeing her leading her children along, was reported to have inquired: "What in the world are you going to do, Phoebe?" "To surrender," was her reply. "Never," exclaimed the indomitable Sally Buchanan, "as long as there is life in this body! Go back to your room and keep out of the way; we will whip the Indians!" and back the helpless, nerveless woman went. Only eleven days later Mrs. Buchanan gave birth to her first child. These incidents bring into relief the fact that pioneer men and women were normal people and reacted normally to frontier surroundings. Some were "all wool and a yard wide"; others were "shoddy." The rigors of frontier life brought out the inherent quality of the female of the species.

On many a night Mrs. James Robertson ran bullets and loaded rifles for the men when Indians were hovering around the fort. Very frequently when the fort was short-handed the women put on hats and hunting shirts and showed themselves, thus deceiving the Indians as to the strength of the post. From this strategy comes the saying to make a "show of hats." At times some of the women took their place at a loophole and filled a rifleman's role.

That the women had a sense of humor is shown by the following incident. The men at a fort had become very careless and would all go out and play ball. Even those who did not play ball would go out and lie down without their guns. Mrs. Boone, her two daughters, and three or four other women determined to teach the men a lesson. They loaded several guns light as the Indians did and, taking them out the opposite side of the fort from where the men were, fired them to simulate an attack. They then ran in and slammed the two big gates of the fort. The men fled toward the fort in a panic. Some made such haste that they ran right through a pond. Only one young man got in before the gates swung shut. Wet, bedraggled, discomfited because of the ungraceful part they had played, the men were exceedingly angry and some wanted to send the women away. The dispute became so sharp that the men fell to fighting among themselves about it. After two or three fights, however, the situation cooled down to normal.

Out on the cutting edge of the frontier, after the Indian wars were largely over, as the isolated family lived in a little cabin in the midst of a tiny clearing, shut out from civilization by towering forest trees, life was lonely indeed. Once in a while business—a trip to the mill or the trading post or a hunt for horses—called the man away from home. Rarely did his wife escape from the strait social surroundings. Some girls grew to womanhood without ever having been inside a store, hardly knowing there was such a thing except by hearsay.

Michaux in 1802 stopped at a house in Kentucky where the woman told him she had lived there three years and for eighteen months had not seen any person except her own family. On the Skillet Fork, in Indiana, Birkbeck found a nice-looking woman sitting in the shade by the cabin spinning. Her husband was absent on business that would keep him away several weeks. She had no family and no company except her husband's dog. She said she was quite overcome with "lone." Many times her husband took even the dog and was away bear-hunting for days. She urged the travelers to tie their horses up and sit awhile with her during the heat of the day.

Daniel Drake's liveliest recollections as an elderly man were of the pleasure that his mother and the children enjoyed when anyone came in sight.

Captain J. E. Alexander found himself at a loss to know how to gain the good graces of the backwoods women he met. He tried it by praising their children and their houses, but seldom or never could he elicit a smile. They were, to his mind, always dull, cold, and melancholy. He thought it would be very difficult to make love to one of these forest women. Once he went up to a young mother and said: "What a nice garden you've got!" After a stare and a long pause she inquired: "What say ye?" When he repeated the remark, she merely replied: "Tolerable." Their lonely existence made them shy and quiet to strangers.[1]

The womenfolk of the hunter-squatter pioneers lived in a different world from that to which the traveler who visited

[1] Captain J. E. Alexander: *Transatlantic Sketches* (London, 1833), p. 275.

them was accustomed. When Schoolcraft toured the Ozarks in 1818, he tried to engage his hostess and her daughters in small talk such as was common in social circles, but could find nothing of that sort to raise a conversation. He said they could talk only of bears, hunting, and such things. The rude pursuits and coarse enjoyments of the hunter life were all they knew. When he stopped at a cabin, the woman was able to tell him about the geography of the country. She also told him that their guns were not well adapted to the journey, that they should have rifles, and pointed out other errors in equipment, dress, and mode of traveling while they stood in open-mouthed astonishment to hear a woman inform them in matters that they had considered a man's realm.[2]

The lonely isolated cottage was an easy prey of the Indians during the time of the wars. The cabin of John Merrill, of Nelson County, Kentucky, was attacked by the Indians at midnight. In response to the barking of the dog, Merrill got up and cautiously opened the door to see what was the matter. He was greeted with a volley of shots. An arm and a thigh were broken. As he fell by the open door, he called to his wife to shut it. She succeeded in doing this, but the Indians chopped a hole in the stout clapboard door and attempted to crawl in. Mrs. Merrill, stout in strength and courage, stood to one side with an ax and struck at the head of each Indian as it appeared. She killed or badly wounded four in this way. Enraged at being baffled, they lifted two of their number to the roof, prepared to drop down the chimney. Mrs. Merrill heard the ominous sounds and, guessing their meaning, seized her only feather bed, ripped it open, and tossed its contents on the smoldering fire just as the two Indians started down the chimney. The highly inflammable material caused the flames and stifling smoke to leap up the chimney. In a moment the two warriors, half-

[2] Henry R. Schoolcraft: *Journal of a Tour into the Interior of Missouri and Arkansas* (London, 1821), pp. 6, 31, 32.

smothered and singed by this surprise attack, dropped into the fireplace, where they lay blinded momentarily. Seizing the ax, she dispatched them and was immediately called to the door, where another Indian had been trying to gain entrance. She gave him a blow which so severely wounded him that he beat a hasty retreat to the Indian town of Chillicothe, where, according to a prisoner, he gave an exaggerated report of the ferocity of the "long-knife squaw."

Not all were so fortunate or plucky as Mrs. Merrill, and the lonely cabin with no male protector fell a prey to the Indians. The babies were brained by a blow from a tomahawk and the children large enough to walk were hurried along at top speed to prevent pursuers from overtaking them. Should a child cry repeatedly or become too weak to keep up, he was killed without ceremony. Some noble women clung to their babies and carried them for whole days and nights until they were so utterly exhausted that they dropped in their tracks at a halting-spot. Even when they arrived in the Indian village, there awaited them the horrible decision of whether they would be adopted or tortured to death. If they were fortunate enough to live, they had to make the final separation from their children if any survived. The case of a certain Mrs. Martin gives a picture of the pitiful condition of such a captive. In Virginia in 1782 Jonathan Alder, when a mere boy, was taken prisoner and adopted into an Indian family. About a year after he had been captured the Indian family went to boil salt at a salt spring, and there he met Mrs. Martin. His account follows:

It was now better than a year after I was taken prisoner, when the Indians started off to the Scioto salt-springs, near Chillicothe, to make salt, and took me along with them. Here I got to see Mrs. Martin, that was taken prisoner at the same time I was, and this was the first time that I had seen her since we were separated, at the council-house. When she saw me, she came smiling and asked me if it was

me. I told her it was. She asked me how I had been. I told
her I had been very unwell, for I had had the fever and ague
for a long time. So she took me off to a log, and there we sat
down; and she combed my head, and asked me a great many
questions about how I lived, and if I didn't want to see my
mother and little brothers. I told her that I should be glad
to see them, but never expected to again. She then pulled
out some pieces of her daughter's scalp, that she said were
some trimmings they had trimmed off the night after she
was killed, and that she meant to keep them as long as she
lived. She then talked and cried about her family, that was
all destroyed and gone, except the remaining bits of her
daughter's scalp. We staid here a considerable time, and
meanwhile, took many a cry together; and when we parted
again, took our last and final farewell, for I never saw her
again.[3]

Infrequently a husband was captured, and since the wife
never knew whether he was alive as a captive or had been
killed, the question of her marital status arose. Single women
were at a premium on the frontier, and widows were not allowed to enjoy single bliss very long. Soon the supposed
widow was courted by a number of honorable eligible men.
Usually before long it was ascertained whether the husband was really dead or not. A good many instances, however, occurred where the husband came back to find his
wife married to another. In one famous case of a group of
twelve men captured at the Battle of Blue Licks, eleven
were killed and one was allowed to live. For over a year his
wife awaited his return, hopeful against all arguments, put
forward by a suitor, that he was dead. She finally accepted
this man on condition that her husband did not return. She
postponed the marriage from time to time, however, de-
claring that she could not escape the belief that her husband
would yet return. Her friends finally persuaded her that

[3] Henry Howe: *Historical Collections of Ohio* (Cincinnati, 1875),
pp. 263–4.

her course was foolish, and reluctantly she set the wedding day. At dawn on that day the crack of a rifle was heard near her lonely cabin, and at the sound she leaped out like a liberated wild doe, crying as she ran: "That's John's gun! That's John's gun!" And it was his gun! The trained ear of the woodswoman had detected the familiar sound. In an instant the woman was in her husband's arms. Strangely enough, nine years later, at St. Clair's defeat, that same husband was killed and the same persevering lover won the faithful widow.

It is sometimes stated that thread was spun by fair hands. As a matter of truth those hands were almost universally hardened with toil and browned from exposure.

In addition to the housework the woman provided the garden "sass," hunted greens, picked wild berries, and helped gather nuts for the winter's store. She gathered herbs and made most of the simple home medicines used by the family. After her morning's work was done, she took her place beside her husband, piling brush as he trimmed the fallen trees. And it was the boast of many a pioneer that his wife could run as straight a furrow as any man. Often she plowed with the family cow until evening and then drove her home to milk her for the children's supper.

The task that took a major portion of a woman's time at other than the crop season was that of clothing the family. After the first few years, when all were clothed in the skins of animals, the family began to come out of the hunting and fishing stage in the matter of apparel. A little patch of flax provided the raw material for linen. It was rotted in a nearby creek and then broken by the men. The women then spun it into thread on a small wheel.

In time, when the bears and wolves were sufficiently killed off in a neighborhood, a few sheep were raised. After the sheep had been thoroughly washed in the creek, a small boy would hold the meek animal on its back while the mother sheared it with big scissors. The wool was then carded, spun, and woven.

By 1825 cotton-spinning and weaving came in. After the seeds had been removed, the fiber was carded. This process straightened the fibers out in such a way that they lay parallel. A card was simply a piece of hardwood board about four by ten inches in size and a quarter of an inch thick. One side of the board was covered with a soft leather in which were thickly set fine wire teeth a half inch long. The cotton was spread over these teeth and another card was raked over it. A card was held in each hand, and the raking of one over the other was known as carding. This was done by a series of quick jerks. Then the cotton was rolled up in rolls about as large as a man's thumb and ten inches long. These the woman placed one by one in a heap on the floor beside her until she had enough to spin a "cut" of thread. When enough rolls had been made—every woman knew exactly how many it took to make a cut—she laid down her cards and spun the cut. This gave a change of position and a rest from the cramped position in which she sat. A cut was simply a thread 160 yards long. A woman considered carding and spinning six cuts a day's work.

In spinning, a woman had to stand or walk back and forth as the rolls were drawn into thread and twisted by the turning of the wheel. The hum of the wheel could be heard several hundred feet away and was a characteristic sound of the log cabin from before daylight to nine or ten at night much of the year. Often two women worked together. One carded and the other spun. They changed places after every cut. After the thread was spun, it was dyed in a tub.

When Indians were seen coming, the sons of an Alabama widow named Cobb unhooked their horses from the plow and dashed to the house to take their mother to the fort. As she passed her chimney corner, she saw her dye tub with indigo blue. She quickly turned the whole contents into her lap, jumped up behind her son, and rode eight miles to the fort. When they arrived, they were blue from head to foot. The only thing they saved from the house was the thread in the dye. The women in the fort had looms and made a piece of blue cloth for her.

Not everyone owned a loom for it was a large mechanism for the one-room log cabin. Enough were owned in a neighborhood to weave cloth for all, however.

In addition to the ordinary house duties of cooking, sewing, making candles, and making soap, women made their own starch. They raised flint corn and at a certain stage, when it was still soft, it was taken to the spring, crushed, put into iron pots filled with water, left standing for a time, and then boiled down.

In addition to all these household duties, there was the everpresent matter of childbearing and child-rearing. In many homes a child was born almost every year. The typical frontier woman had a numerous brood at her heels, one or two not yet able to walk, and still another expected to swell the ever increasing circle. Then the day came when a boy was sent for the neighborhood midwife. All of the children were sent to visit a neighboring family, and on their return they found another inmate of the little cabin. When children were born without the aid of anesthetic, amidst the unsanitary conditions of a log cabin, with no medical attention for either mother or child except that of the untutored midwife, it is remarkable that any mother lived to an old age.

A stranger who visited a backwoods home in the late pioneer days before the Civil War said that upon his arrival the daughter of the home, about eighteen, disappeared out of doors for a few minutes and returned from her wide-open dressing-room wearing a clean homespun dress. She was barefooted. After the dishes were done, she moved over to the mantel above the fireplace, took down a cob pipe, reached into a spacious pocket, drew forth some home-cured tobacco, lighted her pipe, and sat down by the fireplace. Soon a large column of smoke rose from around her head as gracefully as that from the most expensive cigar smoked by a congressman. As a matter of record, a cob or clay pipe was quite commonly smoked by the frontier women, young and old, before the Civil War.

XXVII

Border Food

FOR the first few years the settler was largely dependent upon game, wild fruit, corn, nuts, honey, and a little garden truck for food. Often game alone furnished the only food for months until a crop could be raised. The first settlers west of the mountains found plenty of buffalo. Unfortunately these were soon killed and most of their flesh wantonly wasted. While they lasted, however, they were the chief source of food. The tongue was a dainty morsel and was often roasted in the embers of the campfire or fireplace hearth. In June 1778, when Daniel Boone was returning from captivity among the Indians and killed a buffalo, he did not even in his hunger forget to save the tongue and take this delicacy home to his eight-year-old son, Daniel Morgan Boone.[1] The hump was another choice cut. Around the hunter's campfire the marrow bones were especially appreciated. The large leg bones were boiled or roasted in the embers and when done were cracked wide open with an ax and the long rolls of marrow were eaten with zest by the hungry hunter. When the buffalo were gone, venison, readily secured everywhere, was the staple diet. The breast of the wild turkey served as a substitute for bread.

[1] Bakeless: *Boone*, p. 183.

Beaver were to be found in many places, and the beaver tail was a special treat. It was cooked by roasting before the fire. Then the skin would peel off and the delicate meat was eaten with salt. Its flavor was described by Schoolcraft as mellow, luscious, melting in the mouth, somewhat like marrow. It was sometimes used for soup also. In the summer the strong musky taste rendered it unfit for food.

Bear meat was highly appreciated. The bears fed on honey, fruit, and nuts in the autumn and were killed just before going into hibernation while they were fat. They took the place of swine. The oil was used in place of lard, and it was said one could not eat enough to make him sick, for it "never turned on a person's stomach." The oil often furnished fuel for lamps. The hindquarters were made into hams. The claws, roasted in the embers, were considered a special goody. J. B. Finley said that roasted bear claws constituted the richest conceivable delicacy and, although some considered beaver's tail or buffalo marrow better, he begged leave to differ. Some thought panther was the best of all, and to the mind of many, and especially to the colored people, a " 'simmon-fattened possum" was in a class all by itself. A tureen of squirrel broth often graced the table, also.

As wild animals became scarcer and domestic animals became more numerous, the staple frontier meat was pork. Salt pork, bacon, or ham was almost the only meat, day in and day out. At butchering time in the winter there was fresh pork or beef for a while. Sausage was made by pounding the trimmings of the meat on a solid block of wood. At the proper time salt and pepper were added and, when thoroughly macerated, the meat was packed away in vessels or put into hog intestines which had been washed for that purpose, and hung up in the smokehouse.

As a matter of fact, the fare of the first few years was more varied, owing to an abundant supply of game, than that later on. There was a tendency, however, to settle into the easy ways of the hunter's life and to make too little pro-

vision for raising crops and domestic animals. Long before
spring, settlers were surfeited on salt meat and looked forward to the first appearance of spring greens. Turnips,
planted early, furnished the famous Southern dish of turnip
greens. The little truck patch was often neglected, but
furnished some vegetables. Sweet potatoes, known simply as
potatoes, were a staple product. They were generally baked
in the hot ashes. Irish potatoes, less frequently used, were
called white potatoes to distinguish them from the other
variety. Various other vegetables were raised by the thrifty,
but most pioneers were not thrifty. When raised, these vegetables were used unsparingly in summer and dried for
winter. Peppers, string beans, shucky beans, and pumpkins
were dried and hung on strings overhead in the cabin.
Pumpkins were buried under hay to protect them from
freezing or cut in large circular slices and hung on poles or
strings.

Next to meat, corn was the most important item of diet.
Many times for the first year the settlers were almost nau-
seated with the constant diet of meat and they watched the
developing corn with watering mouths. Joyfully the first
roasting ears, pronounced "rosneers," were hailed by a
carbohydrate-starved population. For days corn on the cob
was the principal and welcomed diet. Corn was also dried
for winter use. When the kernels grew more mature and
hard, the ears were rubbed over the rough side of a piece of
tin studded with nail holes. This was called "gritting" (grat-
ing) and made the sweetest corn meal imaginable, according
to the testimony of the pioneers. Throughout the South
coarsely ground corn is still called hominy grits from this
process, and it is still a popular dish. As the grain grew drier
and more flinty, it had to be beaten into bits in the hominy
block or other crude mill. The fine portions were used for
corn meal and the coarser part was boiled and used for
hominy grits, sometimes simply called hominy.

For years almost every particle of breadstuff was made

of corn meal. Ash cake was rolled into small portions and baked in the hot ashes. Sometimes such cake was placed on a clean board in front of the fire and cooked. This was called a johnnycake. Sometimes a hoe was used instead of a board and the product was known as hoe cake. Corn pone was corn bread made into cakes or small loaves. It, or parched corn, was carried on hunts or military expeditions for subsistence. Sometimes these small corn cakes were called corn dodgers. So-called light bread was made of corn meal and baked in Dutch ovens or skillets. Professor Albert Burton Moore tells us that corn light bread was sometimes called Presbyterian bread because the practice of the good Presbyterian "mothers in Israel" was to bake up a quantity of it on Saturdays to avoid breaking the "Sabbath's rest" by cooking ash cakes on Sunday. Others, of course, cooked only enough bread for each meal.

Corn-meal mush was a regular supper dish. In the spring it was made with maple sap and was known as sap porridge. If the scanty supply of milk from the browse-fed cows warranted it, they had milk on their mush. If not, nut oil, bear's grease, or pork cracklings were eaten with it. Lye hominy was made by soaking the whole grains of corn in lye water to remove the hulls and then boiling and seasoning the swollen grains with lard or bear's oil. Bacon or other pork products were such a common accompaniment of this kind of corn that the monotonous diet was often referred to as "hog and hominy." In short, corn was the staff of life in the era before wheat was easily raised. When the first white flour came into use, white bread was like manna from heaven, a food fit for the gods.

In the evening as the family sat around the cheery fire they often cracked and ate nuts. When hickory was burned, a sweet sap boiled out of the end of a burning log. This "hickory goody" was often wiped off on the fingers of the children and from there found its way into their mouths. A trencher of raw turnips was often brought in and the whole group sat around eating them. A cultured German immigrant of Missouri wrote, in 1835, that his American pioneer neighbors ate raw potatoes as they ate apples in Germany and that one neighbor complained that his children had eaten nearly all his potatoes in the field before digging time. He said they ate many other things raw: beets, turnip tops, cabbage leaves, hickory bark, and so on.

From the Indians the settlers of Mississippi got the idea of seasoning foods with nuts. A dish known as sof-ky to the Indians, but Americanized into "Tom Fuller" by the settlers, was made by cracking the shells of certain nuts very fine and putting them, shell and kernel, into a pot containing peas, corn, dry venison, and beans. The nuts furnished the grease for seasoning. When served, the dish was of a consistency of thick soup. It was similar to the succotash of the Northern Indians—a mixture of corn and beans.

Other forest products were plums, haws, grapes, persimmons, and all sorts of berries. The winter grapes and persimmons were not good until frost. In some places in the lower South after a few years rice was grown.

Sweetening came almost wholly from the forest. The so-called "long sweetening" was honey obtained from bee trees. "Short sweetening," or maple sugar, was also obtained in its raw state from the trees. In Louisiana, because of the favorable climate, sugar-making came in before the frontier era had passed, and supplied the settlers with the luxury of a dark sugar. In most places, however, sugar was so scarce it was saved for the use of the sick, to sweeten a dram, or for special occasions such as a wedding.[2]

A foreigner in Alabama mentioned that a great deal of sour milk was used there. Clabber was eaten with a spoon. Cheese and butter were made at each home where a cow was in milk.

Before 1840 the popular table drinks were almost unknown in the new country. A Presbyterian minister making a tour

[2] Moore: *History of Alabama*, p. 137.

of the West, fearing that he might not always be able to get tea, took a pound in his saddlebags. When he reached a home where it was not obtainable, he took the tea and handed it unopened to the housewife. Such was her utter ignorance of its use that she served it to him on a plate as she would a dish of greens. When he asked her about the broth from it, he found she had thrown that out.

When Schoolcraft prepared some Chinese tea as a treat for his Ozark hostess, he was surprised when she rejected it as a bitter herb. She preferred their drinks of sassafras, dittany, and spicewood. By 1840 black coffee was coming into use as a beverage.

Whisky was universally used and a person no more thought of acting the host to a visitor, be he preacher or statesman, without a dram or eggnog than he would of hunting without a gun. Anne Royall said: "I am afraid my brave Tennesseans indulge too great a fondness for whiskey. When I was in Virginia it was too much whiskey—in Ohio, too much whiskey—in Tennessee, it is too, too much whiskey!"

Whisky was often drunk at the table in the way coffee or tea is today. In Missouri just before the Civil War, it was so common for travelers to carry a jug that the Kansas free-state men on their way through the proslavery blockade to the abolitionists in the East carried their papers safely through that hostile slave state openly in a jug.

A correspondent of the *Prairie Farmer* saw this Missouri sign: "Hunny in the come." Inside, a jingling of glasses and a babble of voices from the crowd indicated a brisk retail trade, while the wholesale capacity of the place was indicated by a sign done in relief on a cottonwood board with the point of a jackknife: "Licker fer sail by the BoRL." In all the hotels, first-, second-, third-, and no-class, he said, Bacchus had his temple, shrine, and devotees. The proportion of buildings in the Missouri town devoted to the sale of liquor was truly great.

XXVIII

Pioneer Dress

IN no particular did the impact of savagery upon the whites show its influence more markedly than in the matter of dress. For years the hunting shirt was universally worn. This was a kind of loose frock reaching about halfway down the thighs and drawn in at the waist by a broad leather belt. It was held together in front by two or three buttons or hooks. The sleeves were large and the garment was so wide it lapped over a foot or more when belted. It had an upright collar and a small full cape. Ordinarily it was made of linsey-woolsey. William Newnham Blane described one which was dyed blue and bound round the collar, cuffs, cape, and edges with red fringe. He pronounced the dress one of the most commodious, serviceable, and at the same time becoming and elegant he had ever seen. Less frequently it was made of buckskin, which although very durable for wear in the brush, shrank when wet and was very cold and uncomfortable in wet weather. The bosom of the shirt served as a wallet to hold pieces of jerked meat, corn pone, tow for wiping the rifle barrel, or any other necessity for the hunter or scout in the field. The belt was always fastened behind. In cold weather mittens were tucked under it in front of the body. From it hung a shot-pouch. On the right side was suspended a tomahawk and on the left a sheathed scalping knife.

Leggings covered the legs and lower thighs, but often no breeches were worn. Cresswell noted in his diary on June 10, 1775: "I believe there is but two pair of Breeches in the company, one belonging to Mr. Tilling and the other to myself. The rest wear breech-clouts, leggings and hunting shirts, which have never been washed only by the rain since they were made." [1]

William Hickman in writing of Harrodsburg on April 1, 1776 says that "a poor town it was in those days, a row or two of smoky cabins, dirty women, men with their britch clouts, greasy hunting shirts, leggings and moccasins."

The breech clout of the savage covered the breech and loins. Secured by a girdle at the waist, it was formed of a piece of linen nearly a yard long and eight or ten inches wide, which passed through the crotch with the two ends carried under the belt in front and behind and allowed to hang down over the girdle behind, and in front forming ornamental flaps. These flaps were often trimmed with coarse embroidery. The leggings were attached by straps or suspenders to the same girdle. When this belt, as was often the case, passed over the hunting shirt, the upper thighs and buttocks were partially exposed. The young warrior was proud of this Indian-like dress. In time, when society had advanced beyond the semibarbaric stage indicated here, this costume, formed of dressed buckskin, was adopted by the young men as a fancy dress to display their fine forms and persons.[2] Like the Western cowboy costume, it remained long afterward a symbol of an epoch.[3] The leggings were made of dressed deerskin.

[1] Willard Rouse Jillson: *Early Frankfort and Franklin County, Kentucky 1750–1850* (Louisville, 1936), p. 22.

[2] Henry Howe: *Historical Collections of the Great West* (Cincinnati, 1856), II, 188.

[3] John W. Monette: *History of the Discovery and Settlement of the Valley of the Mississippi* (New York, 1846), II, 2–3.

Many did not fully adopt the Indian breech cloth but wore pantaloons or breeches, following the custom of their forebears. Even these wore the hunting shirt as an overcoat. Under it were perhaps a shirt and vest. Sometimes a deerskin hunting shirt was ornamented with tassels and leather bands of fringed deerskin around the shirt and cape and the wrist and shoulders of the sleeves.

Shoe-packs and moccasins served for footwear. Moccasins were made of a single piece of buffalo or deerskin with a gathering seam along the top of the foot and another seam without gathers from the bottom of the heel as high as the ankle joint or a little above. Flaps were left on each side to reach some distance up the legs. Thongs attached to these were wrapped about the legs, securing the ankles and lower legs against snow, dust, or gravel getting into the moccasins. It took but a few hours to make them. The only tools necessary were a knife and a moccasin awl made from the back spring of an old clasp knife. This instrument with its buckhorn handle, together with a roll of buckskin for repairing moccasins, was always carried on the shot-pouch strap. On a long campaign repair work was a frequent task by the campfire. The moccasins were sewed together and patched with deerskin strings or "whang" leather, as it was called. During cold weather as a substitute for stockings the moccasins were stuffed with deer hair or dry leaves. This kept the feet fairly comfortable in dry weather, but it was a common saying that wearing moccasins when it was wet underfoot was "a decent way of going barefooted." The porous nature of the leather readily admitted moisture. The shoe-pack probably had a sole and was made of home-processed leather. In warm weather nearly everyone went barefoot. A Captain Cumming, while a candidate for the legislature, canvassed Conecuh County, Alabama, on horseback with nothing on his feet but what he had been born with. It was not unusual to meet men on horseback with their bare feet armed with a rude pair of wooden spurs. It was entirely permissible to attend church barefoot. Even the women went barefoot. When dress shoes were finally secured, often in order to save them the young lady would walk barefoot while her beau carried her shoes. Near the church she would sit down on a log, brush the dust from her feet, put on her stockings and shoes, and they would go on to divine service.

A man's cap was often made of coonskin with the tail dangling down behind, or of bear, fox, or wolf skin. Sometimes if the skin of a smaller animal was used, the feet were left on it. Instead of wearing hats in the summer, men sometimes wore handkerchiefs around their heads. Hats of plaited grass or straw were also worn.

In winter over the hunting shirt a blanket or bearskin robe was worn Indian-fashion and pinned under the chin. At night the robe made a good bed. Sometimes an old hunter would make himself a winter coat of a large bearskin in the following way: Beginning at the nose, he would split the skin down the belly to the tail. He next split the skin on the inside of the hind legs and stripped it off the body, but without opening up the front legs. As these were skinned, the skin was left whole, turned, and pulled over them and the head. The forelegs, when turned, served as sleeves, and the head as a cap. In curing such a hide, salt was sprinkled on it and the cows allowed to lick it. They would lick out most of the grease.

Gradually as the frontier moved west, by 1825, the hunting shirt and buckskin attire began to disappear and were worn only by the old hunters on the extreme edge of the frontier. Almost everybody still went barefoot and shoes were not common. A shoemaker in each community began to make "fine shoes" of calfskin for special occasions. The men in each home made the rough everyday footwear, known as shoe-packs.

As settlement pushed into the region of milder climate below Tennessee, lighter clothing was worn. Goods of flax were worn by white people and tow by the Negroes. On formal occasions, especially at weddings, white suits were worn by the rising planter aristocracy. In winter jeans, linsey-woolsey, and other homespun took the place of leather clothing. Men's "fine" coats were often made of yard goods such as ladies used for dresses. One old man recorded that he had grubbed three days at twenty-five cents a day to get calico to make him a coat to go to see the young lady who later became his wife.[4]

Men and boys never wore coats or shoes at any gathering in summer. White cotton or linen shirts ornamented with brown suspenders colored with copperas and fastened to the trousers in front and behind by large horn or pewter buttons were usual.

Under the age of six, girls and boys were dressed exactly alike. Their hair was cropped short. A little girl with long hair would have been an object of general comment. Boys until they were in their teens wore nothing but a single garment, a "wamus" or shirt that reached down nearly to the ankles. Early the wamus was of buckskin, later of tow. Both boys and girls wore Virginia poke bonnets or sunbonnets.

On the raw frontier, women's clothing, like men's, was made of buckskin. Soon by means of their own handicraft they began to furnish their wardrobe from wool, cotton, or flax. A linsey-woolsey petticoat and a "bed gown" were the usual dress of the women in early times. In the winter they wore woolen stockings. In summer linen or straw sundowns (sunbonnets) were the normal headgear. In 1823 on the Indiana frontier caps made of dark, coarse knotted twine "like a cabbage net" were worn, as the women said, "to save slickin' up and to hide dirt."[5] Sometimes broad-brimmed straw hats were worn. The hair was either tied in a hard knot on the nape of the neck or plaited and done up on top

[4] Virginia Clay McClure: "The Settlement of the Kentucky Appalachian Highlands," MS. (Doctor's thesis, University of Kentucky, 1933), p. 115.

[5] J. A. Woodburn: "Local Life and Color in the New Purchase," *Indiana Magazine of History*, IX, 224.

of the head. Dresses extended from neck to heels, and there was seldom a ruffle, flounce, or other ornamental device.

Seldom did store goods make their appearance in the backwoods. When Audubon attended a barbecue in Kentucky in 1810 he noticed that all the fair ones were clad in pure white, and as they jumped lightly from their horses and advanced, they resembled a procession of nymphs, and their buckskin escorts disguised divinities.

Milburn recorded that at one frolic a backwoods beauty who had sent her father to the city fifty miles away for a dress was the center of attraction. What catastrophes take place when men are entrusted with the responsibility of purchasing women's clothes! He bought calico, a luxurious fabric for the backwoods, but unfortunately this was a lurid red furniture calico with very large figures. The hunters stood about staring and admiring this ravishing beauty. The young women were envious, the young men attentive, and the older women winking and whispering to one another that "that gal's extravagance will spile the whole family." Certainly it took a very little finery purchased from some peddler to create great excitement in a neighborhood.

In the rural area the women dressed much better than did the men, who had a tendency to cling to the old hunting shirt long after the women had begun to wear store finery.

The well-to-do in town after a few years could, and did, buy silks, satins, and velvets, and ribbons and plumes for their hats. As early as 1784, at Louisville, St. John de Crèvecœur noticed a boat carrying seventeen people, of whom all the men had on silk stockings and all the ladies had parasols. A planter's wife wrote from Columbia, Missouri, in 1835 that the people dressed well and very fashionably. She thought most of them carried it to an extreme. Straw bonnets and Circassian dresses with large capes trimmed with black cord or braid, tassels, and silk belts were fashionable among the upper class in that boom period.

XXIX

Frontier Ways

THE ways of the frontier were those brought from the East, conditioned by contacts with the primitive. When the first half-famished settlers joyfully saw the interminable winter drawing to a close, the women followed the cows out along the little streams to see what they found to eat and in that way learned what greens to pick for their families.

The dishes were few, heavy, and homely. A few pewter vessels found their way west amidst the other "plunder," but for the most part tableware consisted of a set of trenchers of different sizes hewn from logs. In time, glazed earthen vessels or crockery, known as delf, came into use. This was the famous blue tableware of the early and middle nineteenth century. At first there was much criticism of this new tableware by the old backwoodsmen. They objected that the hard surface dulled their scalping knives, and furthermore the fork would not stick into the hard surface, but slipped about and sometimes flipped the meat out of the plate onto the table.

A "meat trough" was a canoe-shaped trough made from a log. It was used to hold pork while it was taking salt.

Washing was almost invariably done out of doors. In rainy seasons it was possible to catch enough rain water to do the washing. A large log was split in half and dug out to form two huge troughs. These were set under the eaves and caught quantities of soft rain water. When coopers established their shops, rain barrels were placed at one or two corners and the roof water was led into these reservoirs by means of troughs made of bark or halves of small hollow trees.

If water was not available at the house, the washing was done by the spring or little stream, often some distance from the house. A big iron kettle was inverted and kept there. Often it was necessary to "break" this water by adding potash from the ash leech. The clothes were well smeared with soft soap and then thoroughly boiled in the big kettle, which was swung under a tripod. Then the clothes were laid on a block or heavy bench and the dirt pounded out with a batting or "battling" paddle. Old-timers say this "battling" could be heard fully a quarter of a mile away. After the clothes had been beaten, they were put into hot water and smeared with soap again; then the women rubbed them vigorously between their knuckles. Another boiling and rinsing completed the program. Lines were often not available and the clothes were hung on rail fences or on the boughs of trees. These neighborhood laundering areas often became social centers in the sense that the young folk frequently came with the elders to help wash, and the trees in the vicinity were covered with inscriptions and little rhymes bearing messages of love and flirtation. A typical washday was characterized by flying smoke, squalling children, and slavish labor.

The cabin in the evening was ordinarily lighted by the flames of the fireplace, but in case of sickness or on other special occasions lamps were improvised. One such, called a "slut," consisted of a saucer or similar vessel filled with bear's oil or other fat. A strip of cotton cloth was then inserted, allowing one end to lie over the edge. This end of the wick was lighted. Sometimes in place of the cloth small split sticks were tied into a bundle and set on end in the fat as a substitute for a wick. A cob lamp was sometimes used, consisting of a wick, fifteen or twenty feet long, dipped in rosin and beeswax and wound around a corncob. The wick was drawn up through the hole in the center where the pith had been taken out of the cob. From time to time the wick was pulled up through the cob.

For lanterns, shellbark hickory torches or "light wood" made of small split sticks of pitch pine were used. Frequently a slave or two walked along the trace ahead of a party, bearing aloft these hickory torches, which lighted up the narrow woodland trail on the darkest night.

Beds were often removable. Some of the more primitive were made in the corner of the cabin and could be removed by taking out the one post in the cabin and taking down the bed rails. Bear or buffalo skins were used at first. Ticks were filled with cattails or oak leaves until enough corn or wheat was raised to fill them with shucks or straw. Feather beds were used in the winter, especially in the upper South. Featherstonhaugh found at a judge's home in southwestern Arkansas a bed with two sheets. He remarked that it was the first time he had seen such a phenomenon in several months' travel in Missouri and Arkansas, and he had spent some time in Little Rock.[1]

Until he went away to Cincinnati to study medicine, Daniel Drake had never seen a scrubbing brush. In their home a split broom had always been used. He had spent many rainy days and evenings making them. A hickory sapling furnished the raw material. The stick was stood on end and thin pieces were split down the outside of the stick eight or ten inches with a jackknife pressed with the right thumb. These were bent back and held down with the other hand. When the heart was reached and there was no more flexible wood, the central part of the stick was sawed off and the splits turned back up to their original place and tied

[1] Featherstonhaugh: *Excursion through the Slave States*, p. 118.

with a tow string. The stick was then inverted and the portion of the pole above the splits was shaved to the size of a
handle. A lighter broom for more genteel use was a short
hand-broom known as a scrub. It was made exactly like the
larger broom except that it was made from a smaller sapling and was shorter. When Dr. Drake was twelve, he was
dexterous in the manufacture and use of both.

Hickory and pawpaw were used in a surprising number of
ways as a substitute for iron. Ropes and harness traces were
made of the bark of hickory and pawpaw. The so-called
"Missouri hitch" consisted in fastening the vehicle to a knot
tied in the tail of the horse. Buffalo hide was cut into strips
and used for rope.

Kentuckians dried the sinews of the buffalo and divided
them into small fibers. These were used for fiddlestrings
and for sewing moccasins. Buffalo horns served for drinking
cups, were used to make combs, and were blown. Conch
shells and large cow horns or tin trumpets were used also
for family and neighborhood signaling. Blasts from these
brought the father and the boys from the clearing for meals.
Children were called from the woods to the hearth by the
horn or a youngster was called to do a chore. The neighbor
who had promised to act as midwife was summoned by horn,
whereupon she mounted her steed and rode to her neighbor's place. Upon the arrival of the new citizen, she gave the
prearranged signal on the horn to let her waiting family
know that all was well. Everybody knew the tone of everyone else's horn, and even a woman or child could blow it so
it could be heard long distances.

The door of the cabin was fastened with a latch on the
inside. A deerskin cord attached to it ran through the door
and always hung on the outside except in time of an Indian
scare; hence the expression that to this day signifies the
utmost in hospitality: "The latchstring hangs out." Such
was the primitive simplicity that there were no locks. The

first lock in one community was bought by a farmer and attached to the door of his corn-crib. This aroused such indignation among the whole neighborhood that a mass meeting compelled him to remove it. Public opinion held that his action was a reflection upon the honesty of the neighborhood and an insult to the whole community. It was freely acknowledged that he had a perfect right to lock things from his own children in his house, but to turn a key in the face of the whole community was an affront that would not be brooked.

Since the chimney was made of poles and the clay chinking sometimes cracked and dropped off, leaving the thoroughly dry and highly inflammable wood exposed, it was sometimes necessary to "wet down" the fire to keep the chimney from catching on fire. This was done by throwing a pail of water over the backlog and other areas of the fire adjacent to the exposed area. This sent forth clouds of steam and ashes, which at times seemed to threaten the whole household with the fate of Herculaneum and Pompeii. Should the chimney catch on fire (and the colder the night, the heavier the firing and the more likely a conflagration), it was necessary to get out in the wintry blasts and pour on water. As a last resort in order to save the house, a pole that was kept in readiness was used to push the chimney away from the building and thus save the home.

Too often, however, the house caught on fire before the danger was discovered, and burned to the ground. There was no such thing as insurance, but the warm-hearted sympathy of the community rose to an emergency so effectually that almost a one hundred per cent coverage was effected. When one suffered a loss, all lamented. A personal calamity was a neighborhood misfortune, and sympathy was not a mere form of empty words. The unfortunate family was taken to the shelter of a near neighbor's home, and there the women wept with and for the sufferers. A list of articles needed to furnish a new home completely was made out and such as the neighbors could not give were made by the women and their menfolk.

In the meantime the whole neighborhood as one man came together at the scene of the loss and began to erect another cabin. In such an emergency a house was completed in a day and a night.

When it was ready for occupancy the whole community came together again. Each brought a gift by way of furnishing the new home. One brought a gourd of lard, another a ham, others quilts, chairs, stools, a water bucket, cooking vessels, and clothing.

One man wrote in reminiscence:

> My father's house burned about the middle of one cold night in December. Notwithstanding the severity of the weather, by sun-down the second day after the fire, and before the place where the old house sat had cooled off or quit smoking, we were all comfortably housed in a new cabin, with as much furniture as we lost in the fire.

It was amazing to a foreigner what a backwoodsman could make with a few simple tools. A washtub, piggin, or water pail was often made with no other tools than a broadax and a scalping knife. The latter, fastened in a stick of timber that was hewed and made as straight as possible in imitation of a carpenter's plane, was known as a jointer.

As a result of a certain feeling of superiority due to their European background, foreigners, especially those with an education, when coming in contact with the backwoodsmen were inclined to look down on the crudities of the frontier and to slow the speed of their adjustment to an environment so different from that of the Old World. A German immigrant, Gert Goebel, learned this lesson the hard way and afterward wrote:

> Much of the work done by the natives looked so simple, that we thought we could easily do it. We soon learned

that every trade and occupation requires a certain skill. For example, we observed how our neighbors cut their corn fodder and set it up in shocks. We undertook to do the same, but in spite of all our toil we had scarcely begun the second shock, when the first had already fallen down. While thus engaged in cutting corn Caleb Bailey, who said he was our nearest neighbor, came over and made us understand, that the dry cornstalks which we were cutting had no value as fodder so we desisted from this irksome task.

Another lesson which we had to learn pertained to the simple principle of splitting fence rails. I had suggested to my father that he had better hire one of our neighbors for a day, and let him show us how it was done. My father, however, responded that the splitting of wood was such a simple matter, that with a little thinking, we would soon understand it, just as well as our ignorant American neighbors.

It is true, that mathematical and astronomical problems can be solved by hard thinking. It is also true that the splitting of fence rails does not require any scientific training for most of our skilled woodsmen could neither read nor write, nevertheless the work in which these men showed so much skill required an infinite amount of practice and the most varied experience. Mere thinking could never teach us that the beautiful, slender sycamore could not be split by any man, that of the different elms only a single variety can sometimes be split, that of the black gums, which sometimes grow forty to fifty feet absolutely straight before the branches begin, not even a short log can be cleft in two. We did not know that the kind of timber most commonly used for rails was the different varieties of oak, nor did we know that even these did not always split well.

A hillside near our field had been almost completely deforested. Only here and there we found a few large black oak and white oak trees standing. To any one initiated into the mystery of the forest it would have been clear that there was a reason why these fine trees had been spared. We in our ignorance undertook to fell them but could not get a decent chip out. We hacked all around the trunk until it finally came down. The stump looked as if beavers had gnawed it off. This sample of our skill was for a long time an object of amusement to the passing Americans. By noon my father had his hands full of blisters, so that he had to give up the work. During the afternoon I succeeded in felling two more trees in spite of my aching hands. On the following days these trees were to be cut into ten foot rail lengths. In spite of all of our efforts, the second day saw only seven rail lengths cut. But our effort at splitting the logs capped the climax. Instead of setting our first wedge at the larger end of the log we set it at the smaller, pounded away at it until it was driven entirely into the wood. By this time the maul was a wreck. Ferdinand was sent to get another maul from Boing. In the meantime we set to work to make a maul ourselves. Unfortunately we chose the most useless kind of wood for this sort of an implement, namely black walnut. We chopped out our wedge and set it in a new place. Presently it, too, stuck tight, without having produced even a slight split, while our new maul lay in splinters. Again we chopped our wedge out, and again proceeded to drive it with Boing's maul, which Ferdinand had in the meantime brought. By the end of the day we had all our wedges chopped out again, Boing's maul lay in ruins, but not a single fence rail did we have to show for. The following day we were very much downcast and physically sore.

The next day Tom and Bill Bailey visited us. We told them what we had done. They only laughed and asked us to get our axes and to go with them. They took us to a part of the woods where black oaks abounded, selected a particularly straight one, placed themselves on opposite sides of the tree and began to chop. With every blow chips as large as your hand flew in every direction. In less than five minutes the oak lay on the ground. They measured off four lengths. Each of the lads sprang on the log and they began to cut it in two. One side of the cut was as straight as if it had been sawed. Then they selected a tough young white oak for a maul, cut it off close to the ground, trimmed the handle with their ax and smoothed it with their pocket knives. With even more skill and ease they made a couple of wedges from another tough tree. The iron wedge was set in the larger end of the log. A few blows sank it in and the log was half split open. Following up with the wooden wedges, the log lay in halves. This was all done in an incredibly short time. The halves and the quarters of the log were handled in the described manner. In less than two hours they had finished between forty and fifty rails. We had learned more in those two hours than we could have acquired by several months of hard thinking.[2]

When a preacher or other man known for his piety visited a home, it was customary to ask him in a manner peculiar to the South and the Old Southwest to lead in family religious activities. An invitation to lead family prayers was given in this fashion: the host handed his guest the Bible and hymn book saying: "Will you take the books, sir?" He gave an invitation to offer thanks at table: "Will you make a beginning, sir?" Then all reverently bowed their heads while the blessing was being asked.[3]

In the early days there were no watches or clocks. People depended upon the sun to indicate more or less the time of day. A Louisiana woman upon being asked the time of day by a traveler walked across her puncheon floor to where she had her sun mark and brought back word that it was a puncheon and a half until twelve o'clock. Some had hourglasses. Some made a sundial on the top of a stone or stump. Calendars were scarce also. Often people counted time from some noted event, as two years after the cold winter or the year before the big flood.

Mail routes were scarce in the sparsely settled areas, and since government mail was not available, most letters were carried by private messenger. This seems to have had the effect of making messages more or less public business. John Floyd, of Kentucky, wrote a correspondent, on December

[2] William G. Bek: "The Followers of Duden," *Missouri Historical Review*, XVI, 379–82.
[3] Pierson: *In the Brush*, pp. 54–5.

8, 1780: "If you write me about it, let it be by some one who will deliver the letter as I scarce ever receive any but what are broke open."

Borrowing was universal. If a man owned a crosscut saw, an augur, or other tool of steel not generally possessed but more valuable than rubies, it virtually became in use and practice the common property of the whole station or neighborhood. Even milk, butter, cream, garden vegetables, and fruits were borrowed. One traveler reported that the thrifty householder would have applications for his garden products before they were ripe and, if disposed to be liberal, would have no chance of tasting them himself.

Hospitality reigned supreme. Once a friend abode for a time with Thomas Sharp Spencer in Tennessee and helped him plant a patch of corn. When he wished to return home, his host went with him as far as the barrens of Kentucky to set him on the right trail, but he had lost his scalping knife and had nothing with which to butcher and skin game. Hospitably, Spencer broke his own knife into two pieces and gave his departing friend a piece of the precious metal worth, under those conditions, more than gold or silver.[4]

Many early settlers did not even have horses and had to plant their crops with mattocks and heavy hoes. There were few wheeled vehicles. When horses were available much hauling was done with a ground sled known as a "land-slide." Built like a sled, it was used at all seasons, even as a family vehicle. A family would ride to the house-raising or spelling school in such a conveyance. Over roots, poles, and logs and through mud holes it was a fairly easy method of travel. A family rode on one or more horses and no violence was done to good form for a young man to offer a blushing maiden a seat behind him on his horse. Sometimes horseback parties would gaily move along with the young men holding umbrellas over their fair partners. All around

[4] Thomas Edwin Matthews: *General James Robertson, Father of Tennessee* (Nashville, 1934), p. 208.

the churches were horse blocks for ladies to mount and dismount from their horses.

Southerners usually rode with a thick blanket—more often white than colored as people began to put on finery—over the saddle, forming a comfortable cushion. In case of rain or cold the blanket was unstrapped and folded about the rider after the manner of the Indians. When he was forced to stay overnight in the woods, this blanket and the one under the saddle served for a bed. A horse was never tied to the trunk of a tree, but always to a bough over his head. This gave the animal more freedom, and a sudden jerk in fighting flies did not break the reins.

In western Georgia, October 1 was known as settling day. On that day accounts for the year were due, although it was freely interpreted as any time between October 1 and Christmas. During all the year until that time, transactions were of the barter type.

To go security for a friend was as much a duty as to sit up with him when he was ill, take care of him when he was feeling happy, or fight for him if he got into a brawl.

An important pastime of the young men, due no doubt to their environment, was practicing imitating the noise of every animal of the forest. In fact, its utility made it an almost necessary part of the education of the backwoodsman. The gobble of the skilled woodsman could bring the keen-eyed, ever watchful turkey up to him. A bleating fawn called the anxious mother to her death. For amusement the hunter often coaxed to his camp a group of owls that sat about screaming in hoarse voices.

Nearly everyone used tobacco. Chewing was widely practiced and many even of the women chewed, dipped snuff, and smoked.

XXX

Frontier Speech

THE distinct flavor of the language spoken over the entire area treated in this volume came from the uplanders and was carried northwest and southwest by them. In Georgia it was known as "cracker" talk. It was brought into southern Ohio, Indiana, and Illinois and known there as Hoosier dialect. Before it was used to designate the citizens of Indiana, the term "Hoosier" was used in the South to describe a rough or uncouth person.[1] Some of the distinct words and phrases came directly from Elizabethan English, are now obsolete, and sound strange for that reason. Others have come into good American use, but most of them are widely used provincialisms today.

The frontiersman was inclined to speak in superlatives. He had the finest dog, the most accurate gun, and the fastest horse imaginable. When speaking of Kentucky, the citizen of that state waxed eloquent. A boatman in singing her praises bragged: "No, stranger, there's no place on the universal 'arth like old Kaintuck; she whips all 'out-west' in prettiness; and you might bile down cr'ation and not get such another state out of it."

[1] Robert La Follette: "Interstate Migration and Indiana Culture," *Mississippi Valley Historical Review,* XVI, 349.

Timothy Flint spoke of a Methodist minister who was attempting to convey to his illiterate auditors some conception of the realm within the pearly gates and, after considerable explaining, wound up his description by saying: "In short, my brethren, to say all in one word, heaven is a Kentuck of a place."

Many expressions were strong metaphors drawn from the hunt, the Indian fight, the steamboat, or other incidents or objects of the savage surroundings. Abraham Lincoln must have used a frontier expression that originated with an animal fight when he wrote from the White House to a general in the field: "Hang on. Chew and choke." A minister on arriving at a certain appointment found the meeting-place where he was to preach occupied that evening by a secret society. The church people commented that the two appointments "locked horns." This undoubtedly came from the buffalo bull or domestic bull fight, or possibly from the strife between male deer, who sometimes got their horns so badly locked that they could not loosen them and both died in the struggle.

When a person or animal pretended to be asleep or dead, he was said to be "playing possum." When an opossum was caught and chewed up by a dog, his bones would crack and he would give every evidence of having expired, but once left alone, he got up and made off. Raccoons were plentiful and the hunters enjoyed the social outlet provided by hunting them in a group. Often people were called coons in good-natured or even affectionate palaver. A man in difficulty would often say: "I'm a gone coon," which meant that he was ruined or lost.

A man, likewise, was often intimately called an "old hoss" (horse). A typical horse-trade conversation was reported thus:

"Well, my old coon," said he, "do you want to swap *hosses*?" "Why, I don't know," replied the stranger; "I believe I've got a beast I'd trade with you for that one, if you like him." "Well, fetch up your nag, my old cock; you're jist the lark I wanted to get hold of. I am perhaps a *leetle*, jist a *leetle*, of the best horse-swap that ever stole *cracklins* out of his mammy's fat gourd. Where's your hoss?" "I'll bring him presently; but I want to examine your horse a little." "Oh! Look at him," said the Blossom, alighting and hitting him a cut; "look at him. He's the best piece of *hoss*-flesh in the thirteen united univarsal worlds. There's no sort o' mistake in little Bullet. He can pick up miles on his feet, and fling 'em behind him as fast as the next man's hoss, I don't care where he comes from. And he can keep at it as long as the sun can shine without resting."

Another figure stemming from the use of horses was that referring to the headquarters of a trader as his stand or stamp or stamping-ground. A stamping-ground was a place where a horse stood for perhaps hours and stamped to scare away the flies.

The action of a man who pretended to do something that he was not really trying to do, or the act of doing something half right, was expressed by the old hunters: "He's shooting at the hump." Hunters knew full well that a shot at the hump of a buffalo really counted for naught. If a man wanted to kill a bison, he shot just behind the foreleg.

When a spy went out and returned with the report that the Indians were near, doubters would say: "He smelled a cold track."

The term "brush" was used a great deal in the highlands to represent a backwoods or rural area. At a ministerial meeting an old pioneer minister was spoken of as "an old brush-breaker." Or it would be said of another: "That is Brother ——. He has broken a right smart chance of brush." When a bishop got a bit confused in his sermon and failed to make himself clear, a minister remarked: "Didn't you think the Bishop got badly brushed in the first part of his sermon?" This meant, of course, that he was lost in the brush.

From spinning came the term "slack twisted." To pronounce a man slack twisted meant that he lacked courage. Cloth made from thread that had been twisted too little made cloth that did not wear well.

A wagoner picked up a bucket, at the same time saying: "Stranger, is this your bucket?" "Yes," returned the other. "Well, I thought it was mine, for I'm a bucket out of pocket." Often people did not speak of splitting rails—they "mauled" them. A man in easy circumstances was spoken of as "not rich, but a good liver."

An English schoolteacher in Alabama reported the following idioms: The term "holler" was applied to almost any kind of noise. When a carpenter bee began to buzz, one said: "How that bee hollers in his hole!" The word "whip" was used as a synonym for "win over" or "overcome"; for example, "He whipped me at running, but I can whip him at jumping." "Tote" was used instead of "carry," and "bucket" instead of "pail." "Right" was used in the old English usage meaning "very"; that is, "a right pretty brook." When offering a wet towel to a guest, a Hoosier landlady apologized that "thar'd been sich a rite down smart chance of rain that her wash wouldn't dry." "Severe" was used to describe a wild or cross animal: "The man has a severe dog." When one wanted to send a person away, one might say: "Make tracks!" When one desired to speak contemptuously of a person, one might say: "He is all sorts of a feller" or "He is no account."

When a man wished to compliment another on his crop, he said: "You've a mighty heap this year." The terms "powerful" and "heap" were both used to indicate the superlative quality of almost any other commodity also: "He had a heap of trouble"; "I'd a heap rather have my claim than his." If a man were just recovering from an illness he might be said to be "powerful weak."

The steamboat and other boats played such a large part in the lives of the people that they were the origin of many phrases, metaphors, and allusions. If one inquired whether a person were reliable or not and it chanced that he was very unreliable, the reply might be: "He won't do to tie to in a calm, let alone a storm." A man who returned safely from a journey by flatboat would say he had made the trip; "to make the trip" then became a universal synonym of success. Of the beginner who attempted to make a stump speech, preach a sermon, or address a jury, people predicted his failure or success by saying: "He'll make the trip" or "He'll never make the trip." When asking a newcomer to take a drink with him, the pioneer would say: "Stranger, will you take in wood?" A boat took on fuel to keep its steam up and a person took in liquor to keep his steam up. To become ardent or jealous was to "raise the steam." To give vent angrily to one's feelings was to "let off steam." To encounter a disaster was to "bust a byler" (boiler). The expression "cut loose" was used for "start" or "go ahead."

When a young man was courting a girl, it was said: "He is setting to her." If his suit was rejected, it was said: "She kicked him." When one suitor was successful to the disappointment of several others, the experience was summed up thus: "The tallest pole takes the persimmon."

At a church meeting in the brush, like many another meeting, the parliamentary machine got completely choked with motions piled on one another, and the greatest confusion prevailed as to the question before the body. When the moderator was appealed to, that worthy, rising to his feet, hesitated a moment and then said: "Brethren, my decision is that you are all ahead of the hounds."

"Sunup" and "sundown" were used instead of "sunrise" and "sunset." In informing a stranger how far west Ohio paper money was good, a citizen said: "It's such good money that it will carry you to sundown." A handsome young girl at a log tavern had so many suitors that it was said that "they came to visit her in *cords*" or that "she flung them off by *cargoes*." A person in financial straits was said to be "in a tight place" or "in a bad fix." When he ran off from his creditors he was said to have "sloped." When a proposed arrangement was difficult to settle, it was said: "It won't do any which-way you may fix it;" or "They can't fix it, anyhow or nohow."

A Huntsville, Alabama, newspaper gave the following dictionary of cracker expressions: "flustrated"—greatly agitated; "jimberjawed"—having one's tongue constantly moving; "chawed up"—having an ear, nose, or lip bitten off; "corn stealer" or "tater grabber"—the thumb and the four digits; "lambasting"—a severe beating; "licking"—blows inflicted with fist; "mosey"—to clear out; "obsquatulate"—to mosey or abscond; "pernickety"—squeamish or fastidious; "ring-tailed roarer"—a most violent fellow, a Crockett; "Rip-roarious" or "rambunctious" or "ripping and tearing"—very outrageous; "sock dologer"—in fighting, a lick that counted; "sarsafari"—legal proceedings of any kind; "to chunk"—to brickbat with chunks of wood, not stones; "tetotally twisted"—greatly contorted.

Often new words were coined or old ones altered to meet new needs. "Explatterate" meant to crush or smash. "Explunctify" meant the same. "Honey-fuggle" was to hang about one and flatter him for some selfish purpose.

The backwoodsman had a keen sense of humor, which manifested itself even under the most adverse circumstances. An unfortunate man in attempting to save the six-dollar pilot's fee for conducting him over rapids, lost his boat and its cargo. By the greatest effort he escaped the clutches of the waves and upon reaching shore stood contemplating the wreckage. As he watched all his earthly possessions swirling beneath the waters he exclaimed: "She's going to be —— anyhow, but she made a most almighty rare [rear] of it didn't she?" He seemed to gain some satisfaction from the fact that if he was to lose all he had, at least it was a good show.

A well-known anecdote was that of the speaker who was discomfited by a heckler in the crowd. During a momentary pause at the summit of a flight of oratory, the heckler bawled out at his back: "Guess he wouldn't talk quite so hifalutenatin' if he knowed how his britches was tore out behind!" The horrified orator, momentarily deceived, clapped a hand to the location indicated and was thereby overthrown—overwhelmed by the inextinguishable laughter.[2]

Another specimen of humor is that represented by the story of the man who had come from Florida. When asked about the country, he replied: "It is the most fertile I ever saw; the land producing forty bushels of frogs to an acre and alligators enough to fence them."

Shortly after the earthquake of 1811, which almost destroyed New Madrid, when the bank of the Mississippi River some miles below caved in and left a dangerous hidden bar, Davy Crockett proposed that they "send up to New Madrid and procure a boatload of earthquake and sink the —— thing."

One European declared that no conversation, however brief, could take place without a due proportion of "anecdotes full of jocoseness," and in less than five minutes generally all listening were convulsed with laughter. A minister reported the story of an old backwoodsman and the difficulty he had with his gun hanging fire one day when he deliberately aimed at a chicken a few yards away. He said:

"She sputtered, an' spootered, and sizzled till the chicken got tired waitin' an' went over in the field to hunt June bugs. I had both eyes shet, fur the sparks wuz jest a b'ilin' out'n the tech hole, an' I dasn't take 'er down from my shoulder, 'cause I knowed she'd go off *some* time that day, an' when she *did* go, I knowed she'd git whatever wuz before 'er. So thar I wuz, as blind as a owl, an' a dodgin' the sparks worse'n a blind mule in a yaller jackets nes', an' 'bout that time a old sheep trotted out before the gun, jest

[2] William Henry Milburn: *The Pioneers, Preachers and People of the Mississippi Valley* (New York, 1860), p. 401.

as she went off, an' got the whole load right behind the
shoulder, an' keeled over deader'n a shad." [3]

If one were to join a circle of settlers, one would most
likely find them discussing the nature of the country, the
advantages and disadvantages of the settlement, the amount
of produce raised, and the means of disposing of it. Often
they argued the respective virtues of the laws of the states
from which they came. Other common topics of conversation were bear and buffalo hunts, narrow escapes from
wolves or panthers, Indian exploits, race horses and .races,
the relative merits of hunting dogs, and adventures on a
flatboat trip to New Orleans.

Often a group engaged in telling tall tales. One such tale
was an exploit of Henry Rhoads, who, according to one
version, took steady aim at a wild turkey and then pulled
the trigger of his flintlock. He had scarcely pulled the
trigger when he heard a panther behind him. The old hunter
swung his gun around, aimed at the panther, then in the
very act of making a long leap from a limb onto the woodsman. But the old scout's lightning move was quicker than
either the discharging powder or the springing panther and
he had the gun aimed at the panther before the bullet left
the rifle and killed the big cat with the load that a split
fraction of a second before was started toward the turkey.
The animal did not fall to the ground, but since it had leaped
and been struck in midair, its spring carried it to the hunter
and it fell harmlessly across his shoulders. He grabbed it,
leisurely walked home, and did not throw the panther down
until he was in front of his house.[4]

According to Birkbeck, the term "elegant" was much
overused and misused to mean useful or eligible and had
nothing to do with taste. A rude log cabin and a few acres
with the trees cut down at a height of three feet and a rail

[3] Srygley: *Seventy Years in Dixie*, p. 59.
[4] Rothert: *History of Muhlenberg County*, p. 34.

fence surrounding the plot was called an elegant improvement. One heard of an elegant tanyard and an elegant mill. Even roads that were barely passable were called elegant. A "clever" person was an amiable or good-tempered one.

A British officer at the Battle of New Orleans afterward told of a fighting Tennessee frontiersman who met him and the remains of his shattered unit on the breastworks. As the officer raised his sword, it was shattered by a rifle ball and at that instant, before he could retreat, the daring old hunter jumped upon the parapet, leveled his deadly rifle at the breast of his enemy, and calmly observed: "Surrender, stranger, or I may perforate ye!" Chagrined, the officer was obliged to deliver to the bold fellow his mutilated sword and pass over into the American lines.

Bowie knives were known in Mississippi as "Arkansas toothpicks." A person wishing to describe something dark said it was "as black as the hinges of midnight."

An Arkansas hunter in conversation with a stranger revealed that he had no use for Little Rock, although he had never been there, because there were so many lawyers. He thought the United States Government was horrible because it sold the lands and ruined the canebrakes for hunting, but he highly approved of Texas, saying that he had "heern there was no sich thing as a government there, and not one varmint of a lawyer in the *hull* place."

When someone was sought to carry the property of an Eastern dramatic company from Maysville to Frankfort, in 1815, a man with a wagon appeared and said he thought he could haul the "plunder." The other said: "What do you mean? Do you take me for a housebreaker? . . ." "I mean I can take your truck for you," said the wagoner. "Look you, my friend," said the showman, "just be so good as to explain what you mean by 'plunder' and 'truck.' I do not understand your outlandish jargon." "Jargon," said the frontiersman, squaring himself and looking the showman in the face. "Look here, my young hoss, thar's no use to begin raring and pitching here, because you can't make nuthin' off o' me in that way." [5]

When asked about the road from Nashville to Huntsville, one frontiersman answered: "I guess you'l find [it] purty much so—tarnation swamps and cedars and mud, takes one a'most up to hub sinkin into that are mire grounds 'tallmost killed my cattle." [6]

It was said that a boatman was half horse and half alligator with a cross of the wildcat (or steamboat, as some versions have it). It was quite customary for the river boatmen to celebrate at various points. A quantity of liquor was almost sure to awaken the lightly sleeping pugnacious spirit of the cocky, fighting, half-savage boatmen. This brought forth inciting, boastful speeches, which were sure to start a fight. A typical braggadocio's speech on such an occasion by a brawny fellow six feet four inches tall is given in Cist's *Miscellany* with the statement that it is not too highly colored. The braggart sprang from the crowd, rolled up his sleeves, and began his tirade:

"This is *me*, and no mistake! Billy Earthquake, Esquire, commonly called Little Billy, all the way from Noth Fork of Muddy Run! I'm a small specimen, as you see,—a ramote circumstance, a mere yearling; but cuss me, if I ain't of true 'imported breed,' and can whip any man in this section of country! Whoop! Won't *nobody* come out and fight me? Come out some of you and die decently, for I am *spileing* for a fight! I han't had one for more than a week, and if you don't come out, I'm fly blown before sundown to a *certaingty!* So come up to taw!

"Maybe you don't know who Little Billy is? I'll tell you: I'm a poor man—it's a fact—and smell like a wet dog; but I can't be run over! I'm the identical man that grinned a whole menagery out of countenance, and made the ribbed nose baboon hang down his head and blush! W-h-o-o-p!

[5] Ludlow: *Dramatic Life*, p. 77; Thomas D. Clark: *Rampaging Frontier* (Indianapolis, 1939), p. 26.
[6] Anne Royall: *Letters from Alabama* (Washington, 1830), p. 29.

I'm the chap too, that towed the 'broadhorn' up Salt River, where the snags were so thick that a fish couldn't swim without rubbing his scales off!—fact, and if anybody denies it just let 'em make their will! Cock-a-doodle-doo! Maybe you never heard of the time the horse kicked me and put both his hips out of jint—if it ain't true, cut me up for cat fish bait! W-h-o-o-o-p! I'm the very infant that refused its milk before its eyes were open and called out for a bottle of old Rye! W-h-o-o-o-p! I'm that little Cupid! Talk to me about grinning the bark off a tree!—'taint nothing; one squint of mine at a Bull's heel would blister it! Cock-a-doodle-de doo! O I'm one of your toughest sort—live for ever, and then turn to a white oak post. Look at me, [said he, slapping his hands on his thighs with the report of a pocket pistol] I'm the *ginewine* article—a *real double acting engine*, and I can out-run, out-jump, out-swim, chaw more tobacco and spit less, and drink more whiskey and keep soberer than any other man in these localities! Cock-a-doodle-doo! Darn it, [said Bill walking off in disgust] if that don't make 'em fight, nothing will. I wish I may be kiln-dried, and split up into wooden shoe pegs, if I believe there is a chap among 'em that's got courage enough to collar a hen. Well! I'll go home and have another *settlement* with Jo Sykes. He's a bad chance for a fight, it's true, seeing as how he's but one eye left to gouge at, and an 'under bit' out of both ears; but poor fellow, he's *willing to do his best*, and will stay a body's appetite till the next shooting match." [7]

[7] Cist's *Miscellany*, II, 134–5.

XXXI

Frontier Characteristics

ON the frontier, that twilight zone where the light of civilization met the darkness of savagery, the impact modified the European character, bringing to the fore certain well-defined characteristics.

During the Indian wars the white man became almost as ruthless and savage as the Indians. He was as wily, cruel, perfidous, and inhumane as the red man. He took scalps and killed prisoners in cold blood. In 1794 when Lieutenant Vincent Hobbs sent the scalp of the Bench, a famous Indian chief, to the Governor of Virginia, the legislature voted him a silver-mounted rifle for his gallantry.

On General George Rogers Clark's expedition into Ohio in 1780 the frontiersmen killed a squaw by brutally ripping her abdomen and otherwise mangling her. They also dug up the bodies of Indians that had been buried several months and scalped them. Twenty-five dollars was the bounty given for each Indian scalp in Kentucky during the Revolutionary War. When Hugh McGary killed an Indian with his stepson's shirt on, he cut up his body and gave it to the dogs. In an Indian attack James Foster was wounded and fell from his horse into a cane thicket. Thomas Smith thought he was dead and observed: "Here's Foster dead, and the Indians shan't have his scalp—I'll have it myself." And he jumped off his horse and drew his knife, but Foster cried: "Don't 'sculp' me, I ain't dead yet." The men put him on the horse in front of Smith, took him home, and he recovered.

Akin to this savage attitude toward the Indian was a wild, crude, rough state of society. Governor John Sevier had a fist fight with his rival Colonel John Tipton in a public place in Jonesborough, Tennessee, shortly after he began his administration as Governor of Franklin. Their families and supporters did the same thing from time to time, losing an ear, an eye, or a nose in the rough-and-tumble fights. The editor of the *Montgomery Republican* on November 8, 1822 said there was too much truth in this complaint of a correspondent:

> The recent transactions in this village are such as would disgrace even Algerine. . . . Shameful and barbarous deeds committed on the nights of the 30th of October and the 6th of November. This is the third, if not the fourth, attempt at homicide that has been made in this place within a few months.

Featherstonhaugh said one of the most respectable inhabitants told him he did not suppose there were a dozen men in Little Rock (in 1834) who ever went into the streets without being armed with pistols or large hunting knives. The secretary and judges of the territory drank whisky with the common drinker at the bar. By 1827 more than a dozen murders had been committed, and it was common practice for the young bucks to take shots with rifles at one another across the street and then dodge behind a door. Daily there was quarreling on the street. During a debate in the house of representatives in 1837 the speaker left the chair, took out his bowie knife, and stabbed another member to death. He then wiped the blood off the knife with his thumb and forefinger and went back to the chair. The offender was later expelled and tried for murder, but was acquitted. This was a farcical trial, during which the prisoner lodged at the same house as the judge and ate three times a day at the same table with him. When he was acquitted, the judge paid for the drinks for the jury and all others there.

Men wore their hats in the house. It was not at all unusual to see a man walk down the church aisle to his pew or even for the minister to walk into the pulpit before removing his hat.

As late as the thirties on the Western steamboats men went to the table in their shirt sleeves and spectators at the theaters put their feet on the balustrade. Mrs. Trollope aroused the anger of Americans by pointing out these things as crudities in American society, but they were true nevertheless. Soon after her book *Domestic Manners of the Americans* appeared (1832), the steamboats made rules forbidding a person to be seated at the table unless properly dressed. As late as the 1830's theater rows occurred. At Louisville in 1837 there was a typical theater brawl. A spectator with his feet hanging over the balustrade fell into a deep sleep and began to snore so loudly he disturbed the audience. Awakened by the catcalls, jeers, and hoots of the audience, he flew into a rage. Noticing a group beneath him with outstretched arms pointing scornfully at him, he swung himself over the balustrade and landed among his tormenters with fists flying. After a short, bloody struggle he was beaten and tramped nearly beyond recognition and, bloody and almost without a stitch of clothing on his body, he was carried from the room. In the meantime the spectators took sides and a general uproar ensued. The actors on the stage stood waiting until the row was over to resume the play.[1]

Invariably the judge and lawyers in frontier courts placed their feet on tables much higher than their heads. It was quite common in company for a man to lean back in his chair so it would bear his weight on its hind legs and put his feet

[1] John Morris: *Wanderings of a Vagabond* (New York, 1873), pp. 14, 15-16, 17.

against the mantelpiece, higher than his head. This was an Americanism not confined to the frontier, but may have been an outcropping of its influence.

People, especially the men, would spit almost constantly anywhere and everywhere. This was rendered unavoidable by the habit of chewing tobacco. Isaac Candler said he had been in a lecture room where the floor was as wet from spitting as though someone had wet it down to sweep it. Philip Lindsley, a Nashville college president from the East, wrote in 1831:

> The other day at church, a well-dressed young fellow, while standing up in prayer time and leaning over into my pew, so wantonly besprinkled every part of my premises with his tobacco distillations, as fairly to put all devotion out of countenance, and made me wish for the *Amen*, as impatiently as ever did hungry urchin during his puritan papa's long grace over a thanksgiving-day's dinner.[2]

In spite of these crude manners the frontier had its own code of rough etiquette and the people were usually polite according to code.

Hospitality was the rule on the fringe of settlement. People were isolated, lonely, hungry for companionship and news, and highly gratified to have an opportunity to meet and talk to someone from outside their little circle. Then, too, all had the same battle to fight against savagery and an inhospitable wilderness and they were drawn together by a common need. Perhaps on occasion they would be away from home and in need of hospitality. Furthermore, it cost a settler little or no cash to entertain. He had no grocery bills to be doubled or tripled by much entertaining. His hogs and cattle running on the range furnished almost free meat. Perhaps he might have to go into the forest a few days sooner to kill some game, but that was a thing he loved

---

[2] LeRoy J. Halsey: *The Works of Philip Lindsley* (Philadelphia, 1866), III, 624–5.

to do. There was almost no market for corn. He could well afford to spare the little necessary to feed company.

Hamilton W. Pierson, a colporteur agent, recorded a typical frontier reception. One evening in search of a place to stay, he rode up as near the settler's cabin as the rail fence would allow him to approach on horseback and shouted in a loud voice: "Hello there!" One hardly dared dismount and knock, for there was a pack of dogs to act as a reception committee. At his shout they set up a loud chorus and came rushing out. They were followed by a group of black pickaninnies from the log kitchen not far from the house. Their mammy followed them to the door and stood with arms akimbo and hands fresh from mixing corn dodger for the family supper. She stood wide-eyed with distended mouth and shining ivory, staring at the stranger with pleased curiosity. Almost as the same moment the mistress of the incipient plantation appeared at the door of her cabin in bare feet, dressed in linsey-woolsey. With a pleased expression, she cordially greeted the visitor: "How d'y, stranger—how d'y, sir? Light [alight], sir—light, sir!" He remained on his horse and asked if he might stay overnight. To this she made the characteristic frontier reply: "Oh, yes, if you can put up with our rough fare. We never turn anybody away." This offer he gladly accepted. The dogs were now called off and he dismounted. His hostess then informed him that her husband was working in the "deadening," but would soon be home.

The naturalist Audubon and a companion in taking a short cut one stormy night became lost. The rain fell in torrents and the night was dark, cold, and dismal. They let their horses have their head and finally came to a house in the forest. In answer to their hallo, a man came to the door and welcomed them. He apologized for not having very good food, saying the visitors would have to make out on bacon and eggs and roast chicken. He was sorry he had no whisky, but his father had some extra good cider and he would ride over and get some. They asked him how far his father lived. He replied that it was only three miles and he would go while his bride of three weeks prepared the supper. He could not be dissuaded from going into the storm at that hour. Meantime his wife had mixed some corn bread and had it on a board before the fire. The servants had cleaned two chickens, which were soon roasting on the spit. Their host at length came in out of the dripping night with two gallons of cider. He said his father was coming shortly to ask the visitors to stay with him that they might have better accommodation. The visitors declined this hospitable offer and stayed with the young couple even though the accommodation was not as good as the father offered. The strangers were astonished at the cordial hospitality they received.

When a brother or sister died leaving orphan children, they were without question adopted as a matter of course into the families of uncles and other kindred who treated them entirely as their own. When Tyrone Power was traveling by stage, the passengers discommoded themselves so that he could have a seat all by himself to lie down and rest. They said he was not used to the rough roads as they were. Faux reported that when he was on his trip in 1819, a sick, moneyless stranger was sent from Kentucky back to Chillicothe, Ohio, on the stage free of all expense and was received and fed at the taverns without cost. Even the driver gave him a dollar. Such humanity and hospitality he found to be a Western trait.

Another characteristic peculiar to Western people was inquisitiveness and a lack of reserve. Unlike the European who kept things strictly to himself, Western people were informal and often intimate with passing acquaintances concerning their private business. In turn, they expected to inquire into the affairs of others. Charles Hoffman, a traveler from the East, was one day riding past the home of a Kentuckian who was saddling a horse when the latter called to the traveler: "Hallo! Stranger, I reckon you and I are cuttin' out for the same place so hold a bit and you shall have company."

Once an acquaintance was struck up, no matter how casual, the backwoodsman began to ply all sorts of questions: Where are you going? Where did you come from? Are you peddling? Is that plunder in those bags or is it goods?

An Englishman found that it was impossible to have a private chat between two persons. He said he had several times imagined himself enjoying a private chit-chat when on raising his eyes he found a little circle formed around the two, fully prepared with suggestion, rejoinder, or observation. This, however, was without any intention of rudeness. When Sir Charles Lyell was pacing the deck with his short-sight glass suspended by a ribbon from his neck, one after another eyed the glass and asked him to read the name of a vessel at an extraordinary distance. Others without permission or apology abruptly brought their heads close to his, seized the glass, and attempted to read something. In the meantime, in the ladies' cabin, ladies took his wife's embroidery out of her hand without leave and examined it with many comments, usually of a complimentary nature.

Backwoodsmen disliked formality and ceremony of all kinds. An Englishman frequently remonstrated with them about the entire absence of forms and ceremonies in the courts. The usual answer was:

> Yes, that may be quite necessary in England, in order to overawe a parcel [pronounced *passel*] of ignorant creatures, who have no share in making the laws; but with us a man's a man, whether he have a silk gown on him or not; and I guess he can decide quite as well without a big wig as with one. You see, we have done with wiggery of all kinds; and if one of our judges were to wear such an appendage, he'd be taken for a merry-andrew, and the court would become a kind of show-box—instead of such arrangements producing with us solemnity they would produce nothing but laughter and the greatest possible irregularity.[3]

[3] Simon Ansley Ferrall: *A Ramble of Six Thousand Miles through the United States of America* (London, 1832), pp. 243-4.

They were especially displeased with a person who put on airs or who they felt acted superior. A general from the East on a Mississippi steamboat in the thirties used a silver fork at his meals. At that time two-pronged forks with buckhorn handles, called "hay-makers," were the only kind in use in that region. A backwoods passenger was incensed at the refinement of the general and made himself a large wooden fork. The next day as the military hero called for his silver one, Old Kentuck produced his wooden one and, sitting directly across the table, ate in open ridicule.

People along the river had a great aversion to brass buttons, and a man who wore them was likely to be insulted. Many people on coming to the West put away broadcloth and lace and put on the homespun or buckskin attire of the West rather than bear the ridicule. If a high official or an overseas visitor, however, wore that sort of attire which the backwoodsman felt it was his place to wear, they conceded it and respected such an individual as entitled to it.

They did despise sham. So austere were they that they even turned thumbs down on fiction. On one occasion the daughter of a fairly well-to-do woods dweller brought home from the boarding school a copy of *Robinson Crusoe*. Night after night she read it to the intense satisfaction of all as they encircled the fireplace, carried in imagination to a tropical island. The father sat entranced, with his chair tipped back against the wall. When the last chapter was finished, the daughter remarked that Daniel Defoe was a great creative genius of his day. The old man looked up: "Defoe? Who was he?" "Why, the man who wrote *Robinson Crusoe*." "What? Didn't old Crusoe write it?" "Oh, no, it was the work of Defoe." "And I have been kept up here night after night listening to a lie? Throw that book behind the fire." His order was imperative and into the fire the volume went, while the children sat there tearfully watching the martyr consumed by the flames.

Closely akin to this was the frontier characteristic of

paucity of speech and particularly of compliments or words of praise. Some even spoke of the frontier fringe as a taciturn people. It was thought that their isolation, surrounded as they were by the great forests, caused this. Words of praise for children were scant and any show of affection in family life was frowned upon. After months of separation the members of a family merely shook hands and said: "How do you do?" It was scarcely different from greeting an entire stranger.

Frederick Gerstaecker had been out hunting with an Arkansas settler for three weeks. There was not the least sign of greeting when they arrived at his home. The wife and children stood looking at them as though they were complete strangers. Finally, when the horse was cared for and they went into the house, the hunter took his youngest child on his lap and then coolly asked: "How do you do, all of you?" Gerstaecker remarked that he had seen men leave home to be absent for months without saying good-by or shaking hands and it was the same on their return.

On one occasion at Boonesborough, when Simon Kenton engaged in an Indian fight not far from the fort, Daniel Boone with ten men rushed out to his rescue. Then the Indians rushed between them and the fort. Captain Boone ordered his men to cut their way through the enemy lines. This was successfully done, but in the fight Boone was shot through the leg, the bone was broken, and he was left lying on the ground. Just as an Indian had his tomahawk raised to dispatch the old fighter, Simon Kenton came to his rescue, killed the Indian, and carried his captain into the fort. After they had got into the fort and the gate was closed, Boone sent for Kenton and eulogized him with these words of scant praise: "Well, Simon, you have behaved like a man today. Indeed, you are a fine fellow."

XXXII

Frontier Characteristics
(*Concluded*)

SHIFTLESSNESS was one of the besetting evils of the frontier. The frontier forts were in many instances not well built, never finished, or left to tumble down. Often the weeds were allowed to grow up close enough to form a protecting screen for the enemy. There many times was no well or other adequate water supply to last over a siege. In countless other ways the frontiersman led a hand-to-mouth existence. Often he had to go out on a cold morning or when the rain was pouring down and cut a backlog before a fire could be made. He would haul water a mile rather than dig a well, get along without pothooks, and cook with one iron skillet, called a cook-all, although pots could readily be had. Birkbeck complained that the people could secure subsistence so easily that there was no stimulus to pursue cultural things, and life was whiled away in a painful state of yawning lassitude.

To Europeans, American pioneers were dirty. Said one, in speaking of a handkerchief: "Such articles are [not] an unknown commodity out here but . . . they are used rather economically, after the major operation has been performed with the fingers."Another said there was no soap in the taverns along the trail through southern Indiana and Illinois and that the farms were neglected, the people indolent, dirty, sickly, wild-looking. There were dirty hands, heads, and faces everywhere. Birkbeck said that cleanliness in houses and too often in person, was neglected to a degree that was very revolting to an Englishman. He found that even in the towns there was slovenliness. He thought that when the settler's wife moved from a log cabin into a brick house she unconsciously retained some of the habits of the dirt-floored cabin.

The settlers often got so far ahead of organized government that they were without law and authority. When such a thing happened, the great Anglo-Saxon genius for self-government was sure to come to the surface. In eastern Tennessee the people set up the Watauga Association and later the state of Franklin, which they intended should be the fourteenth state in the Union. Under Judge Richard Henderson, of the Transylvania Company, a government was set up for the governing of the people. When Judge Henderson's grant was not allowed and Virginia extended her authority over Kentucky, government was so ineffective because of the great distance that the people, as early as 1784 and 1785, held a series of conventions asking for statehood.

Particularly before 1800 there appeared from time to time movements to separate from the nation various areas that lay west of the mountains. James Robertson, head of the Cumberland Settlement, and John Sevier, of the state of Franklin, both dallied with the idea of their settlements' aligning themselves with foreign states. Sevier actually wrote offering to place the state of Franklin under the protection of Spain. This action was aimed at North Carolina rather than the United States. Such sentiments did exist from time to time against the United States, however, even after the new Constitution was adopted. When the settlers did not get their way about Indian removal or the navigation of the Mississippi River, they were ready to flirt with other nations.

They even threatened to rejoin British North America and boasted that, if united to Canada, they would some day be able to conquer the Atlantic commonwealths.[1]

Closely connected with this was a spirit of democracy, which grew as the frontier moved forward. Every man felt as good as anyone else and proudly resented any hint that there was any class distinction. A man of means could hardly get another man to hold permanently a servile position when he could erect a cabin on government land and live on a plane with his employer. In Indiana and Illinois, where white servants were employed, they would not tolerate being called servants. They were known as "the help." When a European asked such a person where his master was, he answered: "I have no master. Do you wish to see Mr. So-and-So [his employer]?" He was astonished to hear white servants called mister and sir. A hired girl who was called a servant or not invited to eat with the family would not brook the insult. When an English traveler asked to stay overnight at a home, the man who was sitting by the fire replied: "I reckon you can," and without rising told him he would find a barn behind the house. The Englishman, who had to take care of his own horse, thought this treatment was pretty hard, but people simply did not place themselves on the level of an old-country servant.

While there was a distinction between classes in Philadelphia and Boston in the thirties, there was almost none on the frontier. Charles A. Murray was astounded to see a steamboat clerk, a grocer, an army officer, and a member of Congress playing cards together and calling each other by their first names. He found it was customary. At a party the major of the militia danced with the hired girl of the tavern-keeper, an English adventurer danced with the wife of a member of the legislature, and the member of the legislature with the daughter of a rough lawless hunter. A judge upon leaving the courthouse shook hands with his fellow citizens

[1] Roosevelt: *Winning of the West*, III, 118, 128, 129, 153.

and retired to his log house. The next day he could be found following his plow. A lawyer who was a captain served in the militia under his neighbor who was a farmer and colonel. A German immigrant to Missouri in the thirties rejoiced that there was no difference in rank and that the poorest and richest mingled on equal terms.

There was a rage for military titles, however, and once a man was elected a captain or colonel, he kept that title among the citizens as long as he lived. Europeans were more than astonished to find a colonel plowing or swinging a hammer in the village blacksmith shop. The equality of economic opportunity with its resultant extreme absence of class distinction naturally affected the political institutions. One astute observer, Francis J. Grund, said that each of the Western states was a nursery of freedom. Each new settlement was, to his mind, already a republic in embryo. He found that they extended their political life in every direction and that every new state was a guarantee for the continuance of the American Constitution. It increased the interest of all in upholding the central government, he said, and made individual success dependent on national prosperity. The frontier was, then, in short, a great nationalizing influence in American history. Its people looked to the central government for protection against the Indians, for postal service, for land, for laws, and eventually for admission to the sisterhood of states with the same rights as the other states. In fact, each new state brought into the Union more democratic constitutions and brought into Congress legislators with more liberal ideas. This was a leavening influence that in time leavened the whole nation with democracy. The Kentucky constitutional convention of 1792 cast aside religious tests for holding office, so common in the East, provided for representation by population rather than by counties as in Virginia, and universal manhood suffrage without property qualifications. Even woman suffrage was proposed. After admission a state could make a new constitution more democratic than the one under which it was admitted. Kentucky, only eight years after admission, adopted a new constitution, substituting for its electoral college in the election of its government direct election by the people.

It would hardly be correct to infer, however, that there were absolutely no classes on the frontier. As a rule the cutting edge or squatters were entirely democratic, but they were enemies of the speculator, lawyer, planter, and more educated frontier city group. These two groups continued the struggle that had existed between the tidewater and back country in colonial days. As time went on, there was a tendency for the gap between classes to widen. The energetic and progressive added acres to their domain and slaves to their force until an aristocracy was formed alongside the small farmers, even while there were great areas still uncleared and in many ways the frontier had not passed.

The spirit of the frontier was a spirit of reckless conquest or exploitation. There were great resources and the settlers felt they were the chosen people to exploit them. The buffalo was soon killed off and most of the meat wasted in spite of protective measures. The giant trees were felled and burned, their lumber possibilities wasted. The lead was dug and smelted with wasteful log-fire furnaces. By scheme and trickery the government was defrauded of much of its land.

The frontiersmen were intensely individualistic. The old saying: "Everybody for himself and the devil take the hindmost," was enacted in the rush to secure the natural resources.

In theory the frontier was an area of equal opportunity. Theoretically, the lucky, industrious, thrifty settler reaped the rewards of his honest laudable efforts. In practice the unscrupulous, the cunning, the hoggish, and downright scoundrels were the ones who as often reaped the rich harvest from a bountiful, developing, virgin region.

Where large opportunity existed and competition was keen, there were sure to congregate the schemer, the creator and manipulator of fictitious values. As events moved swiftly on a developing frontier, there followed in the wake of these individuals a whole host of cheats and petty swindlers. When the frontier had passed and the getting was gone, it was found that the unscrupulous had the major portion of the loot.[2]

Rugged individualism kept the frontier troops from acting together as well-disciplined armies, although they were often effective as raiding parties or when in the field for a short time.

The pioneer was always jealous of creditors. Poor himself (some even fled from creditors in the East), he looked upon the merchant and the banker with anger because they seemed to do less work and still made more money than he did. Many lawsuits were filed for the collection of debts.

Old customs and forms rested lightly on the pioneer. Around Natchez, about 1802, there was no marriage ceremony as there was no one to perform it. Many a lovely forest maiden of the respectable folk became the companion of the young man she loved on his promise to legalize the union at the first opportunity.

Divorce was obtainable by an act of the legislature. The Kentucky legislative session of 1837 granted upward of two hundred divorces. There were few instances in the West of a woman's being refused a divorce. Dislike was very generally considered sufficient reason for granting a woman her freedom.

Foreigners early noticed the tendency of Americans to worship success in money-making. One said:

The most remarkable feature in the American character, and indeed their ruling passion, is a thirst for gain. . . . The avarice of an American, in general, is nothing more than the passion of ambition directed to the acquisition of wealth as the only means of attaining distinction. . . .

[2] W. F. Cash: *The Mind of the South* (New York, 1941), pp. 18, 19.

Others noted that they did not play or give time to fun, but their ardor for adventurous enterprise made them attempt long and arduous journeys and endure great hardship.

People of the West were satisfied with rude accommodations and rarely complained of poor fare or lack of comforts at an inn or on a steamboat. Mrs. Basil Hall in 1828 said:

> The Americans are the most extraordinary people in that respect I ever saw. I have seen them over and over again sit down and eat a dinner barely eatable as to cookery or diet and not above half sufficient for the size of the party without uttering a word of complaint or seeming to find out that anything was wrong.

Frontiersmen were very versatile; Little Rock's first mayor combined with his duties as chief magistrate those of justice of the peace, schoolteacher, bookkeeper, clerk in the post office, house- and sign-painter, glazier, and general tinker. In Alabama, Harriet Martineau saw driving a wagon a man who was a schoolmaster, a lawyer, an almanac-maker, a speculator, and a dealer in eggs, not to mention a few other occupations.

Any word or act that was deemed an impeachment of a man's integrity or honor had to be avenged by combat. In the backwoods this took the form of a rough-and-tumble fight, but as the towns and planter aristocracy began to emerge, nothing but a duel would bring satisfaction. The rough-and-tumble fight at its worst declined into an animal-like combat where anything was fair except weapons. The assailants kicked, bit, and sought to gouge each other's eyeballs from their sockets with their thumbs. Not a few mutilated ears and noses and sockets minus eyeballs testified to the ferocity of these conflicts. It was not considered honorable to use weapons in these affrays, but along the rivers or among town blackguards all too frequently the dirk was slipped from its concealment and into the heart of an assailant. In the thirties almost everybody carried a dirk or a dagger.

There was a highly optimistic outlook on the frontier. Speculators were busy running here and there locating the finest land and townsites obtainable. Squatters selected the richest bottom land, the best mill sites, the most advantageous ferry locations, and the best-watered claims. All of this led to the laying out of townsites and "booming" the country.

The early settlers, too, were very provincial, many never having gone far from their own state. This, together with an unbounded optimism, led the settlers to believe their state the best in the world. Back-country people were notorious braggarts. A typical remark made by a Mississippian illustrates the point: "If the first settlers of Eden had seen the 'Mississippi Bottoms' they would have located there a heap quicker than in the other place." A Kentuckian bragged: "If you plant a nail 'twill come up a spike next morning."

Captain J. E. Alexander reported a conversation with a backwoodsman that revealed the provincial outlook of such a forest dweller. Alexander stopped overnight at a wilderness cabin. After he had finished eating, the host plied him with all sorts of questions, finally prying out the information that his guest was from Scotland. The settler then continued: "Scotch, eh! Why that's far overseas. Are you all quiet there now?" "Yes, very quiet. Did you ever hear of any disturbance there?" "Yes, I've heard of a good deal of fighting and plundering there. Have you got rid of your Indians yet?" "Indians!" cried the astonished old-countryman. "We've no redskins in our country." "No? Why, that's curious enough."

Long before the Civil War there was a genuine dislike for Yankees, as people from New England were called. For years Southern people never knew there was any other kind of Yankee than a damned Yankee, for the proper noun was never used without its inelegant modifier. In a discussion of Yankees in an Alabama paper in 1822 one contributor stated that the term was often heard in that town "from the mouths of gentlemen as well as boors." Another in accounting for the intense dislike for New Englanders mentioned the holierthan-thou attitude of the "damned Yankees," the unscrupulous sale of clocks, horns, gun-flints, wooden nutmegs, wooden cucumber seeds, and other articles; most of all, however, Southerners hated New Englanders for their lack of support of the War of 1812 and their near treachery in threatening to secede from the Union.[3] As a matter of fact, for some years after the War of 1812, Yankees were very unpopular even in Pennsylvania and large areas of the Old Northwest. In going west through Pennsylvania in 1816 the New Englanders were often refused entertainment at taverns and had to stop in the woods.[4]

Strange as it may seem, the upper South was considered the West by the lower South. When boatmen left Mississippi on the Natchez Trace for Kentucky, they were said to be going to the West, when as a matter of fact they were going northeast toward Nashville and Lexington. In 1842 when Alabama challenged Kentucky to a horse-race, it was proclaimed as the South against the West.

The frontiersmen enjoyed a wild, carefree life without restraint. They had but little contact with the government and were exceedingly jealous of their personal liberty. Such liberty was interpreted to mean a republican form of government. Monarchy meant to them a decline in individual liberty. When David Crockett was about to be sworn into the Texas insurgent army, he was asked to take an oath to support the Republic of Texas or any other government that might be established. At that, Crockett refused point-blank and was followed by the others. Said he: "I am a republican, and believe in a republican form of government, and if any other kind of government results from this revolution, I will never support nor defend it." Not until the oath was changed would they take it. In this they exemplified the frontier.

[3] *Montgomery Republican*, January 12, February 2, 1822.
[4] Ebenezer Stedman: "Reminiscences, 1808," MS., Kentucky State Historical Society Library, p. 7.

In the fight against the wilds, brute force was more prized than other endowments and in time education came to be looked upon as unnecessary. Educated and cultured men were likely to conceal their attainments and appear on a level with the ignorant, crude frontiersmen.

In spite of their lack of the education and refinements of the East, backwoods people were of course as intelligent as the more formally educated and, in their own way and for their environment, were really educated. In forest lore and in solving the practical problems of their forest life they surprised the uninitiated. Newspapers circulated widely, and the common people were far better acquainted with the form of local, state, and national government than people of the same class in Europe. It was surprising to the outsider to find men and women in the log cabins ready to defend political opinions or religious beliefs. Since most of them read little, their ability to hold their own with educated people came from reflection, conversation with others, and the information that comes down to each generation as the heritage of the race. With respect to an insight into human nature, many were far in advance of those who were learned in the arts and sciences, and they successfully competed with those who had enjoyed greater educational advantages.

These traits born of that constant struggle against hostile Indians and nature over a period of several generations made of the European immigrant a distinct American type. As the years passed and culture came to the region, the child of the pioneer became in Dixie a Southern American with certain characteristics peculiar to that area.

Bibliography

I. PRIMARY SOURCES

PRINTED DOCUMENTS

American State Papers, Public Lands, Vols. I–VIII.

CARTER, CLARENCE EDWIN: *The Territorial Papers of the United States*. Vols. IV–VI. Washington, 1938.

HULBERT, ARCHER BUTLER (editor): *The Records of the Original Proceedings of the Ohio Company*. Vol. I. Marietta, Ohio, 1917.

Laws of the State of Tennessee. Vol. I, Part II.

Proceedings of the Illinois State Bar Association 1877–80, 1881–4, 1885–7, 1888–91, 1892–3.

Proceedings of the Mississippi Territory as Superintendent of Indian Affairs. Journal of Indian Department 1803–8. Department of Archives and History, Jackson, Miss.

SEVIER, GOVERNOR JOHN: "The Executive Journal of Governor John Sevier," East Tennessee Historical Society *Publications*, (Samuel C. Williams, editor), Vol. I, pp. 95–153; Vol. II, pp. 135–49; Vol. III, pp. 154–82; Vol. IV, pp. 138–67; Vol. V, pp. 155–77; Vol. VI, pp. 104–28; Vol. VII, pp. 128–64.

CONTEMPORARY BOOKS

AMPHLETT, WILLIAM: *The Emigrant's Directory*. London, 1819.

AUDUBON, JOHN JAMES: *Delineations of American Scenery and Character*. New York, 1926.

BAIRD, L.: *View of the Valley of the Mississippi or the Emigrants and Travellers Guide to the West*. Philadelphia, 1834.

BALDWIN, JOSEPH G.: *The Flush Times of Alabama and Mississippi*. Americus, Ga., 1853.

BLUE, M. P.: *City Directory and History of Montgomery, Ala.* Montgomery, Ala., 1878.

BRADFORD, JOHN: *Historical Notes on Kentucky* (G. W. Stipp, compiler). San Francisco, 1932.

BREAZEALE, J. W. M.: *Life as It Is; or Matters and Things in General*. Knoxville, 1842.

BUCKINGHAM, JAMES SILK: *The Slave States of America*. 2 vols. Vol. I. London, Paris [1842].

BUTLER, MANN: *A History of the Commonwealth of Kentucky*. Louisville, Ky., 1834.

CAIRD, JAMES: *Prairie Farming in America*. London, 1859.

COLLINS, S. H.: *The Emigrant's Guide to the United States of America*. Hull, England, 1829.

DRAKE, DANIEL: *A Systematic Treatise, Historical, Etiological, and Practical, on the Principal Diseases of the Interior Valley of North America, as They Appear in the Caucasian, African, Indian, and Esquimaux Varieties of Its Population*. Cincinnati, 1850.

Essay on Camp-Meetings, An. By the author of "The True Evangelist." New York, 1849.

FROST, JOHN: *Heroes and Hunters of the West*. Philadelphia, 1859.

——: *Pioneer Mothers of the West; or, Daring and Heroic Deeds of American Women*. Boston, 1859.

HALL, BAYNARD RUSH (Robert Carleton, pseud.): *The New Purchase: or, Seven and a Half Years in the Far West*. Philadelphia, 1843.

Inaugural Thesis on Endemial Bilious Fever as It Generally Occurs in the Vicinity of Natchez (for degree of Doctor of Medicine, Transylvania University, Lexington, Ky., January 15, 1825).

LEWIS, P. H.: *The Medical History of Alabama*. New Orleans, 1847.

LONGSTREET, AUGUSTUS BALDWIN: *Georgia Scenes, Characters, Incidents, etc. in the First Half Century of the Republic*. New York, 1856.

McDONALD, JOHN: *Biographical Sketches of General Nathaniel Massie, General Duncan McArthur, Captain William Wells, and General Simon Kenton: Who Were Early Settlers in the Western Country*. Cincinnati, 1838.

McKNIGHT, CHARLES: *Our Western Border*. Philadelphia, 1875.

MEEK, ALEXANDER BEAUFORT: *Romantic Passages in Southwestern History*. New York, 1857.

MONETTE, JOHN W.: *History of the Discovery and Settlement of the Valley of the Mississippi*. 2 vols. New York, 1846.

ORD, GEORGE: *Supplement to the American Ornithology of Alexander Wilson*. Philadelphia, 1825.

PICKERING, JOSEPH: *Emigration or No Emigration*. London, 1830.

PIERSON, HAMILTON W.: *In the Brush*. New York, 1881.

SMITH, OLIVER HAMPTON: *Early Indiana Trials; and Sketches*. Cincinnati, 1858.

SMITH, SIDNEY: *The Settler's New Home*. London, 1850.

SPRINGER, JOHN S.: *Forest Life and Forest Trees*. New York, 1851.

STODDARD, MAJOR AMOS: *Sketches Historical and Descriptive of Louisiana*. Philadelphia, 1812.

TILLSON, MRS. CHRISTIANA HOLMES: *A Woman's Story of Pioneer Illinois*. Milo Milton Quaife, editor. Chicago, 1919.

NEWSPAPERS AND PERIODICALS

Alabama Intelligencer (Tuscaloosa, Ala.) 1833–5.

Alabama Intelligencer and State Rights Expositor (Tuscaloosa, Ala.), July 18–October 17, 1835.

Alabama Journal (Montgomery, Ala.), September 8, 1826–July 27, 1827.

Alabama Republican (Huntsville, Ala.), August 5, 1817, September 15, 1820–May 3, 1822.

Alabama Sentinel (Tuscaloosa, Ala.), March 10–July 15, 1826.

American Pioneer (Chillicothe, Ohio), Vol. I, 1842; (Cincinnati, Ohio) Vol. II, 1843.

Arkansas Gazette (Little Rock, Ark.), November 20, 1819, December 18, 1819–December 23, 1823.

Baton Rouge Gazette (Baton Rouge, La.), January 12–March 16, 1822, January 11–February 19, 1823.

Chickasaw Union, (Pontotoc, Miss.), November 23, 1837–March 8, 1838.

Cist's *Miscellany* (Cincinnati, Ohio), 1846.

Clinton Gazette (Clinton, Miss.), September 12, 1835–July 16, 1836 [scattered numbers].

Galenian, The (Galena, Ill.), September 5, October 22, 1836.

Hamilton Intelligencer and Advertiser (Hamilton, Ohio), November 17, 1821–August 19, 1822.

Harper's New Monthly Magazine (New York), Vol. XXXIV, No. 203.

Illinois Advocate (Edwardsville, Ill.), February 23, 1831–January 20, 1832.

Illinois Gazette (Shawneetown, Ill.), February 16, 1822; January 15, March 12, 19, June 25, 1825.

Indianian, The (Jeffersonville, Ind.), November 13, 1819–June 8, 1820 [scattered numbers].

Kentucky Gazette (Lexington, Ky.) 1787–94.

Louisville Monthly Magazine (Louisville, Ky.), January 1819.

Macon Herald (Macon, Miss.), July 17, 1841–May 14, 1842.

Marshall County Republican (Holly Springs, Miss.), August 11, 1838–June 1, 1839.

Missionary Herald (Boston, Mass.), Vols. XVII, XVIII, 1821, 1822.

Mississippi Gazette (Natchez, Miss.), 1832.

Mississippi Statesman (Natchez, Miss.), August 2, 1827.

Montgomery Republican (Montgomery, Ala.), January 6, 1821–May 8, 1821; 1834–6; 1840–3.

Nashville Herald (Nashville, Tenn.), February 1–June 6, 1832.

Natchez Gazette (Natchez, Miss.), June 23–July 28, 1832.

Northern Mississippi Advocate (Aberdeen, Miss.), July 1838.

Observer, The (Oxford, Miss.), August 19, 1843–August 20, 1844.

Observer and Reporter (Lexington, Ky.), February 10–June 27, 1832.

Pearl River Banner (Monticello, Miss.), December 16, 1837–July 28, 1838.

Rodney Telegraph (Rodney, Miss.), December 22, 1838–May 24, 1839.

Southern Advocate (Huntsville, Ala.), April 30–October 2, 1830; May 13, 1825–January 13, 1826; June 23–July 14, 1832.

Southern Planter (Richmond, Va.), Vol. VII, 1847.

Spirit of the Times (New York), March 9, 1839–February 29, 1840; March 5, 1842–February 25, 1843; March 1, 1845–February 14, 1846; February 22, 1851–February 14, 1852; February 18, 1854–February 10, 1855.

Telegraph, The (Tuscumbia, Ala.), October 31, 1827–July 19, 1828.

Washington Republican (Washington, Miss.), May 4, 1813–February 9, 1814.

Weekly Chronicle (Natchez, Miss.), July 6, 1808–February 15, 1809; November 25, 1809–January 22, 1810.

Western Herald (Steubenville, Ohio), March 15, 1823–April 10, 1824.

Western Monthly Review, Timothy Flint, editor (Cincinnati), Vol. I, 1828; Vol. III, 1830.

Western Star (Lebanon, Ohio), March 5–October 1, 1821.

Western World, (Frankfort, Ky.), August 9, 1806–August 6, 1807.

PRINTED DIARIES AND JOURNALS

BEDFORD, DR. JOHN R.: "Journey down the Cumberland," *Tennessee History Magazine*, Vol. V.

CLAIBORNE, J. F. H.: "A Trip through the Piney Woods," *Publications*, Mississippi Historical Society, Vol. IX.

KELLAR, HERBERT A. (editor): "A Journey through the South in 1836: Diary of James D. Davidson," *Journal of Southern History*, Vol. I.

"Captain Newman's Original Journal of St. Clair's Campaign," *Wisconsin Magazine of History*, Vol. II.

RILEY, FRANKLIN L.: "Diary of a Mississippi Planter, January 1, 1840, to April, 1863," *Publications*, Mississippi Historical Society, Vol. X.

"Winthrop Sargeant's Diary While with General Arthur St. Clair's Expedition against the Indians," Ohio Archæological and Historical *Publications*, Vol. XXXIII.

MANUSCRIPTS

1. Documents

Bent Creek Church (Baptist), Jefferson County, Tennessee, *Records*, 1785–1844. MS. (photostated copy), McClung Collection, Lawson-McGhee Library, Knoxville, Tenn.

Buffalo Lick, Ky., Baptist Church *Minutes*, 1805–38. MS. Filson Club Library, Louisville, Ky.

Champaign County, Ohio, *Court Docket*, 1809–14 (Justice of the Peace Court), MS., Ohio State Archæological and Historical Society Library, Columbus, Ohio.

CRAIG, JAMES. *Company Book* Kept in the Creek Campaign of 1813–14. MS., Alabama Department of Archives and History, Montgomery, Ala.

Indian Office *Miscellanies*, United States Indian Affairs. MS., Library of Congress.

Inspection Reports of Posts and Reservations up to 1864. Loose files. National Archives: War Department.

Land Office Treasury Warrant, No. 10,243, issued to Daniel Boone, December 22, 1781.

Letters Received, Surveyor General's Office, 1797–1806, 1835, 1836. National Archives: Records of General Land Office.

Lincoln County, Ky., Court *Order Book*, No. 1, 1781–4. Stanford, Ky., Courthouse.

Lincoln County, Ky., *Will Book* A, 1781–91. Stanford, Ky., Courthouse.

Order Books of the Military Organizations during General Anthony Wayne's campaign. Filson Club Library, Louisville, Ky.

Ouachita Parish District Court *Records*, 1830's. Monroe, La., Parish Courthouse.

Post Revolutionary War *Records*, Books 149, 156, 168. National Archives: War Department.

Probate *Record*, Book A, Ouachita Parish, Monroe, La., Parish Courthouse.

Records of the Proceedings of the Board of Trustees for the Transylvania Seminary, 1796–8. Transylvania College, Lexington, Ky.

Records of the Sixth Regiment of Kentucky Militia, 1803, Stanford, Ky. Filson Club Library, Louisville, Ky.

Tick Creek or Bethel Baptist Church *Record Book*, Shelby County, Ky., 1810–16. MS., Filson Club Library, Louisville, Ky.

2. Journals and Diaries

BRETHETT, JOHN: "Journal on a Journey from Bardstown, Ky., to Washington, D.C., 1805." MS., Tennessee Historical Library, Nashville, Tenn.

BRIDGE, H.: "Journal, March–April 1836, of a trip from New Orleans to Columbia, Pa., via Louisville, Maysville, and Cincinnati." MS., Illinois State Historical Library, Springfield, Ill.

BROWN, WILLIAM: "Original Notes of William Brown's Journey to Kentucky in 1790." MS., Filson Club Library, Louisville, Ky.

——: "Journal of Wm. Brown's Journey to Kentucky in 1790 with changes and additions by him." MS., (photostatic copy), Filson Club Library, Louisville, Ky.

COFFIN, DR. CHARLES: "Tennessee Journals 1800–22." MS. (typewritten copy), McClung Collections, Lawson-McGhee Library, Knoxville, Tenn.

CROGHAN, MAJOR WILLIAM: "Diary of a Trip from Louisville to Nashville." Croghan Papers, I, Draper Manuscripts, Wisconsin State Historical Society Library, Madison, Wis.

"Heads and Tales of a Voyage down the Ohio and Mississippi to New Orleans, January 28–November 24, 1828." MS., Illinois State Historical Library, Springfield, Ill.

"Journal of a Trip from Champaign Co., Ohio, down the Mississippi River to New Orleans with a cargo of flour, November 25, 1805–July 26, 1806." MS., Illinois State Historical Library, Springfield, Ill.

"Journal of the Barge *Lovely*, Nan Lewis West, Master, July 9, 1807–November 20, 1807." MS., Ohio State Archæological and Historical Society Library, Columbus, Ohio.

Kelso, William: "Journal" kept on a trip from Fort Pitt to New Orleans on a flatboat with flour, 1782. MS. (photostatic copy), Ohio Archæological and Historical Society Library, Columbus, Ohio.

Larwill, Joseph H.: "Journal of a Journey from Wooster, Ohio, to Kentucky and Illinois, January 3–February 25, 1823." MS., Illinois State Historical Library, Springfield, Ill.

Leggett, Mary Norwood: "Journal of a Trip from Newark, N.J., to Edwardsville, Ill., September 21, 1819 to January 2, 1820." MS., Illinois State Historical Library, Springfield, Ill.

McAfee, Robert: "A Journal, 1803 & 1807." MS. (typewritten copy), Kentucky State Historical Society, Frankfort, Ky.

"Memoranda on the Road" (during a month and a half tour in the West from Baltimore to Missouri and return in 1836). MS. (typewritten copy), Illinois State Historical Library, Springfield, Ill.

Pears, Sarah: "Account of a Journey from Kentucky to Natchez in 1780." MS., Newberry Library, Chicago.

Roberts, Amelia: "Journal of a Trip from New York to Illinois in 1835." MS., Illinois State Historical Library, Springfield, Ill.

Rodney, Thomas: "Diary." MS., Department of Archives and History, Jackson, Mississippi.

Scott, General Charles: "Journal," 1793. MS., Filson Club Library, Louisville, Ky.

Smith, Mrs. George: "Diary." MS., Mississippi History Collections, Rackham Library, University of Michigan, Ann Arbor, Mich.

Straghan, John: "Journal by River Sea & Land." MS., Ohio

State Archæological and Historical Society, Columbus, Ohio.

TROWBRIDGE, C. C.: "Journal, 1820." MS. (typewritten copy), Burton Collections, Detroit Public Library, Detroit, Mich.

WOOTEN, H. V.: "Private Journal of Life and Doings, 1813–1851." 4 vols. Vols. I and II, MS., Alabama Department of Archives and History, Montgomery, Ala.

3. *Reminiscences*

AUSTILL, MARGARET ERVIN: "Life of Margaret Ervin Austill." MS. (typewritten copy) in Eades folder, Alabama Department of Archives and History, Montgomery, Ala.

DuBOSE, JOHN WITHERSPOON: "Chronicles of the Canebrake," 1817–60. MS. (typewritten copy), Alabama Department of Archives and History, Montgomery, Ala.

GAINES, COLONEL GEORGE S.: "Reminiscences of Early Times in the Mississippi Territory," Second Series. MS., Alabama Department of Archives and History, Montgomery, Ala.

GILMER, GEORGE N.: "Autobiography." MS. (typewritten copy), Alabama Department of Archives and History, Montgomery, Ala.

HITE, PETER: "Reminiscences of Peter Hite," Montebello, Va., September 6, 1919. McCormick Historical Association Library, Chicago, Ill.

"Illinois Women." Letters written by pioneer women of Crawford, Pike, and Sangamon Counties, for World's Columbian Exposition, 1893. MS., Illinois State Historical Library, Springfield, Ill.

McCULLOUGH, SAMUEL D.: "Reminiscences of Lexington." MS., Lexington Public Library, Lexington, Ky.

MOORE, JAMES W.: "Early Times," *Arkansas Pioneers*, October 1913.

NICHOLSON, MRS. A. O. P.: "Reminiscences." MS., Tennessee State Library, Nashville, Tenn.

QUILLIN, MARY HEDGES: "Reminiscences," Illinois Women, Stories of Pioneer Mothers. MS., Illinois State Historical Library, Springfield, Ill.

RAMSEY, REV. A. C.: "A Sketch of the Life and Times of Rev.

A. C. Ramsey" as written by himself in 1879 at the age of 72. MS. (typewritten copy), Alabama Department of Archives and History, Montgomery, Ala.

RAMSEY, J. G. M.: "Autobiography." MS. (typewritten copy), McClung Collections, Lawson-McGhee Library, Knoxville, Tenn.

"Reminiscences of Pioneer Life in Illinois, *ca.* 1830–60." MS., Illinois State Historical Library, Springfield, Ill.

RILEY, FRANKLIN L.: "Diary of a Mississippi Planter," January 1, 1840–December 30, 1841. MS., Department of Archives and History, Jackson, Miss.

STEDMAN, EBENEZER: "Reminiscences, 1808." MS. (typewritten copy), Kentucky State Historical Society Library, Frankfort, Ky.

STONE, BENJAMIN FRANKLIN: "From Rutland to Marietta," Leaves from the Autobiography of Benjamin Franklin Stone. MS. (typewritten copy from manuscript in Campus Martius State Memorial Museum, Marietta, Ohio), Ohio Archæological and Historical Society, Columbus, Ohio.

TAYLOR, THOMAS JONES: "The History of Madison County, Alabama." MS. (typewritten copy), Alabama Department of Archives and History, Montgomery, Ala.

WOODSON, MRS. MARY WILLIS RENNICK: "My Recollections of Frankfort." MS. (typewritten copy), Kentucky State Historical Society Library, Frankfort, Ky.

4. Correspondence

"An Account of the revival of religion [which] began in the Eastern part of Kentucky." Unsigned, undated manuscript. Patterson Papers, Vol. III, No. 105, Draper MSS., Wisconsin State Historical Society, Madison, Wis.

BLOUNT, WILLIAM: "Correspondence of William Blount, 1777–1797." MS. (typewritten copies), McClung Collections, Lawson-McGhee Library, Knoxville, Tenn.

BURTON, ——: A.L.S. to Peter —— (Vermont), Brownsville, Ill., December 13, 1820, MS., Illinois State Historical Library, Springfield, Ill.

COFFEE, MARY: "Papers." Robert Dyes Collection of Coffee

Correspondence, MS., Tennessee Historical Society Library, Nashville, Tenn.

FRANCIS, SIMEON: Letters of, 1831–2, 1840, 1860ff. MS., Illinois State Historical Library, Springfield, Ill.

Franklin Family Letters. MS., Kentucky State Historical Society Library, Frankfort, Ky.

FREELAND, FOSTER: Papers. MS., Mississippi Department of Archives and History, Jackson, Miss.

HILL, ELIZABETH McDOWELL, of Crawford County, Ill.: Letters written by Pioneer Women of Crawford, Pike, and Sangamon Counties. MS., Illinois State Historical Library, Springfield, Ill.

HOPKINS, GENERAL SAMUEL: Correspondence. Letters to various persons, 1798–1811. MS., Kentucky State Historical Society Library, Frankfort, Ky.

———: to his son Samuel G. Hopkins, who was at school at Chapel Hill, North Carolina, from Spring Garden on the Ohio near Louisville, September 1, 1801. MS., Kentucky State Historical Society Library, Frankfort, Ky.

HOWARDS, H. H.: "Observations, Knowledge, etc. of Tennessee," May 8, 1885. MS., Tennessee Historical Society, Nashville, Tenn.

INNES, JUDGE HARRY: to Hon. John Brown, Danville, December 7, 1787. MS., Kentucky State Historical Society Library, Frankfort, Ky.

KNEELAND, CHARLES W.: A.L.S. to John R. Kimball, Griggsville, Ill., August 16, 1837. MS. (copy), Illinois State Historical Library, Springfield, Ill.

LAMB, JAMES L.: A.D.S., Kaskaskia, Ill., April 21, 1825. MS., Illinois State Historical Library, Springfield, Ill.

LEAKE, WALTER: to ——— Smith, Washington, Miss., December 15, 1807. MS., University of Virginia, Charlottesville, Va.

McGAHEY, DANIEL: to Rev. James Smelie, May 22, 1814. MS., Alabama Department of Archives and History, Montgomery, Ala.

MERIWETHER, NICHOLAS: Letters from Nicholas Meriwether to Captain Wm. Meriwether, 1782–6. Meriwether Papers. MSS., Kentucky State Historical Society Library, Frankfort, Ky.

RICHARDS, DR.: to H. A. Kellar, near Island Ford, Va., January
    27, 1919. MS., McCormick Historical Association Library,
    Chicago, Ill.

SEVIER, JOHN: Correspondence. MSS., McClung Collections,
    Lawson-McGhee Library, Knoxville, Tenn.

STERRETT, JAMES B.: A Medical Student at Transylvania Uni-
    versity to His Sister Elizabeth Sterrett, December 5, 1820.
    MS., Transylvania College Library, Lexington, Ky.

TAIT Collection. MSS., Alabama Department of Archives and
    History, Montgomery, Ala.

TAYLOR, JONATHAN: Notebook, 1796. MS., Filson Club Library,
    Louisville, Ky.

——: Papers. MSS., Filson Club Library, Louisville, Ky.

TWYMAN, R. G.: to ——, Crittenden, Ark., January 14, 1861.
    MS., University of Virginia, Charlottesville, Va.

WILKINSON, JAMES: to Hugh M'Ivain, Frankfort, Ky., March
    17, 1791, in Todd: "How Pioneers Marketed Products,"
    Filson Club Library, Louisville, Ky.

WILSON, ALEXANDER: to Alexander Lawson. MS. (typewritten
    copy), Lexington Public Library, Lexington, Ky.

WINCHESTER, GENERAL JAMES: "Journal." MSS., Tennessee His-
    torical Society Library, Nashville, Tenn.

                          5. Miscellaneous

Arithmetic Book (used in Kentucky in 1811). MS., about 50
    pages, Filson Club Library, Louisville, Ky.

"Cahaba." From the *Young American*. In Towns—Cahaba MS.
    (copied from *Dallas Gazette*, February 24, 1854), Alabama
    Department of Archives and History, Montgomery, Ala.

"History of Lowndes County, Mississippi," assembled by
    Bernard Romans Chapter, D.A.R., 1925. MS., Department
    of Archives and History, Jackson, Miss.

MCAFEE, GENERAL ROBERT B.: "History of the Rise and Prog-
    ress of the First Settlements on Salt River, and Establish-
    ment of the New Providence Church," Draper MSS.,
    4CC12–28; 4CC56–68, Wisconsin State Historical Society
    Library, Madison, Wis.

PICKETT, COLONEL A. J.: Papers. "Notes on Alabama," Vol. II.

MSS., Alabama Department of Archives and History, Montgomery, Ala.

Pickett Papers. Conversations with George S. Gaines. MS., Alabama Department of Archives and History, Montgomery, Ala.

ROBERTSON, GENERAL JAMES: Papers. Draper Notes, XXXI. MS., Wisconsin State Historical Society Library, Madison, Wis.

ROBINSON, C. H.: "Our Greatgrandfathers—How They Harvested." MS. (typewritten copy), McCormick Historical Association Library, Chicago, Ill.

Source Material for Mississippi History. Pontotoc County, Part I. Compiled by W.P.A. State-wide Historical Research Project, Susie V. Powell, supervisor. Department of Archives and History, Jackson, Miss.

WHITTINGTON, HIRAM ABIFF: to his brother, April 21, 1827, in *Arkansas Gazette*, April 17, 1932.

TRAVEL ACCOUNTS

ALEXANDER, CAPTAIN J. E.: *Transatlantic Sketches, Comprising Visits to the Most Interesting Scenes in North and South America and the West Indies.* London, 1833.

ARFWEDSON, CARL DAVID: *The United States and Canada in 1832, 1833, and 1834.* 2 vols. Vol. II. London, 1834.

BAILY, FRANCIS: *Journal of a Tour in Unsettled Parts of North America in 1796 and 1797.* London, 1856.

BARTRAM, WILLIAM: *The Travels of Wm. Bartram.* New York, 1928.

BENSON, ADOLPH B. (editor): *Peter Kalms' Travels in North America.* 2 vols. Vols. I and II. New York, 1937.

BIRKBECK, MORRIS: *Notes on a Journey in America.* London, 1818.

BLANE, WILLIAM NEWNHAM: *An Excursion through the United States and Canada, during the Years 1822–23.* London, 1824.

BURNABY, [ANDREW]: *Burnaby's Travels through North America.* R. R. Wilson, editor. New York, 1904.

CANDLER, ISAAC: *A Summary View of America.* London, 1824.

CHASTELLUX, MARQUIS DE: *Travels in North America.* New York, 1827.

COXE, TENCH: *A View of the United States of America.* Philadelphia, 1794.

D'ARUSMONT, FRANCES WRIGHT: *Views of Society and Manners in America.* By an Englishwoman. New York, 1821.

DEWEES, MARY COBURN: *Journal of a Trip from Philadelphia to Lexington in Kentucky.* R. E. Banta, editor. Crawfordsville, Ind., 1936.

DICKENS, CHARLES: *American Notes.* New York, 1926.

FARNHAM, ELIZA WOODSON: *Life in Prairie Land.* New York, 1846.

FAUX, WILLIAM: *Memorable Days in America: Being a Journal of a Tour to the United States.* London, 1823.

FEARON, HENRY BRADSHAW: *Sketches of America.* London, 1819.

FEATHERSTONHAUGH, GEORGE WILLIAM: *Excursion through the Slave States.* 2 vols. New York, 1844.

FERRALL, SIMON ANSLEY: *A Ramble of Six Thousand Miles through the United States of America.* London, 1832.

FLINT, JAMES: *Letters from America, 1818–20.* Edinburgh, 1822.

FLOWER, RICHARD: *Letters from Lexington and the Illinois.* London, 1819. In Reuben Gold Thwaites: *Early Western Travels,* Vol. X.

GERSTAECKER, FREDERICK: *Wild Sports in the Far West.* New York, 1854.

GOSSE, PHILIP HENRY: *Letters from Alabama.* London, 1859.

GREENE, WELCOME ARNOLD: "An Excursion to New Orleans and up the Mississippi and Ohio Rivers Returning through Pennsylvania" (Journal of 1823). MS., Wisconsin State Historical Society Library, Madison, Wis.

GRUND, FRANCIS JOSEPH: *The Americans, in Their Moral, Social, and Political Relations.* Boston, 1837.

HALL, BASIL: *Forty Etchings.* Edinburgh and London, 1829.

——: *Travels in North America, in the Years 1827 and 1828.* 3 vols. Vol. III. Edinburgh, 1829.

HALL, MRS. BASIL: *The Aristocratic Journey.* New York, 1931.

HALL, LIEUTENANT FRANCIS: *Travels in Canada and the United States in 1816 and 1817.* London, 1818.

HALL, FREDERICK: *Letters from the East and from the West.* Washington, 1840.

HARRIS, THADDEUS MASON: *The Journal of a Tour into the Territory Northwest of the Alleghany Mountains; Made in the Spring of the Year 1803.* Boston, 1805. Reprinted in Reuben Gold Thwaites: *Early Western Travels, 1748–1846,* Vol. III. Cleveland, Ohio, 1904.

HODGSON, ADAM: *Letters from North America, Written during a Tour in the United States and Canada.* 2 vols. London, 1824.

HOFFMAN, CHARLES FENNO: *A Winter in the Far West.* 2 vols. London, 1835.

IMLAY: *A Typographical Description of the Western Territory of North America.* London, 1792.

INGRAHAM, J. H.: *The Southwest.* By a Yankee. 2 vols. New York, 1835.

KIRKPATRICK, JOHN ERVIN: *Timothy Flint, Pioneer, Missionary, Author, Editor, 1780–1840.* Cleveland, 1911.

LATROBE, CHARLES JOSEPH: *The Rambler in North America* (1832–3). 2 vols. London, 1836.

LINDLEY, HARLOW (editor): *Indiana as Seen by Early Travelers.* A collection of reprints from books of travel, letters, and diaries prior to 1830. Indianapolis, 1916.

LYELL, SIR CHARLES: *A Second Visit to the United States of North America.* 2 vols. Vol. II. New York and London, 1849.

MARTINEAU, HARRIET: *Society in America.* 3 vols. London, 1837.

MARRYAT, CAPTAIN C. B.: *A Diary in America.* 2 vols. Paris, 1839.

Men and Manners in America. By the Author of *Cyril Thornton.* 2 vols. Vol. II. Philadelphia, 1833.

MERENESS, NEWTON D. (editor): *Travels in the American Colonies.* New York, 1916.

MICHAUX, ANDRÉ: *Travels to the Westward of the Alleghany Mountains, in the States of the Ohio, Kentucky, and Tennessee, and Return to Charlestown, through the Upper Carolinas.* London, 1805.

MORLEIGH (pseud.): *Life in the West: Back-wood Leaves and*

Prairie Flowers: Rough Sketches on the Borders of the Picturesque, the Sublime, and Ridiculous. London, 1842.

MURRAY, CHARLES AUGUSTUS: *Travels in North America during the years 1834, 1835, and 1836.* 2 vols. London, 1839.

NUTTALL, THOMAS: *Journal of Travels into the Arkansas Territory, during the year 1819.* Philadelphia, 1821.

OLMSTED, FREDERICK LAW: *A Journey in the Back Country.* New York and London, 1860.

PARKINSON, MARY WASHBURN: "Travels in Western America in 1837," *Journal of American History,* Vol. III.

PARKINSON, RICHARD: *A Tour in America in 1798, 1799, and 1800.* London, 1805.

PAULDING, JAMES KIRKE: *Letters from the South, Written during an Excursion in the Summer of 1816.* New York, 1817.

POWER, TYRONE: *Impressions of America during the Years 1833, 1834, and 1835.* 2 vols. Philadelphia, 1836.

ROYALL, MRS. ANNE: *Letters from Alabama.* Washington, 1830.

SCHOOLCRAFT, HENRY R.: *Journal of a Tour into the Interior of Missouri and Arkansaw.* London, 1821.

SCHULTZ, CHRISTIAN, JR.: *Travels on an Inland Voyage.* 2 vols. New York, 1810.

STUART, JAMES: *Three Years in North America.* 2 vols. Vol. II. New York, 1833.

SUTCLIFF, ROBERT: *Travels in Some Parts of North America in the Years 1804, 1805, and 1806.* Philadelphia, 1812.

Travels through Canada and the United States of North America in the Years 1806, 1807, and 1808. London, 1814.

WELD, ISAAC: *Travels through the States of North America.* London, 1800.

WOODS, JOHN: *Two Years' Residence in the Settlement on the English Prairie in the Illinois Country, June 25, 1820–July 3, 1821.* London, 1822. In Reuben Gold Thwaites: *Early Western Travels,* Vol. X.

REMINISCENCES

ALLISON, JOHN: *Dropped Stitches in Tennessee History.* Nashville, 1897.

BABCOCK, MRS. BERNIE: *Yesterday and Today in Arkansaw.* Little Rock, 1917.

BABCOCK, RUFUS (editor): *Memoir of John Mason Peck.* Philadelphia, 1864.

BEAUCHAMP, GREEN: "The Early Chronicles of Barbour County," in *Eufaula Times,* 1873. Clippings in Barbour County folder, Alabama Department of Archives and History, Montgomery, Ala.

BEGGS, REV. S. R.: *Pages from the Early History of the West and Northwest.* Cincinnati, 1868.

BRACKENRIDGE, HENRY MARIE: *Recollections of Persons and Places in the West.* Philadelphia, 1868.

BURNET, JACOB: *Notes on the Early Settlement of the Northwestern Territory.* Cincinnati, 1847.

CARTWRIGHT, PETER: *The Backwoods Preacher, an Autobiography of Peter Cartwright.* W. P. Strickland, editor. London, 1858.

CASSEDAY, BEN: *The History of Louisville from Its Earliest Settlement till the Year 1852.* Louisville, 1852.

CLAIBORNE, J. F. H.: *Life and Times of Gen. Sam Dale, the Mississippi Partisan.* New York, 1860.

CLARK, REV. JOHN A.: *Gleanings by the Way.* Philadelphia, New York, 1842.

COLLINS, LEWIS: *Historical Sketches of Kentucky.* Cincinnati, 1847.

CROCKETT, DAVID: *A Narrative of the Life of David Crockett, of the State of Tennessee.* Philadelphia, Baltimore, 1834.

DAVIS, REUBEN: *Recollections of Mississippi and Mississippians.* Boston and New York, 1891.

DODDRIDGE, JOSEPH: *Notes on the Settlement and Indian Wars, of the Western Parts of Virginia and Pennsylvania, from the Year 1763 until the Year 1783 Inclusive.* Wellsburgh, Va., 1824.

DOW, LORENZO: *History of Cosmopolite; or the four volumes of Lorenzo Dow's Journal concentrated in one.* Philadelphia, 1848.

DRAKE, DR. DANIEL: "Memoir of the Miami Country, 1779–1794," Ohio Archæological and Historical *Publications,* XVIII.

——: *Pioneer Life in Kentucky, a Series of Reminiscential Letters*. Cincinnati, 1870.

FINLEY, REV. JAMES B.: *Autobiography or Pioneer Life in the West*. Cincinnati, 1853.

FLINT, TIMOTHY: *Recollections of the Last Ten Years*. Boston, 1826.

FOLSOM, W. H. C.: *Fifty Years in the Northwest*. [St. Paul], 1888.

FOOTE, HENRY S.: *Casket of Reminiscences*. Washington, 1874.
——: *The Bench and Bar of the South and Southwest*. St. Louis, 1876.

FULKERSON, H. S.: *Random Recollections of Early Days in Mississippi*. Vicksburg, 1885.

GOODE, WILLIAM H.: *Outposts of Zion*. Cincinnati, 1863.

GORIN, FRANKLIN: *The Times of Long Ago* (Barren Co., Ky.). Reprinted from series of papers appearing in the *Glasgow Times* in 1876. Louisville, 1929.

GREVE, JEANETTE S.: "Traditions of Gatlinburg," East Tennessee Historical Society *Publications*, No. 3.

GUILD, JO. C.: *Old Times in Tennessee*. Nashville, 1878.

HALSEY, LEROY J.: *The Works of Philip Lindsley*. 3 vols. Vol. III. Philadelphia, 1866.

HENDERSON, JOHN G.: *Early History of the Sangamon Country*. Davenport, Iowa, 1873.

HERNDON, DALLAS T. (compiler): *Annals of Arkansas*. Vols. I–V.

HILDRETH, S. P.: *Biographical and Historical Memoirs of the Early Pioneer Settlers of Ohio, with Narratives of Incidents and Occurrences in 1775*. Cincinnati, 1852.

HOLCOMBE, HOSEA: *A History of the Rise and Progress of the Baptists in Alabama*. Philadelphia, 1840.

HOWELLS, WILLIAM COOPER: *Recollections of Life in Ohio, from 1813 to 1840*. Cincinnati, 1895.

ILES, MAJOR ELIJAH: *Sketches of Early Life and Times in Kentucky, Missouri and Illinois*. Springfield, Ill., 1883.

KENDALL, AMOS: *Autobiography of Amos Kendall*. William Stickney, editor. Boston and New York, 1872.

LAFFERTY, T. M.: "Some Traditions," *The Arkansas Pioneers*, I, January 1913.

LEMCKE, J. A.: *Reminiscences of an Indianian.* Indianapolis, 1905.

LINCECUM, GIDEON: "Autobiography of Gideon Lincecum," *Publications*, Mississippi Historical Society, Vol. VIII.

LOMAS, THOMAS J.: *Recollections of a Busy Life.* Place and date of publication not given.

LUDLOW, N. M.: *Dramatic Life as I Found It.* St. Louis, 1880.

Brother Mason, the Circuit Rider; or Ten Years a Methodist Preacher. Cincinnati, Philadelphia, 1856.

MILBURN, WILLIAM HENRY: *The Pioneer Preacher; Rifle, Axe, and Saddle-bags, and Other Lectures.* New York, 1858.

——: *The Pioneers, Preachers and People of the Mississippi Valley.* New York, 1860.

MORRIS, JOHN: *Wanderings of a Vagabond.* New York, 1873.

NICHOLS, THOMAS LOW: *Forty Years of American Life, 1820–1861.* New York, 1937.

PASCHALL, EDWIN: *Old Times; or Tennessee History.* Nashville, 1869.

POPE, JUDGE WILLIAM F.: *Early Days in Arkansas.* Little Rock, 1895.

PRENTISS, GEORGE L. (editor): *A Memoir of S. S. Prentiss.* 2 vols. New York, 1886.

PRITTS, J.: *Mirror of Olden Time Border Life.* Abingdon, Va., 1849.

REED, SETH: *The Story of My Life.* Cincinnati, 1914.

REYNOLDS, JOHN: *My Own Times: Embracing also the History of My Life.* Chicago, 1879.

ROBBINS, FRANK EGLESTON: "The Personal Reminiscences of General Chauncey Egleston," Ohio Archæological and Historical *Publications*, XLI.

ROBERTSON, W. G.: *Recollections of the Early Settlers of Montgomery County and Their Families.* Montgomery, 1892.

SEMPLE, EMILY VIRGINIA: *Reminiscences of My Early Life and Relatives.* Santa Barbara, Calif., no date given.

SMEDES, SUSAN DABNEY: *A Southern Planter.* New York, 1890.

SMITH, REV. J. C.: *Reminiscences of Early Methodism in Indiana.* Indianapolis, 1879.

SMITH, WILLIAM R.: *Reminiscences of a Long Life: Historical, Political, Personal and Literary.* Vol. I. Washington, 1889.

SPARKS, W. H.: *The Memories of Fifty Years.* Philadelphia, 1870.

SWITZLER, WILLIAM F.: "Missouri Old Settlers' Day Tales," *Missouri Historical Review,* Vol. II.

SRYGLEY, F. D.: *Seventy Years in Dixie.* Recollections and sayings of Thomas W. Caskey and others. Nashville, 1893.

——: *Smiles and Tears, or Larimore and his Boys.* Nashville, 1891.

WEBSTER, J. C.: *Last of the Pioneers, or Old Times in East Tennessee, Being the Life and Reminiscences of Pharaoh Jackson Chesney* (age 120 years). Knoxville, 1902.

WELSH, MARY: "Reminiscences of Old Saint Stephens, of More than Sixty-five Years Ago," *Transactions,* Alabama Historical Society, III.

WELSH, MARY J.: "Recollections of Pioneer Life in Mississippi," *Publications,* Mississippi Historical Society, Vol. IV.

WOODS, MICHAEL LEONARD: "Personal Reminiscences of Colonel Albert James Pickett," *Transactions,* Alabama Historical Society, Vol. IV.

WRIGHT, GENERAL MARCUS JOSEPH: *Reminiscences of the Early Settlement and Early Settlers of McNairy County, Tennessee.* Washington, D.C., 1882.

YOUNG, REV. JACOB: *Autobiography of a Pioneer.* Cincinnati and New York, 1857.

◇◇◇

II. SECONDARY SOURCES

HISTORIES

ABERNETHY, THOMAS PERKINS: *The Formative Period in Alabama, 1815–1828.* Montgomery, Ala., 1922.

——: *Frontier to Plantation in Tennessee.* Chapel Hill, 1932.

BALLAGH, JAMES CURTIS (editor): *Economic History, 1607–1865*. (Volume V of *The South in the Building of the Nation.*) Richmond, Va., 1909.

BARKLEY, A. H.: *Kentucky's Pioneer Lithotomists*. Cincinnati, 1913.

BOGGESS, ARTHUR CLINTON: *The Settlement of Illinois, 1778–1830*. Chicago, 1908.

BOND, BEVERLEY W.: *The Foundations of Ohio*. (Vol. I of *The History of the State of Ohio*, Carl Wittke, editor.) Columbus, Ohio, 1941.

BUCK, SOLON JUSTUS: *Illinois in 1818*. Springfield, 1917.

CAPERS, GERALD M., JR.: *The Biography of a River Town Memphis: Its Heroic Age*. Chapel Hill, N.C., 1939.

CASH, W. F.: *The Mind of the South*. New York, 1941.

CHAMBERS, HENRY E.: *Mississippi Valley Beginnings*. New York and London, 1922.

CHESTER, SAMUEL HILL: *Pioneer Days in Arkansas*. Richmond, Va., [1927].

CLAIBORNE, J. F. H.: *Mississippi, as a Province, Territory and State, with Biographical Notices of Eminent Citizens*. Vol. I (Vol. II never published). Jackson, Miss., 1880.

CLARK, THOMAS D.: *The Kentucky*. New York, 1942.

COLEMAN, J. WINSTON, JR.: *Slavery Times in Kentucky*. Chapel Hill, N.C., 1940.

COTTERILL, R. S.: *History of Pioneer Kentucky*. Cincinnati, 1917.

——: *The Old South*. Glendale, Calif., 1937.

DAVIS, CHARLES SHEPARD: *The Cotton Kingdom in Alabama*. Montgomery, 1939.

DOWRIE, GEORGE WILLIAM: *The Development of Banking in Illinois, 1817–1863*. University of Illinois Studies in the Social Sciences, Vol. II, No. 4. Urbana, Ill., 1913.

DUKE, GENERAL BASIL W.: *History of the Bank of Kentucky, 1792–1895*. Louisville, 1895.

ESAREY, LOGAN: *History of Indiana*. Indianapolis, 1915.

FORD, AMELIA CLEWLEY: *Colonial Precedents of Our National Land System as It Existed in 1800 (Bulletin of the University of Wisconsin, No. 352, History Series, Vol. II, No.*

2) (Ph.D. thesis, University of Wisconsin, 1908). [Madison], 1910.

FORTIER, ALCÉE: *A History of Louisiana.* 4 vols. Vol. III. 1904.

GAYARRÉ, CHARLES: *History of Louisiana.* 4 vols. Vol. IV. New Orleans, 1903.

GRAY, LEWIS CECIL: *History of Agriculture in the Southern United States to 1860.* 2 vols. Vol. II. Washington, 1933.

HANNA, CHARLES A.: *The Scotch-Irish, or The Scot in North Britain, North Ireland, and North America.* 2 vols. Vol. II. New York and London, 1902.

——: *The Wilderness Trail.* 2 vols. Vol. II. New York, 1911.

HAYWOOD, JOHN: *The Civil and Political History of the State of Tennessee from Its Earliest Settlement up to the Year 1796, Including the Boundaries of the State.* Nashville, 1915.

HEISKELL, S. G.: *Andrew Jackson and Early Tennessee History.* Nashville, Tenn., 1920.

HERNDON, DALLAS T.: *Centennial History of Arkansas.* Vol. I. Chicago, Little Rock, 1922.

HINSDALE, BURKE AARON: *The Old Northwest.* New York, 1888.

HOWE, HENRY: *Historical Collections of Ohio.* Cincinnati, 1875.

——: *Historical Collections of the Great West.* Cincinnati, 1856.

HULBERT, ARCHER BUTLER (editor): *Ohio in the Time of the Confederation.* Marietta, Ohio, 1918.

——: *The Ohio River.* New York, 1906.

JILLSON, WILLARD ROUSE: *The Kentucky Land Grants.* Louisville, 1925.

KEMPER, GENERAL WILLIAM HARRISON, M.D.: *A Medical History of the State of Indiana.* Chicago, 1911.

LEVERING, JULIA HENDERSON: *Historic Indiana.* New York and London, 1909.

LEYBURN, JAMES G.: *Frontier Folkways.* New Haven, 1935.

MARSHALL, H.: *History of Kentucky.* 2 vols. Vol. I. Frankfort, 1824.

MARTIN, FRANÇOIS XAVIER: *The History of Louisiana, from the Earliest Period.* 2 vols. Vol. II. New Orleans, 1829.

MATTHEWS, THOMAS EDWIN: *General James Robertson, Father of Tennessee.* Nashville, 1934.

McELROY, ROBERT McNUTT: *Kentucky in the Nation's History.* New York, 1909.

McLendon, Samuel Guyton: *History of the Public Domain of Georgia*. Atlanta, 1924.

Moore, Albert Burton: *History of Alabama*. University, Ala., 1934.

Perkins, James Handasyd: *Annals of the West*. Cincinnati, 1847.

Perrin, William Henry: *The Pioneer Press of Kentucky*. [Louisville], 1888.

Phelan, James: *History of Tennessee*. Boston, New York, 1889.

Phillips, Ulrich Bonnell: *American Negro Slavery*. New York, London, 1918.

——: *Life and Labors in the Old South*. Boston, 1930.

——: *Plantation and Frontier Documents: 1649–1863*. Cleveland, 1909.

Pooley, William Vipond: *The Settlement of Illinois from 1830 to 1850*. Madison, Wis., 1908.

Ramsey, J. G. M.: *The Annals of Tennessee to the End of the Eighteenth Century*. Chattanooga, 1926.

Riley, Rev. B. F.: *History of the Baptists of Alabama*. Birmingham, 1895.

Roosevelt, Theodore: *The Winning of the West*. 4 vols. New York, 1889–96.

Rowland, Dunbar: *Courts, Judges, and Lawyers of Mississippi 1798–1935*. Jackson, Miss., 1935.

——: *History of Mississippi, the Heart of the South*. Chicago, Jackson, 1925.

Spaulding, Oliver Lyman: *The United States Army in War and Peace*. New York, 1937.

Speed, Thomas: *The Wilderness Road*. Louisville, 1886.

Stiles, Henry Reed: *Bundling*. Harrisburg, Pa., 1928.

Thomas, David Y.: *Arkansas and Its People: A History, 1541–1930*. Vol. I. New York, 1930.

Thwaites, R. G., and Kellogg, Louise P.: *Documentary History of Dunmore's War, 1774*. Madison, 1905.

Verhoeff, Mary: *The Kentucky River Navigation*. Louisville, 1917.

Volwiler, Albert Tangeman: *George Croghan and the Westward Movement, 1741–1782*. Cleveland, 1926.

Wertenbaker, Thomas Jefferson: *The Founding of American Civilization*. New York, 1938.

WEST, ANSON: *A History of Methodism in Alabama.* Nashville, 1893.

WILD, J. C.: *Valley of the Mississippi.* St. Louis, 1841.

WILLIAMS, JOSEPH S.: *Old Times in West Tennessee.* Memphis, 1873.

WILLIAMS, SAMUEL COLE: *Beginnings of West Tennessee.* Johnson City, Tenn., 1930.

WILLIAMSON, FREDERICK WILLIAM, and GOODMAN, GEORGE T. (editors): *Eastern Louisiana: a History.* Louisville, 1939.

WRIGHT, RICHARDSON LITTLE: *Hawkers and Walkers in Early America.* Philadelphia, 1927.

Scotch-Irish in America, The. Proceedings and Addresses of the Second Congress at Pittsburgh, Pa., May 29–June 1, 1890. Cincinnati, 1890.

COUNTY AND LOCAL HISTORIES

BALL, TIMOTHY HORTON: *A Glance into the Great South-East, or Clarke County, Alabama, and Its Surroundings, from 1540 to 1877.* Grove Hill, Ala., 1882.

BESON, J. A.: *History of Eufaula, Alabama.* Atlanta, 1875.

BETTS, EDWARD CHAMBERS: *Early History of Huntsville, Alabama, 1804 to 1870.* (Revised edition) Montgomery, 1916.

BROWN, A. J.: *History of Newton County, Mississippi,* from 1834 to 1894. Jackson, Miss., 1894.

BROWN, STERLING SPURLOCK: *History of Woodbury and Cannon County, Tenn.* Manchester, Tenn., 1936.

CARROLL, THOMAS BATTLE: *Historical Sketches of Oktibbeha County.* Gulfport, Miss., 1931.

CISCO, JAY GUY: *Historic Sumner Co., Tenn.* Nashville, 1909.

COOK, ANNA MARIA GREEN: *History of Baldwin Co., Georgia.* Anderson, S.C., 1925.

COTTINGHAM, E. B., SR.: *A History of Caldwell Parish, Louisiana.* Kelly, La., 1938.

DAVIS, JAMES D.: *History of Memphis.* Memphis, 1873.

DOMBHART, JOHN MARTIN: *History of Walker County* [Alabama]. Thornton, Ark., 1937.

DURRETT, REUBEN T.: *The Centenary of Louisville.* Louisville, 1893.

GRAHAM, JOHN SIMPSON: *History of Clarke County*. Birmingham, 1923.

GRAHAM, KATHLEEN: *Notes on a History of Lincoln Parish, Louisiana*. (No place or date of publication given.)

HALE, WILL T.: *Early History of Warren County* [Tenn.]. McMinnville, Tenn., 1930.

——: *History of DeKalb County, Tennessee*. Nashville, 1915.

HAWKINS, HENRY G.: *Methodism in Natchez*. Jackson, Miss., 1937.

HAYS, LOUISE FREDERICK: *History of Macon County, Georgia*. Atlanta, 1933.

History of Cole County, Illinois, The. Chicago, 1879.

History of Daviess County, Kentucky. Chicago, 1883.

History of Henry County, Illinois, The. Chicago, 1877.

History of Washington County, Ohio. Cleveland, 1881.

HOPKINS, MOLLY GLASS: *Early Chronicles of Valley Creek Community*. (Place and date of publication not given.)

HUNT, THOMAS JAMES DE LA: *Perry County: A History* [Indiana]. Indianapolis, 1916.

Jefferson County and Birmingham, Ala. Birmingham, 1887.

JOHNSON, L. F.: *The History of Franklin County, Kentucky*. Frankfort, 1912.

KENNAMER, JOHN ROBERT: *History of Jackson County, Alabama*. Winchester, Tenn., 1935.

LANG, JOHN H.: *History of Harrison County, Mississippi*. Gulfport, Miss., 1936.

LANGFORD, ELLA MOLLOY: *History of Johnson County, Arkansas*. Clarksville, Ark., 1921.

LEFTWICH, NINA: *Two Hundred Years at Muscle Shoals*. Tuscumbia, Ala., 1935.

LENOIR, W. B.: *History of Sweetwater Valley*. Sweetwater, Tenn., 1916.

LITTLE, JOHN BUCKNER: *The History of Butler County, Alabama, 1815–1885*. Cincinnati, 1895.

LOGAN, JOHN H.: *A History of the Upper Country of South Carolina, from the Earliest Periods to the Close of the War of Independence*. Charleston, S.C., 1859.

MARLIN, L. G.: *The History of Cherokee County, Georgia*. Atlanta, 1932.

McCALLUM, JAMES: *A Brief Sketch of the Settlement and Early History of Giles County, Tennessee.* Pulaski, Tenn., 1928.

NEUMAN, FRED G.: *The Story of Paducah* [Kentucky]. Paducah, Ky., 1927.

O'PRY, MAUDE HEARN: *Chronicles of Shreveport.* Shreveport, La., 1928.

PAGE, O. J.: *History of Massac County, Illinois.* (Place of publication not given), 1900.

PIRTLE, ALFRED: *James Chenoweth, the Story of One of the Earliest Boys of Louisville and Where Louisville Started.* Louisville, Ky., 1921.

POSEY, WALTER BROWNLOW: *La Grange, Alabama's Earliest College.* Birmingham-Southern College *Bulletin,* Vol. XXVI, No. 6. Birmingham, 1933.

POWELL, NETTIE: *History of Marion County, Georgia.* Columbus, 1931.

RANCK, GEORGE W.: *Boonesborough.* Louisville, 1901.

——: *History of Lexington.* Cincinnati, 1872.

RIDENOUR, GEORGE L.: *Early Times in Meade County, Kentucky.* Louisville, 1929.

RILEY, BENJAMIN FRANKLIN: *History of Conecuh County, Alabama.* Columbus, Ga., 1881.

ROTHERT, OTTO A.: *A History of Muhlenberg County.* Louisville, 1913.

ROWLAND, MRS. DUNBAR (ERON O.): *History of Hinds County, Mississippi, 1821–1922.* Jackson, Miss., 1922.

SARTAIN, JAMES ALFRED: *History of Walker County, Georgia.* Vol. I. Dalton, Ga., 1932.

SAUNDERS, COLONEL JAMES EDMONDS: *Early Settlers of Alabama* (Lawrence Co., Ala.). New Orleans, 1899.

SEALS, REV. MONROE: *History of White County.* (Place of publication not given), 1935.

SHANNON, KARR: *A History of Izard County* [Arkansas]. Melbourne, Ark. (No date given.)

SHIELDS, JOSEPH DUNBAR: *Natchez, Its Early History.* Louisville, 1930.

SHIRAS, FRANCES H.: *History of Baxter County* [Arkansas]. (Place and date of publication not given.)

SMARTT, EUGENIA PERSONS: *History of Eufaula, Alabama.* Birmingham, 1930.

SMITH, NELSON F.: *History of Pickens County, Ala.* Carrollton, Ala., 1856.

STOCKARD, S. W.: *The History of Lawrence, Jackson, Independence and Stone Counties of the Third Judicial District of Arkansas.* Little Rock, 1904.

TAYLOR, OLIVER: *Historic Sullivan* [Tennessee]. Bristol, Tenn., 1909.

TEMPLE, SARAH BLACKWELL GOBER: *The First Hundred Years, a Short History of Cobb County in Georgia.* Atlanta, 1935.

THOMAS, BENJAMIN P.: *Lincoln's New Salem.* Crawfordsville, Ind., and Chicago, 1934.

THOMPSON, MATTIE THOMAS: *History of Barbour County, Alabama.* Eufaula, Ala., 1939.

TOWNES, S. A.: *The History of Marion, Sketches of Life &c in Perry County, Ala.* Marion, Ala., 1844.

VAN COURT, CATHERINE: *In Old Natchez.* Garden City, N.Y., 1938.

WALKER, ANNE KENDRICK: *Backtracking in Barbour County.* Richmond, Va., 1941.

WEBB, ROBERT T.: *History and Traditions of Clay County, Arkansas.* Mountain Home, Ark., 1933.

WILLIAMS, HARRY LEE: *History of Craighead County, Arkansas.* Little Rock, 1930.

WILLIS, GEORGE L., SR.: *History of Shelby County, Kentucky.* Louisville, 1929.

YOUNG, BENNETT H.: *A History of Jessamine County, Kentucky.* Louisville, 1898.

MANUSCRIPTS

1. Theses

ALEXANDER, THERON: "The Covenanters Come to East Tennessee." MS., Master's thesis, University of Tennessee, 1939.

ALLINSON, MAY: "Conditions in the Illinois County, 1787–1800." MS., Master's thesis, University of Illinois, 1907.

BRUMBAUGH, ALICE LOUISE: "The Regulator Movement in Illinois." MS., Master's thesis, University of Illinois, 1927.

CARMANY, HAROLD G.: "The History of the Evangelical Church in Fairfield County, Ohio." MS., Master's thesis, Ohio State University, 1938.

CLEARY, THOMAS FRANCIS: "The History of the Catholic Church in Illinois from 1763 to 1844." MS., Doctor's thesis, University of Illinois, 1932.

COE, ROBERT H. C.: "Banjamin Hawkins, Indian Agent from 1796 to 1817." MS., Master's thesis, University of Tennessee, 1926.

COTTON, JULIANA MARIA SOFIA: "Social Life and Conditions in the Mississippi Valley, 1826–1840." MS., Master's thesis, University of Wisconsin, 1926.

COUNCE, PAUL A.: "Social and Economic History of Kingsport before 1908." MS., Master's thesis, University of Tennessee, 1939.

CROUCH, WILLIAM W.: "Missionary Activities among the Cherokee Indians, 1757–1838." MS., Master's thesis, University of Tennessee, 1932.

DANEY, CHARLES ALBERT: "Amusements and Diversions in Ohio from 1788 to 1850." MS., Master's thesis, Ohio State University, 1940.

DELCAMP, MARY ESTELLE: "The Early Life of Lexington before the year 1820." MS., Master's thesis, Transylvania College, 1916.

DISBROW, NATALIE JARBOE: "Thomas Walker, Man of Affairs." MS., Master's thesis, University of Virginia, 1940.

DOWNES, RANDOLPH CHANDLER: "Frontier Ohio, 1788–1803." MS., Master's thesis, Ohio State University, 1929.

EAGLE, DELBERT P.: "Aspects of the Kentucky Frontier." MS., Master's thesis, University of Kentucky, 1938.

EDWARDS, LAWRENCE: "History of the Baptists of Tennessee with Particular Attention to the Primitive Baptists of East Tennessee." MS., Master's thesis, University of Tennessee, 1941.

FINK, MIRIAM: "Some Phases of the Social and Economic History of Jonesboro, Tennessee, Prior to the Civil War." MS., Master's thesis, University of Tennessee, 1934.

FITZRANDOLPH, LURA MAE: "The History of Arkansas to 1836." MS., Master's thesis, University of Wisconsin, 1935.

FLISCH, JULIA ANNA: "Land Legislation in Georgia." MS., Master's thesis, University of Wisconsin, 1908.

GIDDENS, LUCIEN: "The Development of Colleges for Women in the South to 1885." MS., Master's thesis, Vanderbilt University, 1937.

GORDON, FRANCIS MARION: "Early History of Hocking County." MS., Master's thesis, Ohio State University, 1940.

GRAY, CLARENCE E.: "Washington as a Promoter of Westward Expansion." MS., Master's thesis, Ohio State University, 1933.

HALL, ROBERT GREEN: "The Natchez Trace." MS., Master's thesis, University of Wisconsin, 1914.

HARRIS, GERALDINE C.: "The History of the Theatre in Ohio, 1815–1850." MS., Master's thesis, Ohio State University, 1937.

HEIDELBERG, NELL ANGELA: "The Frontier in Mississippi." MS., Master's thesis, Louisiana State University and Agricultural and Mechanical College, 1940.

HILLIER, FRANCIS RICHARDSON: "The Hite Family and the Settlement of the West." MS., Master's thesis, University of Virginia.

HOLDER, RAY: "The Autobiography of William Winans." MS., Master's thesis, University of Mississippi.

HOLT, ALBERT C.: "The Economic and Social Beginnings of Tennessee." MS., Doctor's thesis, George Peabody College, Nashville, 1923.

HOPKINS, JAMES FRANKLIN: "A History of the Hemp Industry in Kentucky." MS., Master's thesis, University of Kentucky, 1938.

HOWARD, HUGH ASHER: "Chapters in the Economic History of Knox County, Kentucky." MS., Master's thesis, University of Kentucky, 1937.

HURLEY, WILLIAM MARVIN: "Socializing Forces in the History of Pope County, Arkansas." MS., Master's thesis, University of Arkansas, 1931.

JAMISON, LENA MITCHELL: "The Natchez Trace." MS., Master's thesis, University of Wisconsin, 1938.

KERSHAW, MARY CATHERINE: "Early History of Shawneetown, Illinois, from 1812 to 1832." MS., Master's thesis, University of Illinois, 1941.

LAMB, AVIS M.: "The Ohio Valley as Seen by Early Travelers 1788–1820." MS., Master's thesis, Ohio State University, 1932.

LAWRENCE, MATTHEW: "John Mason Peck, a Biographical Sketch." MS., Master's thesis, University of Illinois, 1914.

LEDFORD, ALLEN JAMES: "Methodism in Tennessee 1783–1866." MS., Master's thesis, University of Tennessee, 1941.

LESTER, WILLIAM STEWART, SR.: "The Transylvania Colony." MS., Doctor's thesis, University of Kentucky, 1934.

MARTEL, GLENN GARDNER: "Early Days in Columbia County, Arkansas." MS., Master's thesis, University of Arkansas, 1933.

MARTIN, MARY FRANKLIN: "Kentucky the Growth of a Personality." MS., Master's thesis, University of Kentucky, 1938.

McCLURE, VIRGINIA CLAY: "The Settlement of the Kentucky Appalachian Highlands." MS., Doctor's thesis, University of Kentucky, 1933.

McKINLEY, HENRY CARROLL: "Some Aspects of the History of Logan County, Ohio." MS., Master's thesis, Ohio State University, 1934.

McLENDON, JAMES HAYS: "A History of Simpson County, Mississippi, to 1865." MS., Master's thesis, University of Texas.

MOONEY, CHASE CURRAN: "Slavery in Tennessee." MS., Doctor's thesis, Vanderbilt University, 1939.

MORRILL, JENNY HUGHES: "The Settlement of Alabama, 1820–1830." MS., Master's thesis, University of Wisconsin, 1905.

MUSGRAVE, MRS. BONITA: "A Study of the Home and Local Crafts of the Pioneers of Washington County, Arkansas." MS., Master's thesis, University of Arkansas, 1929.

NAYLOR, RALPH E.: "A History of Athens College, Athens, Alabama." MS., Master's thesis, Vanderbilt University.

OLIVER, KENNETH L.: "Columbus, the Town That Wanted to be the Nation's Capital." MS., Master's thesis, University of Kentucky, 1938.

PATTON, J. FRED: "History of Fort Smith, Arkansas." MS., Master's thesis, University of Arkansas, 1936.

PAULLIN, MARJORIE RUTH: "New Salem: A Typical Frontier Settlement." MS., Master's thesis, University of Illinois, 1942.

PORTER, JEAN H.: "The Frontier and Lord Dunmore's War." MS., Master's thesis, University of Kentucky, 1943.

RICE, MARY LOUISE: "The Role of the Osage Orange Hedge in the Occupation of the Great Plains." MS., Master's thesis, University of Illinois, 1937.

ROBBINS, ROY MARVIN: "A History of the Pre-emption of Public Lands." MS., Doctor's thesis, University of Wisconsin, 1928.

ROGERS, WILLIAM FLINN: "Life on the Kentucky-Tennessee Frontier near the End of the Eighteenth Century." MS., Master's thesis, University of Tennessee, 1925.

ROLAND, CLIFFORD P.: "History of the Disciples of Christ in Tennessee to 1850." MS., Master's thesis, Vanderbilt University, 1931.

SEEBER, R. CLIFFORD: "A History of Anderson County, Tennessee." MS., Master's thesis, University of Tennessee, 1928.

SHAW, HAZEL YEARSLEY: "The Ohio River Trade 1788–1830." MS., Master's thesis, University of Illinois, 1908.

SMITH, BEATRICE MERLE: "Sam Houston in Tennessee." MS., Master's thesis, University of Tennessee, 1932.

SMITH, PAUL TINCHER: "Organized Militia in the United States from 1846 to 1860." MS., Master's thesis, University of Wisconsin, 1918.

STARNS, EFFIE COX: "German, French, and Dutch Settlers in Kentucky." MS., Master's thesis, University of Kentucky, 1931.

STROKER, FRANCIS M.: "Money and Currency in Kentucky before 1865." MS., Master's thesis, University of Kentucky, 1942.

TAYLOR, FLORANCE WALTON: "Culture in Illinois in Lincoln's Day." MS., Master's thesis, University of Illinois, 1933.

TAYLOR, GEORGE F.: "Suffrage in Early Kentucky." MS., Master's thesis, University of Kentucky, 1925.

WATKINS, VIOLET JANE: "Pioneer Medicine in the Tennessee-

Kentucky Frontier Region." MS., Master's thesis, Vanderbilt University, 1941.

WILEY, BELL IRVIN: "Cotton and Slavery in the History of West Tennessee." MS., Master's thesis, University of Kentucky, 1929.

WOODSON, ELIZABETH G.: "John May and His Brothers." MS., Master's thesis, University of Virginia.

YOUNG, JAMES HARVEY: "Disease and Patent Medicine in Southern Illinois before 1840." MS., Master's thesis, University of Illinois, 1938.

2. Miscellaneous

BROWN, MATTIE: "A History of River Transportation in Arkansas from 1819–1880." MS., University of Arkansas, Fayetteville, Ark.

HENDERSON, JOHN G.: "Early History of the Sangamon Country." MS., Illinois State Historical Library, Springfield, Ill.

ILES, ELIJAH: "Early Life and Times of Maj. Elijah Iles." MS., Illinois State Historical Library, Springfield, Ill.

TODD, GEORGE D.: "How the Pioneers of the West Marketed Their Products." MS., Filson Club Library, Louisville, Ky.

——: "How the Pioneers of the West Obtained Their Supplies prior to 1800 and What They Paid for Them." MS., Filson Club Library, Louisville, Ky.

WILLIAMS, CLANTON W.: "Early Ante-Bellum Montgomery—a Black-Belt Constituency." MS. (typewritten), Alabama Department of Archives and History, Montgomery, Ala.

PAMPHLETS

Centenary of Kentucky, The. Proceedings at the Celebration. By the Filson Club. Louisville, 1892.

HERNDON, DALLAS T.: *History of the Arkansas Gazette.* Little Rock, November 20, 1919. (Supplement commemorating the founding of Arkansas' first newspaper.)

——: *Why Little Rock was Born.* Little Rock, 1833.

LEWIS, P. H.: *The Medical History of Alabama.* New Orleans, 1847.

McClellan, Captain R. A.: *Early History of Limestone County*. Tennessee State Library, Nashville, Tenn.

Scotch-Irish in America, The. Proceedings of the Scotch-Irish Congress at Columbia, Tenn., May 8–11, 1889. Cincinnati, 1889.

Wharton, A. C.: *The Founder of Port Gibson*. Port Gibson, Miss., February 18, 1887.

COLLECTIONS

Alabama Historical Quarterly, Vols. I–V.

American Historical Magazine, Vols. I–II.

Arkansas Historical Quarterly, Vols. I–III.

East Tennessee Historical Society Publications, Nos. I–XVI.

Filson Club History Quarterly, Vols. I–XVIII.

Georgia Historical Quarterly, Vols. I–XII.

Georgia Historical Review, Vols. I–XII.

Illinois State Historical Collections, Vols. I–1925.

Indiana Historical Society Publications, Vols. I–XXV.

Journal of Mississippi History, The, Vols. I–V.

Journal of Southern History, Vols. V–VII.

Kentucky State Historical Register, Vols. I–XLII.

Louisiana Historical Quarterly, Vols. I–XXVI.

Magazine of American History, December 1883.

Mississippi Valley Historical Review, Vols. I–XXXII.

Missouri Historical Review, Vols. I–XXXI.

Ohio Archæological and Historical Publications, Vols. I–XLIV.

Publications, Alabama Historical Society, Vol. I.

Publications, Arkansas Historical Association, Vols. I–III.

Publications, Mississippi Historical Society, Vols. I–XI.

Publications, Southern History Association, Vols. I–XI.

Tennessee Historical Magazine, Vols. I–IX; Series 2, Vols. I–III.

Tennessee Historical Quarterly, Vol. I.

Transactions, Alabama Historical Society, Vols. I–IV.

BIOGRAPHY

Allsopp, Fred W.: *Albert Pike: a Biography*. Little Rock, 1928.

Bakeless, John: *Daniel Boone*. New York, 1939.

CHAMBERS, KATE WALLER: *Chronicles of a Worth-while Family Chambers-Stout.* New York, 1919.

COULTER, ELLIS MERTON: *William G. Brownlow.* Chapel Hill, 1937.

GREEN, REV. WILLIAM M.: *Life and Papers of A. L. P. Green, D.D.* Nashville, 1877.

MEYER, LELAND WINFIELD: *The Life and Times of Colonel Richard M. Johnson of Kentucky.* New York, 1932.

PUTNAM, A. W.: *History of Middle Tennessee; or Life and Times of General James Robertson.* Nashville, 1859.

Shields, Joseph D.: *The Life and Times of Seargent Smith Prentiss.* Philadelphia, 1883.

SHINN, JOSIAH H.: *Pioneers and Makers of Arkansas.* Little Rock, 1908.

STEPHENSON, WENDELL HOLMES: *Alexander Porter, Whig Planter of Old Louisiana.* Baton Rouge, 1934.

——: *Isaac Franklin, Slave Trader and Planter of the Old South.* University, La., 1938.

SWEARINGEN, MACK: *The Early Life of George Poindexter, a Story of the First Southwest.* New Orleans, 1934.

SYDNOR, CHARLES S.: *A Gentleman of the Old Natchez Region, Benjamin L. C. Wailes.* Durham, N.C., 1938.

TROWBRIDGE, M. E. D.: *Pioneer Days, the Life Story of Gershom and Elizabeth Day.* Philadelphia, 1895.

Index

Aberdeen, Ala., 57

Academy, 177, 180

Accidents, treatment, 216, 217; in digging well, 220

Account of Christian Perfection, 190

Acrobat, 159

Ague, 221

Alabama, 11, 24, 26, 27, 30, 36, 53, 57, 59, 60, 62, 63, 65, 66, 69, 70, 71, 73, 74, 76, 88, 110, 117, 118, 123, 150, 151, 152, 181, 199, 207, 234, 242, 247, 284, 291, 336, 337, 338

Alabama (city), Ala., 151

Alabama River, 12, 79, 114, 118, 168

Alamance, Battle of, 13

Alder, Jonathan, 281

Alexander, Captain J. E., 213–14, 279, 337

Allegheny Mountains, 159, 170, 178, 179, 182, 237

Allen, R. L., 86

Alton, Ill., 210

American Agriculturist, 86

American Bible Society, 122, 191

Amherst County, Va., 56

Ammunition, 41, 42, 244, 263

Amphitheater, 159

Amusements: school, 175; muster, 271; horseback parties, 308

Andersontown, Ind., 211

Animals: wild, 4; roamed streets, 152; trained, 158

Appalachian Mountains, 3, 220

Apple: scions destroyed, 16; brought by boat, 110; paring, 130; butter, 130; grown in Kentucky and Tennessee, 255

Aquasca, Md., 57

Architecture, 28

Arfwedson, Carl David, 150

Ark: described, 19; same as Kentucky boats, 109

Arkansas, 22, 24, 27, 31, 59, 74, 75, 78, 83, 105, 132, 159, 181, 206, 213, 226, 237, 246, 301

Arkansas Gazette, 206, 268

Armstrong mill, 249

Articles of agreement, 171, 173

Asbury, Bishop, 135, 182, 193

Ash leech, 300

Ashley, Colonel, 246

Auctions: land, 68, 72; town lots, 149

Audubon, John James, 118, 143, 298, 325
Avery, Henry, 135

Bailey, Caleb, 305, 306
Bailey, Tom, 306
Baily, Frances, 111, 212
Bakeless, John, 47
Baldwin, Joseph G., 164, 229, 232
Ball, 146
Baltimore, 108, 118
Banjo, 128, 129
Bank: discount, 117; closed, 123; wild-cat, 123
Bank of Kentucky, 117
Baptist, 181, 182, 185, 186, 190, 194, 196, 198
Barbecues, 95, 137–8, 240
Barefeet, 285, 295–6
Barges, 119
Bark: in place of leather, 32; harness, 302; rope, 302
Barking exercise, 198
Barn, 98
Basket: used to carry children, 16; meetings, 203
Bastrop, Baron de, 75
Batesville News, 159
Battle of Alamance, 13
Battle of Blue Licks, 282
Battle of King's Mountain, 272
Battle of New Orleans, 318
Battle of Nickajack, 40
"Battling," 300
Bean, Russell, 227
Bear, 4, 34, 50, 105, 139, 158, 283, 288
Bear Grass, Ky., 49
Bear-hunter, 31
Bear hunting, 34
Bear skins, 29, 30
Bear's oil, 30, 107, 115, 253, 288, 300
"Beats," 243
Beaver, 115, 288
Bedford, John, 112

Beds: of squatter, 29; feather, 51, 301; types, 301
Bee: gums, 30, hunting, 36–7; tree, 37
Beef: divided into quarters, 144; fresh, 288
Bees: log-rolling, 125; house-raising, 127–8; house-warming, 128; corn-shucking, 128–9; cotton-picking, 130; flax-pulling, 130; sap-collecting, 130; sugaring-off, 130; wood-chopping, 130; apple-paring, 130; apple butter "biling," 130; road-building, 130; quilting, 131
Beeswax, 107, 115, 117, 121
Bell, 42
Bench (Indian chief), 321
Bent Creek Church, 187
Benton, Jesse, 9
Benton, Senator Thomas Hart, 123
Bergu, 127
Berry, Captain, 211–12
Bible agent, 241
Bibles, 122, 181–2, 192, 194, 307
Big Bone Cave, 247
Big Bottom, Mo., 24
Big Prairie, Ind., 24
Billy Earthquake, 319
Birkbeck, Morris, 279, 317, 331
Bit (money), 116
Biting, 140
Black family, 58
Black Fox, 267
Blacksmith, 253, 271
Blacksmith shop, 122, 143, 333
Blackstone, Sir William, 230
Bland, James, 89
Blane, William Newnham, 143, 257, 293
Blanket, 296, 309
Bledsoe, Abraham, 4
Bleeding, 220
Blockhouse, 39
Blount, Governor, 66, 205

Blount County, Ala., 135
Blount County, Tenn., 108
Blue Licks, Ky., 244
Blue Ridge Mountains, 38, 57
Boasting, 319
Boatmen: described, 113; cared for by Indians, 113; returned overland, 113; defense going overland, 113; returned by steamboat, 114; celebrated, 319
Boats: ark, 19, 109; Kentucky, 109; barge, 119; *Fastgoing Mary*, 119; *Industry*, 119; *Lovely*, 119; *Willing Maid*, 119; *Monroe*, 152; *General Jackson*, 221; sunk to thwart Indians, 265; leather, 272; rawhide, 272; speech colored by life on, 313–14. *See also* Flatboats, Keelboats, Steamboats.
Boing, Mr., 306
Bonny Kate, 51
Books, 31
Boone, Daniel: on buffalo, 4; lone hunter, 5; singing, 6; habits on trail, 6; on being lost, 7; gone from home, 7; field notes, 9; lost landholdings, 10; on keeping the country, 13; escaped creditors, 13–14; laid out Wilderness Road, 15, 204; letter from, 17–18; on moving, 25; dug ginseng, 32; sought to protect buffalo, 33; rescued daughter, 45; wrote Governor of Virginia, 50; held Spanish land grant, 75; good shot, 143; operated on Squire, 216; remedy for scalded feet, 218; went to salt lick, 244; lead in salt-manufacturing in Missouri, 246; made gunpowder, 246; captured and released, 256; ran gantlet, 259; killed buffalo,

Boone, Daniel (*Continued*)
287; rescued by Simon Kenton, 329
Boone, Daniel Morgan, 287
Boone, Jemima: captured, 44–5; married, 135
Boone, Rebecca, 274, 278
Boone, Squire, 6, 47, 148, 216
Boone's Lick, Mo., 246
Boonesborough, 39, 44, 45, 48, 49, 148, 216, 329
Borderer, 32
Borrowing, 308
Boston, 332
Bourbon County, Ky., 187, 202
Bowie, John or James, 74
Boyd, Lynn, 241
Bragging, 310
Bran dance, 131
Breech-clouts, 294
Brethett, John, 158
Bride, 128, 135–7. *See also* Wedding.
British, 39, 54, 74, 332
British Proclamation of 1763, 14
Broom, 301–2
Brown, E. A., 73
Brown (gambler), 168
Brown, Dr. Samuel, 222
Brush: fence, 103; preachers, 194; scrubbing, 301; backwoods, 312
Brush-breaker, 312
Buchanan, Sally, 277
Buchanan's Station, 267, 277
Bucket brigade, 154
Buckskin, 297
Buffalo: 4, 32–3, 50, 287, 312; hunting, 33; wool, 252; skins, 301; hides, 302; horns, 302; hunts, 317
Buffalo Lick Baptist church, 186–7, 188
Bullets, molding, 277
Bundling, 134
Burgoo, 127, 129
Burial, 222, 223

Burleigh plantation, 92
Butchering, 288
Butler County, Ala., 69
Butter, 109, 291
Butting poles, 28
Buzzard's Roost (tavern), 209

Cabin rights, 25, 66
Cabins in station, 38
Cadron, Ark., 156
Cahaba, Ala., 65, 69, 151
Caldwell Parish, La., 99
Calendars, 307
Calico, 298
California, 121, 209
Calk, William, diary, 17
Calloway, Elizabeth, 44–5, 134
Calloway, Fanny, 135
Calloway, Flanders, 45
Campaigns, political, 239
Camp-ground, 199
Camp-meeting: whites and
   blacks attended, 96; product
   of frontier, 195; standard pat-
   tern, 199; brush arbor, 199;
   pulpit-stand, 199; altar, 199;
   penitent's pen, 199; tents, 199;
   daily program, 200; decorum,
   200; attendance, 201; behav-
   ior, 201–2; duration, 202; Cane
   Ridge, 202
Canada, 332
Candidates for office: tactics,
   239, 242; treated, 241;
   speeches, 241; still hunt, 241;
   at militia muster, 271
Candler, Isaac, 324
Cane, 3, 4, 5, 82, 83, 99, 265
Cane Ridge camp-meeting, 202
Canebrakes, 3, 34, 241, 318
Cannon, wooden, 46
Canvassers, 122
Caps, 296, 297
Captain Slick's Company, 234
Caravan, of planter, 60

Cards: gamblers, 166; three-card
   monte, 167; all classes played,
   332
Carolinas, 21, 58, 59
Carpet, 31
"Carry Me Back to Ole Vir-
   ginny," 89
Carter, James, 187
Cartwright, Peter, 192, 202
Casket, 222–3
Cassiday, Michael, 40–1, 242
Caste system in slavery, 89
Castleman, Abe, 265, 267
Cattle: sensed Indians near, 50;
   shelter for, 98; driven to mar-
   ket, 108; on boats, 110
Cave, 34, 87, 246
Cemetery, 222
Chair, travel by, 55
Chapman, 164
Charcoal, 246
Chariton, Mo., 24
Charleston, 118
Chateau's pond (St. Louis), 152
Chattahoochee River, 114, 150
Cheese, 291
Cherokees, 50, 65, 66
Chestnut Hill, 84
Chickasaw, 66, 260
Chickens, 110
Childbirth, 14, 275, 278, 285, 302
Children: carried in baskets on
   trail, 16; appearance, 24, 29;
   preached, 198; dress, 297;
   work, 302
Chimney, 28, 303
Chillicothe (Indian town), 281
Chillicothe, Ohio, 326
Choctaw, 260
Christian Repository, 191
Christmas, 35, 62, 95, 137, 173,
   176, 219, 309
Church of England, 198
Churches: squatters did not
   have, 30; slaves attended, 96;
   membership, 181; meeting-
   house built, 182; description,

Churches (*Continued*)
182–3; out of doors, 183; attendance, 183; preaching appointments, 183; customs, 183; announcements, 184–5; music, 186–9; duties of membership, 186; communion tickets, 186; business meetings, 186; rules of order, 187; sectarianism, 187; trials, 187; discipline, 187; problems of order, 188; attitude toward liquor, 188–9; music, 189; offering, 189; worship informal, 189; love feast, 189–90; behavior, 324

Cincinnati, 273, 301

Circuit courts, 225; cases tried, 225

Circuit judge, 227

Circuit riders, 193

Circus, 159; boats, 122

Cist's *Miscellany*, 319

Claiborne, Ala., 3

Claims, land: methods of holding, 8; not valid, 9; club, 69; floating, 76

Clark County, Ark., 260, 261

Clark, George Rogers, 8, 40, 267, 272, 321

Clark, Lucy, 187

Clarke County, Ala., 59

Clay County, Mo., 140, 237

Clearing, making, 98, 99

Clinch River, 18

Clocks, 121, 307

Clothing: taken by pioneers, 14; made of nettles, 251; buffalo hair, 252; hemp, 252; flax, 252; cotton, 252; wool, 252; from skins, 253; repair, 295. *See also* Dress.

Clown, 159

Coach, Concord, 206; driver, 208. *See also* Stagecoach.

Coate, William, 59

Cobb, Mr. 284

Cochuma, Miss., 71

Cock fighting, 145, 271

Cockrell, Simon, 237

Coeducation, 178–9

Coffee, 292

Coffin, 222–3

Cold Water expedition, 271

Collar, horse, 32

Colleges, 177–9; library, 177–8; laboratory equipment, 178; entrance requirements, 178; Transylvania, 178; Cumberland, 178; La Grange, 178; coeducation, 178–9; Judson, 179; women's, 179; subjects taught, 179; business, 179; tuition, 179; medical, 220

Colporteurs, 122, 241, 325

Columbia, Mo., 95, 120, 153, 177, 298

Columbus, Ga., 88, 150

Columbus, Miss., 72, 219

Commission merchants, 117

Commissioner of Public Lands, 78

Communion, 186

Concord, N. H., 206

Concordia Parish, La., 82, 227

Conechu County, Ala., 118, 295

Confectioneries, 118

Confections, 120

Conjurers, 216

Connecticut, 120, 121

Conversation: full of anecdotes, 316; topics of, 317. *See also* Speech.

Coonskins, used for specie, 115

Cooper Run Baptist Church, 187

Coopers, 300

Coosa River, 114

Copperas, 120, 297

Cordelling, 119

Corn, 24, 32, 82, 83, 107, 110, 128, 254, 289–91; planting, 99; checking, 100; harvesting, 100–1; fed to cows, 105; right, 8, 66; shocking, 305

Cornbread, 290

Cornmeal mush, 290

Corn-shuckings, 95, 101, 128–9, 224

Cotton: prices, 53; cultivation, 82; picking, 91, 92, 130; boat loads of, 110; ginner's receipts, 116; gin, 252–3; seeding, 252; spinning, 284; carding, 284

Cotton kingdom, 78

Counterfeiting, 233–4

County: fairs, 108; formed, 149; court, 237–8

County-seat: located, 149, 238; fights, 151

Court, 173; week, 108, 177; punishments, 226; county, 237–8; scene, 228–9; procedures, 228–9; manners, 323

Court martial, 268, 270

Courthouse, 228

Courtland, Ala., 151

Courtship: bundling, 134; noosing, 134; privacy lacking in, 133–4; in stations, 277; references to, 314

Covington, Leonard, 57

Cowan, Captain John, 48

Cows: feed, 104–5; dead, 152; lead way to greens, 299

Cox, Nathaniel, 54

Crab Orchard, Ky., 88, 205

Cradle, 101, 102

Creek Nation, 162

Creeks, 11

Cresswell diary, 294

Creswell, James, 238

Crèvecœur, St. John de, 298

Crimes: adultery, 225; fornication, 225; debt, 225; assault and battery, 225, 227; horse-stealing, 226, 232–3; rape, 226; murder, 233; counterfeiting, 233; slave stealing, 233; stealing, 234; murder of Indians, 257–8

Crockett, David: famous bear-hunter, 34; member of legislature, 34; drove stock, 108; meager schooling late, 170; ignorant of governmental affairs, 237; winning ways, 239, 240; lost his fortune, 251; quipped about earthquake, 316; would not take oath, 338

Crops, 83

Cumberland area, 15, 18, 50, 195, 331

Cumberland College, 178

Cumberland Gap, 14, 18, 204

Cumberland Mountains, 256

Cumberland River, 14, 112, 204, 205

Cumberland Road, 204

Cuming, Fortesque, 131

Cumming, Captain, 295

Curfew, 153

"Cut and call," 33

"Cut" money, 117

Cutlery, 299

Dabney, Colonel Thomas, 58, 61

Dameron, George W., 21

Dams, 251

Dances: slave, 95, 96; at frolic, 127, 128; types, 131; bran, 131; square, 131; "hops," 131; week-long, 131, 132; "White Cockade," 132; "Flowers of Edinboro," 132; wedding, 136; churches frowned on, 187

Danville, Ky., 222

Daubeny, Charles, 80, 85

Davidson, James, 207

Dead, preparation for burial, 222

"Dead falls," 165

Deadening, 98

Death, violent, 49

Debating societies, 138

Deer, 50; hunting, 35; skins, 6, 27, 29; antlers, 29

Defoe, Daniel, 328

Democracy, spirit of, 332

Denominations, 182. *See also* Baptists, Church of England, Disciples of Christ, Methodists, Presbyterians.

Detroit, 45

Dialect, 310

Dickens, Charles, 207–8, 214

Dictionary of expressions, 315

Disciples of Christ, 192

Diseases: prevalent, 221; treatment of, 221

Dishes, 29, 299

Distilling, 254–5

Divorce, 335

Doak, Samuel, 177, 182, 197

Doctor book, 217

Doctors: scarce, 215–18; Indian, 215; old women, 215; conjurers, 216; called only in extremity, 216; influx, 218; unlicensed, 218; training, 218–19; profited financially, 219; number in Lowndesboro, Ala., 219; college training, 220; quacks, 220; allopathic, 220; Thompsonian, 220, 234; ignorant, 221–2; progressive, 222

Doggeries, 118

Dogs: hunting, 28–9, 33–6; killed, 30; fought Indians, 50; scouting, 50; saved Nashboro, 51; saved Negroes, 57; possum, 96; fought bears, 139; acting, 158; aided spies, 266; subject of conversation, 317

Domestic Manners of the Americans, 323

Domestic Medicine, 217

Donaldson, Israel, 260

Doors, 27, 39

Dow, Lorenzo, 197, 198

Drake, Daniel, 104, 128, 174, 219, 221, 279, 301–2

Drake, Sr., Samuel, 161, 162

Drake, Rev. Silas, 188

Drama, societies, 161; troupes, 161; critics, 163; company, 318

Dress: hunting shirt, 293; leggings, 294; breech-clouts, 294; shoe-packs, 295; pantaloons, 295; moccasins, 295; caps, 296–7; blanket, 296; robe, 296; shoes, 296; for mild climate, 296; at weddings, 297; of aristocracy, 297–8; children, 297; buckskin, 297; hats, 297; styles, 298; finery, 298

Drinking, 210, 292

Drives: made in fall, 108; hog, cattle, horse, 108

Dromedary, 158

Drugs, 120

Drury Allen district, S. C., 59

Dry goods, 120

Duels, 141, 156, 336

Durant, Benjamin, 11–12

Dyeing, 284–5

Earmarks, of hogs, 36

Earthquake, Billy, 319

East Alabama (city), Ala., 151

Easter, 95

Education, 339

Election: educational and social institution, 239; days, 242; ballot, 242; viva voce, 242; fights, 242; beats, 243

Electioneering, 239; "still hunts," 241

Elephant, 158

Elizabeth City, N. C., 55

Elk, 4

Ellett, Jim, 164

Emigrants: parties, 15; on the journey, 15–16; number on Wilderness Road, 18; turn back, 18

Estill, Capt. James, 87

Estill's Station, 87, 88

Eufaula, Ala., 88

Exercises, religious: falling, 196; jerks, 197; barking, 198; holy laugh, 198; holy dance, 198

Expeditions: hunting and trapping, 5; Cold Water, 271

Express: riders, 205; mail, 209

Exportation: salt, 246; pork, 246

Eyeglasses, 327

"Falling exercise," 196

Farm implements, 99

Farmer's Gazette, 96

Faro, 164

Fastgoing Mary, 119

Featherstonhaugh, George William, 61, 141, 301, 322

Federal Road, 204

Feed: for cattle and horses, 105; for pack horses, 107

Fences: brush, 103; rail, 103–4, 305–7; worm, snake, Virginia, 104

Ferries, 149

Fever, 221

Fiddle, 128, 129, 159, 242

Fiddler's contest, 132

Fight: at corn-shucking, 129; biting, 140; gouging matches, 140; man and beast, 140; rough-and-tumble, 140, 322, 336; with knives, 140; wolf and dog, 140; of road builders, 145; in frontier towns, 155; over state capital, 156; at school, 174; on frontier, 225; at fort, 278; boatman's challenge, 319

Filson, 4

Finley, J. B., 197, 288

Fire: at siege of Boonesborough, 46; protection, 154; from chimney, 303–4

Fireplace, 27, 300

Fireworks display, 160

Fitch, John, 122

Flatboat: appearance, 19; construction, 19; cost, 19; described, 19; ark, 19, 109; used on Ohio, 19; travel, 20; hazards of travel, 21, 112; Kentucky boats, 109; number on Mississippi, 110; life on, 110–12; lashed together, 111; broken up in New Orleans, 113; blacksmith shops, 122; circus, 122; stores, 122; tin shops, 122; used by peddlers, 122

Flax, 252, 283, 296

Flax-pulling, 130

"Flinging the rail," 145

Flint, James, 200–1

Flint, Timothy, 19, 96, 114, 181, 182, 203, 242, 311

Floating claims, 76

Floating mills, 250

Floating rights, 73

Floating theater, 164

Florence, Ala., 218

Florida, 62, 161, 316

Flour, 110

Floyd, Colonel John, 13, 16, 49, 307

Flush Times of Mississippi, 232

Fodder-pulling, 173

Food: dried, 30; from forest, 50, 275; scarce, 52, 80; of slaves, 83; raised on plantation, 84; for pack-horse drivers, 107; brought on boats, 110, 120; at taverns, 214; early pioneer, 287; game, 287–8; vegetables, 289; meat, 288; corn, 289–90; nuts, 290; sap porridge, 290; "Tom Fuller," 291; succotash, 291; fruit, 291; rice, 291; sof-ky, 291; sweetening, 291; dairy products, 291; beverages, 291–2; greens, 299

Forge, 254

Fort Jefferson, 275

Fort Leavenworth, 66

Fort Miro, 151

Fort Smith, 204

Forts, 38ff.; not kept up, 330

Fortune-teller, 170

Foster, James, 321–2

Fourth of July, 95, 138

Frankfort, Ky., 109, 153, 162, 318

Franklin, state of, 182, 236, 331

Franklin County, Mo., 269

Fraud: land company, 64; land sales, 70, 72; pre-emption, 73; land, 74, 75; land offices, 76; marketing goods in New Orleans, 109; corn-shucking, 129

Freighting, 114

French, 54, 247

French and Indian War, 8, 38

French Broad River, 257

Frolic, 127, 130, 131, 134, 151, 298

Frontier characteristics: inventiveness, 32; neighborliness, 303–4; skill with tools, 304; borrowing, 308; hospitality, 308, 324; going security, 309; sense of humor, 315–16; savagery, 321; went armed, 322; crude manners, 322–4; inquisitiveness, 326; lack of respect for privacy, 327; dislike of formality, 327; despised sham, 328; paucity of speech, 329; scant show of affection and praise, 329; shiftlessness, 330; lack of cleanliness, 330–1; self-government, 331; spirit of democracy, 332; rage for military titles, 333; lack of class distinctions, 333–4; exploitation, 334; individualism, 334–5; jealousy of creditors, 335; worshipped financial success, 335; willingness to endure hardship, 336; uncomplaining, 336; versatility, 336; personal honor, 336; optimism, 337; provincialism, 337;

Frontier characteristics (Continued)
dislike of Yankees, 337; jealous of personal liberty, 338; lack of education and refinement, 339; intelligent, 339; nationalizing influence, 333; area of equal opportunity, 334–5

Fruit: dried, 110; raising, 255; forest products, 291

Fulsome, James, 226

Funeral: church-regulated, 188; how conducted, 223; sermon, 224; spiritual institution, 224; attendance, 224; business event, 224

Gallatin, Miss., 161

Gallatin County, Ill. Terr., 89

Gambling, 164–9; laws against, 164; on river fronts, 165; on steamboats, 165, 166

Game, wild, 4, 5, 24, 25, 50, 85, 136, 287, 288

Games: kissing, 132, 176; "picking grapes," 132; "hanging onto the doorknob," 132; party, 132; snick-a-snack, 140; "long bullets," 145; ball, 146; billiards, 146; "rattle and snap," 146; fives, 146; at school, 176

Gander pull, 141–2

Gate, 39, 43, 51

General Jackson, 221

Georgia, 10, 11, 24, 57, 58, 59, 60, 63, 82, 88, 141, 150, 174, 204, 207, 228, 309, 310

German, 291, 304, 333

Gerstaecker, Frederick, 329

Gibson, Samuel, 43, 84

Gilmer, George N., 83

Ginseng ("sang"), 31–2, 107, 115, 121

Gouging, 140

Goebel, Ferdinand, 306

Goebel, Gert, 304

"Going abroad," 137

Gosse, Philip Henry, 80, 174

Gourds, 29–30, 127

Government: provided escorts to emigrants, 15; self, 236, 331; beginnings of state, 236; local, 237–8; territorial, 237; efforts to form, 331

Governor: of Alabama (territorial), 81; of Arkansas, 31, 270; of Franklin, 322; of Indiana, 211; of Mississippi, 264; of Virginia, 50, 321

Graining of hides, 6

Granada, Ala., 151

Granary, 128

Graves, 222–3; robber, 223

Graveyard, 183

Great migration, 58, 59, 149

Great Revival, 187, 195–203

Greeneville, Tenn., 162

Grenada, Miss., 153

Groceries, 118, 120

Groom, 128, 135–7. *See also* Wedding.

Grund, Francis J., 333

Guild, J. C., 231

Guion, Parish Judge George S., 227

Gulf of Mexico, 110

"Gull," 168

Gum, 30

Gunn's *Domestic Medicine,* 217

Gunpowder, 87, 246, 247

Guns: Old Beelzebub, 29; rifle, 40, 142, 143; Old Nancy, 41; Old Blood Letter, 144; Old Hair-splitter, 144; Old Panther-cooler, 144

Gunsmith, 271

Hall, Basil, 62, 150

Hall, Mrs. Basil, 213, 336

Ham, 109

Hamilton, Colonel John, 55

Hamilton, General (British), 45

Hampton, General Wade, 67

Hand mill, 250

Handspikes, 126

Hanging, 226

"Hanging onto the doorknob," 132, 133

Hanks, Abraham, 17

Hanson, Thomas, 3

"Happy Valley," 53

Hardware, 120

Harness, 32

Harrisonville, Ill., 210

Harrodsburg, 39, 48, 87, 135, 146, 148, 267, 294

Hart, David and Nathaniel, 16

Harvest, 101–2, 173

Hats, 296, 297, 323

Haywood, Judge John, 231

Health, 215

Heating, 27–8

Hemp, 110, 252

Henderson, Judge Richard, 331

Henderson, Samuel, 45, 134

Henry County, Mo., 260

Henry, Patrick, land speculator, 8

Hiwassee: country, 7; river, 118

Hickman, William, 294

Hickory Ground, 11

Hides: price, 6; preparation for market, 6; storing, 6; baled, 7; for export, 107; curing, 296

Hippodrome, 159

Hobbs, Lieutenant Vincent, 321

Hodgson, Adam, 60

Hoes, 308

Hoffman, Charles, 326

"Hog Drivers," 132

Hogs, 35–6, 82, 105, 108, 110, 152

Hogsheads, 58–9, 234

Holder, John, 45, 47

Holston, 46, 47, 118, 177

Homesteads, 8ff.

Hominy: block, 249; pounder, 250, lye, 290

Honey, 30, 36–7, 292

Holy dance, 198

Holy laugh, 198

Hoosier, 24, 310, 313

Hopkins, General Samuel, 116

Hornbook, 175

Horns, 302

Horse: col‗ar, 32; captured by Indians, 44; sensed Indians near, 50, travel by, 55, 308–9; shelter for, 98; wild, 105; driven to market, 108; brought to boat, 110; trading, 146, 271, 311–12; dead, 152; pulled circus, 159; stealing, 226, 232–3; aided spies, 266; lack of, 308; blocks, 309; stamping ground, 312

Horseraces, 146–7, 229, 317

Hospitality, 85, 308, 324–6

Hotel, 209, 292

House: skin, 5; half-faced camp, 26; rock, 26; pole, 26; log, 27, 81; saddlebag, 28, 117; raising, 81, 98, 127–8, 224, 308; planter, 81; two-pen log, 81; warming, 128; on wheels for moving, 150

Houston, Sam, 172

Howell, Henry, 73

Hubbard, Colonel James, 257

Humor, 315

Hunter-farmer, 25

Hunter-trapper, 23

Hunters: delighted in Kentucky, 4; methods used, 33; game procured, 50; on Indian lands, 256; shooting at the hump, 312

"Hunters of Kentucky, The," 163

Hunting: opportunities for, 5; of squatter, 32; buffalo, 33; methods, 33; division of the kill, 33; bear, 34; dogs, 34; deer, 35; turkey, 35; wild hogs, 35–6; bees, 36–7; of Negroes, 95; possum, 96; stories, 138; shirt, 293, 298

Huntington, Collis P., 121

Hunts: squirrel frolic, 146; wolf-hunt, 146

Huntsville, Ala., 70, 154, 163, 217, 315, 319

Hutchins, John, 106

Ice, 157

Ice cream, 157

Idioms, 313

Illinois, 21, 24, 31, 32, 40, 110, 141, 268, 310, 332

Illumination, 153, 300–1

Imitating noises, 41, 309

Improvements: on claims, 8; land, 69

Indenture laws, 89

Indian: agent, 24, 257; countrymen, 11, 12, 23; policy, 64; title, 24

Indiana, 21, 24, 40, 149, 279, 310, 332

Indians: wars, 8; Creeks, 11; effect of Indian countrymen on, 11; burned cabin, 16; scouts sought to intercept, 16–17; doing mischief in Kentucky, 18; attacked flatboat, 19, 20; tricked whites, 20, 44, 50–1; countrymen lived with, 23; crowded by squatters, 24; attacks 1775–83, 39; incited by British, 39–40; raids, 40; peace made with, 40; treatment of captives, 40; methods of warfare, 40–1; imitated sounds, 41; ruses to kill whites, 41, 42, 44; loaded guns light, 42, 278; caused settlers to go to stations, 43–4; method of attack on forts, 45; captured Jemima Boone, 45; attacks frequent, 48–50; Cherokees, 50, 65, 66; affected settlement, 50; fear of dogs, 50; depredations in Kentucky and Tennessee, 50; rights disregarded, 65; em-

Indians (*Continued*)
  ployed to hold claims, 73;
  land title, 74; treaties with,
  75; uprising because of land
  frauds, 75; attacked Estill's
  station, 87–8; defeated in
  nineties, 108; cared for ill
  boatman, 113; captured girl,
  134; skilled in throwing tomahawks, 145; hostilities ceased,
  148, 233; Creek Nation, 162;
  early conquest of, 170; school
  children guarded from, 174;
  attacked express rider, 205;
  kept inns, 205; wounded
  Squire Boone, 216; troupe of,
  219; friendly, 256, 260; considered pelts theirs, 256; defended fellow wrongdoers,
  256–7; murdered, 257–8; none
  good but dead ones, 257;
  whites hated, 257–8; disfigure-
  ment of foes, 258; enslaved,
  258; taking of prisoners, 258-
  9; torturing prisoners, 258;
  running the gantlet, 259;
  adopted white prisoners, 259;
  never violated women, 259;
  Choctaw, 260; Chickasaw,
  260; expert traders, 260; rescued lost white boy, 260–1;
  sense of humor, 261; beggars,
  261; scouted by spies, 265;
  signs, 266–7; snuffed by
  horses and dogs, 266; hated
  spies, 267; attacked Buchanan's Station, 267, 277; spies
  warned whites of attack, 267;
  loot divided, 272; fighting
  with, 272; bloody battle at
  Cincinnati, 273; attacked Fort
  Jefferson, 275; deceived by
  strategy of women, 278; attacked isolated cabins, 280–1;
  captured women, 281; treatment of captive children, 281;
  captured Jonathan Alder, 281;

Indians (*Continued*)
  captured men, 282; type of
  dress, 294–5; Bench, 321; at-
  tacked Boonesborough, 329;
  government protected against,
  333
Indigo, **83**
Industry, **119**
Infare, 136
Infidels, 182
Ingraham, J. H., 96
Inn, 209
Innes, Judge Harry, 18, 50
Intruders War, 66
Iron, 107; manufacturing, 253;
  works, 253; forge, 253;
  bloomery, 254; furnace, 254
Irvine's Lick, 146
Itch, 213
Itinerant preacher, 185, 193–4
Izard County, Ark., 238
Jackson, Andrew, 54, 147, 163,
  227
Jackson, Miss., 211

Jail-breaking, 155
Jails, 226, 227–8, 258
Jarman, Colonel, 264
Javelin throw, 145
Jefferson, President Thomas, 70
Jerks, 197
Johnson, Andrew, 240
Johnson, General, 264
Johnston, John, 257
Jokes, 51–2, 126–7, 315–16
Jones, Robert, 42
Jonesborough, Tenn., 226, 227,
  250, 322
Judicial circuit, 230
Judicial districts, 225
Judge, 229, 230
Judson College, 179
Jury, 228, 233
Justice: through courts, 225–6;
  without regard to law, 226;
  thwarted, 225–6; quashing,
  232

Kalebah Hatchee (river), 162
Kansas, 292
Kaskaskia, Ind., 267
Keelboat: described, 119; crew, 119; speed, 119–20; used by soldiers, 272
Kemey, Peter, 36
Kenton, Simon, 259, 265, 329
Kentucky, 3, 4, 5, 8, 9, 10, 11, 14, 15, 16, 19, 20, 21, 26, 33, 34, 36, 39, 49, 50, 53, 55, 63, 75, 78, 83, 87, 92, 106, 107, 108, 110, 113, 116, 134, 135, 148, 153, 158, 161, 163, 181, 182, 187, 188, 193, 195, 196, 204, 217, 223, 225, 228, 236, 237, 239, 255, 256, 258, 260, 262, 265, 268, 272, 274, 275, 276, 279, 298, 307, 308, 310, 321, 326, 331, 333, 334, 335, 337, 338
Kentucky Gazette, 146, 204
Kentucky River, 33, 45, 109
Kingsport, Tenn., 253
Kissing, 129, 130, 132, 137, 176, 187, 190
Knives: scalping, 294, 299, 308; bowie, 155, 318
Knoblick, Ky., 220
Knox, James, 5
Knoxville, Tenn., 57, 148, 155, 205

Laboratory, 178
La Grange College, 178
Lamps, 300–1
Land: hunger, 7, 13; speculators, 8; claims, 8, 9; office, 9, 10, 11, 64, 76, 77, 78, 79; laws, 10, 74; hunter, 24; policy, 63, 64; public, 63; hunting, 64; survey, 64; looking, 26, 64; sales, 64, 65, 70, 71, 72; company, 64, 70, 71–2; frauds, 64, 74, 75; price, 64, 68, 72; corn rights, 66; sugar-camp rights, 66; tomahawk rights,

Land (*Continued*)
66; cabin rights, 66; illegal removal to, 67; auctions, 68; improvements, 69; claim club, 69; rush, 70; speculation, 70; commissioner, 73; boom, 74; squatter rights, 74; grants, 74; commission, 75; locators, 75; graduation act, 76, 77; receiver, 76, 78, 79; cleared by slaves, 81
Lanterns, 301
Latchstring, 302
Laughter, 316
Laundry, 300
Lawlessness: promoted by scarcity of women, 225; promoted by influx of undesirables, 225; subdued, 227; of whites toward Indians, 257
Laws: land, 74; apprenticeship, 89; slavery, 94; enforcement difficult, 226; governing territories, 237
Lawsuits, 10
Lawyers: Alexander Porter, 54; at an inn, 211–12; at court, 229–30; on circuit, 230; training, 231; financial success, 231; admittance to bar, 231; apprenticeship, 231; reading law, 231; quashing, 232; worked up cases, 232; shams, 232; unscrupulous practices, 232–3; hunter's aversion to, 318; squatters enemies of, 334; combined with other professions, 336
Lead, 107, 110, 120, 144, 247
Leather: breeches, 32; "whang," 295
Leggings, 294
Legislators: dress, 237; unlearned, 237; ignorant, 240
Legislatures, 237
Leitensdorfer, Eugene, 160
Lemon, James, 32

Lenoir, Walter, 95
Letters from Alabama, 80
Lexington, Ky., 56, 57, 92, 106, 117, 152, 155, 162
Liberty, personal, 338
Liberty, Mo., 237
Library, 177-8
Lick log, 105
Licking River, Ky., 253
Licks, 33
Light, 300-1
Limestone, Ky., 20, 21, 56
Limestone County, Ala., 30
Lincecum, Gideon, 174, 219, 220
Lincoln, Abraham, 17, 311
Lindsley, Philip, 324
Linen, 117
Linsey-woolsey, 117, 252, 293
Lion, 158
Liquor, 94, 128, 129, 188, 210, 225, 254, 292, 319. *See also* Whisky.
Literacy: in the area, 170; among women, 175
Little Rock, Ark., 141, 152, 156, 206, 270, 301, 322, 336
Livestock, 108
Lizard wagon, 106
Locks, 302-3
"Log tote," 126
Logan, General, 49
Log-rolling, 99, 125, 224
Logs, snaking into house, 128
Long Hunter, 4, 5
Loopholes, 39
Louisiana, 27, 32, 35, 36, 54, 55, 59, 73, 74, 75, 76, 79, 80, 83, 105, 106, 111, 114, 175, 180, 221, 238, 291, 307
Louisville, Ky., 19, 49, 118, 162, 210, 273, 298, 323
Love feast, 189
Love, Colonel Robert, 147
Lovely, 119
Lowes family, 99
Lowndesboro, Ala., 219
Luckey, J., 274

Ludlow, N. M., 162, 163
Lumber, 110
Lyell, Sir Charles, 212, 327
Lynching, 234

Macon, Miss., *Herald*, 155
Mad stone, 217
Madison, President James, 67
Magician, 160-1, 170
Mail service, 155, 205-9, 307-8
Malaria, 221
Mammoth Cave, 34, 246
Mansco, 6
Mansker, Kasper, 41-2
Manufactures: most needed, 244; gunpowder, 246, 247; lead, 247; maple sugar, 247; molasses, 248; clothing, 251-3; iron, 253; distilling, 254-5; soap, 255
Maple: syrup, 37; sugar, 247-8, 291
Marriage: of slaves, 92; first in Kentucky, 134; first at Harrodsburg, 135; first in Blount County, Ala., 135; extra-legal, 135; first in Henry County, Mo., 135; second, 223; in station, 277
Market: needed for agriculture, 108-9; for goods at New Orleans, 109; going to, 110, 112; glutted, 112; produce, 155
Market Street (St. Louis), 152
Marksmanship, 143
Martin, François Xavier, 55
Martin, Mrs. (Indian captive), 281
Martin, William, 140
Martin Academy, 177
Martineau, Harriet, 155, 336
Maryland, 57, 58, 182
Maryville, Tenn., 172
Maury County, Tenn., 3, 179
Mayslick, Ky., 276
Maysville, Ky., 158, 318

McAfee families: preparation for migration, 14; confinement of Mrs. George, 14
McCracken, Sarah, 134
McDowell, Dr. Ephraim, 222
McGary, Hugh, 146, 321
McGee, James, 195
McGee, John, 195–6
McGillivray, Chief, 11, 12
McGillivray, Sophia, 11–12
M'Gready, Rev. James, 195
Meade, David, 20, 56
Meadows, 3
Meat trough, 299
Medical: colleges, 220; practices, 220–2
Medicine show, 164
Meetings: camp, 200–3; protracted, 203; basket, 203
Meigs, R. J., 66
Memphis, 204
Menagerie, 158–9
Mercer County, Ky., 187
Merchants, 119
Meredith, Colonel Samuel, 56
Merrill, John, 280–1
Merrill, Mrs. John, 280–1
Metaphors, 311
Methodists, 20, 31, 182, 185, 186, 188, 189, 190, 195, 196, 198, 311
Michaux, F. A., 108, 279
Midwife, 302
Migration: preparation, 14; streams of, 14; volume, 18, 21; waves of, 23; reasons for, 53; into lower South, 54; routes, 57; line of march, 59; method of transportation, 59; hardships, 61, 62; influx to Mississippi, 79; influx into Alabama, 80
Milburn, William Henry, 298
Military Road, 204
Militia: muster, 140, 243, 264; organization, 262–3; service, 263; drafting, 263; service required by necessity, 263; duties, 264–5; inspection, 264; uniform, 264; officers, 268; Sixth Regiment Kentucky, 268; discipline, 271; formidable in a crisis, 271; provisions, 272; tactics, 272
Milk, 291
Milking, 104
Mill: sites, 149; floating, 250; hominy block, 249; Armstrong mill, 249; rock mortars, 249; water-power sweep mortars, 249; hand mills, 249; hominy pounder, 250; "slow john," 250; steel mill, 250; ox or horse, 250; water-power, 250; waiting at, 251; saw, 251; carding, 251
Miller, I. B., 21
Mine a'Burton, 246
Ministers: nurtured schools, 177; educational requirements, 190; overcome with emotion, 195; work at campmeeting, 201; funeral sermons, 224; brush-breaker, 312. See also Preachers.
Missionary, 23
Mississippi, 11, 25, 27, 53, 54, 57, 58, 59, 63, 64, 65, 67, 71, 74, 76, 79, 80, 84, 91, 116, 117, 123, 199, 208, 229, 231, 232, 234, 242, 291, 318, 337, 338
Mississippi River, 4, 55, 57, 109, 110, 111, 119, 182, 316, 328, 331
Mississippi Valley, 96, 177
Missouri, 3, 21, 22, 27, 31, 66, 74, 78, 83, 95, 98, 106, 108, 110, 115, 123, 141, 171, 214, 221, 226, 234, 237, 246–7, 265, 291, 292, 301, 333
Missouri River, 33
Mittens, 128
Mobile, Ala., 119

Moccasins, 128, 265, 295

Molasses, manufacturing, 248-9

Money: at discount, 9, 123; coonskins, 115; substitutes for, 115-16; "bit," 116; "cut," 116; paper abundant, 123; kind used, 123; hidden for safekeeping, 124; "banked" in logs, 124; paper, 233; counterfeit, 233

Monk (Negro slave), 87-8

Monkey, 158

Monongahela River, 56

Monroe, 152

Monroe, La., 152

Monroe County, Miss. Terr., 67-8

Montgomery, Ala., 57, 118, 119, 145-6, 151, 152, 162, 207

Montgomery *Republican*, 145, 152, 155, 322

Moore, Albert Burton, 224

Morehouse, Abraham, 75, 79-80

Morehouse Parish, La., 80

Morris, John, 89

Mortar and pestle, 249

Moulton, Ala., 164, 264

Mountains, 14

Mountjoy, George, 226-7

Mourning, 223

Muddy Run, 319

Murder, 322

Murray, Charles A., 332

Muscle Shoals, 57, 130

Music: "Sugar in the Gourd," 132; "Possum up a Stump," 132; "Leather Britches," 132; "Hog Drivers," 132; "Old Sister Phoebe," 132; circus, 159; Negro, 186; quarrels over, 189

Muster: militia, 268; company, 268; battalion, 268; when effective, 268; description of, 268-72; firearms, 268; lack of discipline, 269, 270; in Franklin County, Mo., 269; uni-

Muster (*Continued*)
form, 270-1; at Little Rock, 270; maneuvers, 271; amusements, 271; who attended, 271

Nails, absence of, 39

Nashboro, 39, 50, 148

Nashboro compact, 236

Nashville, 4, 50, 54, 119, 155, 162, 204, 205, 206, 212, 213, 231, 255, 267, 319, 324, 338

Natchez, Miss., 54, 57, 79, 106, 110, 160, 204, 205, 206, 233, 275, 276, 335

Natchez Trace, 55, 113, 204, 205, 338

Natchitoches, La., 246

National Road, 108

Neighborliness, 216, 303-4

Negroe Mountain, 56

Negroes: offered to Colonel Preston, 13; among emigrants, 15; fond of homes, 58; treatment by planters, 57-8; in traveling, 61; employed by speculators, 73; huts, 80; cooked barbecue, 137; trained horses, 147; worked on streets, 152; church attendance, 185; preachers, 185; at hanging, 226; testimony against whites, 233; stolen, 233; tramped cotton, 253; dress, 296. See also Slaves.

Nelson County, Ky., 280

Nettles, 251

New Albany, Miss., 208

Newbury district, S. C., 59

Newcastle, Ky., 144-5

New England, 171

New Englanders, 338

New Madrid, 316

New Orleans, La., 86, 109, 110, 112, 113, 119, 163, 164, 180, 209, 272, 317

Newspapers, 85, 315, 339

Newton County, Miss., 164

New Year, 35
New York, 110, 209
Nicholson, mother of Mrs. A. O. P., 3; A. O. P., 179
"Niggering off," 126
Nightshirt, 211
Niter, 246
Nixon, Frank, 30
Noosing, 134
Norfolk County, Va., 61
North Carolina, 8, 10, 13, 14, 21, 55, 57, 66, 177, 179, 236, 257, 267, 331
Northwest Territory, 122
Nuts, 290, 291
Nuttall, Thomas, 132, 226

Oak Lawn, La., 86
Obion River, 34
Ohio, 21, 40, 76, 237, 292, 310, 314, 321
Ohio River, 4, 14, 18, 19, 21, 22, 23, 33, 56, 57, 63, 69, 71, 76, 113, 164, 207, 242, 259, 265, 275, 276
Ohio Valley, 244
Okoa River, 118
"Old field" schools, 172
Old Hickory, 54
Old Northwest, 8, 39, 89, 237
Old Southwest, 11, 38, 307
Olmsted, Frederick Law, 80, 85, 94, 211
Opelousas, La., 73, 74
Optimism, 337
Opossum, 311
Osage, Mo., 206
Ouachita Parish, La., 32, 106
Ouachita River, 151, 260
Overland freighting, 114
Owen, Rev. John, 61
Owsley, Harriet and Frank, 79
Ozark, 274, 280, 292

Pacific, Mo., 209
Pack horses: carried hides, 6; carried necessities, 16; required on Wilderness Road,

Pack horses (*Continued*)
19; carried planter goods, 58; used early, 106; load, 107; carried merchant goods, 118; used by salt makers, 118
Paine, Robert C., 118
Palisade, 38
Panic of 1837, 123
Panthers, 4, 28, 288, **317**
Paper money, 9
Paper towns, 151
Paris, Ky., 115, 226
Parish police jury, **238**
Patrols, 94, 153
Paxson, F. L., 78
"Paying in trade," **117**
Peaches, 255
Pearl River, 114
Pears, Mrs., 275–6
Peck, John Mason, 182, **185**
Peddlers, 120–2
Pelts, 107, 110
Pennsylvania, 66, 338
Peppers, 289
Performers, strolling, **160**
Pharmacy, 219
Philadelphia, Ala., 151
Philadelphia, Pa., 117, 118, 133, 332
Picnics, 95
Piedmont, 53
Pierson, Hamilton W., **325**
Pike, Albert, 171
Pillory, 226
Piqua, Ohio, 272
Pitfall, 139
Pittsburg, Miss., 151
Pittsburgh, Pa., 19, 56
Plantation: system transplanted, 62; system, 78; house, 80; Negro huts, 80; size, 80, 84; became estate, 84; described, 84; names, 84; Oakwood, 84; self-sustaining, 84; life, 85, 86; slave life, 91; work, 91; ladies had maids, 93; patrols, 94

Planters: reason for migrating, 53; investigated before moving, 55; sent slaves ahead, 55; mode of travel, 55, 60; hardships of travel, 56, 57; routes of travel, 57; considered slaves, 57–8; caravan, 60; brought family physician and teacher, 61; treatment of slaves, 61, 83; patrolled camp, 61; squatters, 78; fewer than farmers, 79; owned many slaves, 79; establishment of home, 80; house, 80; house-raising, 81; slaves built house, 81; worked with slaves, 82; aristocracy, 85; life of, 85; overseers, 90; abuse of slaves, 95; squatter enemies, 334

Platte Purchase, 66
Plow, 99–100
Plowing contest, 130
"Plunder," 318
Polk, President James K., 222
Pontotoc County, Miss., 129
Pony express, 209
Pork, 110, 288, 299
Port Gibson, Miss., 84
Porter, Alexander, 54
Porter, Judge, 85
Possum, 96, 288
"Possum up a Stump," 132
Potatoes, 110, 289, 291
Potosi, Mo., 206
Pottinger's Creek, 182
Powder, 107
Powder-horn, 128
Power, Tyrone, 207, 326
Prairie Farmer, 292
Prairies, 3
Prayer, 307
Preachers: driven off, 181; itinerant, 185; Negro, 185; against ornaments, 188; drank, 189; lead singing, 189; ignorance, 191; manner of speaking, 191–2; practices, 193; itin-

Preachers (Continued)
erants, 193; circuit riders, 193; "brush," 194. See also Ministers.
Preaching: appointments, 183; attendance, 183; of Negroes, 185–6; breaking exercise, 186; description, 191–2; type, 191–2; children, 198; at camp-meeting, 200
Pre-emption: size of, and cost, 8; rights allowed to squatters, 67; act, 68, 69, 72; weaknesses of acts, 73; float, 73; fraud, 73
Presbyterian, 177, 182, 186, 189, 190, 195, 196, 197, 291
Preston, Colonel, 13
Prince George County, Va., 56
Princeton University, 182
Prisoners: difficult to hold in custody, 227; methods of holding, 228
Privacy: lacking, 134; disregarded, 327
Protracted meetings, 203
Public domain, 11, 63
Pulaski County, Ky., 36
Pumpkins, 289
Punishment: school, 173; court, 225–6; forms of, 225–6, 228; "coach" ride, 234; of militiamen, 265
Pushpin, 146

Quakers, 198
Quashing, 232
Quilting bee, 132

Raccoons, 311
Race for the bottle, 136
Rafts, 114, 164
Rail: fence, 103–4; splitting, 104, 305–7
Rain barrels, 300
Ramsay family, 25
Rangers, 264
Razor strops, 258

Receiver, land, 78, **79**
Red River, La., 114
Red River Parish, 246
Redstone, 56
Register of county, 10
Regulators, 13, 233, 234
Reid, Peter, 75
Religion: lack of, 181; interest in, 181; early church bodies, 182; common plane, 185; sectarianism, 187; family prayers, 307
Religious phenomena: falling exercise, 196; jerks, 197; barking exercise, 198; holy laugh, 198; holy dance, 198; children preaching, 198; visions, 198–9
Revival, 187; of 1800, 195–203
River travel: difficulties, 21; hardships, 56; day of flatboats, 109–14; going to market, 110; extent, 110; obstructions, 114; falls, 149; fords, 149
Revolutionary War, 8, 18, 40, 79, 138, 144, 257, 264, 272, 321
Reynolds, won Sarah McCracken, 134
Rhoads, Henry, 317
Rice, 83, 291
Richmond, Va., 61, 267
Richmond *Enquirer*, 149
Rifle, 142, 143
Rights: corn, 66; sugar-camp, 66; tomahawk, 66; cabin, 66; floating, 73
Road-building bee, 130
Robertson, James, 13, 16, 50, 205, 267, 271, 331
Robertson, Mrs. James, 278
Robertson, Jonathan, 16
Robinson Crusoe, 328
Robinson, John, 159
Rocky Mountains, 6
Roofs, 28, 39
Roots, Dr. Philip, 56
Ropes, 32, 110, 226, 302
Rorer, David, 213

Roy, James, 51
Royal British Proclamation of 1763, 14
Royall, Anne, 218, 292
Running the gantlet, 259
Russell, James, 205
Rye Cove, 48

Saddles, 32
St. Charles, Mo., 139, 181
St. Clair, 283
St. Louis, 77, 152, 156, 160, 161, 182, 213
St. Stephens, Ala., 78, 181
Saltpeter, 87, 246
Salt: for cattle, 105; brought to settlements, 107; deposit, 149; manufacturing early, 244; methods of manufacture, 244–5; protected by government, 246; exported, 246; works, 246; hardened soap, 255; springs, 281; made by Indians, 281
Salt River, 320
Sandbars, 21, 112
Sap-collecting, 130
Savannah, 118
Sawmill, 251
Scalp: restoration, 222; taking of, 258; knife, 294, 299, 308
Schoolcraft, Henry R., 24, 30–1, 246, 279, 288, 292
Schoolhouse, 172
Schoolmaster, 336. *See also* Teacher.
Schools: squatters did not have, 30; centered in teacher, 171; private, 171; tuition, 171; forest, 172; old field, 172; subscription, 172, 177; classes, 173; discipline, 173; punishments, 173; procedures, 173; "blab," 174; fights, 174; manners taught, 174; play-hours, 174; hours, 174–5; practices, 175; equipment, 175; amuse-

Schools (*Continued*)
ments, 175; few girls, 175;
games, 176; barring out the
master, 176; public examina-
tion, 177; tutoring, 177, 179;
private academy, 177, 180;
colleges, 177–9; in Louisiana,
180; organized, 224
Schultz, Christian, 4
Scioto, 281
Scotland, 337
Scouts: of emigrant parties, 16;
warned of Indians, 40; Kasper
Mansker, 41; mission, 263; de-
tail sent, 264–5; Henry
Rhoads, 317
Seat of justice, 228
Sectarianism, 187, 196
Security, 309
Self-government, 331
Sermons, 191–2
Settling day, 309
Sevier, John, 7, 40, 51, 66, 131,
132, 146, 217–18, 322, 331
Shakes, 26
Shaw, John, 220
Shawnee Springs, 48
Sheep, 105, 252
Sheep shearing, 283–4
Sheriff, 227
Sherrill, Kate, "Bonny Kate," 51
"Shin plasters," 124
Shirts, 297
Shoemaker, 296
Shoe-packs, 295, 296
Shoes, 120, 296
Shooting at a mark, 257
"Shooting for the beef," 144
Shooting match, 171, 271, 320
Shot-pouch, 128, 293
Shot put, 145
Shot towers, 247
Show boat, 164
Shows: professional, 158; ani-
mal, 158; circus, 159; theatri-
cals, 160–4; magic, 160–1;

Shows (*Continued*)
medicine, 164; floating thea-
ter, 164
Shreve, Henry M., 114
Sickle, 101
Sickness, 216, 221–2
Siege of Boonesborough, 41,
45–8, 216
Siege of Watauga, 51
Signs, Indian, 266, 267
Silks, 298
Singing, 6, 58, 138. *See also*
Music.
Skillet Fork, 279
Skin-house, 5
Skin packs, 7
Skin piles, 6–7
Skins, 29, 115, 117, 121, 253
Slavery: transplanted, 62; caste
system, 89; in Old Northwest,
89, 237; laws regarding, 94.
See also Negroes.
Slaves: number of emigrant, 21;
helped hunt deer, 35; planter
brought few, 53–4; as pioneers, 55–6; treatment, 57–8,
96; given choice about migrating, 58; sang, 58; of planters,
79; of settlers in lower South,
79; built master's house, 81;
cleared land, 81; followed
"task system," 82; worked
with whites, 82; food, 83; life
on plantation, 83; duties on
plantation, 84; rejoiced at
master's return, 85; in Kentucky early, 87; feeling at
leaving old home, 88; protected family from Indians,
88; saved girl from Indians,
88; terms used for, 89; classes,
89–90; aristocracy, 90; esprit
d'corps, 90; work, 91–2; marriage, 92; morality, 92; work
of women, 92; wedding, 92–3;
influence on whites, 93; relation to masters, 93; forbidden

Slaves (*Continued*)
liquor, 94; watched by patrols, 94; uprisings, 94; allowed to hunt, 95–6; families separated, 95; liberties, 95; no recourse to law, 95; attended balls, 96; church privileges, 96; overland freight drivers, 114; attended shucking, 130; observed curfew, 153; paid half-price at circus, 159; greeted returned planter son, 179–80; worshipped with owners, 185; marital status, 188; at taverns, 210; stealing, 233; insurrection, 234; Monk made gunpowder, 246; carried torches, 301. *See also* Negroes.

Sled, "land-slide," 308
Sleight-of-hand, 160
Slicker War, 234
"Slow-john," 250
Slut, 300
Smith, A. J., 31
Smith, James, 217
Smith, Sol, 123, 162–3
Smith, Thomas, 321
Snags, 21, 56, 112
Snake fence, 104
Snick-a-snack, 140
Soap, 300
Soap-making, 255, 285
Society, rough, 155–6, 322, 323
Societies: dramatic, 161; Thespian, 161
Socks, 128
Songs, 132, 138, 159, 163, 189. *See also* Music.
South Carolina, 59, 108, 122
Southwest Point, Tenn., 205
Spain, 331
Spanish: early settlers mingled with, 54; employed by speculators, 73; land grants, 74, 75; government, 79; territory, 109; opened lead mines, 247

Sparta, Ga., 96
Specie: lack of, 115; Spanish, 116
Speech: "cracker talk," 310; superlatives, 310, 313; where it came from, 310; metaphors, 311; idioms, 313; allusions, 313–14; dictionary of expressions, 315; new words, 315; anecdotes, 316; humor, 315–16; boasting, 319–20; paucity of, 329
Speculation, 7
Speculators, 18, 54, 55, 68, 70, 75, 149, 156, 334, 336
Spelling schools, 138, 308
Spencer, Thomas Sharp, 308
Spies: played trick, 51–2; duties, 265; appointment, 265; aided by dogs and horses, 266; life depended on their skill, 266; life, 266; read "signs," 266–7; habits, 267; equipment, 267; hated by Indians, 267; work, 267; practices, 268; report of, 312
Spinning, 312
Spitting, 324
Sports: bear-baiting, 139; dog-fighting, 139; gander-pulling, 139, 141; cock-fighting, 139, 145, 146; wolf and dog fights, 139, 140; rough-and-tumble fights, 139, 140; shooting for the beef, 139, 144; turkey-shoot, 139; horse-racing, 139, 146–7; ring tournament, 139, 147; playing games, 139; athletic contests, 139; throwing "shoulder stones," 145; "flinging the rail," 145; horse swapping, 146
Spring Creek, Ala., 130
Squatters: described, 23–4; troubles, 24; moved, 24, 25; by preference, 25; easy-going, 25; through misfortune, 25;

Squatters (*Continued*)
   building of homes, 26–8;
   homes, 26, 30; hospitable, 29;
   interior of home, 29–30; intellectual status, 30–1; inventive,
   32; makeshift, 32; professional,
   54, 55; opened path of settlement, 55; ordered off land,
   65; moved onto best land, 66;
   pre-emption rights, 67; sought
   special concessions, 68; club,
   69; rights, 74; on townsite,
   150
Squaw-man, 23
Squirrel, 288
Squirrel frolic, 146
Stage-coach, 206, 208–9
Stagner, Barney, 49
Staking board, 6
Stamping-ground, 312
Starch making, 285
State capital fight, 156
Stations: described, 38–9; life,
   42, 277; poorly kept up, 44;
   had to maintain constant vigi-
   lance, 48; in lots, 148; out lots,
   148; new ones established, 148
Steamboats, 22, 119, 122, 221,
   313–14, 323, 328. *See also*
   Boats.
Stockings, 298
Stone, Barton, 187
Store: country, 117; trading at,
   117; tramp vending, 118;
   keeper treated customers, 118;
   settlers, 117; early ones de-
   scribed, 118; volume of busi-
   ness, 120; on flatboats, 122
Story-telling, 138, 317
Streets, 152, 153
Sturdevant (minister), 181
Subscription school, 177
Sugar, 291
Sugaring off, 130
Suggsville, Ala., 3
Sulphur, 87, 246
Sunbonnets, 297

Superstition, 31, 217–18, 220
Surgery, 222
Surveyor, 9, 10, 65
Surveys: descriptions vague, 9;
   no system, 9; overlap, 9; rec-
   ords not available 9; rectan-
   gular system, 11, 63; townsite,
   150; railroad, 153
Swaney, John Lee, 205
Sweet potato, 289
Sweetening, 291
Sykes, Jo, 320

"Task system," 82
Tavern, 209; "stand," 209; "ordinary," 209; advertisements,
   209, 210; described, 210; toilet
   facilities, 210; furnishings, 211;
   customs, 211; practices, 211–
   13; lack of privacy, 212;
   vermin, 213; meals, 213–14;
   haste in eating, 213; cooking
   privileges, 214; price of meal,
   214
Tax: vehicle, 156; property, 156;
   poll, 156; licenses, 156; shows,
   156; sales, 157; paid in produce, 239; collector, 239
Taylor family, 60
Tea, 292
Teacher: examinations, 171; articles of agreement, 171; qualifications, 171; boarded round,
   172; salary, 172; barring out,
   176
Tecumseh, 258
Telling time, 307
Temperance, 189
Tennessee, 5, 7, 8, 10, 11, 14, 15,
   21, 22, 27, 34, 41, 42, 50, 55,
   59, 61, 63, 65, 66, 68, 70, 71,
   78, 80, 83, 95, 107, 108, 110,
   113, 116, 118, 140, 146, 148,
   177, 182, 194, 197, 204, 227,
   231, 236, 237, 239, 247, 250,
   251, 255, 257, 258, 262, 264,

Tennessee (*Continued*)
265, 267, 292, 296, 308, 318, 331

Tennessee River, 14, 33, 70, 80, 272

Tennessee River Valley, 53

Tensaw River, 54

Texas, 59, 232, 318, 338

Theater: floating, 164; brawl, 323

Theatricals: company, 123, 318; professional, 160; troupe, 161, 162; taken seriously, 163

Theobold, Thomas, 226

Thomas, Seth, 121

Threshing, 102–3

Tick Creek Church, 188

Tilling, Mr., 294

Tin shops, 122

Tinder-box, 128

Tipton, Colonel John, 322

Tobacco, 53, 109, 110, 116, 183, 309, 323

Tomahawk: claims, 8; rights, 8; improvements, 66; pioneers carried, 294

Tombigbee River, 79, 114

Tombigbee settlements, 57

Tools, 99

Torches, 301

Toulmin, Judge Harry, 67

Tournament, 147

Towel, 210

Town: companies, 130, 149; preceded settlement, 148; established, 149; boom, 149, 150; founding, 150; rapid growth, 150–1; competition, 151; lots sold, 151; paper, 151; rivalry, 151; frontier appearance, 152; streets, 152; patrol, 153; curfew, 153; no street lights, 153; watchman, 153; constable, 153; illumination, 153; water supply, 153; waterworks, 153; fire protection, 154; fights, 155; mail service, 155; market,

Town (*Continued*)
155; financial support, 156; luxuries, 157

Townsite: described, 150; survey, 150

Trader, 23

Trading, opportunities for, 5

Trails: obliterated, 6; marked, 15; early, 204; Wilderness, 204; Cumberland Road, 204; Federal Road, 204; Natchez Trace, 204; Military Road, 204; dangerous, 204; limited to travel by horse, 205; express riders, 205

Transylvania: legislative assembly, 33; College, 178; University, 178, 220; Colony, 222, 236; Company, 331

Trapeze, 159

Trapping, 5

Travel: through wilderness hazardous, 17; volume on Wilderness Road, 18; routes, 57; hardships, 56, 57, 61, 62; by stage, 326

Treaty of Fort Greenville, 40

"Treeing," 41

Trees: marked survey boundaries, 9; kinds used for splitting rails, 305–6

Tricks, played on settlers, 51–2

Trollope, Mrs., 323

Tucker, Rev., 20

Tullahoma, Miss., 151

Turkeys, 4, 35, 110, 287, 317

Turnips, 290, 291

Tuscaloosa, Ala., 62, 79, 153, 157, 160, 173, 233

Tuscumbia, Ala., 165, 179

Tutor, 179

Umbrellas, 61

University, 179, 180

Vance, Dr. Patrick, 222

Vegetables, 289, 291

Vehicles: early, 206; Concord coach, 206; wheeled, 308

Venison, 287

Ventriloquist, 160

Vermin, 213

Virginia, 4, 5, 8, 14, 21, 58, 66, 108, 118, 131, 182, 207, 225, 244, 262, 281, 292, 331, 333

Virginia fence, 104

Visits, 137

Voting: by ballot, 242; viva voce, 242

Wagon: travel on Wilderness Road, 15, 19; wooden, 32, 106; types, 106; lizard, 106

Walker, Dr. Thomas, 26, 256

Wallace, Sir William, 160

Wamus, 297

Wapetonmace River, 258

Warping, 119

Warrants, land, 8

War of 1812, 21, 53, 80, 149, 239, 338

Washing, 299–300

Washington College, 177

Washington, George, land speculator, 8

Washington, La., 76

Wasson, James, 106

Watauga: region settled, 14; famous, 39; siege, 51; Association, 236, 331

Watches, 307

Watchman, 152, 153

Water: supply at stations, 44; supply for towns, 153; stored, 300; works, 153–4

Waterman, W., and Company, 159

Wax-figure exhibit, 160

Wayne, General, 40

Weaving, 284, 285

Wedding: slave, 92–3; social occasion, 125; backwoods, 135–6; feast, 136; plantation, 137; sugar for, 291; dress, 297

Wells, 44

Well-digging, 220

Wesley's *Account of Christian Perfection*, 190

Wheat: early Louisiana crop, 83; raising, 101–3; planting, 101; harvesting, 101–2; threshing, 102–3; winnowing, 102–3

Wheeling, W. Va., 56

Whelan, Father M., 182

Whipping, 226

Whirlpools, 21

Whisky, 65, 95, 102, 110, 118, 127, 129, 131, 132, 136, 138, 183, 187, 202, 218, 241, 242, 254, 292

Whist, 138

Whitcomb, James, 211–12

Whites: hated Indians, 257; mutilated Indians, 258; taking of prisoners, 258; prisoners escaped, 259–60; at peace with Indians, 260; boy found by Indians, 260–1; friends of Indians, 261; scalped Indians, 321

Whitney, Eli, 252

Widows, 135, 223–4, 282

Wild-cat banks, 123

Wilderness Road (or Trail): described, 15; laid out by Daniel Boone, 15; mode of travel on, 16; hazards, 17; numbers who traveled, 18; poured immigrants into Kentucky, 18; traveled by planters, 56; droves of stock on, 108; famous, 204; dangerous, 204–5

Wilkinson, General James, 109

Williams, Joseph, 59, 80

Willing Maid, 119

Wilson, David, 42

Wilson, Hugh, 135

Wilson, John, 140, 226

Windows, 27, 39, 80

Winton, estate of Samuel Meredith, 56
Witchcraft, 31
Wolf hunt, 146
Wolf pit, 106
"Wolf traps," gambling house, 165
Wolves, 4, 28, 140, 283
Women: married young, 134, 135; did not attend sports events, 147; colleges, 179; typical frontier, 274; courageous leadership of, 275–7; sense of humor, 278; lonely life, 279; shy, 279; informed on frontier matters, 280; courageous defense against Indians, 280–1; captives, 281; uncertain of husband's fate, 282; second

Women (*Continued*)
marriage, 282–3; toilworn hands, 283; work, 283; made clothing, 283; barefoot, 285; child-bearing, 285; smoked, 285–6; gathered greens, 299
Wood-chopping, 130
Woods, Hannah, 88
Woodsmen, quiet, 42
Wool, 252, 284
Wooten, Dr. H. V., 137, 219
Worm fence, 104
Wrestling match, 127

Yankees, 337–8
Yazoo Land Company, 64
Yazoo River, 114
Yellowroot, 32
Young, Jacob, 20, 197